The World of

COL.
JOHN W.
THOMASON
USMC

The World of
COL.
JOHN W.
THOMASON
USMC

Martha Anne Turner

EAKIN PRESS
Austin, Texas

A percentage of the royalties from the sale of this book
has been assigned by the author to
The Colonel John W. Thomason Room
of the Sam Houston State University Library.

FIRST EDITION
Second Printing
Copyright © 1984
By Martha Anne Turner

Published in the United States of America
By EAKIN PRESS, P.O. Box 23066, Austin, Texas 78735

ISBN 089015-439-2

To Leda Thomason of Terrell, Texas
and
To the memory of Sue Hayes Goree Thomason
This volume is dedicated

Books by Martha Anne Turner

White Dawn Salutes Tomorrow

The City and Other Poems

Tools of the Earthmover
(Edited by Martha Anne Turner)

Sam Houston and His Twelve Women

The Life and Times of Jane Long

The Yellow Rose of Texas: The Story of a Song

William Barret Travis: His Sword and His Pen

Women of Texas
(In collaboration with others)

Texas Epic

The Yellow Rose of Texas: Her Saga and Her Song

Old Nacogdoches in the Jazz Age

Richard Bennett Hubbard: An American Life

Clara Driscoll: An American Tradition

The World of Colonel John W. Thomason USMC

Contents

Acknowledgments		vii
Preface		xi

PART ONE

1.	Nineteenth-Century Huntsville	3
2.	A Good Place for a Boy	19
3.	Period of Exploration	33
4.	A Marine Takes a Bride	61

PART TWO

5.	A Marine Goes to War	77
6.	Pearl of the Antilles	96
7.	Man of Words and Windy Periods	110
8.	Of Forgotten Fighting Men	120

PART THREE

9.	A Ship Is a Man's World	175
10.	Potomac Potpourri	201
11.	With the Legation Guard in Peking	225
12.	Horse-and-Buggy Man	257

PART FOUR

13.	Literary Editor of the *American Mercury*	277
14.	Into this Peace . . .	297
15.	Pearl Harbor and *Lone Star Preacher*	311
16.	*Semper Fidelis*	332
	Bibliography and Thomason Checklist	369
	Index	387

Acknowledgments

My interest in John W. Thomason dates back more than three decades. I first became seriously interested in the author in 1944 when I was a graduate fellow teaching freshman English on the campus of the University of Texas at Austin. I had read a few of Thomason's books. But it was not until I read his essay *The Old South Myth* in the anthology I was using as a text that I became aware of his impact on American literature and embarked on a course that ultimately resulted in this study.

I have been fortunate in the help that I have had in writing this biography. I have enjoyed what seemed like a rare collaboration — that with John W. Thomason himself. From the inception of this study to its completion, I have felt that he was looking over my shoulder. Not only did I find an abundance of material in Thomason's works, I had the privilege of using the fabulous Thomason Collection, which Sam Houston State University has the honor to house and administer.

The collection, assembled in the elegant walnut-paneled centerpiece of the university library, designed to accommodate it and named to memorialize the author-artist-Marine, is one of the most extraordinary in the nation. It is comprised of first editions of Thomason's works and publications he illustrated for others, books to which he contributed, presentation copies, manuscripts, paintings and sketches, scrapbooks, sketchbooks, notebooks, original documents, cases of newspaper clippings relating to every phase of his career, periodicals and vertical file materials pertaining to the Marine Corps per se, letters written by and to Thomason, citations of awards, photographs, and assorted ephemera.

Most valuable of the materials were the letters written by the author to his parents over a period of more than four decades; correspondence from readers; letters from Thomason to his close friend, the novelist James Boyd of Southern Pines, North Carolina; and other communications from people of the publishing and literary fields, among them the legendary editor Maxwell E. Perkins.

Undoubtedly, Thomason was one of the most prolific letter writers of his time, and no topic was too insignificant or controversial to elude his all-inclusive pen. For that matter, perhaps no one was in closer touch with the era in which he lived — an epoch that spanned two world wars and in which he, as a Marine officer, observed humanity from far-flung areas of the globe. Because of this fact, many of his contemporaries have made substantial contributions to this study: Perkins and Boyd, H. L. Mencken, Alexander Woollcott, Laurence Stallings, Roy Chapman Andrews, Colonel Henry L. Roosevelt, Frazier Hunt, Ernest Hemingway, and J. Frank Dobie.

My debt to Leda Thomason is immense. It is not too much to say that without her cooperation this book would never have become a reality. She has been exceedingly generous in granting me permission to quote the author-artist, has approved my unrestricted use of all of the materials comprising the Thomason Collection, has shared her treasured memorabilia with me, and entertained me as a guest in her home in Terrell, Texas.

Other members of the Thomason family have been generous in assisting me with this project. I am indebted to Sue Thomason Noordberg and Margaret Thomason Cole, the author's sisters of Huntsville, and to Emily Thomason Petersen, another sister who lives in Houston, for their untiring efforts to help me.

At Sam Houston State University in 1946 I introduced a course called Literature of the Southwest in which I included the works of Thomason as part of the format. When Sue Goree Thomason, the author's mother who lived in Huntsville, learned of the fact, she was appreciative.

Mrs. Thomason and I became friends, and much of the detail in this book stems directly from her. John's mother talked much about her famous son and firstborn. She recalled with amazing accuracy what Huntsville was like in 1893, the year of his birth. She had vivid recollections of John as a boy and of how the servants spoiled him. She reminisced about his love for books and the hours he spent in his father's library. Nor did John Thomason's mother forget his unusual experiences as a reporter for the *Houston Chronicle*, for which she had many a chuckle.

This great Southern lady prized her collection of first editions of her son's books and his art adorning the walls of her home, along with her accumulation of letters and photographs covering his entire lifespan. She meticulously preserved every letter the family received, from the first John wrote at five years of age to the last he wrote before his death at fifty-one. She attached special sentiment to that first letter John wrote from Galveston in 1898, while he was visiting her parents, as she did to his first drawing—a pencil sketch of a duck he made a year later at six.

Once asked which she considered John's greater gift—his art or his writing, Mrs. Thomason replied: "To me there could be no choice. He was equally great as a writer as he was an artist. But when she spoke she was gazing tenderly at her son's first Christmas card designed when he was scarcely eleven—a composition of two birds perched on a limb, ready for flight.

I should like to make my manners to Dr. Herbert T. Hayes, John's cousin, of Conroe, Texas, who has been kind enough to correspond with me about him. Dr. Hayes, now an octogenarian, and John, who was a year younger, grew up together. The doctor likes to recall their fishing and hunting trips and how, as boys, the two sometimes ate at the "Keep" house in Huntsville just to hear the Confederate veterans of the Civil War, who boarded there, talk of their experiences and review the battles.

My indebtedness to the staff of the Sam Houston State University library is prodigious. I am particularly grateful to Charles L. Dwyer, special collections librarian in charge of the Thomason Room; Donald H. Ko, interlibrary loan librarian; and John P. Nunelee, former director, for the hours they devoted to this work. It would not be possible to enumerate the many courtesies these gentlemen extended to me while this biography was in progress, all in addition to the professional expertise they exerted in my behalf. Dwyer, one of the finest research librarians in this nation, was unstinted in his devotion of time and effort to this study. Dr. Rush Miller, present director of Sam Houston State University Library, also deserves my thanks.

I appreciate the courtesy of Mary Pat Mclaughlin, director of special collections, Cody Memorial Library, Southwestern University, for honoring my request for the use of the university yearbook, the 1910 edition of the *Sou'westor* containing specimens of John Thomason's prose and drawings. I am particularly grateful to Mr. Kirk Treible, vice president of fiscal affairs, Southwestern University, for permission to use the material in any way I wished. It is with this official permission that I quote Thomason's "Revised Version of 23rd Psalm" in Chapter III.

My gratitude goes to Mr. Lauren Brown, special collections librarian, Woodson Research Center, The Fondren Library, Rice University, for his assistance in research related to Thomason's newspaper work.

I also wish to make grateful acknowledgment to Charles Scribner's Sons for permission to quote brief excerpts of material, pages xi and xvii, from the Introduction (by Robert Leckie) to *Fix Bayonets!*, copyright 1970, along with that of Leda Thomason for 1959.

My thanks go also to my secretary, Jeanette Koger, for her excellent services, and to Westen McCoy of the Sam Houston State University Graphic Arts Department for processing photographs for this volume.

Finally, I wish to express appreciation to the United States Marine Corps and particularly to Lieutenant Colonel Robert W. Smith, USMC (retired), former editor of *Marine Corps Gazette*, for reading the manuscript and for permission to use some of the text and illustrations from my article "Legend and Legacy of John W. Thomason," which appeared in the 204th anniversary issue of the magazine in November of 1979.

I acknowledge further indebtedness to the Marine Corps for permission to quote from articles by Thomason which appeared in earlier issues of the *Gazette*.

Martha Anne Turner
Huntsville, Texas

Preface

It has been said that John W. Thomason made the United States Marines. Certainly his influence on the history and spirit of the Corps is irrefutable. One of the most vivid writers of his time, Thomason is acclaimed today as the latest, and greatest, in the line of American military artists since Frederick Remington. Not only was his influence on the combat art of World War II and Korea notable, his impact on the combat art of Vietnam was unmistakable.

It is equally true that the Marines made John Thomason. A legend in the armed forces and literary world before he was forty, Thomason found his identity in the Marine Corps during World War I. Moreover, he confirmed his three-dimensional talent — that of Marine officer, artist, and writer — as the war progressed in 1918, and was charged with helping to cultivate his own substantial saga.

For instance, he liked to appear different, was individual in his dress and manner. While he took much pride in the fit and flawless tailoring of his uniform — and cut a fine figure for his height of five feet, ten inches, and weight of one hundred, sixty-five pounds — he removed the wire grosset from his cap to give it a softer appearance and make it droop around the edges.

In civilian attire he had a penchant for slacks and unusual jackets and a predilection for short Wellington boots. Also in civilian dress he preferred a broader-brimmed felt hat than most men and wore it with the brim turned down at a rakish angle. His horn-rimmed glasses were attached to a narrow black silk ribbon suspended from his neck, after the fashion of other officers of the American Expeditionary Force. His pipe was almost as much a part of his colophon as were his pencils and sketching pad, and he invariably lit up as he worked.

In customary stance Thomason's military bearing was evident. Still at times he was inclined to demonstrate an almost contrived nonchalance in his posture with thumbs tucked inside his belt and his right knee bent slightly forward. His pride in the Corps could be measured by a kind of "swank" or "swagger" in his walk.

Thomason's nonconformity was not restricted to idiosyncrasies and to dress. The Marine officer allowed his salary checks to collect over long periods as he and his family subsisted off royalties and fees from illustrating books for others and an occasional sale of an oil painting or a watercolor. As a result, paymasters and disbursing agents of the Corps, who balanced their books twice during a fiscal year, urged Thomason to cash or deposit his government checks so as to avoid confusion. He was also accused of either refusing, or being unable, to march in step with the music in parades.

Despite individual characteristics, Thomason in demeanor was dignified, in manner friendly. He had the utmost respect of the men under his command and was extremely popular. An impeccable officer, he observed military discipline rigidly according to regulation. His perceptive blue-grey eyes sparkled upon the least provocation. On the other hand, they snapped when he was displeased. His square jaw, firm chin, and strong mouth set him apart as a man's man and masculine to the core. Fine facial wrinkles and a weathered complexion stamped him as an outdoorsman and added distinction to his physical appearance.

Thomason had a quality which some people term *charisma*, for lack of a better word. It was said by those who knew him best that when he joined a group or entered a room he brought to it instantly an intangible quality of glamour. This, they said, was particularly true of social gatherings. The dullest cocktail party infested with international bores would begin to swing the minute John Thomason walked through the door.

Thomason was attracted to men and women alike. But it was for women that he had profound appreciation. Beautiful women were to Thomason like fine works of art — great paintings or exquisite sculptures — in which proportion, color, and rhythm were brought into perfect harmony.

His knowledge of anatomy was apparent in his sketches of women from their shapely legs and derrieres to the curve of a shoulder and the tilt of a chin. Not only that, he portrayed the barefoot squaw and the native woman of the tropics transporting laundry on her head with the same skill and dedication that he exercised in depicting elegant ladies at affairs of state.

Thomason has been called the greatest paper conservationist of his time. The statement, taken out of context, is misleading. The truth is the artist — a compulsive sketcher — was constantly exhausting his materials. In addition to his sketchpads, he used anything available — odd scraps of paper, leaves from old ledgers, canvas board, stationery of all kinds (U.S. Marine Corps, War College, Navy College, Pacific Fleet, etc.) — and frequently every inch of space, along with both sides of a sheet or canvas. A frustrated publisher of one of the nation's most important magazines got in touch with Mrs. Thomason and insisted that the next time the artist ran out of paper she should contact him immediately and the publisher would rush a supply to him.

A significant aspect of Thomason's legend was his ability to concentrate on two or more levels at the same time. Thus he could listen to a classroom lecture or discussion on one plane as he sketched in his notebooks on another. He could command a platoon of Marines in combat while recording on a sketchpad what was happening. He could direct a Special Service Squadron landing operation and draw details of the maneuver or its participants simultaneously.

As the Marine's legend mushroomed so did fictional moss accumulate. Whether he lacked the time or was merely indulgent, he neither denied nor corrected the embroidered stories and colorful allegations attributed to him. There was the anecdote about the author's first literary speech. The occasion was a tea honoring the famous alumnus of Sam Houston Normal Institute, shortly after the publication of *Fix Bayonets!* By that time the school's name had been changed to Sam Houston State

Teachers College, but some of Thomason's former instructors were still on campus.

Requested to speak, the author, who later drafted addresses for Colonel Henry L. Roosevelt and Admiral Chester Nimitz and gained a reputation as a reconteur himself, arose and shyly looked around the room. Without preamble, he singled out his teachers present. This one, he said, had guided him through the intricacies of mathematics. That one had expounded the truths of history to him. Another had taught him English, and so on.

Then he paused. "But none of you taught me how to make a speech."

A later anecdote illustrates Thomason's occasional unpredictability. One day during the tour in Peking, he rushed into his quarters and informed Leda that he had bad news for her. Aware of the swiftness with which death strikes in the Orient, Leda steeled herself against the possible news of the tragic death of a close friend or a member of the Legation Guard.

When her husband seemed groping for words to diminish the blow, "Well, what is the bad news?" she asked.

"I don't intend to play another damned bridge game in my life," he told her emphatically. His wife was, of course, an addict who genuinely enjoyed the game.

Although he was essentially a realist in his art, Thomason, like some of his characters, inclined occasionally toward the romantic and the dramatic. But he never let ostentation interfere with his sense of values. The following incident was supposed to have occurred on one of the inspection tours Thomason made in 1941 to naval attaché posts in the South American republics.

His visit to one of the South American capitals was concurrent with a three-day ceremony staged for a visitor of state. Thomason attended all of the official functions — reviews, receptions, dinners — arranged to honor the dignitary.

On the morning of the fourth day, as he was boarding the aircraft to return to his base in Panama, the effusive wife of an American diplomat asked if he had not been impressed with the display and if he were not envious of the members of the diplomatic corps to whom such grand affairs were common occurrences.

Without intending to be rude, Thomason replied, as he adjusted his parachute harness: "Madam, I'd turn it all in on a good trottin' horse."

Much has been made of Thomason's fatalistic philosophy which he developed during World War I. In spite of it, or possibly because of it, he was known to joke in the face of death and danger. His sketches and stories in *Fix Bayonets!* are cases in point. This dry wit crossed over into his peacetime routine. A typical specimen involving nautical problems recorded in his notebook is this:

"You are officer of the deck in a heavy fog. You hear 1 long blast and 2 short whistles directly ahead; you have been hearing it for some time. Solution: Jump overboard."

An inherent member of the Old Breed, Thomason was a Southerner and an East Texan. Idol of the big magazines in the thirties and early forties and the author of three masterpieces — *Fix Bayonets!*, *Jeb Stuart*, and *Lone Star Preacher*, all bearing the stamp of his art — Thomason was invited to propose a toast at a function of national note. His toast, completely original, must have astonished the elite of the writing and publishing world.

John W. Thomason raised his glass: "Here's to East Texans and their way of life. They marry their women, pay their poll taxes, and attend all wars that the people in Washington get us mixed up in. They go early and stay late. They don't shoot quail on the ground, whip horses with bridles, or lay violent hands on women."

THE MARINES' HYMN

From the Halls of Montezuma
To the shores of Tripoli;
We fight our country's battles
On the land as on the sea;
First to fight for right and freedom,
And to keep our honor clean;
We are proud to claim the title
Of United States Marine.

Our flag's unfurl'd to every breeze
From dawn to setting sun;
We have fought in every clime and place
Where we could take a gun;
In the snow of far-off Northern lands
And in sunny tropic scenes;
You will find us always on the job —
The United States Marines.

Here's health to you and to our Corps
Which we are proud to serve;
In many a strife we've fought for life
And never lost our nerve;
If the Army and the Navy
Ever gaze on Heaven's scenes;
They will find the streets are guarded
By United States Marines.

John W. Thomason, Jr. at the time of his graduation from high school. He was 16.

— *Courtesy Sue Thomason Noordberg*

1 *Nineteenth-Century Huntsville*

Founded six years before the Texas Revolution, nourished by tradition, and garnished by the culture of the Deep South — that was Huntsville in the nineteenth century. Located in the center of Walker County, Texas, Huntsville lies seventy-five miles north of the city of Houston.

Attracted by the artesian springs, where he stopped to water his horses, Pleasant Gray established a trading post on the site of Huntsville in 1830. He named the location for his former home in Alabama and carried on a profitable trade with the amicable Bedias Indians until 1848. Then lured by tales of gold in California, he headed for the West Coast with his family, only to die en route.

As early as 1837, one year after Texas won its independence, advertisements of the new town appeared in Alabama and in New Orleans newspapers, and posters proclaiming the location's assets were displayed in steamboat offices. Gray had laid a better foundation than he realized.

Consequently settlers migrated to Huntsville in a constant stream from Mississippi and North Alabama and Georgia. Unlike Gray, they were not interested in prospecting for gold. They were seeking land and homesites. People of solidarity and refinement, gentle and soft-voiced, they possessed wealth and expertise. So they came to the spot well-watered by artesian springs, where wooded red clay hills rolled gently down to the sand of the valleys, where fish flashed in the winding streams, and wild turkey and deer enriched a native habitat.

Some came on horseback. A few freighted the family silver and china by oxcart. Most came in caravans of canopied wagons transporting their families and chattels and household goods: professional people, skilled craftsmen — printers and saddlemakers and millwrights — mercantilers and financiers, astute planters who recognized the excellent pasture land and the suitability of the soil for the production of cotton and tobacco. Overland in hooded wagons they came to the site where Gray had built his trading post in a grove of oaks facing westward toward a prairie. They traveled with vision and such names as Bush, Elkins, Josey, Gibbs, Smither, Yoakum, and Thomason were conspicuous among them.

A few, like the Elkins and Joseys, later moved on to give an economical boost to a town seventy-five miles south named for Sam Houston, but they got their first millions together in the little town of Huntsville.

These settlers put down permanent roots and built graceful two and three-story dwellings with pillared verandas to catch the Gulf breeze, and later Victorian mansions. They mapped the area and laid out a town around a central square identified by the artesian springs. From north to south they named the streets pleasantly: Milam, Fannin, Cedar, Spring, and Tyler; and from east to west, Travis, Burton, Main, Jackson, Bell, and Farris. In 1846, when Walker County was lopped off the northern portion of Montgomery and Huntsville was named the county seat, they put a handsome courthouse in the center of the square bordered by Cedar, Main, Spring, and Jackson streets. Clustered around the rectangle business places marked points of intersections: identified as Barrett's, Foster's, Smither's, and Gibbs' corners.

The Henry Opera House — popular with the carriage trade and dilettantes — occupied an important position in the rectangle as did the City Hall. The wagon yard, south of the square, where in proximity gaming, drinking, and wenching flourished, was not one of the town's redeeming features. When ladies passed it, they lifted their skirts slightly as if to avoid contagion and admonished their young fry not to go near it, especially on Saturdays or tradesdays. Merchants and shopkeepers built wooden porches in front of their businesses for the convenience of their customers and attached hitching posts to take care of parking. For many years the rhythmic clop-clop of horse-drawn vehicles churning the mud and dust of the unpaved, tree-lined streets was familiar to Huntsvillians. Moreover, the acrid odor of livery stables, fused with the smell of saddle leather, was accepted as a necessary adjunct of civilization.

By 1850 enterprising Huntsville became the stagecoach capital of East Texas. Contributing vitally to the place as a commercial distributing point were the fine inns which specialized in Southern cooking and provided clean, comfortable rooms. The first frame building was the old "Globe Tavern," built around 1841 on Jackson Street from lumber whip-sawed by hand by "Old Father William Weser," who established a mill on the Trinity. The famous Keenan House went up in 1848 on the corner of Spring and Jackson streets — an old-fashioned country tavern, whose main structure and stables occupied almost half a block. In 1859 the Keenan House was destroyed by fire and not rebuilt. The Eutaw House, erected by B. S. Wilson in 1850, was for fifty years the town's most luxurious hostelry.

Although it was uncommon for ladies to engage in business in nineteenth-century Huntsville, Mrs. Lizzie Gibbs opened her inn — "Keep" — in the 1870s and operated it successfully for many years. Mrs. Gibbs endeared herself to the young people by opening her spacious inn to them for festive holiday dances and parties.

Another stimulus to Huntsville economy in the early nineteenth century was the river port of the thriving town and stage stop of Cincinnati, fifteen miles to the northeast on the Trinity. Supplies for Huntsville were shipped to Cincinnati by boat and hauled inland. Huntsville planters and businessmen also used the port as an outlet, particularly for the shipping of their tobacco and cotton crops. Because of its strategic location, the port of Cincinnati served points between Northeast Texas and Houston as well as Huntsville and Montgomery.

The very first business, other than Gray's trading post, was opened in a loghouse on the corner of Cedar and Jackson streets in 1841 by Thomas Gibbs. The second was erected by Robert Smither, a retail and wholesale mercantiler, who housed his business in a brick building as early as 1850. Still earlier, in 1845, the town published its first newspaper, the *Montgomery Patriot*, which was succeeded by *The Texas Banner*. The latter was the forerunner of *The Huntsville Item*, founded by George Robinson in 1850.

Testifying further to those plush years in historic Huntsville were the administration building of the main unit of the State Prison System established in 1837 by the Congress of the Republic of Texas (this was before the erection of the walls); the Austin College and the Old Main buildings on the Sam Houston Normal Institute campus, dating from 1853 and 1890, successively; the depot of the spur to the I. & G. N. Railroad, circa, 1893; and a number of residences, some of which predated the Civil War. These latter included the two homes of Sam Houston: his favorite, the story-and-a-half dwelling with the dogtrot erected in Smedes Valley in 1847, across from the Normal Institute, and the Steamboat house to which he retired after he was deposed as governor in 1861.

Nineteenth-century Huntsville was religious. There were five churches within the city limits, some dating from the mid-century. The Presbyterians got started in 1848; the Baptists in 1852; the Christian Church in 1854; the Methodist Episcopalians in 1857; and the Episcopalians in 1868.

The Presbyterians and the Methodists brought to Huntsville the two most important educational institutions — Austin College, for men, and Andrew Female College, for women. In 1851 the Presbyterians founded Austin College on Capitol Hill, the site formerly offered without success to the Republic of Texas as an inducement for the location of the capitol in Huntsville.

Chartered in 1849 and operated under the direct supervision of the Texas Synod of the Presbyterian Church, the institution was a training school for theologians. On Saint John's Day, June 24, 1851, the cornerstone was laid with formal ceremonies sponsored by the Grand Lodge of the Masonic Order in session at the time. Dr. Samuel McKinney, who became the college's first president, gave the dedicatory address. Civic-minded citizens initiated the event with a march in the torrid sun from the town square to the hill. As McKinney's lofty rhetoric churned the air and the standing audience continually mopped its collective brow, none other than General Houston himself held an umbrella over the speaker to shield him from the sun.

Although the institution was Presbyterian, prominent citizens of other denominations supported it wholeheartedly. For instance, the first board of trustees represented different religious affiliations and sounded like an early Texas Who's Who: Daniel Baker, Robert Smither, John Hume, George C. Reed, Henderson Yoakum, John Branch, Sam Houston, Hugh Wilson, and J. C. Smith. In addition to sectarian instruction, the college offered strong academic courses and established a Department of Law under the supervision of Royal T. Wheeler of the Texas Supreme Court and Henderson Yoakum. Austin College operated for a quarter of a century before its removal to Sherman in 1876.

In 1852 the Methodists established Andrew Female College on "Cotton Gin Hill," adjacent to Oakwood Cemetery, on the opposite side of town from Austin College. Chartered in 1853 and named for Bishop James Osgood Andrew, the institution became one of the best known early schools for Southern young ladies in this area. Like Austin College, it was enthusiastically supported by Huntsville citizens regardless of church affiliation.

Set in the midst of a densely wooded plot surrounded by a four-foot fence of open design, the campus was entered by means of quaint stiles. In addition to the usual preparatory and academic curricula, the college fostered an "Ornamental Department," offering instruction in music, art, and embroidery. Graduates were awarded the "Title and Degree of Mistress of

Polite Literature.'' Throughout the area the school was noted
for its high academic standards.

Although the institution was affected by the yellow fever
epidemic, it continued to operate until shortly before Sam
Houston Normal Institute was opened in 1879.

The war between the North and South left its impact. It
depleted the student body of Austin College leaving only the
younger boys and instructors. It interfered with the steamboat
traffic on the Trinity. Fewer and fewer boats plied the river's
reaches and finally disappeared. Cotton production diminished
from the loss of manpower to cultivate the crops.

Texas sent over 75,000 men to the Civil War who saw action
on one side or the other. Moreover, Huntsville did its part by
the Southern armies. The Fourth and Fifth Regiments of Hood's
Texas Brigade of the Army of Northern Virginia were recruited
from the vicinity of Huntsville. During the conflict the penitentiary and its manufacturing facilities proved to be a tremendous
asset. As the men went to war, the prison population decreased
and the space was used to hold Yankee prisoners: Banks' men
from the fiasco of the Battle of Mansfield, Louisiana; captives
taken by John Magruder at Galveston and Dick Dowling at Sa-
bine Pass. Many oldtimers remembered that Union sympathizer
Houston, who repaired to Huntsville in 1861 to nurse his political wounds and contemplate the futility of the war, often
pushed through the big iron gate to shout words of encourage-
ment to the boys in blue, while his son Sam fought for the Confederates and was wounded at Shiloh.

Two years after the Civil War ended, the yellow fever epidemic struck. The year 1867 engraved on many headstones in
Oakwood Cemetery in Huntsville testifies to the extent of its
ravages. Yellow fever decimated the port of Cincinnati and one
hundred fifty persons succumbed to it in Huntsville. Many of
the institutions, including Andrew Female College, were hastily
converted into hospitals and doctors were kept busy around the
clock. So numerous were the fatalities that multiple burials were

necessary. In some instances bodies of the victims were wrapped in sheets and the caskets laid out in lines to expedite the numerous burials.

But Huntsville survived both disasters. The very land itself proved to be a catalyst — the land and the people. The town retained its position as a commercial center for the surrounding counties and even though the International and Great Northern Railroad had bypassed Huntsville, the seven-mile spur that connected the town with the main line at Phelps Junction was put to good use. When the I. & G. N. Railroad first demanded a bonus of $10,000 to put the line through Huntsville, some of the citizens objected and later had to pay substantially more to get the branch line. Even this was only a temporary setback.

By 1898–1899, despite the fact that the population stood at only 2,500, "the Mount Vernon of Texas," as Huntsville became known, was making progress. In that year the town supported two banks, one daily and three weekly newspapers, fifty business enterprises, controlled the cattle market in the vicinity, produced 30,000 pounds of cured tobacco, from which half a million cigars were manufactured, and exported 20,000 bales of cotton. The two state institutions — the penitentiary and the Sam Houston Normal Institute — contributed to the economy.

Precursor to Sam Houston State University, the Sam Houston Normal Institute, named for the town's most famous citizen, had opened its doors on October 10, 1879 — the first institution of its kind in the state. To secure its permanent location on the site opposite the Houston homestead, Huntsville citizens purchased the Austin College building and donated it to the state.

On the faculty roster in 1898 were such interesting names as Dr. Harry Fishburne Estill, who taught Latin, school management, and civics; Professor J. L. Pritchett, who taught mathematics; and Miss Bertha Kirkley, who taught Latin and history.

Dr. Estill, a Virginian, who was one of the Institute's first graduates in 1880, succeeded his father on the faculty and would later become one of the school's most beloved presidents. A well-known historian, Dr. Estill wrote two history texts, one of which emphasized the Southern view of the Civil War. Professor J. L. Pritchett was a Missourian from an old and distinguished family. His brother, Henry Carr Pritchett, headed the school in 1898.

Until her death in 1949, Miss Kirkley, who had retired a decade earlier, was a provocative link between the nineteenth century and modern times. A native Texan and the daughter of Dr. J. E. Kirkley — a surgeon in the Confederate army — "Miss Bertha," as she was fondly called, was connected with the institution for half a century.

A familiar figure about the streets, leaning upon her stick, as she called her cane, "Miss Bertha" could walk faster than many a pedestrian forty years younger. An authority on American history whose keen memory rarely failed her, the gnome-like little creature had a reputation for being peppery and outspoken. When a person got in her way — or in her hair — she spewed out a string of expletives that would discourage the proverbial sailor. When words proved ineffectual, legend had it that she was equally skilled with her stick. No one ever heard of her using it, however, except as a pointer. Not averse to a bit of liquid refreshment now and then, when the brand name escaped her in a package store, she would point to the bottle behind the counter with her cane. "Miss Bertha" was endowed with a magnanimous spirit that attracted people. Her impact on Huntsville will remain for at least another century, because "Miss Bertha" was a breed apart. There was no one else like her.

The South lost the war and the old social order changed. Still many of the gracious customs of the vanishing era remained in socially oriented Huntsville.

Not only was the home a man's castle, it was his domain over which he was absolute master and supreme arbiter. He indulged his womenfolk and lavished luxuries upon them. Woman's place in the home, rearing children and supervising the household servants, or performing the domestic chores herself, was sacrosanct. Her role left her little time to consider money and business or national and international affairs. These mundane things were relegated to her mate.

In this masculine-dominated atmosphere rarely did the names of sheltered ladies appear in print. Ladies' initials were used to shield them from publicity.

In nineteenth-century Huntsville the gallants waited upon the ladies or paid their addresses with proper missives usually delivered by hand, gifts of flowers, and the age-old serenade. No lady attended evening devotions unescorted, and the request to accompany her had to be made at least a day in advance. The more aggressive gay blades made so bold as to take the young ladies for drives behind their spirited trotters in fancy buckboards or in flashy light, high buggies. But this intimate custom was usually pursued only by engaged couples.

The Beau Brummells competed in tournaments in which they rode horses at full gallop to snatch a succession of tiny rings on a long thin rod for the privilege of naming a lady as queen of youth and beauty. It was a contest that required tremendous skill and cooperation between the rider and his mount.

Whole families enjoyed Sunday afternoon drives in the family carriage or a newer vehicle called a surrey with a former slave or uniformed coachman in the driver's seat. Substantial citizens prided themselves upon the quality of their horseflesh.

Social calls were paid to all newcomers to the town who were expected to return the courtesy within two weeks. Visits were customary on Christmas morning among families and close friends, and Christmas dinner was a midday feast, to which numerous guests were invited. Open house was observed on New Year's afternoon, when the family's treasured recipes for Old English eggnog and special Southern delicacies vied for attention.

Young people enjoyed dancing in their homes and on holidays, or special occasions, in a downtown hostelry or in another public place. For instance in 1893, when the spur to Phelps was completed, a fancy masked ball was held in the courthouse to mark the event. Favorite dances were the polka, the schottisch, and the waltz. Promenading was also popular with the ladies as cutting the pigeon wing was with the gentlemen. Sam Houston himself was adept at cutting the pigeon wing. By the 1870s the Grecian Bend and the Boston Dip were introduced. New dance

steps were imported from the Mardi Gras in Galveston and the
fairs and fiestas in Houston.

Huntsvillians also welcomed the traveling troupes of players who performed in the courthouse and in tents. The most
popular of these was the "Bailey Family Troupe," of which
Mollie was the leading lady, soloist, and organist.

Both Mollie and her husband, Gus, had contributed substantially to the Southern cause. A talented cornetist who helped
to compose the marching song "The Old Gray Mare," Gus had
enlisted in the Forty-fourth Alabama Infantry, then later was
transferred to a regiment in Hood's Texas Brigade. He became a
leader of the regiment's band and performed with "Hood's
Minstrels." Mollie also sang and danced with the troupe. Consequently, many of the Huntsville veterans had known both
Mollie, whom they called "Aunt Mollie," and Gus personally.

Memorial celebrations and military reunions were gala
events in Huntsville. On memorial days citizens displayed the
Confederate flag prominently from windows and porches and
the "cemetery flowered in the blue and red of the Confederate
markers the sexton set up." Frequently these celebrations were
day-long affairs beginning with a formal agenda of addresses
and music and ending with military parades, topped off by bar-
becues. Usually a few veteran generals attended to add a touch
of glamour, and occasionally Jefferson Davis himself was spotted
among the guests or seated on the speakers' platform.

Reunions particularly were grand affairs. At a reunion of
Hood's Texas Brigade held in Huntsville in 1875 an immense
platform was set up in a grove west of the Andrew Female College for the occasion, and people attended from the surrounding country. Morning festivities got underway with a welcoming
address by Judge Benton Randolph. Methodist minister F. T.
Mitchell delivered the keynote address and several poems composed for the event were read. Among these was one read by the
veteran of General Longstreet's staff, Major Thomas J. Goree.

The afternoon's activities began with a barbecue followed
by additional speeches and music. If an occasional rebel yell split
the air, it was tolerated but frowned upon by the more dignified
citizens. The affair was climaxed by a grand ball that evening.

Visible among Galveston's resplendently uniformed Lone Star Rifles and such Civil War notables as Color Sergeant Norman G. Kittrell, Major E. Charles Hume, and General Felix H. Robertson, were a few tired grey jackets as the veterans went through the less exacting, and more pleasant maneuvers, of the polka and the schottisch.

Nor was nineteenth-century Huntsville any the less proud of its Texas heritage. The town's greatest links with the Republic were Houston and Yoakum, though one came before and the other afterward.

Despite Houston's unpopularity during the Civil War, he and Yoakum were Huntsville's heroes. Furthermore, citizens transmitted to their children a profound respect for both men: the one who is credited with the creation of the Republic and the other who wrote its definitive history — a two-volume work and astronomical achievement after the manner of the supreme Southwestern historian, Hubert Howe Bancroft.

Houston himself made available to the Tennessean, who came to Texas in 1845, much of the material from his official files — primary documents that later found their way into the state archives. He also gave the historian a first-hand account of the Battle of San Jacinto when the two covered the grounds in a buggy and Houston pointed out where strategic incidents occurred.

Outstanding citizens who affiliated themselves with every civic and cultural activity Huntsville espoused, both men were soldiers, statesmen, and attorneys. A West Point graduate and military careerist, Yoakum had probably seen more action on the battlefield than Houston. Enlisting in the U.S. Army in 1836, he served as a colonel in the Tennessee Infantry and was a veteran of the Cherokee and the Mexican wars.

Yoakum, who had married Miss Eveline Connor of Roane County, Tennessee, in 1833, lived with his large family at Shepherd's Valley, seven miles from Huntsville, while Houston and his household occupied an estate at Raven Hill, near Coldspring. The former preceded Houston in death by seven years on November 29, 1856, the same year his history of the Republic was

published. Houston was among those who took up a public sub-
scription to erect the stately granite obelisk that identifies Yoakum's burial site. Houston's gravesite near Yoakum's was selected by Mrs. Houston because she felt that Houston would
have wanted it that way.

The gaudy monument above Houston's grave (which nineteenth-century Huntsville did not provide) bears the inscription
attributed to Andrew Jackson: "The World Will Take Care of
Houston's Fame." Yoakum's monument is inscribed: "In testimony of the high appreciation of his character as a man, his usefulness as a citizen, and his ability as a lawyer — his fellow citizens have erected this monument."

Nineteenth-century Huntsville spawned legends. These involve the educational institutions, the penal system, and the
town and people themselves. There is the one concerning the
punctuality of Professor J. L. Prichtett of Sam Houston Normal
Institute. "Professor Joe," a prime favorite with the students,
was so punctilious that they synchronized their watches by his
movements. When he arrived by horseback on the campus each
morning to tether his mount invariably under the same tree —
"Professor Joe's tree" — it was precisely seven forty-five. "Professor Joe" allowed himself five minutes to remove the saddle,
fold the pad, and hang both on a limb. When he inserted his
key in the door of the administration building, waiting students
set their watches at ten minutes of eight.

Naturally the gentlemen of Austin College "waited upon"
the girls of Andrew Female College. It was said one day the gentlemen playfully trained a powerful telescope from their labora-
tory on the ladies of the opposite hill, a mile away, to spy on
their girl friends. To their amazement, they discovered that the
young ladies were equally curious about them and were engaged
in the same clandestine activity.

One of the town's legendary characters who served Huntsville and Walker County before and after the Civil War was old
Dr. T. W. Markham. An atypical nineteenth-century doctor,
who preferred a single mount to the horse and buggy, Dr. Markham was said to prefer quinine to sugar in his coffee. He be-

lieved so strongly in the preventive efficacies and healing qualities of the drug that he carried quantities loose in his saddlebags and administered doses of it from the blade of his pocketknife. Besides his saddlebags containing his medications, Dr. Markham was never without his fiddle case. When all else failed, it was said that he could hasten the arrival of an infant by inducing delayed labor pains with his resin and bow.

Another unusual character was the conductor of the train of the seven-mile spur connecting Huntsville with the main line of the I. & G. N. Railroad — J. Bob Tilley, familiarly known as "Old Horse." Because Tilley operated the line to suit himself, it was facetiously known as "Tilley's Tap."

Conductor Tilley frequently ignored regular schedules. For instance, if he were engaged in a game of dominoes, he would finish the game despite the loud blasts of the engineer to remind him that it was time to make the run. A lake near Phelps became a monument of sorts to Tilley. He stocked the lake and thought nothing of stopping the train to catch a few trout while the crew and the passengers waited impatiently for him to complete the trip. By the same token, Tilley would hold the train up almost indefinitely for belated passenger friends.

It must be reported to Tilley's credit that once when the "carknocker," whose duty it was to couple the air hose, test the brakes, and make minor repairs, went on strike, Tilley performed these chores himself and took his "Tap" to Phelps as usual. Still the conductor, who also had a reputation as a funster and yarnspinner, was so original in the operation of the spur that "Tilley's Tap" became the butt of quips for traveling shows and minstrels and even inspired doggerel.

At least once Tilley made an unscheduled run. Four convicts planned to use the train in a break for freedom as the depot was only two blocks from the penitentiary. One felon was killed, but three made it to the depot and commandeered the train. At Phelps Junction the inmates hoped to escape on the main line. Tilley's train was not noted for speed, and it is possible that he made the run more slowly on purpose. At any rate, when the train arrived at Phelps, mounted prison officials who easily outran it were waiting for the convicts.

To save time, Huntsville merchants often ordered a whole season's supplies on one invoice. This tale concerns a teamster employed to bring in a wagon load of hams from Houston. After waiting a reasonable length of time for the teamster, the merchant wrote a letter of inquiry to his supplier. The wholesaler replied that the order had been promptly filled and the wagon driver had left with it in record time.

After several weeks passed, the teamster finally arrived. When his employer angrily demanded an explanation for the delay, the man coolly informed him that he had stopped by his farm in Montgomery County to work out his crop.

The muddy streets of Huntsville became a part of the town's legend. The streets were so muddy that at one time, after the installation of the tap railroad, incoming freight had to be transported to the business section by wheelbarrow. At the same time country people coming to town to buy provisions and to sell their produce had to use as many as eight or ten oxen to pull their wagons through the streets. Then Main Street from the hill on which the Normal Institute was located to the courthouse square was so deep in mud that horses were unable to pull an empty wagon through it. Legend has it that signs placed in the biggest holes warned citizens that it was against the law to fish in the pools of water standing in the streets. Later this same street was the scene of Huntsville's first "paving." Where the mud was deepest the citizens installed small logs and covered them with tanbark.

Sam Houston was the greatest legendary figure of the time. A giant of a man towering over six feet, six, he generated stories by his very presence. One concerning him and his Indian friends is possibly not so well known as others. When he and his family were residing at Smedes Valley, his Indian friends, who delighted in racing their ponies up and down Main Street over the log paving to make the tan barks fly, visited him frequently. Houston entertained his redskinned guests privately out in the open, away from the residence, to avoid offending his wife, Margaret Lea. Outside the Houston residence, he smoked the peace pipe with them and worked convivially through several bottles of liquor. There was always, according to the legend, one particular condition that was rigidly observed.

The Indians determined by lot the one among them who was deprived of having any fun. The Indian thus chosen had to remain sober so as to take care of his inebriated contemporaries and see that they arrived at the reservation safely.

Legend and fact are sometimes inseperable. An example involves Huntsville's unknown soldiers. In Oakwood Cemetery there are seven graves in a row with cryptic inscriptions barely decipherable on indentical headboards. The inscriptions, seven times carved, read "U.S. Soldiers Unknown."

Who were the seven soldiers and why were they buried in a civilian cemetery in the nineteenth century? Only legend remains to suggest answers, one says that they were Union soldiers stationed at Old Cincinnati on the Trinity who succumbed to the yellow fever in 1867. Their identities were lost, so the story goes, in the transportation of their bodies to Huntsville.

Another legend identifies the seven as "Captain Stuart and the six unknown soldiers—" insisting that they were federal soldiers who died in the state penitentiary as a result of the epidemic.

An even less probable story comprises a third legend. This states that the seven were guards of an earlier day at the state prison. During a break, they were murdered, so the legend continues, and their bodies mutilated beyond recognition. Hence the anonymity. However, in that case, the word "soldiers" should have been "guards."

Still another assumption is that the seven men were replacements en route to a new military post who were victims of a band of marauders. Attacked, robbed, and summarily slain, they were buried unceremoniously where they fell.

The Unknown Soldier at Arlington, despite its symbolism, or possibly because of it, is to all Americans a memorable fact. The Unknown Soldier at Arlington is never without an honor guard and a wreath. Huntsville's unknown soldiers — whoever they were and however they fell — meet the rain and sun, unheralded and unadorned except for a mantle of autumn leaves tossed by the wind.

That was Huntsville in the nineteenth century — Huntsville from where, seven years before the advent of the twentieth century, the town's most illustrious son emerged. Into this town John W. Thomason, Jr., was born on February 28, 1893.

2 *A Good Place For a Boy . . .*

John W. Thomason, Jr., the first son of Dr. and Mrs. John W. Thomason, was born in the family residence, on Avenue J, two blocks east of the town square. Dr. Thomason had built the house in 1891 as a wedding present for his bride, Sue Hayes Goree Thomason, whom he married in 1892. The couple had moved into their new home in Huntsville after a honeymoon spent in New York, where they tarried long enough for the groom to take advantage of a short medical course and the bride to take piano lessons.

At the time of John's arrival the Victorian dwelling was a one-story structure. But as the family increased to nine children — four boys and five girls — a second story was added. It was in this spacious white house, with its 18-foot ceilings, bright-colored and curiously shaped transoms, and wide verandas — set in a plot of indigenous trees — that John Thomason grew to manhood and to which he returned throughout his adult life from faraway corners of the world.

John Thomason's forebears gave him a solid foundation. For more than a century before his birth, his ancestors had inhabited North America. In Pennsylvania before the American Revolution, they first migrated to North Carolina, then later to Western Georgia, and thence to Northern Alabama. Of Scotch-Irish extraction, John's paternal grandfather, Joshua Allen Thomason, of St. Clair, Alabama, was a physician and surgeon who was graduated from the University of Pennsylvania in 1837. as a young man of twenty-seven, he began his practice in North Central Alabama, where he married Emily Jane Fisher in October of 1841. Dr. and Mrs. Joshua Allen Thomason were among the early settlers who came to Huntsville in covered wagons in the mid-nineteenth century.

They settled on a plantation comprised of fifteen square miles west of Huntsville. One of the most extensive plantations of the time, it supported a domestic population of more than a hundred families. In 1861 Dr. Thomason built on the site the pretentious residence of Oakland, so-called because of the ancient trees wooding the acreage. Oakland became the ancestral Thomason home occupied by members of the family through several generations and the central gathering place for Thomason reunions and festive occasions.

It was there that the Thomasons' son, John W. Thomason, was born in 1864. The son followed his father in the medical profession and initiated a tradition that was preserved through several generations. John W. Thomason took basic academic courses at Austin College and pre-medical work at Texas A&M University before his graduation from the Medical School of the University of Virginia in 1887. Soon afterward Dr. John William Thomason began his medical career in Huntsville.

John Thomason, Jr.'s maternal grandparents were Major Thomas Jewett Goree, a native Texan born at Midway in Madison County, and Eliza Nolley Goree, the daughter of a prominent Mississippi family. The Gorees were married in 1867 or shortly before. Sue Hayes Goree, John's mother, who was born at Midway, was one of five children and the only daughter of the couple.

Major Goree, who moved to Huntsville to open a law office when his daughter Sue was three and later served as superintendent of the Texas Prison System from 1870 to 1890, had been a distinguished officer in the Civil War. First he served as an independent scout on the staff of General Pierre Gustave Beauregard of the Confederate States Provisional Army and afterward as special staff officer to General James Longstreet, one of General Lee's ablest corps commanders. Goree's long enlistment of over four years extended from Bull Run to Gettysburg and from Chickamauga through the Wilderness Campaigns to the final surrender at Appomattox.

Major Goree and General Longstreet maintained a lifelong friendship. Goree was also an intimate friend of Sam Houston, the two having read law together and discussed their cases.

John's maternal grandmother — a poet and intellectual — had been a member of the faculty of Andrew Female College for several years. Shortly before her marriage to Major Goree, Miss Nolley replaced the president of the institution, who succumbed to yellow fever. The Thomason family recalled stories of Miss Nolley's experiences when she was forced to perform the tripartite role as instructor, administrator, and nurse during that tragic period in Huntsville's history.

Before the end of the century the Gorees moved to Galveston, where he served as a city official and the couple became a viable part of the town's civic and social life.

Next to John's mother, his grandfather Goree exerted the greatest influence on his life. Major Goree transmitted to his grandson a love of chivalry and romance, along with an affinity for history. He inducted him into the mysteries of the woods, introduced him to the excitement of the hunt, and taught him how to handle a gun. He accepted the boy as an equal and the two spent much time together both before and after the Gorees moved to Galveston. Since Major Goree occupied a special place in his grandson's life, John addressed him affectionately as Dad. By the same token, he reserved for his maternal grandmother the pet name of Manda.

Young John Thomason's parents provided him with a stimulating background and a warm sense of home that never left him. But each made the contribution in an entirely different way.

Starting out as a general practitioner and surgeon, Dr. Thomason limited his practice in 1900 to the treatment of diseases of the eye, ear, nose, and throat. Throughout his career the doctor — a Fellow of the American College of Surgeons, member of the American Medical Association, and the State Medical Board—kept abreast of advances in the science of medicine and medical research and was outstanding in his field. In addition to his private practice, he also served as medical adviser to the state penitentiary and the Normal Institute and was active in the Walker County Medical Society and other professional organizations.

But Dr. Thomason managed time for other interests. A civic-minded man and dedicated churchman, he served the Methodist Church as steward for fifty years and as Sunday school superintendent for twenty-five. He was a Thirty-second Degree Mason, York Rite, and a zealous prohibitionist. As a young man during the harsh Reconstruction Era, he observed the idleness and the immoderation of youth, along with the injustices imposed by the United States government, all of which had an austere effect upon him and colored his views. Consequently, he was overly solicitous for the Thomason children. He supervised the children's conduct and taught them lessons of responsibility. To achieve this end, each child was assigned a light family chore to perform.

Following their children's completion of public school, both parents planned for them to have the very best educations available on both the undergraduate and graduate levels. Not only did Dr. Thomason set high standards of achievement for the children, he expected them to excel in their studies at school. He wanted his children to be able to take their places in society well prepared to contribute culturally and professionally to the communities where they would eventually locate. He was especially concerned about the success of his sons. He let the boys know that he was expecting them to compete and that he would be disappointed if they failed to measure up to the high goals he upheld for them.

Thus Dr. Thomason's chief interest, outside the medical profession, was the moral development and educational progress of the Thomason offspring. Both a bibliophile and bibliolater, he assembled one of the finest libraries in his section of the state and encouraged his children early to read the classics and the Bible.

Even before the children were old enough to read they were exposed to books. Before John entered public school he spent much time in the library poring over books with lavish color plates: The Doré editions of the Bible, Dante's *Inferno,* reproductions of the Old Masters in portfolio. Other favorites were a book containing halftones of the exhibitions at the Chicago World's Fair, a heavy Civil War folio of lithographs and engravings, and a profusely embellished biography of Napoleon Bonaparte that was serialized in the *Century* in the nineties. As a boy he examined these treasures lying on his stomach on the rug and taking care not to "break the backs." At the same time he was curious about the printing under the pictures.

Before the children were enrolled in school, they were introduced to good literature through listening to their parents read aloud. Years later John Thomason remembered the library as his favorite room in the house, cherished those winter evenings before the crackling logs of the familiar green-tiled fireplace when he and his brothers and sisters were fed large portions of the Bullfinch mythologies, of Homer and Plutarch, and the Old Testament.

Whenever it was possible Dr. Thomason provided his family with the classics in sets: Balzac, Dickens, Thackeray, Scott, Hugo, Tolstoy, and Shakespeare. He procured first editions of such authors as Mark Twain and Rudyard Kipling as they came out. He had collected many books dealing with Napoleon. He stocked his shelves with volumes of natural history and outdoor life, along with bound copies of such magazines as the *Century* and *McClures.* Innumerable biographies and memoirs of the Confederate leaders, including everything published on Robert E. Lee, graced the floor-to-ceiling shelves. Among his prized autographed copies was Longstreet's *From Manassas to Appomattox.* Prominent among the poets, in addition to Kipling and Shakespeare, were Byron, Tennyson, and Longfellow. Nor was the German titan Goethe overlooked.

After the Thomason children learned to read, Dr. Thomason prescribed a comprehensive — and obligatory — reading pro-

gram for them. As they advanced in school, so did he adjust the
reading schedule. As a part of the literary regimen, he encouraged the children to commit to memory a passage of Shakespeare weekly.

He specified a certain number of Bible chapters to be read
and reported on during the week and additional chapters on
Sunday. It took John a year to read the scriptures through. He
would later write of the experience:

> I learned to quote high music from the book of Job, and
> I felt the richness of the Song of Solomon without the least
> understanding it . . . we read much aloud in that library.

In future years he would remember the God of Dr. Thomason's
Bible as a deity of wars.

Sometimes reading late in the evenings, under the profile
portrait of General Lee — the face he knew before any other in a
picture — and in the presence of two statuettes of Napoleon,
John Thomason would extinguish the light, then rest his eyes a
few minutes before mounting the stairs for bed. John could not
remember when he first learned to read. But his father must
have taught him the simple fundamentals two or three years before he began school. At scarcely five he was writing legible letters home from Galveston, where he visited his maternal grandparents.

The daughter of a Confederate officer and endued with the
wealth of Southern idealism and gentility, Sue Thomason would
live to see history unfold through five generations and survive
her scholarly husband by twenty-two years. Reared in a cultural
atmosphere, she was equally influenced by her mother, a lover
of the arts.

A patroness of the arts herself and gifted musician in her
youth, Mrs. Thomason was a graduate of Coronal Institute of
San Marcos, a co-educational school founded in 1865 and later
acquired by the Methodist Church.

A devoted mother and wife, she concentrated on running a
smooth household in the manner of the Old South and implanted within her children the same principles of respect for
heritage, family loyalty, and obedience that had been her legacy. Realizing that her husband had a broader literary back-

ground than she, she approved of his monitoring the children's reading habits. Like her husband, she, too, was deeply religious and heartily endorsed the children's reading of the Bible.

So while Dr. Thomason took care of the children's minds and molded their characters, Sue Thomason — quieter and less assertive — interested herself in their bodies. She fed and clothed them properly; and if they needed medicine or nursing, she saw that these needs were met. More than anything else, she wanted her children to have good health and to be happy.

There were times, when the doctor's profession necessitated frequent and long absences from the home, that she had to act for both and see that the children were measuring up to family expectations. Above all, she was a gentle and loving mother and her children adored her — particularly her first-born and favorite, John, who, she thought, took mostly after her side of the family, with his flair for sketching and devotion to poetry and to the classics.

Like most mothers of the time, Mrs. Thomason taught her children the social amenities and respect for their elders — "to mind their manners," as it were. In the old pleasant way of their Southern forebears the children prefaced their answers to adults with the deferential "Yes, mam" and "No, mam" and "Yes, sir" and "No, sir."

Mrs. Thomason also instructed her children to be unobtrusive in the company of visitors, especially when the presiding elder of the Methodist Church came to dine or kinsfolk or brigadiers of the Civil War sat at the long table, elegantly laden with fragrant food around hog-killing time in the winter. The massive rectangular mahogany table, an heirloom transported from Alabama by oxcart in the early fifties, with its high spindle-backed chairs she had acquired as a bride and its old silver and white napery, was to Mrs. Thomason a source of domestic pride when twenty or more people sat around it in her home. At such times the children sitting toward their mother's end of the board were trained "to be seen and not heard." Such food, such eaters, and such conversation, John recalled, had no equal.

Mrs. Thomason insisted that the children show kindness and consideration for the servants. She herself never failed to look after the domestics when they or their children became ill or needed anything. The servants could always count on "Miss Sue," as they fondly called her, to contribute to their various "causes," often dubious enough.

In addressing the servants, the children likewise adhered to the old custom inherited from the days of servitude — "Aunt Jane Ward," "Uncle Sandy," "Uncle Tip," and "Aunt Sue Simms." John was a favorite with the servants. For instance, "Aunt Sue Simms," the principal cook, reserved for herself the privilege of preparing the wild game he brought in from his frequent hunting trips.

John's relationship to his brothers and sisters was another happy aspect of his boyhood that contributed to his formative years. He fondly recalled the haylofts where they dramatized scenes and impersonated characters from their favorite books — Long John Silver, Ivanhoe, Robinson Crusoe, and where they engaged in mock battles. They crossed the line with Travis and all fell courageously. They resurrected themselves in time to rout the Mexicans at San Jacinto with Bowie knives and pistol butts.

There were the horses the children rode; the ducks and upland game fowl the brothers hunted together.

From the outset the children were taught to respect each other as individuals and avoid foolish sibling rivalries. Actually they grew up in a rather harmonious atmosphere, and much of the extraordinary unity binding them together was directly traceable to the gentle influence of Sue Goree Thomason.

John Thomason's Southern heritage had a profound effect on his boyhood. When he moved onto the scene in 1893, his grandfather Tom Goree's friend Houston had been dead thirty years and the Civil War had been over twenty-eight. But in the mellow nineteenth century these distances were measured with a less exacting mental yardstick and viewed with closer scrutiny than the statistics indicate.

John himself was to write years later that Huntsville at the time of his birth was almost the same place that existed when its youth went to "Virginia behind John Bell Hood" and that "It was a good place for a boy."

Huntsville was primarily a good place for John Thomason because he got to know directly from his maternal grandfather, four great uncles, and another uncle on his father's side what the Civil War was like. One of the uncles, Robert Daniel Goree, served in the Trans-Mississippi theater of operations. The other three — Langston James Goree, who was wounded in 1863 and returned to Huntsville; Pleasant Kittrell Goree, who was affectionately known as "Uncle Scrap;" and Edwin King Goree, who sustained a severe leg injury that left him crippled for life — were members of Company H, Fifth Texas Volunteer Infantry, Hood's Texas Brigade, Longstreet's Corps, the Army of Northern Virginia. The other uncle, J. Mark Smither, was a sergeant major of Company D, Fifth Texas. These were the old soldiers

> . . . who had brought him up to tales of Lee's Army of Northern Virginia . . . great battles, glamorous attacks, full of the color and the highhearted elan of chivalry, Jackson at Chancellorsville; Pickett at Gettysburg . . . the red Southern battleflags, leading like fierce brightwinged birds the locked ranks of fifteen gray brigades . . . and the field music, fife and drum, rattling out 'The Girl I Left Behind Me':
>
> > Oh, if ever I get through this war,
> > And the Lincoln boys don't find me,
> > I'm goin' to go right back again
> > To the girl I left behind me —
> > — John W. Thomason, *Fix Bayonets!*

Never had the old soldiers who congregated around the courthouse in the center of the square in Huntsville a more wide-eyed audience. John Thomason relished their tales of Longstreet and Nathan Bedford Forrest and Stonewall Jackson. He listened to the men who followed them as they talked of Gaines' Mill and Second Manassas, of Gettysburg and Chickamauga and the Wilderness.

> . . . *If old Longstreet hadn't stopped at the Emmittsburg Road — if he'd just let Hood go on and take the Round Tops in the morning of the second day like we wanted to — !*

Not only did the Civil War veterans excite the impressionable boy's imagination, they took him with them to the veter-

ans' reunions and commemorative services, where he saw real
Confederate generals, heard the rebel yell, and waxed spell-
bound at the glowing oratory extolling the fallen martyrs of the
lost cause:

> *The Confederate battleflag, wrapped in everlasting glory*
> *— (Then all the old gentlemen with the bronze crosses on*
> *their lapels would get up in their seats and yell in shrill thin*
> *voices that made your back-hair stiffen: and the ladies would*
> *wipe their eyes . . .)*

Almost invariably some speaker would quote the lines of
the memorial plaque at the University of Virginia inscribed to
the young college men who volunteered unanimously:

> *They shall grow not old as we who are left grow old. Age shall*
> *not wither them, nor the years condemn, But at the setting of*
> *the sun, and in the morning, We shall remember them . . .*

Young John Thomason learned what it meant when a flank
guided true. "Guide Center" was the phrase the veterans of the
Civil War called it. Nor did he ever forget that his maternal
grandfather, Major Goree, who died in 1905 when John was
twelve, had stood with Longstreet and Lee at Appomattox when
the Confederate flag was furled and Lee surrendered his sword
to General Grant:

> *You walk softly at Appomattox, where uncouth markers*
> *. . . indicate the site of the McLean House, and where the*
> *trees stand gaunt . . . from the pleasant Virginia countryside*
> *because of what they saw take place. By Appomattox in the*
> *cold mist of the April evenings pass long files of ghosts; and*
> *they are not all of the Army of Northern Virginia.*
> —John W. Thomason, *The Old South Myth*

Nature had a hand in shaping the clay of John W. Thomason. As the oldest son, he took care of the family livestock. Behind the residence were barns and stables and a sty where milk
cows, horses, and "in those innocent days. . . a wallow of hogs"
were maintained. There in the stalls were kept John's grey pony
Nellie; Daisy, the blooded saddle mare; Ruby, Mrs. Thomason's
buggy horse; the two bays that drew the family carriage; another

pair for odd jobs; and the mules for heavy hauling on the farm. The chore gave John a valuable knowledge of animals and permitted him to spend much time out-of-doors.

One of his principal duties was driving the cows to and from the pasture west of town. He took the animals out early and on school days he went at four to bring them in. He rode through the square and past the last dwellings and into the country to the west. At such times it was exciting to encounter bluejays and flickers in the tall trees, red-headed woodpeckers across the road, and bluebirds and chickadees nesting in old fence posts. Several years later he recalled these trips vividly:

> Mockingbirds and cardinals sang in the orchards and the thickets. I watched for blue darters, and sharp-shinned hawks that quartered over the sedge-grass by the creek; and I admired the field larks that piped tunefully in the pasture, yellow breast and black gorget blazing in the sun . . . and to this day the wild-goose cry wakes a vague, pleasant restlessness in me. I remember now long wedges of them . . . against the cold reds of the autumn sunsets.

He had learned a great deal about birds from Ernest Thompson Seton's *Two Little Savages,* which his grandfather Tom Goree had given him the last Christmas of his life, as well as from his father's encyclopedias and nature books.

John Thomason had hunted as soon as he could point a gun. He remembered his first big green-head mallard, which he had bagged in the slough beyond Town Creek and his first Canada goose, which he had taken on a tank in the pasture, and his first big red fox squirrel shot from a pin-oak tree.

John Thomason acquired a special love for the woods where he rode: "the murmurous tall pines that made me, riding beneath them, my pony's hooves silent on the fragrant fallen needles, feel more religious than has any church."

He loved to recall the fields where the corn stood tall and "the cotton rows marched off like the files of a battalion in mass; the hay fields, rippling like water . . . and the great sun of Texas; and the first yellow star in the west on winter evenings."

From his earliest years John had shown a talent for drawing and painting with watercolors. He had experimented with charcoal, as well as with pen and ink, and had learned to combine his media. For instance, he would first sketch with either charcoal or pen and ink such birds as cardinals and bluejays, woodpeckers and larks, mockingbirds and hawks, ducks and quail. Then he would brush in the proper colors with paints from his palette. He produced hundreds of these colorful wildlife specimens in live scenes on cards, calendars, and odd scraps of paper.

At the outset his parents, particularly his mother, aware of his artistic leanings, encouraged him. They provided the boy with the essential paraphernalia and materials, along with art books, helped him set up a temporary studio in the corridor of the second story above the entrance, overlooking the magnolia trees in the front yard. Although they indulged him, it is possible that neither took their son's addiction to art too seriously at first. He was so young and had all of his life before him.

Frequently he was late driving the cows to and from the pasture as he stopped to sketch mallards on the surface of the pond or an exquisite formation of wild geese in flight, v-shaped against the dusk of a winter sky.

Nor could he resist sketching with pencil in the classroom after he started to school, even though he tried to do it surreptitiously. Sometimes it was the current topic under discussion that motivated him. A case in point was the day that his history class was discussing the incident of Martin Luther's routing the devil with an inkpot. As usual twelve-year-old John took no part in the talk, but he was drawing something in his notebook furiously.

When the period ended he ripped the drawing out of his notebook and presented it to his teacher. The sketch depicted Luther in his cell, with huge ink spots splattering the wall and the heels of the retreating devil visible from the doorway. One of Luther's hands hung over the edge of his desk, cluthing an almost empty liquor bottle.

As a schoolboy, John discovered that drawing was more fun than recitation or committing to memory the multiplication tables or the rules of grammar. School routine was a drudgery except for reading and history. As for the authors he was required to read in school — Scott, Cooper, Hawthorne, Stevenson, Twain—he had already become acquainted with them in his father's library. Though introduced to the reading of the classics by order, John had long since found reading to be one of his greatest pleasures.

John especially loved to draw horses. His interest in the animals began when he started taking care of the stock and increased when he drove the buggy for his father on house calls to his patients and the family carriage for his mother and sisters. By his twelfth birthday, the same year he had portrayed Martin Luther's encounter with Satan, he had had the pleasure of seeing a sketch of his pony Nellie published in a Sunday edition of the *Houston Post.*

John Thomason finished high school in 1909 without having excelled in his studies as his father expected. Dr. Thomason delivered the commencement address and awarded the diplomas.

The study habits of Dr. Thomason's son had not altered appreciably during his high school years. Even though an occasional English theme revealed that he had a better-than-average vocabulary and demonstrated flashes of brilliance, many of John's teachers almost despaired of him because of his seeming lack of interest. They charged him with being a dreamer. Not only did they prohibit his sketching in class, they considered it a waste of time. Even Dr. Thomason tried to explain to his son the difference between a pleasant avocation detrimental to learning and genuine talent indicative of a future profession. It was one thing to engage in a harmless pastime; to become obsessed with it was something else.

Besides, Dr. Thomason, who had permitted his son to observe some minor surgery performed in his clinic, in order to sharpen his knowledge of anatomy, had quietly hoped that his oldest son and namesake would choose a career in medicine and follow his lead as indeed he had succeeded his father in the profession. Two other sons would later preserve the tradition.

Characteristically, John showed no outward signs of resentment at his father's attempt to discipline him . . .

For with its classic books and Bible battles to read; its birds to sketch and paint; the secrets of its deep, dark woods to explore — and old soldiers' romantic tales of chivalry re-echoing from field to stream, Huntsville was a good place . . . *Huntsville was a good place for John Thomason.*

3   *Period of Exploration*

Like other gifted youth of his generation, John Thomason went through a period of exploration before settling down. For seven years he searched for identity with indifferent success. His experiences ranged from enrollment in three colleges, without taking a degree, and serious art study in New York City to teaching at three different schools and working as a reporter on the *Houston Chronicle*.

John had finished high school in his sixteenth year. As indicated, Dr. Thomason had hoped that his oldest son would follow him in the medical profession. In any case, if he had no inclination toward medicine, Dr. Thomason expected John to choose a comparable profession befitting a gentleman and to establish himself in a reputable career.

Dr. Thomason was aware that his son had an excellent mind and could have made a better record in high school had he tried. So John's father gave considerable thought to his problem and finally decided to enroll his son in Southwestern University. Accordingly, in the fall of 1909 John Thomason entered the school at Georgetown, Texas. The fact that it was a Methodist

institution recommended it and the size was right. A year away
from home in a university small enough to accommodate his im-
maturity and not so large that he would get lost in the shuffle
might be just the antidote to cure John of his dreaming and lead
him to decide on a career.

At Southwestern John's academic progress failed to keep
abreast of his social success. He was popular, dated the prettiest
girls of the Annex, as the women's dormitory was called, and
pledged the Kappa Sigma fraternity even before he absolved entrance requirements. He was active in the Athletic Association,
the Tennis Club, and the Camping Club.

He continued to sketch and paint and occasionally sold his
impressions of Indian heads for a dollar a piece to his classmates.
He feasted upon the scenery around San Gabriel River, where he
also hunted infrequently with a borrowed gun. Dr. Thomason
had prohibited him from having his own rifle at school, apprehensive that it would cause him to neglect his studies.

John H. McGinnis, Thomason's English instructor, who
later became the book editor for the *Dallas Morning News,* sheds
light on what John was like as a student.

> When he came to Southwestern he was a slender youth,
> refined in feature and a little absentminded in manner; hard-
> ly military [McGinnis wrote in the *News* later when he re-
> viewed Thomason's *Fix Bayonets!*] He made a creditable rec-
> ord, but he could not have called himself an earnest student.
> He would sit in his freshman English class and sketch in the
> back of his notebook or tap with his pencil on the desk, look
> furtively at his watch or eye the girls across the room. He kept
> up with what was being discussed but sometimes seemed
> bored by the discussion.

When the instructor assigned a theme on the topic "How
to Make Ice" and suggested that the members of the class visit
the local ice plant as an aid to preparation, John ignored it. Instead of following instructions, "John Thomason handed in a
narrative of a duck hunt," according to McGinnis, "and wild
ducks were flying all through the pages, in the margins, between the paragraphs, and on the backs. It was pen-and-ink

work, but even without colors you could tell well enough the teal from the mallards.''

To McGinnis' credit, he complimented the drawings and let the method of making ice go. He conceded that he failed to teach young Thomason how to write the exposition of a process. He went further — he did not suppose that he had taught him anything at all. Still McGinnis believed he had a stake in his former student's fame:

> He pretty well had it in him to do what he has done when I saw him first. But considering how young a teacher I was . . . I think I deserve some credit for not trying to make him stop drawing those ducks.

As a matter of fact, John McGinnis not only accepted John Thomason's nonconformity, he soon recognized his flashes of genius and later the two became close friends.

But if Thomason impressed his English instructor with the magic of his word pictures and stories embellished with pen-and-ink drawings, he had the opposite effect upon his mathematics teacher. Deficient in the subject to begin with, John was unable to cope with his professor's unsympathetic attitude and unorthodox methods of instruction. Also as director of the Fitting School at the institution, the instructor was in direct supervision of Thomason as he proceeded to remove entrance conditions.

The chasm of incompatibility between the two widened to the extent that John decided to do something about it. His opportunity came when he was invited to contribute to the *Sou'wester,* the university's yearbook published toward the close of the spring semester. John's contributions included an essay entitled ''Classroom Manners,'' which would have done credit to an upperclassman, and several illustrative and comic pen-and-ink sketches. One of the latter was a caricature of the mathematics instructor portrayed as a devil in hell, accompanied by a satiric parody of the Twenty-Third Psalm and signed by the fictitious name of a minister.

Revised Version of 23rd Psalm

Crip is my shepherd; I shall not want.

He maketh me to lie down beside the Prep; he fills my head with his old Math. 2.

But if I walk through the valley of the San Gabriel, I will fear no evil; for Crip is not with me.

He prepareth a table before me in the presence of mine Dutchmen: he anointeth my head with Mess Hall grease; my cup runneth over with watered milk.

Surelly goodness and mercy shall follow me all the days of my life; for I will not dwell in the House of Crip forever.

(Preacher) Dawson.

Plainly it was just a bit of schoolboy foolishness, and no doubt the "maligned" academician resented the indignity more for its being permanently recorded in the university yearbook than for any other reason. Still, John's choice of a biblical passage as a framework for his idea was considered by some of the faculty to be blasphemous, and it was said the authorities actually met to consider expulsion of young Thomason. Fortunately for him, however, all of them had been boys themselves once and some still remembered the fact.

There was on the Southwestern University campus in that academic year of 1909-1910 another maverick, who would not establish his own identity until several years later. Five years older than John and a member of the graduating class of 1910, he was so far off his course as to think of law as a possible profession. Despite the age difference between the freshman of 17 and the senior of 22, the students knew each other and later became admirers of each other's writings.

Interestingly, they had much in common, including the major influences in their lives: literature, the land itself and its creatures, and their parents. The other maverick's first work would be a collection of stories entitled *Legends of Texas*, published by the Texas Folklore Society in 1924. His name was J. Frank Dobie.

At the end of the spring term Thomason was greatly relieved to return to Huntsville for the summer vacation. At seventeen he clung to the old, leisurely ways of his boyhood and his interest in art was fast becoming an obsession.

In the fall of 1910, following a luxurious summer of idleness, tempered with the reading of his father's books and drawing and sketching, John enrolled at Sam Houston Normal Institute. He had not really cared to return to Southwestern and his grades hardly justified his matriculation at a larger institution. Besides, it was less expensive to live at home and attend the local school; and, more important, it would allow Dr. Thomason to keep an eye on John.

The Normal Institute emphasized teaching techniques. While John was still trying to make up his mind about the choice of a career, there was nothing wrong with the teaching profession. There was always the possibility, too, that at a different school he might find an innovative teacher or have an unusual experience that might bring him around. The good doctor had heard of such miracles.

At Sam Houston Normal Institute John Thomason did not undergo the regeneration that his father desired. Again he showed only mediocre ability in the classroom while excelling in extracurricular activities in the field of the arts. He did manage to pass his courses, however, and his reward was a piece of paper that certified that John Thomason was a teacher. The teaching certificate was issued automatically with his diploma.

In the fall of 1911, with two years of college behind him and a document entitling him to teach school, 18-year-old John Thomason secured a position as principal of a small rural school in Smith County, Texas, not far from the county seat of Tyler.

Intrigued at first with the newness and novelty of his surroundings, the young schoolman was fired with an almost overwhelming ambition to become the biggest man in the community. Soon, however, this goal gave way to disenchantment, and the young aristocrat found rural life almost intolerable: the absence of indoor plumbing, a monotonous diet of fat bacon and biscuit, and the lack of a congenial social life. In addition, the pressures that built up from his daily grind of attempting to hear twenty-five lessons, with shivering pupils often huddled around a potbellied, drafty, wood-burning stove in zero weather, were insuperable.

The sole antidote for these problems was the occasional hunting trips Thomason took with sportsmen of the community. The abundance of quail, geese, and duck was the little community's one redeeming quality. But that was not enough. Thomason was relieved to terminate what to him was like 'penal servitude' when the seven-months' school session closed on April 12, 1912.

At the expiration of his first experience in the classroom, the youth, dispirited and suffering from exhaustion, took a long vacation in which he visited relatives and friends in Midland, Texas. There in the soothing atmosphere of Paradise Lake he not only repaired his bruised spirit and regained his equanimity. He found ample opportunity to satisfy his almost insatiate desire to fish and camp out. There also he was able to participate in an exciting cattle roundup and drive and even engage in a bit of boyish skulduggery.

One evening he and two contemporaries attended a Pentacostal church service, and at the height of the frenzied demonstrations, peculiar to the sect, made an original contribution themselves. Although the value of the act was questionable, its efficacy was undeniable.

As John later described the incident in a detailed and painstakingly illustrated report to his mother, ''. . . shortly thereafter a pair of dogs sanctified with a brace of tin cans and inspired with highlife descended (out of Heaven doubtless) through a window back of the pulpit and paraded up and down the aisles searching their souls for tongues to tell how holy they were . . .''

Regardless of Mrs. Thomason's reaction to the disruption of the Holiness church service, it was the best testimony she could have of her son's complete recovery from the injurious effect of his first teaching job.

In the fall of 1912 John returned to the halls of academe. This time, accompanied by his brother Herbert, a pre-medical student and two years younger, he enrolled in the University of Texas at Austin. Classified as a junior and with a year of teaching experience, John was expected to demonstrate some maturity. Indeed at the outset he conceded to his father that he had wasted three years and was now determined to make the most of his opportunity. Undoubtedly he was sincere when he made the statement. While the studious Herbert took time out to attend a pep rally on campus, John remained in their room to avoid any outside distractions.

But the custom of neglecting his studies for extracurricular activities had by this time shaped into a pattern, and the comfortable paths of least resistance, especially where his art was involved, were impossible to abandon. Consequently, while he met his classes and maintained a passing average, he devoted his major attention to art. Both the *Brush and Pencil,* a student art club, which met on Thursday evenings under the supervision of an instructor from the university art department, and *The Coyote,* a humorous monthly magazine, provided outlets for John's art. In defense of the *Brush and Pencil* Club, which devoted three hours a week to sketching from live models, John wrote his father: "As Friday is not a heavy day with me, I have joined it and think I will get a good deal of help from it. Of course, I haven't much time for drawing. But I manage to do a little just to keep my hand in."

Even though he minimized his artistic activity to his father, John's talent was recognized by the university faculty and students alike. John could not resist writing home that the noted Professor T. U. Taylor had invited him to contribute a picture to his "big celebration" honoring alumni. As a result he produced a drawing that excited considerable praise. John earned quite a reputation as an artist.

Despite his recognition and popularity, John occasionally succumbed to moods of depression and wished that he could be "settled and steady like Herbert." Whereas Herbert of the scientific mind set himself a goal and attained it, was of Phi Beta Kappa stature, and learned early how to handle money, John of the artistic temperament was a dreamer who by his very innate nature was averse to academic routine and had difficulty in meeting life's daily demands. The ever-increasing "fraternal debt" might have alienated two brothers less devoted to each other. Whether John ever repaid his indebtedness to Herbert in full is conjectural. However, one time after he had begun teaching school, he actually sent his brother $2.00 to apply on an account of several years: "Your tender wailing hath rung in my ears for many weeks. I send you forthwith two shekels." At a slightly later date, John met Herbert's dun with this gem: ". . . My generosity is boundless as the sea, but alas that so frequently I lack the means of expressing it. In my capacious pocket there reposeth at this good hour one quarter and three nickels."

Although the brothers were disparate in nature, their personalities did not clash. On the contrary, they complemented each other. Furthermore, the two had three strong irrevocable links that bound them: pride of family, a tremendous love and respect for one another, and an infectious sense of humor.

While his pleasant relationship with Herbert and his artistry helped him to tolerate the monotonous academic routine, John did not resolve his inner conflict. At the end of his junior year he had barely passed his dull courses and had declined to choose a major subject of study necessary for the earning of an academic degree.

That summer of 1913 John Thomason returned once more to the leisurely life of reading in his father's library, sketching and painting, and pursuing his favorite hobbies of hunting, riding, and fishing. Nor did he neglect the attractive ladies of the community.

But lazy summer passed all too soon and John Thomason was faced with a decision. He could return to the university and take a degree or remain at home and sketch and paint and play. After his third try at three different schools, John was more reluctant than ever to return to the university classroom. As an alternative John reluctantly accepted another teaching job.

John Thomason became the principal of a public school at Penn City in Harris County. At least, it was not a rural school, the patrons would be sophisticated, and there was the compensation of being near the City of Houston and home. Besides John would be self-supporting and worthy of respect.

Located inland on picturesque Buffalo Bayou, between historic Morgan's Point and Harrisburg, Penn City was conducive to painting and sketching, and John's obsession with art increased in proportion.

> . . . the bayou landscape, on a misty grey day, under a dripping sky, has a very definite, if mellowed, beauty — " John wrote his mother, "the tawny sedge, the blue tree line that wells against the clouds, the pale water and the dark sombre pines. It is beautiful — a study in soft grey tones, all of it one color, save perhaps the cold radiance of a February sunset. I have tried hard and often to reproduce it . . . "

As soon as he was established in a boarding place, John wrote his mother that he had provided himself with a large new box of paints and plenty of paper and intended "to settle down to my usual time-killing activities as soon as the weather gets cold enough to discourage flies and mosquitoes . . . "

How he was able to manage the time must have been quite a problem, for he was pursuing a rather strict regimen. His schedule called for him to arise at 6:30, be at school by 8:30, and teach until 12:30 (noon) from Monday through Saturday. School resumed at 2:00 in the afternoon, after the lunch break and ran until 4:00 on week days with Saturday afternoon free. John's somewhat unusual curriculum included Latin, Greek, German, English literature, physics, and chemistry. Whereas only three hours a week were devoted to English, more than twice the time was spent on chemistry. Before the year ended John found himself also teaching Bible as he was astonished at the lack of knowledge the children had of such religious heroes as Sampson, David, Solomon, and others.

John also found ample game — doves, quail, and ducks — for hunting and pleasant sportsmen to accompany him. At times, too, he joined the professional hunters of Houston. On one trip to the Lynchburg marsh he and another hunter bagged nine ducks and forty-three smaller birds. He and his friends hunted in season and out and supplied as many as four or more families with game for the table. Sometimes the sportsmen went out by boat to hunt and fish. Since transportation to Houston and Harrisburg was essentially by water, a number of Penn City citizens had their own boats, which they shared with John. He

managed trips to Houston at least once a month to divert himself, visit relatives, and attend to business.

It was at this time that he met two people who were to figure prominently in his later life. One was a friend of Sue's — a
new girl who had moved to Huntsville with her family from Terrell, Texas — Leda Bass. Sidney John Bass, her father — a former
cotton planter and banker — had accepted an appointment as
superintendent of the Texas penal system. He and his family occupied the official residence reserved for them adjacent to the
Thomason home on Avenue J. John met Leda Bass before
Christmas in 1913 on one of his visits home and had apparently
heard her perform on the violin.

In a letter to Sue, dated December 6, 1913, he makes his
first reference to her: "Also I regard it a priceless boon to have,
even for a space so short, invested the same environment as the
ineffable Miss Bass. Give her my tenderest solicitations and
things. She wears her violin with great chic and distinction and
plays the clothes with symptoms of remarkable talent. I mean
she — oh, fiddle — I get mixed."

The other person was John W. Stevens, an octogenarian
who was a Methodist minister and former chaplain of the Confederate Army. A captain in Hood's Texas Brigade, the fighting
parson, like John's uncles and grandfather Goree, had a ready
fund of stories about the war with which he regaled his young
friend, who affectionately called him Uncle John.

Uncle John's favorite story, or the one he narrated with
most gusto, involved the Battle of Second Manassas in which
Hood's men, or rather the men of the Fourth Texas Regiment,
defeated the Zouve Regiment of Louisiana. The Confederate
veteran's feeling about the war surfaced violently one evening
when a Union veteran of that particular battle visited the home
in which he and Thomason were boarding.

The Battle of Second Manassas, also identified as Second
Bull Run, had been over for more than half a century, but the
two antagonists were as intensively loyal to their respective sides
as if the smoke of the battle had scarcely settled. History records
that McClellan's assault on the Confederate position was easily

halted by the Fourth Texas Regiment, which swept Pope from the field in a powerful counterstroke.

The two opposing veterans discussed the battle with restraint until the Yankee asserted that Lincoln's greatness exceeded that of Lee's, Davis', and everybody else's save that of Fighting Joe Hooker. The reference to Hooker, like the waving of the proverbial red flag, was the signal for action. But let John, who described the incident to his father, recount it:

> Whereupon the hoary valor of Gaines' Mill and Sharpsburg and Little Round Top unlimbered and went into action with Homeric thunder. For three hours they fought the war and reviewed the characters and attainments of the mighty ones to my edification. The skirmish was spectacular. After Uncle John conclusively demonstrated that if his men had had an allowance of one square meal a month, Lee would have driven Grant into Hudson Bay and dictated terms of peace from the Canada lines. Our Northern Brother, long since shouted down, observed 'But ye surrendered, goldarn ye!' and Uncle John, in spite of his eighty-two years, charged home to the Yankee's throat . . .

It required the combined efforts of John and the host to prohibit the Reverend Stevens from "finishing the job begun at Manassas in '62."

It was shortly before John terminated his employment at Penn City, when war with Mexico appeared to be imminent, that he first professed an interest in warfare as an alternative to a profession.

> . . . I confess, there's something in me — maybe a heritage — that is beginning to stir rather strongly. Well, *Dulce et Decorum est pro Patria Mori* — if your life don't happen to be fit for anything else and yet — to go and be shot like a gentleman would solve a lot of worries, wouldn't it? War is very old and very cruel, but as long as we are half barbarous we will want to play what Kipling calls 'the lordliest game on earth'. . . .

Despite the fact that John had taken advantage of his opportunities to hunt and fish to his heart's delight and had made lasting friends at Penn City, his brown moods returned occasionally. He had continued his painting and sketching despite every obstacle. His frustration increased as he recognized his own ambivalence. Above everything else, he realized that teaching was merely a temporary occupation. The fact remained that he really did not enjoy schoolroom routine and felt unable to cope with its attendant pressures and problems. If possible, he was more averse to it than ever. Not only did he decline reelection to his teaching job, he managed to close school a month early. By the first week in May he was back in Huntsville.

At home again, John apparently took his mother into his confidence and convinced her that all he ever wanted to do was to become an artist and pursue the medium professionally. He felt that he was temperamentally unsuited to the classroom and that, under the circumstances, to return to a university to earn a liberal arts degree would only be a waste of time. Consequently, with his mother's assistance, he prevailed upon his father to permit him to attend the Art Students League in New York City. Dr. Thomason, savant and scientist that he was, consented reluctantly. Still, if his son were determined to pursue art as a profession, the doctor recognized the necessity of formal preparation for it.

Accordingly in May of 1914 John embarked on the *San Jacinto* from Galveston and arrived in New York on the sixteenth. For his first night or so he checked into the YMCA at 318 W. 57th Street and registered almost immediately at the Art Students League at 215 W. 57th Street. Direct from the small Texas town of Huntsville, John did not adjust to metropolitan atmosphere easily. By May 22 he had moved into a place at 344 W. 57th Street, and only a few days later moved again — to 356 W. 57th. Two contributing factors to his frustration at the outset were that his trunk was delayed for several days and he had to maintain himself on a strict budget.

It is not surprising that he developed an intense aversion to the city at the start. Whereas in Huntsville, Texas, he was the eldest son of Dr. J. W. Thomason, well-known physician and surgeon, whose professional stature and political weight were recognized in the state, in brisk and objective New York he was just another commuter on the subway, an unknown face in

Times Square. "When I first came here," he wrote Manda, "it was hot and dirty, and I did perspire exceedingly and meditate with longing on Penn City and the State Tank. Indeed, I put in about three months disliking it so heartily that I turned my face to the wall and refused it the light of my countenance."

In July John had moved again—this time to a room at 501 W. 121st Street in the area of Riverside Drive, which was a considerable distance from the League and necessitated his taking the subway across town. He had made the change partially to accommodate his former Huntsville friend Owen Brown, who was living in New York at the time. Owen took his vacation in July and asked John to move into his place so that he could hold it— a matter of six weeks.

The many moves were frowned upon by Dr. Thomason, who requested an explanation or, at least, some kind of justification. In a letter dated July 11, 1914, John defended himself thus:

> I have been here two days and am very favorably impressed. Most of the people here are from the South — my landlady, Mrs. Young, is a Southerner—Georgia. The meals are good — $3.50 per week. The room, which is about two and one-half times the size of the first one on 57th Street is $4.00, and my lunch at the Students League about the same — a sandwich and a glass of milk. So that is less than $9.00. I can live here within the limits of the first location. The subway is unpleasant but endurable and so far as danger goes, I incur that every time I cross the street. Also it is clearner and quiet and cool out here, and Riverside Drive is only two blocks away . . . The very atmosphere is different. . . .

By December John was moving again, this time to an apartment at 400 W. 57th Street. It was his third location on 57th Street, where the League was situated. In the new living arrangement his expenses would amount to practically the same except for money for art supplies and to pay for eating out. Soon after settling into the new place, he wrote home that the quarters were quite comfortable with two large windows, and a steam radiator "with a high tenor voice."

Although John had tried to live within his budget, even

hoped "to eke it out with something on the side," such savings would have been at the expense of his study. "But since I have been painting . . . it's only by doing without certain things . . . I've worn dirtier linen longer this fall than I ever did before in my life, and more delapidated socks — that I have been able to keep in paints, etc. at all," he wrote Dr. Thomason

To Herbert, John facetiously wrote three months after enrolling " 'Tis a long and weary road, but there is consolation in the thought that Raphael got hungry and had to roll his own cigarettes just like anybody else!" He even joked about his tight circumstances: "I lead a blameless life, practically so anyway, for . . . Brother, the high cost of Sin is greater in New York than anywhere on earth."

But while the young artist was neglecting his laundry to purchase paints and shivering in his unheated garret, his dream of eventual success never wavered. ". . . I am taking my first faltering footsteps in the enchanted country that I have heretofore only seen from a great distance," he confided in a letter to Manda. "As yet the enchantment lies a good way ahead. And there be grievous rocks and thorns. But my feet are in the road, and if I keep on long enough, the search is sure . . ."

He drew or painted one or more pictures outside of his League work every day and devoted at least one day a week to sketching scenes of the city and various persons he encountered on the streets or in public places. Sometimes that dream led him to do boyish things. For instance, when he went to the Hotel Astor on Times Square to sketch manservants and maidservants (whom he "stared out of countenance" as they stood and waited to be tipped), he wrote Herbert about it on the hotel's elegant letterhead stationery.

Moreover, as the weeks and months passed and he began to feel the pulse of the metropolis, he derived much satisfaction from his work. One Saturday morning he and another art student began sketching the Italian chapel of the Cathedral of St. John the Divine; and before they realized it, it was late afternoon. Neither had even thought about lunch and had worked eight hours straight!

"But I never attempted such an absorbing study," John wrote his mother, "or such a difficult one . . . and it was splendid practice in proportion and perspective." While he discussed the mundane subject of finances candidly with both parents, he wrote his mother about his art as if she were an artist herself:

> The cathedral is a tremendous building and as it stands now, is less than two-thirds its intended size. It has been building twenty-odd years, and they say they expect to spend forty years more on it before it arrives at completion. There is much beauty and impressiveness in it and much that is not so pleasing. For one thing, inside and out, it is a bewildering mixture of Romanesque and Gothic and heaven knows how many other schools. Some of it suggests Mission! But there are certain corners and turns in it that, as pictures, are perfect jewels.

John also found the scenery along Riverside Drive, overlooking the Hudson River, inspiring to sketch and paint — "the Drive, where sights are to be seen that put Niagara Falls into second place." His attraction for ships possibly dated from this period in New York. He enjoyed sketching the vessels docked in the Brooklyn Naval Yard and the ships comprising the United States Atlantic Fleet, which were anchored in the Hudson River.

As an art student, Thomason was dedicated. He arose around eight each morning, frequently after having sketched or painted until midnight, and was on campus by nine. As his work advanced, he selected whole sections of the city to explore for material and inspiration. On one such day-long expedition he and an artist friend chose Blackwell's Island (now called Welfare), where the city's prisons and hospitals were located.

The artists found the small island both beautiful and interesting. But what to John was most evocative was a cross-section of slum area attached to it. He and the friend had covered the area on foot, pushing their way "over, under, and around swarms of the dirtiest children you ever saw in a nightmare and the noisiest . . . besides push carts, fruit stands, bootblacking joints and so on to infinity and beyond," he wrote his mother. And, in spite of the fact that "it had a smell you could lean against," he got some fine impressions of various types of humanity: "women that called to mind Titian's and Raphael's madonnas — creatures that might hae stepped out of Doré's *Inferno*." John cherished a copy of Dante's *Inferno*, which Paul Gustave Doré, late nineteenth-century artist noted for his wood engraved illustrations, had published in 1861.

If not phenomenal, John's progress was consistent. In his painting class under Dumond, in a short time he advanced from the bottom to the fifth place in a class of thirty-odd. Two months later he ranked close to the top. In the drawing class he ranked higher and held the top place.

The young art student felt particularly indebted to George Bridgeman, instructor of his life class. Bridgeman praised John's bird studies and his nudes and encouraged him to return to the League for further study or spend at least a year in the country teaching himself through experience before attempting to launch himself on a professional career. Bridgeman, who had himself studied for six years in Paris under Jean Leon Gerome, the world's greatest draughtsman and the artist who painted the masterpiece *Bonaparte before the Sphinx*, was convinced that he had learned more in six months painting on his own than he had in the atelier in Paris in six years.

Bridgeman had likewise taught John how best to work from models. Years later Thomason would write in the *American Mercury* that Bridgeman had said unless the artist followed his model with extreme care, he would usually draw a self-portrait. Thomason would likewise recall later how true his teacher's prediction was: "And I remember a portly Marine officer . . . saying that he wished I would draw some Marines with a little more meat on their bones and not fellows with legs like kildees or sandhill cranes."

The two major influences on Thomason's art and indeed upon Thomason, the person — outside the League — were the war in Europe and the City of New York itself. The impact of the war was profound. ". . . There are wars and rumors of wars," he wrote his father on August 5. "The newspapers are having a wonderful time wallowing in red ink, adjectives, and cartoons. The cry of the 'extra' is heard in the land morning, noon, and night, and between times! and everybody is talking battle, murder, and sudden death.

"I watched the crowd before the *Times* Bulletin Board this morning, French and Germans being very conspicuous in the throng and extremely enthusiastic. The *Marseilles* was sung, but as every item that came recorded a German reverse, the sons of the Fatherland were rather silent."

In Battery Park, where John had spent the morning sketching, a crowd of Serbian reservists were waiting to go out to one of the liners. Already shipping from the metropolitan port had felt the ill effects of French, German, and English men-of-war reported to be lying outside the harbor.

The people who congregated before the Times Square Bulletin Board fascinated John. One night he walked from Washington Square — 4th Street — to Times Square — 42nd Street — just to watch the people. Everywhere he was confronted with audible and dramatic reminders of war. "A covey of newsies by every corner yelping hoarsely of battle and death . . . ," he wrote home. "Dense crowds before every bulletin board watching for news — great maps of the theatres of war in shop windows with the positions of the armies and navies indicated by their national flags."

The report came out that France was sweeping across Germany seventy miles over the frontier of Alsace, with the enemy fleeing before her. In the battle Germany had sustained 35,000 casualties to France's 15,000. The news was greeted by handclapping, yells, songs, and cries of "On to Berlin — *a Berlin! a Berlin! A bas les Kaiserliche (Down with the Kaiser)!*" The crowd, according to John, was a Broadway gathering of both sexes — a "typical richman, poor-man, beggar-man-thief" assembly. He found it strange that so much anti-German sentiment prevailed in a place extensively populated by Teutons.

"Up here the war continues to be the topic of the hour," John wrote his father a day or so later. "And I suppose it will be for months to come, though it's hard to believe that it can last very long. Why, where Napoleon killed his thousands, they'll kill their tens of thousands. It's all horrible and revolting, but it's like a big fire, you can't help taking an interest."

The actual effect of the war on John's art was mixed. In one sense the war situation nourished it. Despite the horrible subway jams and intense heat, John found raw material for his studies in anatomy. There were in "these hideous throngs — an arm, a neck, an ear, a mop of auburn hair, a pair of shoulders, an expression" that he was inspired to record later on his sketchpad or on canvas. "One thing about art," he said, "you can study it anywhere you turn."

On the other hand, the war posed difficulties. A part of John's failure to interest editors of such magazines as *Recreation* and *St. Nicholas* was traceable to the adverse impact of the war upon newspapers and magazines in general.

". . . You can have no idea how hard this wartime is on artists and writers," he wrote his mother shortly before he severed relations with the League in May of 1915. "All the papers are running on curtailed staffs. War means dead loss to them financially. Some of the big men in the writing game are doing hackwork, just as big illustrators are forced to making automobile and piano ads — and the little men are starving."

In November John's interest in the war prompted him and his friend Paul Jones to inspect the American dreadnaughts *Wyoming* and *Florida* docked at the Brooklyn Navy Yard. Through the courtesy of the retired commander Hulme, whom John had met at the League, the two were permitted to see more of the battleships than ordinary visitors.

The inspection of the dreadnaughts recalled in John's mind an article he had recently read in the *Times*. The German officer, who wrote it, said "that the simple stone over the grave of a battle-slain German private was of more value, gravity, and meaning to humanity than all the sky-piercing Gothic edifices ever reared by the hands of man."

Finally Thomason saw the war's impetus on art per se and certain artists in particular. "This war's end will see the world center of art shift to the New World," he wrote his mother in December, "for art loves not cinders and dead men's bones — and J. W. T., Jr., Sid Lewis, Bud Ross, K. Beck, E. S. R. Von Soltzer, L. Apenelli, Fat Gottlieb, and certain other League Vagabonds will be just in time to hop on the bandwagon . . .

Engrave these names on your memory. They will be famous.''

(As will be seen, John W. Thomason did not ''hop on the bandwagon.'' Some eleven years hence he took a secure seat in the more substantial and permanent vehicles of American art.)

But the city itself that had bewildered John at first influenced his psychological and artistic promise. Indeed he had recognized the metropolis as the artistic center of America within six months after his arrival. ''New York is the center,'' he wrote Mrs. Thomason. ''. . . Politics, medicine, art, education, business — nearly everything, especially art. There are artists and near artists here by the ten thousand, all the big ones and most of the little ones. . . .''

On still another occasion he conceded to his mother that

New York is a wonderful place for an artist to begin . . . I cannot conceive of any surroundings more calculated to stimulate both eyes and imagination. All the emotions, save happiness, one sees them in a single block. I like it better than when I first came, that is, I endure it better. I do not think I can ever really care for the city or the life here. But it's the greatest school on earth—this Melting Pot of the Nations.

Sometime later he wrote his brother Herbert:

I am not a New Yorker. I never will be . . . But, nevertheless, it is some place. There is a fascination about it that gets into your blood, after a time; and New York becomes a habit, just like whiskey or wearing sideburns . . . Every part of it is different from every other part . . . The bum that asks you for a dime down at the Battery is not like the beggar in Central Park. Nor yet like the panhandler in Madison Square, yet they're all New Yorkers. Wall Street is Wall Street, and Broadway is far, far from Fifth Avenue. And between them and 125th Street there is a great gulf fixed. Yet each is definitely New York. You have the white light district — Broadway in the forties and go through a side street to Eighth Avenue and you're in a different world — cross to Ninth and it's the same.

Funny how this city lies. On the water fronts, North and East rivers, the scum, the vilest possible dregs of mankind — the sweepings of Manhattan and all the world. Then you

work in from either side, and the scale rises as you go to
Broadway on one side with its bejeweled and bedizened
splendor and Fifth Avenue, on the other, with its opulence
and respectability to the nth degree. . . .

But the more deeply immersed in art Thomason became,
and the more he explored the city, the more his evolving philosophy sustained him and his smalltown provincialism gave way to
urban sophistication. "I realize that I am going just now
through a period — not of change — but growth," he wrote his
mother. "I am beginning to see things . . . in certain matters
my views are not nearly as hidebound as they were."

Thus New York had been not only the testing ground for
John Thomason's art, the city had dangled before him a new horizon. Startled at it, he was still a youth, still a romanticist. But he
had turned his eyes away from provinciality to fix them on a
cosmos of challenge — a metaphorical ocean — demanding talent,
perseverance, production, even heartbreak, and often defeat.

John Thomason's classes closed at the League on May 9,
1915. He remained in New York a few days to visit friends and
to see the fleet of the United States Navy, consisting of sixteen
dreadnaughts and fifty auxiliary vessels, anchor in the Hudson
River for review.

". . . I have never . . . seen a more impressive sight than
the succession of great grey hulks lying black against the sunset
on this noble river . . .," John wrote his mother. "There is
nothing more grim and powerful in appearance than the big
Texas, for instance, off Grant's tomb.

The news of Germany's sinking of the Cunard liner *Lusitania* on May 7, drowning 1,189 people, including 128 Americans,
added significance to the review of the American fleet. "Feeling
runs very high here," John reported to the home front.

Before leaving New York, he warned the family not to expect him to have many pictures to show as he had been doing
mostly studies. Since canvas and drawing board were so expensive and could be recovered, he usually painted a thing out as
soon as he finished it and worked another on the same surface.

By the middle of May John was reunited with the Thomason family in Huntsville. The following month of June he was engrossed in helping the hired hands bale hay and walk the fence lines of the farm. After his twelve months at the League, the farm work, along with tennis, riding, hunting, and fishing typified a welcome change.

Meanwhile he had found a new playmate to enjoy these activities with him — a girl, whom he had met earlier but whose time had seemed to be well taken care of as he, himself, was writing off a previous love affair. She was popular and attractive Leda Bass, the daughter of the Thomasons' neighbors, Mr. and Mrs. Sidney John Bass. Leda had lately returned from a year's study at Brenau College, Gainesville, Georgia, and was attending Sam Houston Normal Institute. A capable horsewoman, who could also handle a gun and enjoyed sports, Leda Bass was apparently John Thomason's ideal.

> . . . There never was a girl like this [John would describe her later in his story *Luck*], like a flower and like a flame; a girl who'd get up early to play tennis or go duck-shooting on the lake, a girl who shot and rode like a slim, quick boy, gracious, and merry, and born to tall, white-columned Southern porches; a girl of his own people . . .

Furthermore, she possessed literary knowledge and, like himself, enjoyed poetry. So the artist who returned to Huntsville to sketch and paint his way to fame and fortune divided his time between his absorbing new interest and art. And duck hunting at the State Tank at Wynne Prison Farm became more exciting than ever before.

John had returned home a much improved artist. He had mastered the principles of anatomy, the techniques of landscape drawing. Even though he deplored commercial art, he had become adept at illustration. His sketches became increasingly less static and assumed the professional proportions of real life and movement. His attention to detail increased perceptibly. It was incredible what he could accomplish with even one or two slashing lines. He practiced on the family as models for portraiture and had hopes of painting a serious portrait of Manda if sittings could be arranged. He concentrated on sketching horses, continued to excel on his duck drawings and paintings of other species of wildlife.

But as rewarding as Thomason's work was to him as an artist and regardless of what his training had cost him in time and comfort, it had failed to solve his immediate problem. While he had returned home a better artist, there was no denying that he was a young man of twenty-two without a productive profession. It was too early in his career to depend upon his art for support, and there was nothing else he wished to do.

Whether real or imagined, John felt his father's disfavor of his seeming idleness, and his old feelings of frustration returned. He sketched and painted through the summer and autumn, but he felt restrained and inhibited. Thus at Christmastime, always a joyous, festive occasion in the Thomason home, John decided to seek outside employment.

Almost before he had time to look around, a sudden vacancy occurred in South End Junior High School of Houston and John was offered the position. The position required the teaching of five forty-minute classes daily in, of all detested subjects — algebra — and ancient and medieval history. When John informed the trustees that he was incapable of handling the algebra, that he even disliked the subject, they were impressed with his candor, dangled a higher figure before him, and urged him to accept the position anyway. With nothing else in view, John took the job in sheer desperation.

Although South End Junior High School was one of the best in the city — "the Blue Stocking School," John called it — and his associates were congenial, the routine was like excruciating punishment.

At the same time John was the recipient of other offers. Dr. John T. Moore of Houston commissioned him to execute surgical illustrations in watercolor of a delicate operation he performed. John accepted the commission only because Dr. Moore was a close friend of his father. Waddell's, the furniture store, tried unsuccessfully to employ John to do furniture posters. John did accept an assignment from the *Chronicle* at this time to write a series of special articles on various subjects.

"Was ever one so badgered?" he complained to his mother. "All that I want is a horse, a gun, some books, and some
paints, and a few prescribed creature comforts. . . ."

Since he was temperamentally unsuited to teaching and the
position interfered with the romance he had begun with the
green-eyed girl next door, his moodiness reoccurred.

The United States had not entered the First World War as
yet. But the Mexican outlaw Pancho Villa's raids on the border
of New Mexico evoked concern. When the bandit and his men
put the torch to a portion of the town of Columbus on March 9,
1916, three troops of United States cavalry incurred substantial
casualties in an exchange of gunfire. President Wilson sent General John J. Pershing on a punitive expedition into the interior
of Mexico in retaliation. John Thomason watched these developments with avid interest.

Tension mounted in Texas as the old Texas-Mexican war
wounds were reopened and citizens became apprehensive lest
the bandits cross the Rio Grande and start another war. As the
politicians fumed clamoring for troops and Pershing chased Villa through the mountainous Mexican terrain without success,
the National Guard from Maine to California was mobilized to
meet the emergency. Some 110,000 officers and enlisted guardsmen were assigned patrol and garrison duties at strategic points
on the border, with 40,000 undergoing training in three Texas
camps — Fort Brown, Fort Sam Houston, and Fort Bliss — and
one — Fort Huachuca, in Arizona.

Congress passed the National Defense Act in June of 1915,
expanding both the regular Army and the National Guard. In
addition, the act provided for citizens' military training camps
throughout the nation.

Fort Sam Houston at San Antonio set up one of these
camps in Texas; and Thomason, who was now free of his irksome
teaching duties, enrolled and spent the month of June in training. It was excellent physical therapy for young Thomason.
". . . I am hardening up and coloring like a Meerschaum pipe,"
he boasted to his mother, "and eating most enormously and
sleeping with a profundity that I never knew before." The outfit arose at five-thirty in the mornings, engaged in battle maneu-

vers several hours daily and practiced cavalry drills in the afternoon. In the evenings the men sat around camp and swapped stories. As he had always enjoyed outdoor living, camp life, coupled with military training, was particularly invigorating. Additional target practice at Leon Springs, near San Antonio, added materially to his enjoyment.

For once, at least, Thomason had found something other than sketching and painting that appealed to him. Another thing, the few weeks of military training dissipated for good any further agony in the schoolroom. Whether he was aware of it or not, John Thomason had just passed a notable milestone.

When he returned to Huntsville in July in glowing health and with mental spirits soaring, the family could hardly believe it. Camp routine had forced him to neglect his art, but he resumed it with renewed fervor.

By July 15 he was back in Houston, where he began work as a reporter for the *Chronicle*. Publisher Lester B. Colby remembered favorably John's articles written for the paper earlier and accepted him immediately when he applied as a reporter.

Although the stereotype has often been hung on him, John Thomason did not begin newspapering as a cub reporter. He joined the *Chronicle* staff in time to inherit the job of covering the political campaigns that waxed hot in the month of July — an assignment usually handled by seasoned newspapermen. Despite the long and gruelling hours and writer's cramp from pounding the typewriter keys, he liked the work. "I'm glad I came down here and started this thing on my own," he wrote his parents at the end of his first week. "It is most fitting that I should."

From routine political coverage Thomason advanced to special assignments and feature writing for the Sunday edition, with focus on human interest. The special assignments included interviewing such celebrities as opera stars, motion picture actors, statesmen, and sports figures. It was said that because of his addiction to fine food and as a means of boosting his economy, he arranged for the interviews to coincide with meal times as nearly as possible.

One of his first special assignments was a story on his Grandfather Goree's friend Sam Houston and his famous Colt revolvers (on display at the Houston Memorial Museum) accompanied by pen-and-ink illustrations. He later gave the originals for the illustrations to one of his former teachers and both are in the Thomason Collection at Sam Houston State University Library.

Another of these byline pieces involved John's first airplane ride over the city of Houston. Even though later, he came to prefer other means of transportation to flying, the experience of observing Houston from the air was one he cherished. "There is a sense of exhilaration about riding on the wind," he wrote Mrs. Thomason, "so high that the wheeling buzzard below you looks the size of a chicadee . . . and soaring like an archangel above certain insignificant groups of pigmies that are men — that is fascinating."

He was, he said, exceedingly diverted by the sight of Rice Institute, as the institution was then called. It reminded him of "Margaret's [alphabet] blocks scattered on the grass." Margaret, the baby sister, was then three or four.

Another special assignment proved to be nostalgic. John was instructed by his city editor to hound the footsteps of the Farmers Union, which was inspecting a building site on Buffalo Bayou. In the party that made the trip downstream to Penn City were Houston mayor Campbell and other officials. "At Penn City there was enough fried chicken and things for a regiment," John wrote his mother, "and afterwards we got in cars and wandered over the country that I hunted over three years ago."

Among his Sunday feature articles were subjects as diverse as ships, historic characters, and springtime. "20,000 Sightseers Visit Ships At Turning Basin: Hard Day For Jackies" appeared in the edition of March 26, 1917. The destroyers on view at the Turning Basin were the *Reid* and the *Monaghan,* about which Kipling wrote a poem in 1898. A sidebox centering the feature was titled "Tips for Everybody." In addition to instructions on how to reach the Basin, the tips itemized "What not to do": "Don't fall overboard; Don't put your initials on the guns; Don't tip the officers; and Don't try to smuggle a kodak aboard."

A typical feature on an historic figure was one captioned "Washington Was a Man Long Before He Became a Hero." By this time the young reporter had mastered the technique of writing a good simple declarative sentence. His lead: "Americans are long on hero worship." Second sentence: "It is the best thing they do." Concluding paragraph:

> And the grave of Washington is not at Mount Vernon, where his bones lie awaiting the resurrection in which he had an old-fashioned and orthodox belief — but in the heart of every loyal American citizen on earth, wherever he wanders. And these United States are the monument that stands to him.

The head of the article on spring, which ran in the Sunday edition of March 25, 1917, was "Read This And Know Just What Spring Is Like." It carried two subtitles: "Romantic Reporter Is Given an Assignment to Find Out the Views of the Public" and "He Interviews Indiscriminately From Stenographers to Bartenders and Finds New Philosophy."

The article was doubly refreshing because of the personal note interjected into it. Moreover, Thomason learned that spring meant different things to different people and very few of them concurred with Noah Webster's definition. But the most satisfying commentary on the meaning of spring [at least to the romantic writer] was that made by a lady, whom he declined to identify by name: "I went 300 miles [Terrell] to ask a certain very lovely lady what she thought about spring and things; but that's nobody else's business but ours. And if you really want to know what spring is — that's it."

No doubt Leda Bass, whose family had moved back to Terrell, read the piece with interest.

But not all of Thomason's newspaper work was pleasant and exciting. One assignment in particular he recalled with mixed feelings. The *Chronicle* was conducting a crusade against the legalized red light district of the city and the young newspaperman was assigned to cover it. His graphic reports of the ladies of the evening, who populated Houston's "Dollar Row," attracted widespread attention both in the press and in the pulpit and the crusade was a success.

"I sometime think of that vice crusade and wish very strongly that I could retract some of the stuff I wrote. I now have better sense," he was quoted in the *New York Herald Tribune*, July 9, 1927.

Nor did Thomason neglect his art at this time. Sundays he was frequently seen in the company of Paul Wakefield, another *Chronicle* reporter who maintained quarters with him at the YMCA, and the editor W. W. Ferguson traveling to the Gulf Coast or hiking over the umber-tufted salt domes, destined to yield millions in Texas oil, to paint landscapes and seascapes.

Perhaps the extra activity that brought most genuine satisfaction during Thomason's days as a reporter was the commission to paint several war posters which he secured through his army friend, Captain Lewis Maverick, on duty at the time in Houston. Wakefield served as the artist's model and the two shared the pay equally. As the former later remembered it, it was one of their lucky windfalls since neither made a large salary. Wearing a borrowed O.D. blouse and holding a rifle from the local recruiting station, Wakefield did his best to impersonate a soldier "take a trench," while John — invariably an expert with a weapon — laughed at his model's awkwardness.

When the posters were finished, the fellows celebrated in the customary legal manner of the time at the taproom of the Bender Hotel.

Not only did the nine months on the *Chronicle* provide John Thomason with invaluable experience, it was a splendid ego builder. With his confidence restored, he considered becoming a professional journalist. He very well might have, too, had it not been for world developments. There was an element of daring in newspaper work that could be translated into something glamorous, and the click of typewriters in the city news room and the smell of printer's ink commanded respect.

But Thomason's stint on the *Chronicle* was more than a boost to self-esteem. It typified another milestone. Coincidental with the appearance of his final feature, under dateline of March 25, 1917, was an announcement in the paper by Major General George Barnett, of the United States Marine Corps, that applications for 150 young men to obtain commissions as second lieutenants in the Corps, were being accepted. Since Thomason had enrolled in the officers training program at San Antonio, shortly before his employment on the *Chronicle*, he read the announcement with more than ordinary interest.

No sooner did John Thomason pocket his last paycheck at the *Chronicle* building than he walked across Congress Avenue to the Rice Hotel to enlist in the United States Marines. It was April 6, 1917 — *the day the United States declared war on Germany.*

4 *A Marine Takes a Bride*

After his enlistment, John Thomason was assigned to the First Texas Battalion, along with other units, and was called into federal service for basic training in New Orleans, where he applied for his reserve commission.

Until his commission as second lieutenant came through on April 19, retroactive from April 10, Thomason in the capacity of gunnery sergeant — a non-commissioned officer of the first rating — drilled the men from five to seven hours daily besides doing other work. He started the day's drills with the "Fall in" order at 5:45 in the morning to march the men to breakfast. While another sergeant, "a fat and yielding person," marched at the head of the line, Thomason ran up and down the sides shouting such admonitions as *Keep your fins down, you unfortunate and perfected pollywog . . . Silence in ranks, you onery Soup-Hounds . . . Get in step, you poor accident, you!* By the time the men reached the mess hall, they represented a decent line.

In almost every letter home John reassured his mother that there was small likelihood of his being sent overseas. ". . . As for war, have no uneasiness. I do not think that we will get any for quite a while. Even in the event of sending a force in Europe, the officers here do not believe that Marines will be sent." There were not enough to make a showing, he said. The entire corps numbered only seventeen thousand.

As for the rigorous military discipline and rough living, thanks to his "misspent life," John was faring better than most of the men and was more physically fit than he had been in a long time.

Several months before he joined the Marine Corps, John and Leda had become engaged. As the two families were close friends and neighbors, they welcomed the prospect of union. But Mr. and Mrs. Bass wondered if it would not be in their daughter's best interest to wait until the end of the war to marry because of the uncertain situation and the chance that John would be shipped overseas in a short time.

As favorably disposed as he was toward the match, Dr. Thomason wanted to make certain that John understood the obligation that marriage incurred. Not only was he concerned about John, he was likewise thinking of Leda, the youngest of the four Bass children, who had enjoyed all the advantages that her well-to-do parents could provide and upon whom much affection had been lavished. Above everything else, he hoped that the marriage would be happy and satisfactory but he could not refrain from considering the economy involved.

As early as January, 1917, John had discussed with Dr. Thomason his intentions to wed. Undoubtedly, his father laid before him some of the facts and responsibilities that such a step would entail. John appreciated his father's counsel.

". . . The ideas you have advanced are, as always, full of reason," he wrote him. "I cannot expect to make provision as you were able to make. I can guarantee necessities and something over, and I believe that I have sound reason to feel confident of the future. Needless to say the one most interested is fully informed as to what may be expected; we [he and Leda] have contemplated it for some time and know what we are doing as well as two young people can be expected to know . . .

"It [marriage] is rather a fearsome thing when you contemplate it, however; and there will be nothing particularly easy about it — but I am not especially looking for easy things. . . ."

At twenty-three John Thomason, still a dreamer of sorts, had much to learn about life and living. Undoubtedly he was glad that he had recognized an earlier infatuation for what it was and had put it behind him. But he had fixed his eyes on an expanding horizon — and now Leda Bass had become an integral part of it.

"Meantime, the spring goes on in much beauty to summer," he wrote his mother. "This is a country [New Orleans] of mockingbirds and roses and a blue sky wonderfully tender and soft at evening." It was the statement of a youth deeply in love, a soldier to whom mockingbirds and roses held special meaning. The mockingbird, particularly, had become a symbol of that evening when the lovers had first committed themselves to each other. Etched in his memory at the moment, the scene, only slightly fictionized and moved forward in time, would be recorded later in his story *Luck* for all the world to see:

> The intimate shadow of the box-elders held them. His white uniform and the filmy dress she wore were one pale blue where they sat . . .
>
> Then a finger of moonlight drew across her face and, leaning close, he saw that her eyes were darkly luminous and very tender. His heart turned over inside him, and he put his arms around her and kissed her . . . holding her tightly, he talked at length — And when a word lacked, her mouth, shyly responsive, was near enough.
>
> Then there were no more words, and the world lay away from them like an opalescent mist pierced through . . . by the silvery jets of the mockingbird's ecstasy. The perfume of her hair was in his nostrils, and a strand of it lay across his cheek, and in the silence he knew that her heart was beating against his . . .

In April John obtained leave from his company in New Orleans to visit Leda in Terrell. She may have told him at that time that her parents were insisting that she wait until the war's end to marry him. "I had a visit to Terrell that will stay in my memory as long as I have a memory," he wrote his mother on April 16.

"Slowly through many painful things — but surely through the wonder and the beauty, I come to understanding." Only three days later he received the notification of his commission and on April 20 Company C was transferred to the Marine Barracks, Navy Yard, Charleston, South Carolina, for further training.

With the reserve commission of second lieutenant Thomason's monthly salary was $146 per month, or $1700 a year. He had written his mother that he still planned to marry before the year was out or as soon as he could see some ground to stand on. "I will not give up that hope until all the avenues are closed — and not then, unless she [Leda] so directs." Though not excessive, the second lieutenant's salary was encouraging.

In his letters Thomason paraphrased a line from Goethe's *Die Leiden des jungen Werther (The Sorrows of Young Werther)* — "It is principally a world of sorrows" — especially when he felt uncertain about something or was weighted down with a problem.

But as John's prospects improved, so did his morale. "I would delight your eye now," he wrote Mrs. Thomason soon after arriving at Charleston, "I have a military haircut, a pair of leather leggings, ancient army trousers, a lovely O.D. shirt — tunic is the word — that I bought out of my few remaining funds, and a hat much too big for me."

In June Thomason was further encouraged by the notification that his reserve commission in the Marine Corps Branch of the National Naval Volunteers had been replaced by a regular commission in the United States Marine Corps. The new appointment was prestigious and carried more weight than a commission in the Volunteers.

Meanwhile, the war in Europe still dominated the American press. A Marine officer, recently returned from France and under secret orders in Washington, reported that the Allies were "licked to a frazzle and just hanging on by the skin of their teeth." England, he said, could grow no stronger and France, weakening every day, hung on by a sort of spiritual strength. "In France . . . for the last two years, they have never asked *if* the Americans will join the Allies. They ask *when* the United States will throw her forces in."

Although Thomason kept trying to reassure his mother that he did not expect to be sent overseas, he no longer deluded himself. At this time the Fifth Regiment of Marines was already stationed in France attached to the First Division, American Expeditionary Force; and Thomason's chances of an overseas assignment were increasing almost hourly. He realized that any day now he was subject to transfer for specialized training before being assigned to a combat unit.

In view of these developments, Thomason wished more than ever to hasten his marriage in order to spend the remainder of his time in the states with Leda. Luckily she and a party of friends went to New York for a vacation in August. When he learned of the fact, he contacted her and secured leave to arrange for a wedding to be solemnized in Washington, D.C.

As there was so little time, he did not have the opportunity to invite members of his family to witness the ceremony. As soon as Leda consented, she telephoned her parents in Texas, who came for the wedding. After the ceremony, solemnized on August 24, 1917, John sent his mother the following telegram from Washington, D.C.:

> Married Leda in Rhyland Methodist Church 7 o'clock This Evening Mr. and Mrs. Bass Present Also Paul Everybody Happy Leave For Charleston Tonight.

The next day he wrote both parents of the details. "A fat-faced divine with leonine hair and orotund voice joined us in holy matrimony. And it was over before I got out of my daze — and I'm not quite out of it yet." For the ceremony Thomason was in regulation field service uniform, khaki blouse and breeches, puttees and cap. Paul Jones, who served as best man, wore white serge. The bride was attired in dark shimmering blue and carried a bouquet of roses like gold of Ophir — "And, oh well, she was Leda, quite the loveliest bride the world has ever seen . . . It seems to me the church was done violently in red, but I'm not sure. It had pillars in front anyway.

"We drove a little afterwards through twilight Washington and it was beautiful. There was no crush, no mob, no full dress or other agonies — we just got married."

Thomason conceded that he now had another commanding officer and that it had taken some fancy finagling between
himself and the post commanding officer to arrange for his leave
and for him to perfect the details necessary for the event in the
short time that he had.

The couple did not have a honeymoon. There was no time
for it. They proceeded immediately to John's base in Charleston, where they spent the fall.

Now John began to fill his letters home with accounts of
their married life, sometimes referring to Leda as Divinity, at
others calling her the Rose of all the World. For instance, "the
pellucid waters of the pleasant life led by the Divinity and myself."

The sorrows of young Werther had been replaced by the
joys of matrimony, the days passed "like the links of a golden
chain, drawn smoothly through langurous fingers. Quantico
looms as ever afar off. Meantime, it is well. We are enjoying
what they say is the best month of the year in these latitudes.
October — and sufficient unto the day is the evil thereof."

Like a slightly belated wedding gift — and indeed a thrice-
welcome one — Thomason received his promotion to first lieutenant in October. Naturally he could hardly wait to share the
news with his mother: "The main excuse for this letter . . . is to
impart the merry tidings that your illustrious, talented, and
war-like son, John W. and so forth, has been commissioned a
first lieutenant in the so-glorious United States Marine Corps.
The Senate ratified his nomination August 7, 1917, so that I
have back pay (some $24 plus per month being the difference
between the pittance of a second lt. and the opulence of a
first!)."

John did not rush home immediately to inform Leda of
their good fortune. Having work that needed his attention, he
awaited until noon to "rejoice her [with] the gladsome event."
In the interim one of the other officers had slipped off to tell his
wife and she, in turn, "feloniously traipsed up to Leda and
slipped her the information." The incident may have provided
the occasion for the couple's first spat. Leda thought that her
husband should have been the first purveyor of the news, but

"the Divinity admits," he confided to his mother, "that I am the best husband she ever had."

In characteristically modest John W. Thomason fashion, the lieutenant concluded his letter to his mother with "I am about as fit to be a first lieutenant, second in command over 250 fighting men — as a pig is to lecture on the Higher Pantheism!"

Then in November, as the leaves came sailing down and the bare branches stood stark against the winter sky, Thomason received his transfer to Quantico, Virginia, to affiliate with the Marine Corps Training Center. Located forty miles south of Washington on the Potomac River, the Officers School at Quantico was an austere place consisting essentially of a long bunkhouse at the far end of the infantry camp that began with the railroad station. To get to it you went down half a mile of dusty street and crossed a rutted parade, and there before you stood the barracks, grim and immutable.

The Advanced Base Force was in the process of being organized at the post to serve either in the Caribbean or in Europe; and young officers, like Thomason, were undergoing training for combat with the Marine Brigade in France. As a student officer, Thomason began a comprehensive 90-day course of instruction. Ever mindful that his separation from Leda was imminent, John wrote his father that Quantico was nearer to the war than Charleston.

Since no quarters were available for married officers at the post or its immediate vicinity, Leda — given her choice of Washington and Fredericksburg — chose the latter. Only fifteen miles from the base, Fredericksburg was closer to the training camp and the cost of living less expensive than at the nation's capital. Furthermore, the charming antiquity of the town and its historic atmosphere appealed to the couple, together with the fact that its rolling hills reminded them of Huntsville.

They found a satisfactory apartment at the popular inn, operated by Mrs. Louise Coates, on Prince Edward Street. Because of the nature of the course and the stiff competition it entailed, Thomason was forced to live at the base with the other officers and returned to Fredericksburg for the weekends. At the time the only means of transportation available was the pedestrian Richmond, Fredericksburg, and Potomac Railroad which took him directly to the post.

John could have wished for a better living arrangement. But, even so, Leda was highly adaptable and enjoyed the social contact with the other officers' wives and families who patronized the hotel.

Thanksgiving passed pleasantly enough. After the bountiful repast set before her guests by their buxom landlady, Mrs. Coates, John and Leda seized the opportunity to visit the historic sites of Fredericksburg: Kenmore, Rising Sun Tavern, the Washington home and farm, Chatham, the headquarters of General Burnside in 1862. Their favorite points of interest were the Confederate and national cemeteries, the latter being the site of the Battle of Fredericksburg, where General Burnside and his Army of the Potomac had met decisive defeat at the hands of Lee. Whereas Union losses were 1,300 dead and thousands wounded, Confederate casualties stood at less than half of that figure.

The battle site held personal interest for John because of his grandfather Goree's participation in the battle. John took the occasion to write to Manda of his appreciation:

> I have walked with the Rose of All the World on Marye's Heights and around Brompton, where a national cemetery marks the position that the Confederate South held against Burnside and the North half a century ago. Here was stretched the line of grey riflemen. Hood and Cobb and Hill and Barksdale under Longstreet and Meagher's furious Irishmen — and here at Lee's headquarters rode and stood my grandfather later, Major, C.S.A., with his commanding officer, on such a winter day as this, in 1862.
>
> Well, the place that I shall fight, if I do fight, is a world's width away. But I think Dad [Major Goree] will go along, just as debonairly as he set his face against the Yankees a long lifetime ago . . .

Sleighs cutting through Fredericksburg's deep snowdrifts, their silver harness bells jangling merrily, under the frosty stars, reminded John and Leda that Christmas was approaching. Leda loved the sleighing and sledding while John, who had had to adjust to the cold and discomforts of the Quantico barracks, preferred the bright open flames and crackling logs.

John failed to obtain the ten-day leave he had applied for and so had to cancel plans to spend Christmas in Texas. He did get four days, beginning with Saturday, and one day for New Year's. That Saturday he arrived home in time to lunch with Leda and join her in their Christmas shopping that afternoon. What fun it was! But "Lord . . . it comes high to cultivate the spirit of the merry Yuletide as it should be cherished in this year of grace 1917 — wartimes," John averred.

John and Leda devoted Sunday to the business of wrapping up their gifts to send to their families in Texas. Nor did they forget Uncle Ed — the man of all work in the Thomason menage — and Aunt Sue Simms — the finest creator of Southern cuisine in the world. John's Christmas letter, with his gifts entrusted to his parents for delivery, merits repetition here. The superscription:

> To The House of Thomason
> Mr. Edward Franklin, Sr.
> and to
> Mrs. Sue Simms,
> with respects
> The contents of this envelope are worshipfully dedicated
> Christmas 1917

The text: To Ed and To Aunt Sue, of happy memories and pleasant recollections:

> O our very good and faithful Friends, if the Lieutenant and his bride had been there you would have caught us 'Christmas Gift.' That we are not there, but far away from Ed's warm fires and Aunt Sue's good things to eat, is not your fault. So here's a bottle of snuff for Aunt Sue and two-bits' worth of red stick candy for Ed and a Merry Christmas to you both.
>
> The Lieutenant   and Miss Leda

John and Leda had contemplated taking a little trip to celebrate the holidays — to Baltimore perhaps to see a show; or Washington where they had repeated their wedding vows; or Charleston, where they had taken up married life together. But the days "slid by like a dream," and the luxury of just being with each other was enough. So John and Leda spent their first Christmas together in ancient Fredericksburg. And to mark the event Mother Nature sent them a snowstorm and a blizzard that the oldest inhabitants pronounced the coldest spell the Civil War battle site had known in fifty years.

Sunday morning in weather 4 degrees below zero John and Leda took pictures. To add to their excitement, Herbert, who was attending Johns Hopkins University in Baltimore, braved the snow to spend the New Year's weekend with them.

John had deferred his customary Christmas letter home, awaiting the arrival of the family Christmas box. In postponing the letter until December 31, he had much more to report.

Also, he had hopes of being able to return to Texas sometime in February or by March 1 at the latest. It was like whistling in the dark. "This night a year ago, I was gathering material for a story on 'How the New Year Came to Houston!' " he wrote home. *"Wonder where next Christmas will find me."*

Only Destiny knew where John Thomason would be in December of 1918. One thing for certain he would be where the United States Marine Corps and the American Expeditionary Force designated. In February he completed the intensive training at Quantico. Out of 133 officers, he finished among the top 14. Under the circumstances it was an extraordinary achievement since many of the officers with whom he competed were seasoned men with years of military training.

The first forty officers were automatically assured of overseas billets with the Second and Third battalions. The remainder would serve aboard ship or at stations at home or abroad maintained by the Marine Corps.

Among the hand-picked men, Thomason was assigned to the Third Replacement Battalion to command a platoon of sixty-five men. Elated at the duty he was awarded for overseas, John wrote his father: "I am very proud of my designation — and when they give me my platoon — 65 mighty men — I will be prouder than a peacock with seven tails . . . I think the Rose of

All the World is a little proud, too. She is a good soldier — the Rose of All the World."

Thomason underwent further training involving open and trench warfare. The additional six-weeks devoted to it permitted him to join Leda in Fredericksburg, from where he commuted daily by rail to the post. Arising at 6:30, he took the 7:00 o'clock train to Quantico and returned at 4:30 in the afternoon. Early in March the couple moved into more spacious quarters at Lewis and Princess Anne streets.

Inasmuch as all requests for leaves were disapproved, John invited his parents to visit him and Leda before he was shipped overseas. Professional commitments prevented the doctor from coming, but Mrs. Thomason made the trip to Virginia. Traditionally the wives and sweethearts and mothers of the Marines never said their goodbyes at the ports of embarkation for to do so was thought to bring bad luck. The idyll in Fredericksburg ended in April, and John said his goodbyes in Baltimore, where the three also managed a brief visit with Herbert.

So Leda Thomason, "a good soldier herself," shed tears in private and returned to her family in Terrell — to wait out the war.

John Thomason, together with other officers and enlisted men comprising the Third Replacement Battalion, entrained at Quantico for the Philadelphia Navy Yard, where they boarded the transport *USS Henderson* for overseas duty in France with the Marine Brigade of the Second Division, American Expeditionary Force. On the same ship, which sailed on April 22, 1918, was another young officer, a fellow by the name of Laurence T. Stallings.

Since John was unable to bid farewell to Dr. Thomason in person, he did so by letter four days before sailing. The document is more than a statement made man-to-man. It is eminently more than expression reflecting the father-son relationship. It was the communication at a strategic time in his life that only such a person and son as John Thomason could write to the man who had played the key role in his existence, the third person in the world whom he admired and loved the most.

It is a letter written proudly, gallantly. It is a letter accentuating the end of something . . . a letter hailing the shining advent of something else. Because of its uniqueness, it is quoted here with but slight elision.

18 April 1918

My Dear Father:

Events having been quite crowded of late, there has been little time to write or, indeed, to do anything but attend to the work, strictly in hand, which is good, for work is quite the best anesthetic there is for all mental perturbation . . . I got my assignment to this replacement battalion April 4, and the time of my departure is very near, Very near. I shall communicate with you all by some manner every day — letter or postcard . . . You understand, of course, that any more definite method of communication is strictly forbidden and with the best of reasons.

For the rest of it, I am glad to go. All my life I would be humiliated if I didn't. I have some little intelligence, some little training, and very greatly the will to lead men in this good war and I am more proud than I can say that I am being chosen to lead sixty-five large, healthy Americans against the Boche.

I suppose that it is wise — although never doubt that I intend to come back and that I believe I will come back — for a man who sets out on such a venture to cast up his accounts with life. I have done so. And I find that the big balance in my tangled bookkeeping is all on my side of the ledger. Life, the world — you-all — have been very good to me — and beyond my deserts. For this I am grateful and humble. There are some blots in my ledger, some smears . . . But a careless hand, and not a malicious one, made them. . . . I believe I like the word 'thoughtless' better than 'careless' there — I might have been a better son. I wish I had.

If [I] could atone, all in one sharp minute, for all of the anxieties and disappointments and sorrow that I have caused those who love me, I would — most gladly. Perhaps I can. And if I don't come back, my Father, don't feel bad about it, for more than my share of the good things in this life have come to me — more in my twenty-five years than come to many people in a long lifetime. . . .

It is a sorrow to me that you didn't come up with mother — just as it was wonderful to see her again. Leda goes back with her as far as Longview, I believe. I told them goodbye in Baltimore last night. There are no finer, truer, sweeter women — or braver — on this earth — and their love and faith should make almost a god out of the son of one and the husband of the other. I commend Leda to the love that I know you have already extended her. Wise and tender and very lovely she is, and I am a better man for her — — —.

I would like to see all of you again and home and the rest. But it may be best that I go this way — I never liked goodbyes. They smother me. So say for me — 'Until we meet again' — to my sisters and my brothers and all the rest, and be assured yourself of all my love.

Very respectfully and affectionately,

Your son,

John W. Thomason, Jr.

Lieutenant U.S. Marines

Address unless otherwise given

First Lieutenant John W. Thomason, Jr.
144th Company, 3rd Replacement Battalion
U.S. Marines
American Expeditionary Force
France

Captain John W. Thomason, 1928. This is a favorite family photograph.

— Courtesy Leda Thomason

5 *A Marine Goes to War*

The *USS Henderson* arrived at St. Nazaire in the first week of May, 1918, and within ten days Thomason reported to the Fourth Marine Brigade of the First Battalion, Fifth Marines, under the command of Major Julius S. Turrill. The battalion was training with other elements of the Marine Brigade and the Second Division, A.E.F., in the area of Chaumont-en-Vixen, northwest of Paris.

The metamorphosis of the naive youth into a seasoned soldier and forthright realist, as he identified with the United States Marine Corps, is projected in his frequent letters home. Such a letter typifying the demeanor of the almost incorrigible romantic, before his induction into combat, is the following:

May - France

Dear Folks —

This morning, and unexpectedly, an idle hour turns up and I will put part of it in this letter.

Saturday was half holiday. I went some miles across the country to the nearest town, which same you will find in Du-

mas' "Three Musketeers." They say D'Artangnan fought a
duel here and we had dinner at the inn which harbored him
(maybe). The place is certainly old enough, and romance has
left her travels all over this land anyway. There is a great cha-
teau set on a commanding height — just like a Howard Pyle
drawing with battlements and keep, portcullis and round
tower, and all the other trimmings. I wandered around it and
through a little of it — not much interior, for a general lives
here — and was considerably edified. Behind the castle is an
enchanted wood with its half-obscured winding ways and its
green gloom, and one little terraced lawn hidden away in it
and the voice of the river below it—it was, I believe, the most
beautiful place I have ever seen. One expected soberly pixies
and elves and enchanted fawns waiting for the spell to life —
No description could give you an idea.

A very great event occurred yesterday — no less than a
letter from my wife—the first word I have had from the states
in more than a month! Really, I'm an awful long way from
home. An awfully long way. But now, Leda's letter has established, as it were, communications, and I don't feel nearly so
far as I did. All that is lacking is a letter from you all—which
should turn up very soon. I'm looking forward to it.

Now, mother mine, and all the rest of you, you are hereby
directed to refrain from worrying. Worrying is non regulation
and annoying and calculated to lower morale of troops. Besides, any worries and anxieties of which I may be the subject
will be very much ill bestowed and out of place for months and
months yet. The brave boys from the states have much to learn
before they are sent up to the front.

And by the way, concerning the war, I know infinitely
less about the progress of events than when I was in Quantico.
Over there we had at least the frantic vaporings of the press,
but over here, not only is there no news, but the war is the
last subject anyone ever talks of.

I am quite as well as I could wish to be and in the best
spirits possible — rather busier than I ever was before, from
5:30 to 10:30, approximately, and I would like to write long
letters to you all — but — at night I'm just too tired to write.
So all the fresh and fragrant impressions I am registering must

wait until my return. I hope that won't be long—which is to say that I hope we beat Germany soon. I'll try to write every week anyway.

With all my love —
John

Everywhere through France are soldiers mostly. I presume men on leave — permission in their word. Of the French, it must be admitted that their uniforms do not fit well—indeed, that comfort and utility, rather than the fit of the garment, is the object striven for. But they are clean even when they are worn and faded, and the men who wear them look like fighters, every one.

The color of the line uniform is not unlike the gray of the Confederacy, especially after it has faded some, and a captain of infantry, all dressed up for Sunday—pale blue sets off well with red and gold—is well worth your very snappiest salute.

Taken altogether, they look like what they are — a hard and competent lot who would be at home with the Old Guard and the Grenadiers of the line that Napoleon led.

Thomason's idealism was shortlived. When the Second Division plunged into combat much sooner than he expected, he got a taste of German steel and lead. In fact, on May 27, 1918, when the Germans launched their drive down the Valley of the Marne, intent upon taking Paris, the Second Division was hastily diverted to the vicinity of Meaux. There was no time to lose. General Erich Ludendorff, who had masterminded the German offensive toward Paris, was surprised at his own success. The French themselves had already dispaired of stopping the German advance and were planning to move the seat of government to Bordeau.

By June 1, however, the Second Division had deployed across the Château-Thierry-Paris Road to fill a gap in the French line and the situation reversed itself.

Across the rolling wheat fields, interspersed with rows of blood-red poppies, northwest of Château-Thierry, the Boche were entrenched with infantry and machine guns. They had not expected to engage in a defensive battle at this point. They gave a good account of themselves, however, as the inboard platoons of the 49th and 67th companies attacked fiercely from the wood. Crawling in the enemy's direction through the agitated wheat, lines of fire sweeping forward and backward, the Marines bagged feldwebels in the trees. . . .

Kill that gunner, kill him with your hands. They killed him. Bayonets flashed in as the battle tore through the coppice. The machine gunners and the Prussian infantry were brave men. But brave men die.

Alexander Woollcott, late drama critic and staff member of *Stars and Stripes,* reported stories that leaked through the AEF of a lean, young Marine officer stationed with his crack company just beyond Belleau Wood, who under shellfire sketched hastily, on scraps of paper, Germans impaled on broken tree branches and Marines twisted and dying in the bomb-scarred terrain of a French village.

But Thomason did not spend all of his time sketching. With shells ripping overhead and the kidney-shaped, mile-square, wood alight with flame, he led his men painfully forward with a walk. Here at last was action. He watched his flank to see that it guided true and he thought of the Confederate phrase *guide center,* "the word of the old men who had brought him up to tales of Lee's Army of Northern Virginia, in the War of the Southern Confederacy, great battles, glamorous attacks full of color and the high-spirited elan of chivalry. . . ." Still the Southern gentleman of the classic tradition, Thomason clung tenaciously to his heritage.

Within the next five days Thomason had become a seasoned man of combat. In that time the combined forces had not only blunted the German advance. Toward noon on June 6 the situation around Hill 142, objective of the first attack, had stabilized, and by the end of the month the Marine Brigade had driven the disciplined Boche troops out of Belleau Wood.

Meanwhile, Thomason's first impressions of combat were mixed. Under intense shelling at Château-Thierry, he observes to his father:

> By far the most Christianizing influence that I have run
> across . . . is the German 77 mm shell shrapnel or H. E. [High

Explosive] and chiefly H. E. For H. E. is the stuff that strafes you in your position — when your line is posted and all you have to do is lie low and make yourself as small as you can . . .

The festive Boche 77 has Billy Sunday beat at least eighty-seven ways when it comes to making a man wish that he had led a better life. For you can't run away from a shell, and you can't crawl from under it . . . and you can't hide from it unless you are the blessed possessor of a deep shelter, with eighteen feet of earth between you and the top. . . .

You can hear the cursed things coming, a tearing whine that rises to shrieking crescendo — then the burst. O Lord, that was close! O, Lord, don't let it hit me! . . .

The illustration accompanying the statement and labeled "Hill 142, June 14, 1918" carries this annotation:

Misanthrope in shell hole during violent barrage to fellow refugee —
  'Say, Bill, why the deuce did you ever join this man's outfit and come to war?'
  'Aw, Hell! I wuz dodgin' the draft!'

Later, behind the lines, Thomason grew quite serious again: "But O, my Mother and my Father, it seems to me that God has certainly held His Hand over me. . . ."

(As Thomason remembered only a few years later, "I am one of the very few men alive who threw the 28th Prussian — Brandenburgers — Regiment off that hill and kept them off.")

Trees and heavy foliage provided cover for the huge rocks and ravines infested with machine gun nests. For twenty days the battle had raged with intense fighting. The superior marksmanship of the Marines and soldiers had permitted them to pick off the machine gunners.

Casualties were heavy, but fortunately Thomason was not wounded. Despite heavy losses, the Second Division, of which Thomason's brigade was a focal part, had measured up to its motto — "Second to None." Historians have predicted that the Battle of Belleau Wood will one day stand with Thermopylae and other crucial battles of the world.

The achievements of the Marine Brigade in the Château-Thierry sector were twice recognized by the French government.

The commanding general of the Sixth French Army ordered the name *Bois de Belleau* to be altered to that of *Bois de la Brigade de Marine*. Later General Petain, commander in chief of the Allied forces, cited the Marine Brigade and awarded it the *Croix de Guerre* with Palm.

A letter to Dr. and Mrs. Thomason dated June 28, 1918, affirms that Thomason's transformation from the starry-eyed romantic expecting momentarily to see "soberly pixies, elves and enchanted fawns," into the philosophical realist had begun to take effect. He hoped someday to write a book about the war—if he survived. He doubts his ability, however, "to do justice to this business of war."

Both statements are relevant. Thomason wanted to write a book that would measure the total experience of war as he had known it—not just another war book—but a book that, at the same time, would reflect credit upon the United States Marine Corps. From the outset serving as an officer in the Corps was to Thomason not only a way of life, it was a commitment tantamount to dedication that was almost messianic. That he was later able to fulfill both aspirations is a significant aspect of his legend.

Reared a staunch Methodist, Thomason never strayed from the Christian tenets acquired at the family hearthstone. In the same letter he reasserts his belief that Divine Providence is watching over him. In general, he reflects a tendency toward fatalism — a characteristic he was to retain throughout the remainder of his life. Written on pages torn from a field notebook, the letter concludes significantly with a full-length pencil sketch of a Marine cooking his rations in the trenches. For a brasier the Marine uses a German helmet over which he holds his mess kit. The dugout is at his back. Two riflemen standing guard a few feet away are pleasantly attracted by the odors of the cooking food.

By July 18, 1918, the German offensive was over, and the Allies had commenced a counterattack south of Soissons. Just as they had stopped the Germans at Château-Thierry, within fifty miles of Paris, so did the Marines repeat their victory at Soissons.

And as the fighting progressed so did the stature of John Thomason in combat expand and the author-artist evolve.

Frequently Thomason's letter home was addressed personally to his mother. It was she who had been the more sympathetic of the parents toward his artistic inclinations, she who had never wavered in her faith in him as an artist. It was she who had prevailed upon conservative Dr. Thomason to permit their son to study at the Art Students League in New York; and so a special bond united the two. On July 11, precisely seven days before the Marines and Allies began their counteroffensive, Thomason wrote his mother a letter in which he clarifies his philosophy of war. ". . . war is nobody's picnic—but men can endure it and rise superior to it and live through it. So with the most cheerful possible face we can only 'carry on' and hope for the best."

Simultaneously he calls attention to a lack of materials for artistic expression. ". . . never in all my life have I so vastly wished for drawing materials [the few he possessed were contained in his bedding roll to the rear] "If I just had a bottle of India Ink—or a few colors! But I haven't. If I ever get back to a place where they can be procured I can do some things that you will be glad to have."

Confident artist longing for the means of fulfillment, Thomason is no less the man and Marine capable of measuring up. At this time, he has gained weight. He could easily hike twenty-five kilometers daily, he boasts, carrying a sixty-pound weight of combat gear. At this point he reassures his mother with a pen portrait of himself in "Heavy Marching Order." In connection with his professional military duties, he insists that his first responsibility is the welfare of the men under his command; that personally he is not interested in being awarded a combat decoration for spectacular bravery; and, much as he would like a Distinguished Service Cross, "the souvenir that I want most to get home is me."

The charge at Soissons was intimate and savage. In it Marshal Foch combined the American First and Second Divisions and the First Moroccan Division with French troops to launch his initial major drive. The fighting was so close that much of it was hand-to-hand. The aggregation smashed through the German lines and won another decisive victory. Despite 400 of the Corps killed and 1,500 wounded, the Marine Brigade was again overwhelming.

Executive officer of the 49th Company, Thomason and his men fought in the front line, never out of range of the German guns. "What a barrage there was that morning!" Thomason wrote his father. "It started as we got into position — an awful diaphason of sound that stunned the senses and rocked the solid earth . . . and filled the air with terrible keening noises."

Thomason himself was conspicuous for gallantry in action. Aided by his gunnery sergeant, he destroyed a machine gun nest obstructing the advance, killed thirteen Germans, and captured two heavy Maxim machine guns. For his courage he was awarded the Silver Star by the United States Army. Later the Navy would decorate him with the Navy Cross for the same act of heroism.

The campaign lasted eight weeks. At the end Thomason was especially proud of the fact that his Marines had "written in blood a new and splendid chapter in the history of American arms."

Later he shared with his mother still another experience involving Soissons:

> The day after our attack in July, I found a Boche notebook and some drawing pencils in a Command Post we cleaned out, and got some rather interesting sketches under fire. After we came back, I worked some of them up — all the actual originals I sent home [to Leda] — I think — and the major, who happened by my shelter when I was working on them, commandeered the best of the finished ones to send to Headquarters, U.S. Marine Corps, as a matter of official record. There they will be interred for good. The others — well — there are such difficulties in the way of sending such things home that I have carried them around with me. Anyway some of them are rather crude and brutal. . . . I am well and quite cheerful, considering, and making out fairly well . . . in the profession of arms.

Interestingly, Thomason does not allude here to his feat of heroism in taking out the machine gun nest. Instead he refers to "a Command Post we cleaned out." Naturally the discovery of the drawing materials was important since Thomason worked in several media — oil, watercolors, charcoal, pencil, and pen and ink — and often was reduced to the use of gum wrappers, odd scraps of paper, and even struck matches on the firing line when nothing else was available. It must have been exceedingly frustrating when he had nothing with which to work, because it was as an artist that he was most facile, most at home, and happiest.

The sketches made under fire (spare, stark pictures of soldiers in combat, electric with the drama of death and dying) included scenes of fighting from tree to tree in the woods at Soissons: a Marine lieutenant and German major in hand-to-hand combat; corpses sprawling grotesquely in the shell craters and ravines; a moment caught in the trenches before zero hour; the battalion runner in action; the Boche standing up to bayonet with bayonet and dying that way. . . .

Whereas war had been a business in Thomason's previous letter, it now had become a profession. In his metamorphosis the man had become inured to combat at its fiercest. Thomason, the man, was indeed a professional Marine and even "cheerful" in his recognition of the fact. Furthermore, he must have experienced justifiable pride as an artist in the fact that the "major commandeered" some of his best combat drawings for the official Marine records.

After Soissons the Marine Brigade withdrew to a point on the Moselle River to rebuild the decimated units. Thomason, however, was relieved of duty and assigned to the Army Infantry Specialist School at Andilly.

The assignment to the four weeks' course was intended as an advancement. It would qualify Thomason to serve on the battalion staff as a scouting and intelligence officer. Thomason's leadership in the June and July action around Château-Thierry and at Soissons in the first thrust of General Foch's counteroffensive merited recognition. Even though the rest that withdrawal action made possible was welcome, Thomason preferred straight-line company duty with his men.

From Andilly, on August 24, the first anniversary of his wedding, Thomason called Leda. She was much in his thoughts as he reminisced. To his mother he wrote:

> A man is born, gets married, and dies. These are the three great events in life. If he can add going to war to those three, he can add the great adventure, for that's what war is. . . .
>
> War is certainly the great adventure. It is horrible beyond all words and so hideously and hatefully wasteful and wanton—and yet—you never know what getting down to realities means until you go to war. All a man's pretenses and vanities and such things, as we all wear to mask the inside of us, are quite stripped away . . . Life becomes unbelievably simple and direct. You stand it or you break under it . . . There isn't any middle ground.

Thomason returned to his unit in time to join the St. Mihiel offensive in the Meuse-Argonne sector that began September 12, 1918. He had not become an intelligence officer after all. "The more I thought about leaving my company and the men . . . I had learned to know and gone with into battle," Thomason explained, "the worse I felt. . . ." Accordingly, he pleaded with such vehemence that his request to be left with his company on line duty was honored.

The St. Mihiel operation was the first in the war to be carried out by a complete American army under the control of its own commander in chief, General John J. Pershing. The plan to develop an army in the St. Mihiel region and to reduce the salient as a preliminary to a more decisive action originated with American headquarters soon after American troops arrived in France. As early as January, 1918, certain sectors near St. Mihiel were used to give experience to American divisions to prepare them for action at the front.

Successive German drives in the summer of 1918 had prevented the implementation of the original plan because troops had to be deployed elsewhere as they were needed. With the reduction of the Marne salient, however, General Pershing insisted upon carrying out the original plan and freeing the French citizens who had been held captives since 1914.

Units comprising the army began to concentrate in late August. Approximately twenty-four miles wide at the base and extending fifteen miles into the Allied lines, the salient had remained almost unchanged in shape for the four years of occupation. More than 550,000 Americans, reinforced by 110,000 French, participated in the offensive. German aerial bombing, which was begun earlier to terrorize the civilian population of 2,000 or 3,000, was stepped up as the American and French troops advanced.

"The Rainbow Division had made several unsuccessful attacks there," Thomason recalled later, "and I remember seeing scores of their dead hanging like old clothes on the German wire. There was a lot of marching and fighting after that, as we chased the Boche towards the Meuse. . . ."

The strategy employed by the liberators was not to subject the site to heavy bombardment and aerial shelling to protect the French inhabitants. Instead they surrounded it by penetrations to the east and the north.

Thomason's regiment sustained comparatively light casualties. At the conclusion of the engagement, September 16, the Marine Brigade moved to an area south of Toul — "a place delightful in my recollection," Thomason wrote. "We had a fine mess room with a most worthy lady who had a cellar full of Sauterne, Chablis, and Burgundy of discriminating vintage, and a cook who deserves monuments among the great of the ages. Then we went to the Champagne, and smiled no more thereafter." It was also at this location that Thomason learned of his promotion to captain with accrued pay dating from July 1, 1918.

Almost immediately the Second Division was reassigned to the 21st Corps of the French Fourth Army to continue the Meuse-Argonne offensive. The action had been launched at Champagne, near Somme-Py, but the French soldiers were unable to advance against the heavily entrenched German Fifth Army. Since 1914 the Boche had held Blanc Mont Ridge — a position that dominated the strategic valley of the Arnes and the entire Champagne sector. The ravages of four years of fighting had converted the area into a veritable jungle of barbed wire entanglements, gigantic craters of exploded mines, and an interminable desolation of shell holes.

On the last day of September intermittent drizzle and cold forced Thomason and his men to take such shelters as they could improvise. He and another officer huddled under a corrugated sheet of iron, shivering and wet. Winter clothing had not been issued. On October, another bleak, gray day, the battalion got its battle orders.

Surrounded by their platoon leaders and noncommissioned officers, the two commanding officers of the 49th Company spread a large map on the ground weighting its corners with their revolvers. Second in command, Captain Thomason briefed the men:

> Here, you birds, look at this map. The Frogs have driven the Boche a kilometre and a half north of Somme-Py. You see it here . . . They have gotten into the Prussian trench — this blue line with the wire in front of it . . . a fire trench . . . Behind it is the Essen trench . . . a hum-dinger! . . . The Frogs say it can't be taken from the front — they've tried. We're goin' to take it. On the other side of that is the Elbe trench, and a little to the left the Essen Hook, and in the center the Bois de Vipre . . . We're to take them . . . Next, away up in this corner of the map, is the Blanc Mont Ridge place. Whoever is left when we get that far will take that too. Questions? . . . when we get past the Essen system, we'll be in the open mostly . . . It's goin' to be some party!

With Blanc Mont Ridge as its objective, the Second Division, flanked by the Marine Brigade on the left and the Third Brigade on the right, began the assault on October 3. The morning loomed gray and misty. From midnight until dawn the front has been comparatively quiet. Then promptly at 5:50 a.m. the French and American guns opened with an earth-shattering crash. Seven days of desperate fighting ensued with increasingly stubborn German resistance and fierce counterattacks on both flanks and in front.

The god of battles evidently hovered close during the seven-day siege, because Thomason barely escaped being a casualty.

He would later narrate the incident most vividly in "Marines at Blanc Mont," a chapter in *Fix Bayonets!*

A five-inch shell exploded so near his head that it popped his ear-drums and left him stunned for a few seconds. A warrant officer (gunner) helped Thomason to his feet. The same shell had killed the captain's group and the gunner's platoon. As Thomason regained composure, he realized how close his brush with death had been. His raincoat was torn, his map-case missing, blood stained his hands, and its abrasive taste irritated his mouth.

"The front of the battalion was very narrow, now," but "the support platoons were all in the line." Then miraculously, Thomason and his men had progressed to that point he had indicated as the farthest corner of the map, and trees crowning the crest rose up before them almost close enough to touch!

The Second Division had taken Blanc Mont Ridge, including the infamous Essen Hook, with its lethal machine gunners, and St. Etienne. While the French attack had failed to keep abreast of the Americans, the Second Division had met its objectives. It was a costly victory. Thomason's battalion, the First and Fifth Regiments of Marines, lost about 700 men and 21 officers in two hours of combat. Scarcely more than 100 Marines survived. In the 49th Company only 20 remained alive including Thomason and his company commander.

On the other hand, enemy losses had been extensive. In only two days after the assault was launched, the United States Marines of the Second Division took 2,300 German prisoners.

Once again the Fifth Marines had prevailed even though a few Boche fanatics had elected to die at their machine guns, firing until Americans bayonets or rifle butts silenced them. Increasingly then, the men in heavy green-gray uniforms, under deep helmets, surrendered.

The United States Marines of the Second Division had accomplished an exploit the French, ostensibly masters of the art of war, had to concede was remarkable. They had routed the Boche from Blanc Mont Ridge and liberated the cathedral city of Rheims. They had pierced the Hindenberg line to a depth of four miles and had precipitated the retreat of the Germans to the Aisne. *To put it succinctly, John Thomason's Marines had won the damned war.*

The brilliant performance of the Fifth and Sixth Marine Regiments did not go unrecognized. Marshal Petain, who considered the victory the greatest achievement of the 1918 campaign, ordered citations. The Marines received a second Palm to add to their *Croix de Guerre*. In addition to carrying the streamer of the *Croix de Guerre* on their colors, they were entitled to wear, as a part of their uniforms, the braided and knotted cord known as a *Fourragere* in the same green and red colors of the medal. [They still wear it today.]

By the end of the month the American forces had overrun almost all of the enemy's positions, had advanced beyond the Argonne Forest, and on November 7 had established a bridgehead across the Meuse River. Consequently, with their reserves gone, regiments decimated, and invasion of their country imminent, the Germans negotiated for the cessation of hostilities. Although General John J. Pershing favored unconditional surrender, an armistice ending World War I was officially signed at Compiègne on November 11, 1918, the same night that the Marines crossed the Meuse at Pouilly.

But Thomason did not see action in the few remaining days of the war. He had been evacuated to a hospital camp on the edge of the S.O.S. [Service of Supply]. Toward the end of the Champagne offensive, despite a fever of 104 degrees, Thomason remained in the front lines to regroup his shattered company into fighting shape only to collapse with influenza behind the lines upon being relieved.

Except for the time out at Andilly, it was the only rest he had had since beginning combat duty in May. And while he appreciated it, he longed to be back with his men. From his sickbed on October 25 he wrote Dr. Thomason:

> Odd, the organism of man. I am in comfort and safety.
> But part of me desires very much to return to my own appointed place in that hell of war and fatigue and hunger and cold and wet, where my men are and some of my friends as

are yet alive, even while the rational part of me rejoices in safety and good food and warm shelter.

Thomason was more convinced than ever that the Almighty had played a role in his survival. "I've been through four great battles," he wrote his mother. "I've been over the top in nine attacks, and I haven't had a mark on my body . . . God must be preserving me for something. . . ."

At the same time he had not expected to be spared. As he observed death all around him he had become resigned to it. "Nine times in the last moments before attack — and how many times lying under shellfire I do not know — I have solemnly renounced all hope of ever seeing you that I love again and composed myself as well as I could to meet the uttermost . . . if it were coming."

The C.O. visited the sick Marine officer. When he learned that Thomason was one of the few survivors of the intense summer's campaign and had participated in most of the major battles, he arranged for an extension of Thomason's leave. So on November 12, the day after the signing of the armistice, Thomason was in Paris en route to Marseilles. He learned of the termination of hostilities and obtained the European edition of the *New York Herald,* which announced the event in screaming headlines across its front page: THE WAR IS WON — and sent the copy to his parents.

The celebration by the French, which had been initiated in the capital, had reached gigantic proportions by the time Thomason checked into the Splendide Hotel in Marseilles. Congestion due to the influx of soldiers on leave, like himself, added to the revelry of a brave people who had endured war stoically for four years. Now that the fighting had ended, the uninhibited French were being themselves again — "Gay and volatile, shouting, parading, and making merry with a deep and solemn joy," John wrote his mother. "This was France's war all right, and it is her victory."

But as intense loneliness engulfed him, the revelry and the bibulous masses he encountered everywhere failed to inspire a responsive note. Relieved as he was that the bloodletting was over and that he was alive, Thomason turned his thoughts toward home with the fond hope that there might be a possibility of getting to Texas in time for Christmas.

That hope was dissipated soon afterward, however, when he received orders to report to headquarters for further assignment. His men had already begun the march to the Rhine as members of the American Army of Occupation, and Thomason's instructions were to follow and take command of them.

It took Thomason eleven days to get from headquarters in France to Germany. He was forced to travel as best he could on ration cars, mail cars, trucks, signal trains, and transports. At Metz he discovered that the Boche had resumed passenger train service; so he entrained from there to Bitsburg. At Bitsburg he reported to the provost marshal who drove him to his outfit in time to hike the last hundred kilos with them to the Rhine. On Friday, December 13, 1918, at high noon, Thomason's column filed across the great bridge at Remagen in a downpour of rain.

Later he would recall it in *Fix Bayonets!* graphically: "The men walked silent, remembering the old dead . . . Twelve hundred men hiking to the Rhine and how many ghosts. . . ."

As commander of the 49th Company, First Battalion, Fifth Marines, Thomason was stationed first at Niederbreitbach from mid-December, 1918, to the following April, 1919. The unit's responsibilities consisted of routine guard and patrol duty at small garrisons throughout the occupied territory and training marches between the towns where the troops were billeted.

En route to headquarters the men generally marched all day and billeted for the night in a German town. A representative went ahead of the column to make arrangements with the burgermeister of the particular place or village. Usually the enlisted men were quartered in barns; animals got various places where they could be taken care of; and the officers were billeted in private homes. Since he was a captain, Thomason could usually depend upon the comfort of a bed despite the fact that the second lieutenants were obliged to sleep on the floor.

Occasionally to obtain the simple comforts, officers had to resort to ingenious methods. Arriving at a village during the extreme cold weather of December, Thomason noticed that he and his fellow officers assigned to the residence had only one blanket allotted them. Since his orderly, who spoke German, had left for the evening, Thomason had to rely upon himself to remedy the situation. But he spoke very indifferent German. He asked himself what a German officer would do under similar circumstances. Then he stamped his feet on the floor and shouted loudly.

In a few moments his German hostess, her husband, and some 13 or 14 children "crowded in with great humility." Thomason glared at all of them and pointed scornfully at the one thin blanket. All began to talk at once and he gathered that they were informing him that there were no more blankets. Whereupon he charged around displaying his anger, and they brought another blanket "from somewhere."

Next he kicked two chairs across the room and overturned the table with as much violence as he could muster. The demonstration paid off with another blanket — the third. Then Captain Thomason raged in earnest hurling at them all the profanity at his command in three languages — English, French, and Spanish — and mounting to the oratorical heights in declaiming Daniel Webster and Patrick Henry for a finale. This drama resulted in three blankets — to make a total of six — and the bonus of a down comforter. Thomason regretted his inability to swear in German.

Although the troops had settled down, Christmas in Niederbreitbach was bleak. Promised turkey for Christmas dinner, the Marines had the same "chow as always." Nor were there any Christmas boxes from home to alleviate the situation. The only festive note was contributed by the YMCA: two pieces of chocolate and a package of gum for each man.

Several inches of snow fell, and the "old Boche," who was inured to it, turned out "in his best bib and tucker," while the "little Bochlets" scurried around the countryside merrily gathering Christmas greens. Highly decorated Christmas trees brightened every window, and over all of it melodic German music and holiday songs were heard by the hour.

Sadly, it was one Christmas Thomason had no fruitcake. For that matter, he would have settled for a piece of Aunt Sue

Simms' delicious crackling bread. The one bright note in the
day was provided by two letters from Leda.

But there were antidotes to offset Thomason's increasing
homesickness and loneliness. It was a spotless town and his
quarters were comfortable. His meticulous German landlady
was so addicted to cleanliness that she scoured the floor of his
quarters and washed the windows daily. He had a well disposed
and heedful command. All of his men admired him tremendously and he returned their affection. His junior officers were
able. The nearest thing to an inconvenience was that the water
was unsafe to drink. As a result the Marines bought vintage
champagne by the case at about 35 cents a quart [24 marks] and
drank it as a substitute.

The greatest significance of Thomason's occupation of
Niederbreitbach was that it gave him leisure time in which to
consider his future and added appreciably to his maturation that
began with his entrance into combat.

It was at this time that Thomason definitely committed
himself to the profession of arms in the United States Marine
Corps. He reviewed every battle in which he served as his philosophy by which he was to live evolved, particularly in his letters
to his father. He realized the responsibilities and challenges of
his choice and welcomed them. He had proved to be a leader of
men, a man of unyielding character.

> . . . I like the job, like to handle men, and I like the profes-
> sion of arms, which is, after all the most ancient and honor-
> able profession. It stands to a degree between all the other
> professions as a shield . . . And we have seen how God can
> make it His own weapon.

Certain senior officers had encouraged Thomason to make
application for a permanent commission in the Marine Corps
and Leda had placed her stamp of approval upon it.

Once again the impact that combat had had on Thomason's
regeneration was phenomenal:

> . . . I found God over here . . . It took Château-Thierry to
> show Him to me. It took much death and fear to show me life.
> I do not know to what extent all the men who went up to battle

leaned on Him. Some did. I know I did . . . I remember the morning of July 18 — without food for 3 days — literally — the last water 12 hours gone, on top of 18 hours on camions and a day and a night of marching — we went into battle — and it was a glorious day. . . .

There was one long dark road, and the might of France went on that road in two night marches — the Brigade was part of it — 300,000 men and guns to push them home . . . Such a move it was that Jackson made at Chancellorsville, a thousand times magnified.

From April to July, 1919, Thomason — over his protest and that of his battalion commander — was reassigned to the staff of the 3rd Army Corps attached to the headquarters of the American Army of Occupation in Coblenz. Actually he was billeted at the old fort of Ehrenbreitstein with the official designation of Corps leave officer. Here he observed with interest a different aspect of the military structure — "dapper staff officers in shining boots and spurs and with colonels and majors and generals who have never been sunburned."

During the final week of July, 1919, much to Thomason's pleasure, he was transferred from Coblenz to Brest, France.

When Captain Thomason arrived in New York, with other members of the Marine Brigade of the heroic Second Division, on August 3, 1919, he was twenty-six. But when he was reunited with Leda, who met his ship, and when his brigade was reviewed by the president of the United States in Washington August 12, John Thomason was not just a returning hero, whose years totaled less than three decades.

John Thomason was a man who had met the great adventure . . . *he was a tired warrior come home.*

6 Pearl of the Antilles

After the end of World War I in 1918, trouble in the Caribbean necessitated that the Marines remain active in the area. In Haiti the First Brigade and the Marine-trained *Gendarmerie* — a combined force of 2,700 officers and enlisted men — were engaged in suppressing a *Caco* revolt. In Santo Domingo the Second Provisional Brigade and the native *Guardia Nacional* were faced with an equally difficult problem involving banditry. In eastern Cuba a provisional battalion was maintained to guard the cane fields and protect American interests during the so-called Sugar Intervention, dating from 1917 and extending to the year of 1922.

Although Marine officers normally had little choice in selecting future assignments, Thomason was permitted to elect Cuba over Haiti. Accordingly in 1919 he was assigned as commanding officer of the Thirty-seventh Company, Seventh Marines — a mounted company of the battalion then based in Camaguey.

It was Thomason's introduction to the island which was discovered by Columbus on his first voyage in 1492 and the last

Spanish colony in the Americas to win its independence. "We arrived this morning in Camaguey, which we are assured is what the poet was thinking about when he coined the fetching phrase 'Pearl of the Antilles,' " John wrote his mother, November 25, 1919. He and Leda had sailed from Charleston on the *USS Kittery*, which Thomason identified as "an ancient bucket, built in Hamburg about 1896. She was a fine new boat when she carried troops to fight the Dons in 1898, from Pampa to Guantanamo."

Built expressly for West Indian trade and flat-bottomed to accommodate considerable freight and for convenience in maneuvering the shallow Southern harbors, the vessel was not noted for passenger comfort and frequently rolled. The travelers had good weather on the voyage down, ". . . but the *Kittery* . . . conducted herself in such a manner that most of the ladies and a great many of the gentlemen did not feel like attending meals at all for the first few days." On the morning of November 25 at about 8:30 the vessel docked and the couple took a small conveyance to Camaguey.

Camaguey, the nation's leading sugar province, was a town of about 50,000, whose streetcars and shops reflected on Old World atmosphere. It was spelled Camaquey, Camaguey, and Camagiiy and the natives employed all three. The Marine Corps, however, preferred the second spelling with a *g*. It was a great town for politics and a veritable hotbed of rebellion. "There are two political parties in Cuba," John wrote — "the Ins and Outs. The latter predominate, for unfortunately there are not enough offices to go around at once. Both sides are very bitter and collisions occur, sometimes resulting in bodily injury to bystanders since all Cubans go armed to the teeth."

At the outset the Thomasons took lodgings at the Camaguey Hotel, which had formerly been a cavalry barracks centuries old. They were able to engage an enormous room and a bath with shower for $3.50 a day. Hot water had to be brought in by a domestic. Located on the second floor overlooking a patio, the room was cool and comfortable. With its winding walks, rustic seats, and tropical plants — coconut palms, orange and lemon trees, mangoes, and pawpaws — the patio was like a lovers' paradise. Overall there was a vine that clothed the walls and

hung in great clusters and masses like Japanese wisteria. The natives called it *jumbi vine.*

Thomason's company — the Thirty-seventh — was combined with the Seventy-second Company of the same regiment
to form a provisional battalion. At the outset he was not precisely enchanted with the men under his command. "I have the
47th Company, a graceless set of young thugs who ought to be
at home with their mothers," Thomason assessed them to his
parents. "They are new and green and cocky and need some heroic measures to make them decent. What a pitiful contrast to
the strong fighting men the last I commanded! I'll never have
another command like the men in the old Fifth Regiment, but
these birds present some interesting problems just the same."
Duties consisted specifically of protecting several American-
owned cane plantations and sugar mills in the province.

Nevertheless, within a year's time, Thomason had upgraded
his company's performance. He would stake his reputation on
their dependability and efficiency. ". . . I have a hundred men
who take my orders, as I take the Colonel's, and I have brought
them to such proficiency, with the bayonet, the Browning Automatic Rifle, the V. B. Grenade, the Springfield . . . ," he informed Dr. Thomason, "and I think, in all modesty, that we
would be a very cogent argument for law and order, irregardless
[sic] of whom we argued with — one or 'tother [sic] or both —
that's of no consequence."

American forces had occupied the provinces of Camaguey
and Oriente since 1917, or shortly before entering the war in
Europe. Then, as indicated, unstable political conditions made
it necessary for the United States to maintain the battalion
somewhat longer. The election of Mario Garcia Menocal, a conservative, to the presidency of Cuba in 1917 was contested by his
defeated opponent, José Miguel Gomez, a popular liberal and
former president, who incited a revolutionary movement to oust
his successor. As part of his strategy, Gomez and his followers
destroyed American property in eastern Cuba to force the
United States to interfere in accordance with the Platt Amendment. The Platt Amendment, which the United States Congress
succeeded in attaching as a rider in 1901 to an army appropria-

tions bill, which Cuba was pressured into incorporating into her constitution, gave America the right to intervene in Cuba to preserve its independence and life and property. It further provided that Cuba must lease or sell to the United States lands for naval stations.

In conformity with the Platt Amendment, then, President Woodrow Wilson took action to protect American lives and interests and to safeguard sugar production and exports necessary to the Allies. Simultaneously the United States was in the precarious position of supporting an unpopular president and withholding recognition of the popular leader on the premise that the American Congress could not accept a revolutionary government established by force. The unsettled political climate was such that not until 1919 did the United States see fit to reduce occupation forces in Cuba. However, the Marines performed defensive duties, for the most part, in protecting the major cities and cane fields and left the revolutionists to the regular Cuban troops. Even though Menocal and his successor, Alfredo Zayas, gained control, American Marines occupied part of Cuba until February of 1922.

(History repeated itself in the late 1950s in Cuba. Then, as some thirty years earlier, the United States backed an unpopular and dictatorial president, Batista, against the rising, popular revolutionary star of Fidel Castro. The second time around, however, the United States lost. Castro took Cuba firmly into the Soviet Union's orbit where the island remains today.)

Since the eastern end of the island was placed under martial law and there was scant need for action, Thomason engaged in a number of activities to fill his leisure time. He undertook a broad reading program. Fortunately he discovered a library at Camaguey from which he could read volumes of Kipling, Dickens, Thackeray, Poe, Scott, and Mark Twain — who never got tiresome. In addition he had his mother ship his favorite books, which he had left at home: a three-volume Shakespeare, Aeschylus, Euripides, Swinburne, Homer, and some art books. He directed her to search for a certain book dealing with Michelangelo, as he was seeking to improve his knowledge of anatomy.

He also began an intensive writing and sketching schedule. In the spring of 1920 he submitted a series of articles and short stories relating to his combat experience — about 50,000 words altogether — accompanied by his illustrations, to the big magazines. "At all events before it fades from my mind, I have set down, with some fidelity to truth . . . ," he wrote Dr. Thomason, "a few little pictures of the men who participated in the greatest events this world has ever seen, and in the aftertime they may be found not without value. . . ." He had tried his hand at other subjects, "but the war is about the only thing I can get my heart into."

Thomason's work was uniformly rejected not because of its quality but because the public was tired of war. While praising his submissions, the editors explained that their readers were weary of the war theme.

"I have sent a couple of stories to New York and hear only kind words of them," John wrote his mother on April 14, 1920, "A communication came yesterday concerning one, which is now in the hands of *Scribner's*. It has been 'regretfully returned' by *Harper's*, *Century's*, and the *Saturday Evening Post*. They are agreed that it is 'fascinating,' 'remarkable,' 'the most graphic bit of war stuff yet put out,' 'told in an epic manner,' 'reflecting the soul of the doughboy with masterly fidelity and epic realism' but . . . 'Our readers are not interested in the late conflict.' The opinion seems to be that I can write with rare ability, but that I ought to write about something pleasant."

Thomason took his disappointment in stride, however, and continued to write about his combat experiences. After all, it was history and he had been a part of it. "I shall continue these sketches, however, and in a year or two, or longer, they should be valuable. Meantime, I think I shall polish up some of my old duck hunting tales and try to publish them. The government don't pay me enough to live on." (At the time, Marines were paid on a scale that was considered adequate in 1908. There had been no increase in salaries and benefits since that time. Thomason's pay and allowances in April of 1920 amounted to only $283.00 per month, with $7.00 deducted from that for insurance.)

So Thomason published articles on such prosaic subjects as guinea shooting in Cuba and the flourishing American tourist trade on the islands and consoled himself with the fact that F. Scott Fitzgerald submitted 122 stories before he had an acceptance.

Hunting was excellent in Cuba. The Thomasons and Dr. and Mrs. Cook were congenial hunting companions. They found the jacksnipe, guineafowl, quail, and ducks plentiful. The jacksnipe reminded John of similar birds in Eastham pasture around Huntsville. The quail was a small brunette variety of the Texas bobwhite. The guineafowl was identical with the garden variety of peace destroyers in the states. Wild and sagacious, they were harder to kill than ducks. "— And when they are killed, they don't stay dead," John wrote his father.

But the most exciting sport Thomason found on the island was caiman shooting. He went alligator hunting at Altamira, the 50,000-acre estate of his friend Waterman, nine miles along the Caribbean and fifteen miles inland. Caiman subsisted on stock and cost Waterman some thousands of dollars annually in pigs and young cattle. The animals of assorted sizes, some as big as horses and running to twenty feet in length, occupied the indentations of the coastline, inland along the streams. Each had his favorite stretch of stream or ford and was seldom seen. Caiman seemed to know intuitively how to protect themselves and were not easy to kill. One particular animal had been fired at many times by Waterman's vaqueros with pistols and shotguns. His plates turned the slugs of a soft-nosed .38 easily. Only the steel-jacketed service bullet of the Springfield rifle was effective in most cases.

Since the animal swims with only his eyes exposed, the sportsman has a target about the size of a fifty-cent piece at which to aim. Accuracy and speed are both essential. Then when you shoot one in the water, he sinks; and unless it is shallow you don't get him. Thomason and his orderly shot twenty-odd with their service rifles at one time, but were able to retrieve only eight of them. These were not large, the longest being slightly more than seven feet and the shortest five. The men shot from a boat. Later, however, Thomason shot an alligator

between fifteen and twenty feet in length by ambush — a caiman that Waterman's vaqueros had marked down for him.

Religion on the island assumed a more social function than
spiritual. Since there was no chaplain attached to the post, the
Thomasons and two or three other Marine officers and their
wives attended the only English-speaking church in Camaguey
which was Methodist. The small Protestant church, whose membership consisted essentially of fifty women, was presided over
by three ministers who alternated between preaching and teaching. Thomason took the occasion to comment on the three for
the edification of his father, who had been a steward in the
Methodist Church of Huntsville for fifty years:

> One, Brother Hopkins, addresses his remarks in a confi-
> dential undertone to the long-necked glass vase that stands
> on his pulpit. He is the missionary. Another, Brother Hill,
> from Texas I have not heard. The third, the regular pastor,
> Brother Cunningham, intones comfortable orthodox things
> through his nose in a drawling metallic voice.

Predominantly Catholic, Camaguey observed Holy Week — the
week between Palm Sunday and Easter — with ceremonies, pro-
cessions, prayers, and fastings. Like others, the Thomasons followed the festivities with interest. One night during the week
they visited several of the most pretentious Catholic churches to
get an idea of what it was like. "They all looked about the same.
. . . ," John reported, "ablaze with candles and tinsel and
other gewgaws and bedizened images that flashed and glittered.
All were jammed with the polychromatic population of Camaguey, talking and laughing so that you couldn't hear the inevitable priest in vestments . . . shouting and gesticulating from
some perch near the roof above the altar."

The climax of Holy Week was the enactment on the night
of Good Friday of the resurrection of Christ, the search for the
God figure the next day, and His reunion with the Holy Mother
Mary on Easter Sunday. The spectacle in the form of a procession was peculiar to Camaguey and not observed in the same
manner elsewhere on the island.

Throngs congregated in the well-lighted Plaza to watch the beginning of the procession which originated at one of the cathedrals on the opposite side. There were among them married couples with their innumerable offspring, the old beaus, with their curled and scented beards and waxed mustachios, and the gay young blades and the lovely señoritas. Some stood; others occupied chairs and benches along the walks and all fanned. John invested twenty centavos in chairs for himself and Leda.

Before the procession got underway the young gentlemen and the señoritas appraised each other. The way in which they did it amazed Thomason:

> The young men, very killing in stiff white linen and silver mounted canes, [he wrote] circled in ragged columns of threes and fours around the Plaza, moving clockwise, and the young ladies, lambent-eyed senoritas, clothed wonderfully like the sun in ardent draperies, circled likewise, in counter-clockwise direction. — Dark starry eyes flash a deadly barrage from under silken mantillas—smitten masculine bosoms puff forth passionate clouds of cigarette smoke . . . but not a hand touches — not a word is spoken by the lips — the sexes herd apart — in public, anyway.

Suddenly a scufflement of sound down the street in the direction of the cathedral, accompanied by band music and a Latin chant, announces the beginning of the pageantry. John places a chair at the edge of the crowd for Leda to stand on as the procession passes. Near them a Cuban grandee volunteers to explain as the pageant progresses. Members of the procession transport the crucified Christ through the streets in a silver casket. They place the sepulchrum on the altar of one of the cathedrals, where converts follow for a worship session to last the entire night. On a solid silver throne at the head of the procession is the holy Virgin Mary who is unaware that her Son is no longer with her. On Easter Sunday afternoon when she discovers His absence she goes through the streets on her silver throne searching for Him. The Christ image, now no longer dead, meets the Virgin Mary. The two salute each other and walk together to the Soledad Church. Thomason could not resist reporting the incidents in minute detail to his parents, incorporating the Spanish inflection of the grandee's running explication. "And so with slow, solemn music, with chanting, with a thousand candles along the irregular column, with dark robed priests and red and purple bishops, with painted dolls in precious raiment, the procession passed," Thomason concludes his account.

Regardless of the paganism intermingled with the pageantry, Thomason thought that Ibanez might have extracted some usable material from it.

Thomason and the men of his company covered considerable ground on their mounts, averaging forty miles a day. ". . . We have been to each coast and up and down the line of the railroad." It was important to Thomason for the opportunity it gave him to observe the mores of the rural Cubans firsthand.

On the whole, the Cubans who lived close to the soil were a simple people, quite crude, even primitive in their lifestyle as compared with their urban counterparts. The palm tree figured prominently in their lives. It provided them with houses, horse troughs, and in some instances food. They lived in palm-leafed thatches over palm-log or bamboo frames with dirt floors. They slept mostly in hammocks, beds being rare. Boiled rice was their food staple, supplemented with plantains and roast pork. They consumed much pork when they could get it. Rarely did they eat beef. Plantains took the place of bread.

They drank small quantities of water but imbibed coffee at all hours of the day or night. In every house a pot of coffee was always brewing. It was unthinkable to meet a friend without first drinking coffee with him and paying the proper compliments to its quality. If you rode out to your finca foreman's house to drive his cows out of your garden patch, or to mend a fence, or to go for a doctor, you must first sit down with him and drink coffee ceremoniously.

Usually the rural Cuban was married to the woman who bore his voluminous progeny but not always at the beginning. Frequently a couple would save money and wait to have an impressive wedding at one of the cathedrals after the birth of several children. It saved money if they could combine the christening ceremonies of five or six children with the wedding rites.

The men were alert, wiry little yellowish creatures and usually smaller than their women who inclined to corpulency. All were riders who elevated horse-breaking to an art. But they were not dare-devil horsemen. Almost invariably the men carried pistols and three-foot machetes, ostensibly for their own safety.

Some of the old whiskerandos liked to reminisce about Cuba's ten years' struggle for independence, which was finally realized only after the intervention of the United States in 1899. They told of how *El Vomito*, which they called the yellow fever then so endemic in their society, was employed as a tool of warfare. Since the rural Cubans were largely immune to the disease and the Spanish soldiers were susceptible if forced to live in the open, they burned property to subject the soldiers to contagion. As a result thousands of the garrison died, but the country was left devastated and in the end corruption in the Spanish army became increasingly rampant as the soldiers preyed upon the Cubans and forced them into starvation.

Two outstanding events of personal significance marked the Cuban tour. The first was the birth of the Thomasons' son on June 14, 1920, at Camaguey. The second was Thomason's elevation in rank to a permanent captaincy in 1921, with the date of appointment retroactive to June 4, 1920. Both events dating from the month of June were relevant and *causes célèbres.*

Thomason was particularly proud that he had fathered the first grandchild in the family and the first male heir to perpetuate the Thomason name. Leda had given birth without incident and the family were anticipating the first visit of her parents from Terrell with much pleasure.

Two days after the son's birth the 27-year-old father—and captain of the United States Marine Corps—announced his auspicious arrival to Dr. Thomason of Huntsville:

> Your first grandson, John William Thomason, III, was born Monday night, June 14, at 10:52 PM. He weighs 6¼ pounds, is sound in mind and limb, and is built rather long, like his father—the medico says that he will be bigger in the bones than I am though. Has very dark eyes and considerable dark hair, which curls into drake's tails on his neck. While I

am not experienced enough in such matters to deliver pronouncements, the medico, the nurse, and Leda affirm that he
is quite above the average in conformation and such matters.
He has enough voice to drill a 250-man war-company, but
spends his time sleeping. His expression is bored and cynical.
His features, of which he has the usual number, as usually arranged, are quite pronounced, especially his nose and chin.
They say he looks like me. Although flattered, I don't feel
competent to comment on that. . . .

Within less than a month, on July 4, the remarkable offspring of the proud father was issuing his own bulletins, even
though he conceded that he was unable to work the shift key on
his father's typewriter. Addressing his epistle to "honored and
respected madam," the precocious infant had duly discovered
his parents and was somewhat relieved that they had declined
the aunt's suggestion to name him Oscar.

37 company camaguey cuba 4 july, 1920

honored and respected madam

they tell me that you are the aunt who wrote to me about the
people who wanted to name me oscar. i want to thank you for
not doing it because i would view such a name with alarm.
thats what my father said ell says he jingling his costly spurs
on the floor no son of mine is going to start life with a name
like oscars. i knew a feller named oscar once and he came to a
bad end. ell no, says my father the captain o captains says my
mother you mustnt talk like that around your offspring and
what oscar was it anyway and did they put him in the pen no
woman says the captain they put him in the navy which is
worse says i and oswald would be worse yet says my mother
hes named bueno says my father curling his gold hat cord and
looking fierce right here i want to explain that my name aint
bueno its john the 3 but my father likes to talk like that my
fathers name is john 2 thats a good name, he says it haz been
among them present on 1000 bloody battle fields o john how
can you say such things says my mother like a duck squak i
mean well anyway it has been among those present on 5 re-
plies my father and besides, he looks like me well says my
mother very scornful that wont hurt him as long as hes got his
health i reckon

I know this looks funny but just yet im too little to work
the shift key on my fathers costly typewriter all i can do is
make the letters im not as little as i was though and im growing all the time they issue me rations every 2 hours during the
day and at 10 12 and 2 at night i sleep most of the time except in the afternoon when i take my exercise and at night
when i take my voice culture my parents do pretty well most
of the time but i am looking forward to when i can see my
aunts and uncles and things which my father says i will find
muy sympatico tell her you kiss her hands says my father you
want to be courtly about it you know so i kiss your hands and
present my compliments and regards and evrything from your
nephew

                                                        john william thomason 3

Thomason's extreme pride in his promotion was evident.
"The Marine Corps have at last put its house in order," Thomason wrote his mother on April 10, 1921, "and I received this
week my permanent commission as captain placing me about the
center of the list. If I stay in—and we intend to—I should be major, barring wars, in about six years. And next year I get a ten percent increase of pay, having completed five years service. . . ."
Not the least important part of it was the fact that he could expect
the pay increase.

The Thomasons began calling their son Jack to distinguish
him from his father, and henceforth sent out reports regularly
detailing his progress. By the following September Jack weighed
fourteen pounds and was sitting alone and had to be restrained
from trying to stand on his legs. "His disposition continues
equable, as long as he is humored," John informed Jack's paternal grandmother. "But he is, I regret to state, quite spoiled. He
wants attention all the time — not handling especially — just
somebody around to notice him. . . ."

Meanwhile, the Thomasons had returned to Texas for
Christmas and had had the privilege of showing off the first
Thomason grandson to his two sets of grandparents and his numerous uncles and aunts and cousins. Colonel Hill, who had replaced Colonel Hall, as C.O. managed to keep Thomason pretty
busy. But he had free afternoons which he spent with Leda riding
about the island.

Both parents watched their son's every move avidly. "Jack is eight months old tomorrow, and very bad," John wrote his mother on February 13, 1921. "He is developing an amazing temper — when he don't get what he wants, he takes a deep breath and roars . . . Jack roars. Nothings else describes it." Not only did Jack roar, he was not particular about the time he did it. Two o'clock in the morning was just as good a time as any.

Then again, "Jack now has two teeth and more coming . . . He stood alone for the first time today. All this is encouraging, for it means that before long, I can begin to apply Naval Regulations and Marine Corps Orders to him, and there will be repose and calm in the Casa Thomason again — there will, I say, or he'll stand up to eat."

But by the following June the doting parents had cause for alarm. Just as Jack seemed to be thriving and had begun to take solid foods — mashed potato, toast, etc., he became seriously ill as a result of teething. "Jack has not been so well the first five days," John wrote Dr. Thomason on June 29, 1921. "He started Friday night with high fever . . . and has been very limp and lifeless since. He lost some weight, which he can ill afford, and is still on short rations . . . The medico says it is his teeth — he has four coming through at once . . . I very strongly wish that he was where you could keep an eye on him."

After Jack's difficulty with teething, it was decided that Leda and he should precede John to the states. In preparation for the trip the three visited the capital, Havana. It was Jack's first train ride and he grew excited about it. Thomason booked passage for the two on the United States Fruit Company steamer, the SS *Heredia* bound for New Orleans in July of 1921. "Leda will sail on the United Fruit boat SS *Heredia* on Monday and will reach Terrell Saturday afternoon," John wrote his mother, July 15. "Jack is not as heavy as he ought to be, but barring unintentional digestive upheavals, is well. He is very strong and active all the time, and the medico assures us that it is nothing but his teeth. However, we will feel better when he is out of Cuba. I certainly wish that he could be under Father's care for the next few months."

Before the end of August Leda was able to report that Jack was walking everywhere and gaining weight.

In the last few remaining months of his tour, Thomason witnessed the almost total disintegration of Cuba. Grafters had infiltrated all agencies of government and industry. Crime went unchecked. The railroad strike, bank failures, and the closing down of the sugar mills in 1921 resulted in widespread hunger and banditry. "In her people there is no single element of strength," John wrote his father one month before he left. "They are Negro, Spanish, and Chinese, with all the vices of each race and none of the virtues." In September, when he boarded ship for his return to Texas, Thomason did so without misgivings but with both anger and compassion in his heart for the "Pearl of the Antilles."

7 Man of Words and Windy Periods

At the end of a brief furlough in Texas Thomason assumed the post of base legal officer on the staff of Rear Admiral Hugh Rodman, commander of the Fifth Naval District at Hampton Roads, Virginia — the principal fleet anchorage on the East Coast — in October of 1921.

It is customary in the Marine Corps to appoint officers to billets concerned with the administration of naval justice. Traditionally, aboard ship the commanding officer of the Marine detachment functioned as the captain's legal advisor and the second in command of the Marine guard discharged additional duties as recorded of summary courts-martial. Few officers in the Corps had had formal legal training other than that provided from basic school or acquired through correspondence courses. Even fewer had had active legal experience. However, career officers managed to obtain a practical knowledge of naval law. All had access to such publications as *Navy Regulations,* the *Articles for the Government of the Navy,* and the *Manual for Courts-Martial.*

Thomason's position was a responsible one for a junior Marine officer. Duties included the serving as judge advocate of General Courts-Martial and as a member of Courts of Inquiry and boards of investigations that were convened locally. "I have a staff job—a desk job—," Thomason wrote the family. "I that was a soldier am now a lawyer — a man of words and windy periods."

Even though the routine did not appeal to Thomason, he realized the importance of the work. "I am now Judge Advocate of the General Court here, and am by virtue of my office no mean man, being legal adviser to admirals and things like that," he bragged to his mother. He also let it be known that without undue difficulty he managed to be impressive in the conduct of his duties. "Fortunately, the clerk of the court is old and grey with years passed in GCM work, and when I am consulted I always take time to deliberate maturely — which means to go and ask old Morrison. Then I deliver my pronouncements, and so far, all has gone well. . . ."

Occasionally he served as a witness before General courts-Martial away from the base. One such temporary duty took him to the Naval Yard at Philadelphia. The trial was over by noon and he spent the rest of the day exploring the town, which he had not seen since sailing from it for France in 1918. The experience gave him the opportunity to see Marshall Foch, whom he considered the ablest leader in World War I. A letter to his father dispatched on November 17, 1921, reflects his excitement. "Marshall Foch was there that afternoon, and I had a far glimpse of him in the parade, where he rode in a big grey car . . . That night he went out of the Broad Street station, and quite by accident, I blustered into the crowd waiting for him, and he passed me almost close enough to touch. He looks older than when I saw him in 1919, but he has presence. Certainly he has presence. He has the Napoleonic idea about uniforms. He was in plain field kit—horizon blue—no medals, no batons—only the microscopic silver stars on his sleeves and the red cap with golden oak leaves which a marshall wears, and a little brown stick. His staff, however, are as splendid as French regulations allow, and form an effective foil to his plainness.''

Thomason's stature as a humanitarian had expanded to the extent that he could realize the magnitude of Wilson's vision of a new world, even the nobility of it, though it was impossible of fruition.

But as Thomason's humanitarianism became more clearly defined, so did his philosophy of fatalism become more deeply ingrained. After recovering from a severe duodenal ulcer, he confided to his father: ''. . . my life for the last seven years has made a fatalist of me. I had five straight months of excellent opportunity to get killed in France — five major engagements and fourteen battles I served through as a combat officer. In my battalion that period there were 123 officers — battalion complement is 27. There were three of us who came through without getting hit. Once when we were being shelled, waiting to attack, I was lying in a shell hole. For no reason at all, I got up and moved ten feet over to another hole. A lieutenant in my company . . . jumped up and got into the hole I left. He wasn't settled there. Nor was I down good in my new one when a shell dropped in on him and killed him. There was nothing left but his head and shoulders. I could give you a dozen cases like it. This time, I should have died. I had about 96 chances out of a hundred against me. But I didn't. Like in 1918, it doesn't appear to have been time for me to die. And I have come to the opinion that some Inscrutable Purpose is saving me for some job or other and that I will not get my discharge until I have done that job. I have no idea what it is. It's idle to speculate on it . . . one can merely carry out his orders and leave the rest to Higher Authority. Living is a privilege — not a right.''

During the first year at Hampton Roads the trial docket was so full that Thomason was relieved from standing watch as staff duty officer. However, except at times when the fleet was in and cases increased by the hundreds, Thomason's work was not always time-consuming and permitted him to engage in other activities. As he explained it, he was exceedingly busy about half the time and hardly employed for the remainder. ''That's fortunate," he wrote Manda, his maternal grandmother, "Because I have opportunity to read. Thackeray, Dickens, Dumas, Victor Hugo, various memoirs, and a lot of professional works help me to pass the time very pleasantly. . . ."

Nor did he confine himself to his old favorites. Though he was still reading biographies and was preoccupied with Napoleon, he had begun to identify with such modern poets as Carl Sandburg and Edgar Lee Masters. He hailed the latter's *Spoon River Anthology* as the masterpiece of the day. "He [Masters] writes of homely things with a stark realism that is doubtless more effective in free verse than if he had followed the old classic form, . . ." he wrote to Manda, who was herself a poet and an intellectual. "The moral is . . . that if you have something to say, it doesn't matter a great deal how you say it. So many people have nothing to say, and say that nothing elaborately and beautifully."

Thomason found time for artistic activities. The picturesque atmosphere of the naval base was conducive to painting and sketching. There were always ships for inspiration. A case in point was the old *Iowa,* fighting Bob Evans' flagship, in dock, stripped of her guns and accoutrements, awaiting to serve as a target for maneuvers. "I went down to Pier 7, where she lies, late yesterday afternoon," he wrote his father, "and made a fairly successful oil sketch of her. She was the pride of the Navy in her day, fired the first gun at Santiago, and went around the world in 1908. Admiral Evans entertained the Kaiser aboard her."

The *Iowa* would be scudded to sea with no crew aboard, her steering and operation being controlled by wireless from a destroyer miles away. The fleet ordered to destroy her with gunfire and bombs would be given an area of some 200 square miles in which to sight her. So there she lay in port, all scaly grey and rusting, facing her final performance, and John Thomason recorded with paintbrush the lamentable end of her saga.

At this time Thomason began to exhibit. Miss Ruth Thomas, secretary of the Art Institute of Newport, Rhode Island, was impressed with the artist's work, particularly his watercolors, and arranged for the loan of several for her summer exhibitions.

Thomason's art was much admired and some of it found buyers.

Thomason also found leisure time for drives and short trips in the recently acquired Ford. One weekend he went to Newport News to witness the launching of the *West Virginia*. Intrigued by the spectacle, he submitted an article on the event to his old editor, Marcellous E. Foster of the *Houston Chronicle*. Thomason was trying to recoup some losses. To his dismay, *Outing* magazine had become insolvent and would not be able to pay him for the last two articles he submitted.

One of the family's most enjoyable sidetrips in the vicinity of Hampton Roads was a visit to historic Yorktown. The town — "little and old and quaint," reminded Thomason of Walker County, Texas. He had a weakness for battlesites and liked to imagine the precise action that occurred at such places, splashed with his inevitable feeling for color.

> . . . There is a monument there commemorating the Cornwallis surrender [he wrote his mother], and they show you the cave where the unfortunate general had his headquarters during the investment of the place. It is in the bluff on the York river and is a very charming spot. We ate lunch there, where a little ravine came, heavily wooded, down to the water, and I had no difficulty in visualizing the redcoated Foote and the dragoons with orange helmets and the disgusted seamen in their duck trousers and straw hats, huddling between the river and the hill under the fire of Washington's artillery and the mortar batteries of the Comte De Grasse, with nothing to look at but Rochambeau's blockading fleet and nothing to eat but their wornout horses.

A highlight of the first year at Hampton Roads was the launching of the first helium gas dirigible. "The first helium gas dirigible flew here yesterday — an epochal event in aviation," he reported to the doctor. "By the way that gas is non-flammable and gives lighter than aircraft defensive strength — which they have not had hitherto." The 43,000-cubic foot single-engine H-1 airship served for towing or use as a kite balloon. The J-class — the next naval airship — would be completed the following year. The United States had flown both observation (Kite) balloons and blimps in Europe during World War I.

One of the pleasantest domestic aspects of the Hampton Roads tour was Thomason's observation of his young son's development. No letter went to the parents of Huntsville that failed to include intimate and complete disclosures.

Sometimes his revelations were given with tongue-in-cheek. Leda had provided Jack with an alphabet book and he was "learning to imitate the generic sounds of the cow, dog, and cat with great accuracy — very high order of intelligence." She had also bought him a blue sweater suit in which he appeared "very cunning."

At other times the enclosure of photographs prompted special comment. "He looks a great deal stronger and more solid than when you last saw him," Thomason wrote the doctor, "and he is beginning to frame sentences and express his thoughts very intelligibly. He goes frequently to the park and observes the monkeys and the ducks. He has inherited all my passion for the waterfowl family, and even takes pleasure in a drawing of a canvasback drake, but he doesn't like monkeys at all.

"He is beginning to exhibit a strong individuality and no little temper, and will come in for a great deal of discipline ere long. Leda: Humph!

"Orders are orders and must be carried out; however, as I shall presently instruct him. I have always had well disciplined and heedful companies. I am going to have a well-instructed young olive branch, too (if his mother doesn't interfere with me, Leda: HUMPH)."

Paternity is occasionally overwhelming, but almost never dull, as Thomason's next comment testifies: "Do not be deceived by the seraphic expression on his face as he sits beside the tender Ford. He has exceeded his cracker ration for the day and is planning behind that beatific face, how to circumvent his mother and get further crackers. He has plenty of enterprise in him and will never be so good as to cause alarm. . . ."

At the age of one year and eleven months Jack was "very bad," his father reported, no doubt with a great deal of secret glee, to the child's maternal grandmother, and had "a great taste for riding in the car." The latter fact reminded John of a statement made by his Uncle Mark Smither: "Humph! Never

saw a Thomason in my life that wasn't always ready to go somewhere!'' In that particular the Thomason heir ran true to form.
''He is developing an imperious manner. . . .'' He paid no attention whatever to his nurse, next to none to his mother, but
rendered ''prompt and fairly cheerful obedience'' to his father's
orders—''simply because he knows that I will—and do—spank
him if he don't. . . .''

On June 14, 1923, Jack's parents marked his third milestone with a party. At the remarkable age of three the only
Thomason grandson further projected his extraordinary father
by demonstrating a flair for impressive attire.

During his tour at Hampton Roads, Thomason had the occasion to refresh his memory of his war experiences. His Aunt
Elise, who was planning a trip to Europe, wrote him for an itinerary of the battle sites so that she could visit them.

(Elise, an extremely beautiful and adorable Southern belle,
who had married Thomason's uncle, the rugged individualist
Robert Goree, was a great favorite.)

Although John had no maps at hand to consult, his
memory of the entire combat activity was accurate. His reaction,
after the elapse of four years was notable. He wrote:

> I hope to go back some day — but not for the battle-
> fields. Somehow I have no desire to see them again. Anyway,
> I—nobody—can ever see them again, as they were those days
> that the earth was shaking. You can ride along that long white
> road that goes from Meaux to Chateau-Thierry, but the day
> we went up it, one half was choked with armed men rushing
> to battle, and the other half was a stream of refugees — old
> men and all sorts and conditions of women and children and
> household goods on wheelbarrows and pushcarts, and
> wounded Frenchmen of Degoutte's corps. . . . You will see
> the wheatfields around Bois de Belleau, and the poppies in
> the wheat — the machine guns and the dead men are gone,
> and I suppose the shell holes are all filled up. . . I wonder if
> the grass has grown again in the Champagne? Where we
> were, it was like a great white sea . . . without a tree, or a
> blade of grass — something dead and cursed and cold, all
> shellholes and barbed wire and unburied dead. . . .

At the end of his letter Thomason, who wrote much poetry in his youth, penned these lines of verse:

> All over the world, nursing their scars,
> Sit the old soldiers broke in the wars —
> Sit the old soldiers, surly and grim,
> Mocking the lilt of the conqueror's hymn.
> Over the world, nursing their scars —
> Pity old soldiers broke in the wars!

Thomason's confining routine did not improve with the passing of time. "My court work drags along, keeping me busy enough," he wrote his mother on May 15, 1922, "But I don't like it and will get back to the line at my first opportunity."

The second year at Hampton Roads was more eventful than the first. Not only were the Marines engaged in their own administration of justice at Hampton Roads, the overall situation in the spring of 1922 was fraught with problems including two major investigations of the Corps. As a result of the Washington Conference and the Naval Treaties of 1922, there was imposed a ten-year moratorium on capital ship construction, together with the concomitant provisions to scrap a sizable portion of the navy. On top of this, there was the controversy over the merits of land-based aircraft as compared with ship-mounted ordnance. Resultant speculation raised the question of the future importance of major fleet units. Such conditions could only sow the seeds of consternation, if not downright alarm, among career officers in the naval service.

As if these difficulties were not enough to compound the situation career officers were facing, in 1922 the Marine Corps was subjected to a Naval Court of Inquiry and an investigation conducted by a select committee of the United States Senate. The Marines were charged with alleged atrocities perpetrated in Haiti and Santa Domingo, which comprise the island of Hispaniola in the Caribbean, in suppressing the massive uprisings of 1918-1919 and wholesale banditry. Marine units had been actively engaged in field operations at these underdeveloped countries since 1915, promoting education, establishing sanitation, and constructing railroads. In the first five years of the occupation native casualties had been estimated at 2,250 in comparison with 14 to 15 Marines killed.

Although the Marines survived both investigations, the Corps suffered from the unfavorable publicity. In addition, the organization's future employment as occupational forces in Latin American countries was in jeopardy. Meanwhile the Marines had been ordered by the president of the United States to guard the mails in metropolitan areas. In 1921 the loss by armed robbery was estimated at $7 million, and the Post Office Department had been totally unable to cope with it.

Even though Thomason was not directly involved in the investigations, he could not completely escape the effects. However, his philosophy of making the best of any situation, if possible, insulated him. Besides, he was too busy to give the hearings much attention. In the spring of 1923 he served as recorder of a long and intricate board of investigations at Hampton Roads in which more than one hundred witnesses were examined within the brief space of three weeks. As a result of the strain, he was admitted to the United States Naval Hospital in May for rest. Following his release, he was transferred to the Marine Barracks at Portsmouth (Norfolk) Navy Yard, under the command of Colonel Randolph C. Berkeley.

In Norfolk Thomason was in command of the Barracks Detachment Guard Company. He was greatly relieved to be off Courts-Martial and to be with troops again. The new assignment entailed no more than an hour of office work daily and permitted him to work out of doors the remainder of the time. He drew officer of the day duty which included an eight-mile walking tour in which he visited sentries.

Not only were his working conditions pleasant, his three-story quarters, with two baths and maid's room and completely furnished, were comfortable. As he was expecting Leda and Jack to arrive from Terrell on November 1 or earlier, he left the pictures and ornaments packed.

It was a good thing. Almost immediately he received new orders to report to the Marine Barracks of the Naval Ammunition Depot at Dover, New Jersey. ''I had just gotten comfortable in Norfolk," he wrote his mother. "Big, elegant quarters, room for lots of company which we have always wanted, a golf course right in the front yard . . . and a detail that would have been not too confining or uninteresting. Saturday night my orders came . . . I packed up everything Monday and Tuesday, wired Leda Saturday night — blow to her, poor little sweetheart — and put my car aboard the Baltimore boat Tuesday night. . . ."

Dover? Thomason was not sure that he had ever heard of it.

8 *Of Forgotten Fighting Men*

At Baltimore Thomason retrieved his car on November 2 and drove the 220-odd miles to Dover, New Jersey. He made the trip in ten hours with twenty minutes expended on a puncture and time out for dinner at Morristown, nine miles from his destination. Leda and Jack arrived from Texas on November 5.

Thomason was commanding officer, quartermaster, and post exchange officer of the Marine Barracks attached to the Naval Ammunition Depot five miles northwest of Dover. The Marine detachment consisted of 60-odd men whose duty was to guard the magazine from fire and disorder. Dover, a small manufacturing town and the home of Onyx hosiery, had a population of 9,700. "The station is out in the hills, in a country extremely wild and picturesque," Thomason wrote his mother. "There are many lakes and streams and fine fishing and lots of game, though hunting is not permitted. Roads are excellent. On the army arsenal adjacent there is a 19-hole golf course. The Marines have three saddle horses in poor repair."

Curious as to why he was so peremptorily pulled out of Norfolk and reassigned to his present post, Thomason learned the reason from the Marines' point of view. The naval commander in charge of the depot did not get along with the Leathernecks. Thomason was the third officer to be sent to the ammunition depot that year. The commander brought pressure to bear against the first, along with serious charges, and got him relieved. Headquarters then sent another captain — an officer just returned from sea duty and accustomed to the navy. After six months on the post the officer, whose record was impeccable, requested and was granted a release.

"I suppose it is a compliment to be sent where two captains — the last a very good man — have failed," John said. "I imagine the fact that I got along so well with my last admiral who is known as the hardest person in the navy — is behind the detail. But I hated to leave Norfolk." From the viewpoint of Marines in the guard the commandant was "a very regrettable person indeed." No doubt the story from the other side — the navy — would allege "shocking things against the Corps."

Thus far Thomason's relationship with commanding officers had been exceedingly pleasant. Not everybody who had served under Colonel Terrell, Colonel Hall, Admiral Rodman, and Admiral Andrews had a similar record. For the first few days the naval commander at Dover was noticeably courteous. Then at the first opportunity he demonstrated his irrational nature.

That opportunity presented itself when Captain Thomason decorated the galley walls of the quarters to which he had been assigned with specimens of his art. The commandant threatened to prefer charges against him, including deliberate damage to government property. Thomason took the incident in stride, rose above it. Not only did he succeed with the temperamental naval officer, whom he later categorized as "a vessel of wrath," he did such an outstanding job on the base that his tour was extended to a second year.

Although he was due for sea or foreign duty at the expiration of his tour in the fall, Thomason enjoyed the year at Dover so much that when the inspector of ordnance requested that he be retained for another year (which was contrary to the policy of the Corps), Thomason was glad to remain.

Several factors contributed to the Marine captain's enjoyment of the station. To begin with, he had drawn a contingent of well disciplined men congenial to work with. "Really, my men are so well-behaved that I am puzzled about them," he wrote the doctor. "Prohibition is a great thing for the enlisted personnel, among others. I do not have one drunken man a month . . . and this is very wet territory."

Then the tour permitted him to enjoy the out of doors so vital to his well being. The post required no more than an hour of office work daily, and he could play a few rounds of golf when he desired.

The fact that the area provided splendid fishing and hunting added much to Thomason's enjoyment. Besides the many watering places in the vicinity frequented by vacationers at the resort town, there were a reservoir conveniently located behind the Marine quarters stocked with fine white perch and bass and Lake Pickatinny — one of the best fishing spots in the state — stocked with perch and pickerel. All three of the family enjoyed fishing. Even though shooting was not permitted in the area close to the depot and the army arsenal, duck shooting at Aberdeen, near Harve-de-Grasse, Maryland, was good. Also during the Christmas season of 1924 Thomason and a party of army friends spent six delightful days hunting and fishing on Chesapeake Bay.

Since the post was not too time-consuming, Thomason even took up gardening as a hobby. Though May meant summer in Texas, it heralded the advent of spring in the North. "This is my first spring in the North," Thomason wrote his father. "And I think the season is more beautiful perhaps than in the South, because the contrast is so pronounced." His English peas, carrots, lettuce, and spinach were doing well by the end of May; his cucumbers and corn were due to sprout soon and his okra, while late, was hopeful. What he particularly lacked was black-eyed peas and he requested Dr. Thomason to send him some seed. "These ignorant Yankees have never heard of black-eyed peas. I have been unable to get them anywhere." He hoped the doctor could send enough seeds for a "medium stand" and would also instruct him as to how to plant them. By the 24th of June the black-eyed peas were "up beautifully," John reported.

Of more importance, Thomason's leisure time permitted him to do some writing and devote serious attention to his art. The scenic nature of the lake country and the mountains inspired Thomason to engage in landscape painting. Much of the writing at first was for service publications which did not pay a great deal. Up to this time Thomason had not succeeded greatly at short-story writing. "I have had such unfailing bad luck with the stories that I am trying to develop an essay form," he wrote his mother, February 25, 1924. "My stories simply won't sell."

The station's proximity to New York was an asset. Dover was only 21 miles from Newark, from where it was possible to reach the city by tube in twenty minutes. This made shopping convenient and permitted members of the military community and their families to take advantage of metropolitan social life and entertainment. Leda and her women friends made frequent shopping trips to New York, and she and John attended shows there at least once a month. Moreover, the nearness of New York allowed the Thomasons to make frequent visits to their friends Lieutenant Carl Broaddus, a medico, and his wife Virginia, and son Carl, Jr., who lived in Brooklyn.

New York's proximity also permitted Thomason to exhibit his art in the metropolitan galleries. Ruth Thomas' showing of some of Thomason's paintings the preceding summer at Newark had elicited admiration and brought some sales. As a result, the artist was later invited to exhibit at the galleries of Knoedler's and Ackerman's. Thus some of the best dealers in New York had seen and admired Thomason's art. The directors of the two galleries were enthusiastic in their appraisal of Thomason's combat art. They acclaimed it as being as good as anything that they had seen and superior to most. Still the battle scenes at the point of combat had not found buyers at the time.

Thomason's showing drew a favorable press. It was the press releases that attracted the notice of his former friend of World War I days — the writer and critic Laurence Stallings. Stallings, who trained with Thomason at Quantico and lost a leg at Belleau Wood, is credited with the discovery of the author-artist. Although this has been exaggerated, Stallings did introduce Thomason to important people of the art and publishing world and helped to launch him. "Laurence is quite on the pinnacle of earthly grandeur. He has written a book, *Plumes,* which is selling well, and has a play, *What Price Glory,* that is the hit of the season . . . so my soldiers intrigued him," John wrote his mother on December 11, 1924. "At his solicitation I withdrew all my drawings from the dealers and turned them over to him, and he has gotten the top crust of the artistic and critic crowd in New York interested in them. People like Neysa McMein, Don Marquis, Robert Benchley . . . and they go into fits over my little fighting men; say I get a quality that is unique . . . They are quite sure that I will get some illustrating to do if I want it. . . ."

The way in which Thomason's career as a foremost American author and artist was launched has become an integral part of his legend. Stallings was instrumental in bringing Thomason to the attention of Charles Scribner's Sons, but the introduction to the publishing house was not so simple and direct as it may seem.

The account of his friend Alexander Woollcott ("Introducing Captain Thomason of the Marines," *Vanity Fair,* June, 1925) bears repetition. Stallings remembered Thomason's sketching from the early Quantico days. There was the lean, tawny Texan who drew unceasingly a profusion of deft sketches of soldiers in overcoats. This was puzzling to Stallings. Why was the Marine from the Lone Star State preoccupied with overcoats?

"You see," explained the Texan in an abstracted drawl, "I never did see any soldiers in overcoats before. My details have been in Southern waters, mostly. Then no one had overcoats in Mexico. And the Greeks — those fellows had no overcoats."

The memory of those incisive sketches remained with Stallings and made him restless one night when the Marines drove the Germans out of "a temporary pit of hell" called Bouresches. Later when he was severely wounded, as he led an assault on a German machine gun nest and had to be evacuated, Lieutenant Stallings heard from a sergeant squatting beside him that Captain Thomason was sketching under fire with burnt match ends

Germans impaled on broken tree branches and young Marines twisted and dying in the scarred terrain of a French village. Stallings made a mental note that some day he would reunite with Thomason and see those drawings.

During Stallings' hospitalization and leg amputation, he kept hearing of "how extraordinary a company officer this man [Thomason] was and of his prowess on the hills below Soissons."

Still later — after the war — Stallings would send by every Marine who chanced to stop at his office at the *New York World* the request to Thomason to bring along his sketches if ever a leave should permit him to visit New York.

Then — years later — Thomason finally appeared one afternoon at Stallings' office with his portfolio in hand. After the first shock at seeing his friend again and the waves of excitement subsided, Stallings bundled his hero and his sketches into a cab. Within half an hour the two were in the studio of Miss Neysa McMein, a noted New York artist and designer of magazine covers. Humble in the presence of anyone whose art was superior to hers, Miss McMein called in Blanche Fisher Wright for consultation.

Part of the story insists that Thomason relinquished his portfolio to Miss McMein without hesitation: "I leave these in your care, Ma'am," he said to Miss McMein, who relished his Texan bow. Then he rushed off to take care of more urgent business.

One of his sergeants had gone on a spree [there has to be a first time], and to amuse himself had beaten up three New Jersey policemen. When he had finished the three off, a plainclothesman had come up and clobbered him from the rear. The next day when Captain Thomason got him released from jail, the Marine apologized. Actually he was ashamed of himself. He had not known that the fourth man was a cop, else he'd have worked him over too!

When Miss McMein and Miss Wright concluded their consultation, they decided that *Scribner's Magazine* would be their first port of call. They needed no other.

As a result Stallings and Thomason found themselves in the office of Robert Bridges, director of the Art Department of

Charles Scribner's Sons. Both Bridges and his assistant, Joseph H. Chapin, after a careful examination of the drawings, were impressed. While concurring that the work was excellent, both editors felt that a text to accompany the sketches should be written. They suggested that Stallings and Thomason collaborate on an account of the trench warfare of World War I. Aware of Thomason's talent as a writer, Stallings declined.

Then Thomason, almost self-effacingly modest, ventured that he had also ''done a little writing'' on the war. Whereupon he handed Bridges the first segment of the manuscript. He didn't suppose Scribner's could use the stuff, he said, but they might want to look it over.

The next day, so the legend continues, Scribner's told Miss McMein that her Marine captain could write even better than he could draw.

In a letter to his parents dated January 3, 1925, John Thomason — who preferred the pen and sketching pad to the scalpel and stethoscope and who eschewed the taking of an academic degree — recounted in detail the launching of his career. In his letter — a study in restraint — he gave much credit to the prominent friends who had sponsored him. He acknowledged that he had ''sense enough to see that my poor little pictures of forgotten fighting men would languish forever in the marts, were it not for the influential ladies and gentlemen in high places whom I have met in the course of my misspent life.'' It is an extraordinary statement from a man who when he was rejected, realized the merit of his work and when he was recognized, minimized it and gave the credit to others.

Stallings' difficulty in renewing contact with Thomason was attributable to Thomason's nature; ''He [Stallings] being so up in the world, I hadn't gotten in touch with him, for I have ever gone to extremes to avoid the very appearance of soliciting.''

As he explained it to his parents, ''Scribner's have taken some of my drawings, paying a very nice price for them and holding out prospects that are quite dazzling to a simple captain of the Marines.'' He went on: ''Some other people are after them [his sketches], for I have a telegram from Stallings urging me not to commit myself . . . without seeing him. He says, let him run the show. I am quite content to do this, for I am but a simple soldier, and regard this business stuff with distaste — besides as literary editor of the *New York World,* Laurence is greater than many admirals. He can make or break a book with an idle word, and publishers fawn on him, no less . . . I will probably sell everything I have done and will . . . get some books to illustrate for Scribner's and others.''

That spring he wrote again that Scribner's were holding on to everything he had taken them and that while they had bought outright only one story — *The Battle of Soissons* — and sketches to illustrate it, ''they were dallying with the idea of bringing out a book in the fall . . . I have just finished the illustrations for a story they [Scribner's] sent me and have another story coming in from *Liberty. Liberty* has also asked me to send them a story.''

Meanwhile, Thomason's prominent friends in the literary and art world, especially the latter, were urging him to resign from the service. Undoubtedly he could support himself on income from his art in New York. But he was satisfied with his situation as it was and declined to change it. ''Writing and drawing will combine beautifully with the profession of arms. Nourishing in Uncle Sam's bosom . . . I will never starve . . . Furthermore, I am so organized that I cannot live in the house.''

The initial segment of the combat material entitled *The Charge at Soissons* was scheduled to be published in the June 1925 issue of *Scribner's* magazine. The second article, *Marines at Blanc Mont,* was to be published as the main feature in the September issue. The third installment, *Monkey Meat,* would run in November and a fourth and final segment, *Into Belleau Wood,* was scheduled to be published in March of 1926.

Thus was launched the career of one of America's best known writers and artists, who scarcely a year before had almost despaired of writing short stories and was told that his fellow countrymen were tired of war.

Moreover, as his friends predicted, John Thomason began still another successful career as an illustrator of magazine articles and books for others. Among those were *Geoffrey John of Amiens* by Walter Davenport (*Liberty,* May, 1925); *The Reward of Valor* by Leonard H. Nason (*Liberty*, July, 1925); *The Tank and the Doctor* also by Nason (*Liberty*, September, 1925); *An Uncharted Course* by Harriet Welles (*Scribner's*, August, 1925); *The Doctor's Confession* by Roger Burlingame (*Scribner's*, February, 1926); *The Stranger Woman* by Mrs. Welles (*Scribner's*, December, 1926), and a new edition of Thomas Boyd's *Through the Wheat*, published by Scribner's in 1926.

Thomason maintained good relations with the army personnel operating the arsenal and kept abreast of their experiments involving explosives. One in particular interested him because it transcended everything in existence "like the Almighty's thunderbolts." It was flashless—burned so fast that it was practically invisible, even at night. It had more power than anything then known. He described it to his father:

> It is all a matter of chemistry. So a greasy fellow in a dugout 40 kilometres away with his table of logarhythms, his formulas, and his maps, can press a button and erase a whole battalion of gallant fighting men whom he never saw—and who never saw him. It is disgusting—sentient men against cold machines and formulas that do not bleed or suffer.
>
> . . . Yet in the end machines cannot conquer and man, at a very terrible and ever-increasing price, is superior to the things he makes.

Two memorable Christmases marked the Thomasons' stay in Dover, each accompanied by snow. Jack, who was almost four, in December of 1923, found both exciting. "Our family now consists of one automobile, Jack's size, one sled ditto, one tricycle, two cats, and one puppy, two months old," John wrote his father on December 27, 1923.

The only discordant note in an otherwise perfect Christmas was Jack's accent. In Virginia he had acquired a delightful Virginian inflection. He came up from Texas speaking the drawl of the Far South, "like a scholar and a gentleman." Now, however, his speech faithfully reflected a combination of Yankee twang and Third Avenue, New Yorkese.

The second Christmas in 1924 was enlivened by house guests: Carl and Virginia Broaddus and Carl, Jr., who was about

Jack's age. The visitors fared sumptuously on canvasback ducks and wild geese and other spoils of Thomason's successful hunting expeditions. There was a Christmas tree in the home and the Marines had one in the barracks. "Jack and Carl, Jr. went almost crazy," John wrote his parents, "and all my young men stayed sober and out of jail."

A highlight of the Dover tour was the production of *What Price Glory*. John and Leda attended the production at the Plymouth Theatre in New York in 1924. "I had to be in New York a day last week on court martial duty and took Leda and Jack with me. We spent the night at the St. George in Brooklyn . . . and went on complimentary tickets," John wrote his mother. The couple would not have been able to see the performance without complimentary tickets as the show was sold out weeks ahead and tickets could be obtained only at inflated prices from speculators.

Thomason, who was wearing civilian clothes, went to the head of the line and requested "tickets for Captain Thomason" from the attendant. Immediately the attendant bawled out to the man behind the ticket window: "Gimme them seats for Captain Thomason!"

Thomason was embarrassed as the incident attracted the attention of those in line. Someone behind him said to somebody else: "Wonder if he's a Marine officer?"

"Might be; maybe so," the other person answered. "He's sure got a mean eye."

"Yeah. And look how sunburnt!"

"The play is a great one . . . though not a pleasant one," Thomason wrote his mother. It had incited unfavorable comment from the pulpit, welfare workers, and Admiral Plunkett, who "were insensed by the disclosure that American fighting men . . . drank and swore. . . ."

Whether he was aware of it or not, it has been said that Thomason himself was the model for Lieutenant Cunningham. When Flagg, the protagonist, asks, "You from Texas?" Cunningham answers, "You hit it." Then —

Flagg: Now I get you. So we've got another damned Texan in this outfit wanting to fight anybody that ain't from Texas.

Cunningham: Yep, and I ain't no Goddam college boy either.

Reference has been made to Thomason's belief in fatalism. It has even been said that he bore a charmed life. Whether it was Providence, Fate or merely luck — some force was beneficent to him. Less than a year after his transfer from Dover, the Naval Ammunition Depot was struck by lightning. Following several fires and violent detonations, the shocks being felt as far away as New York and Philadelphia, a major portion of the installation was totally destroyed. Thomason's relief at Dover, Captain Burwell H. Clarke, and eleven enlisted Marines died in the holocaust and thirty-six others were seriously injured.

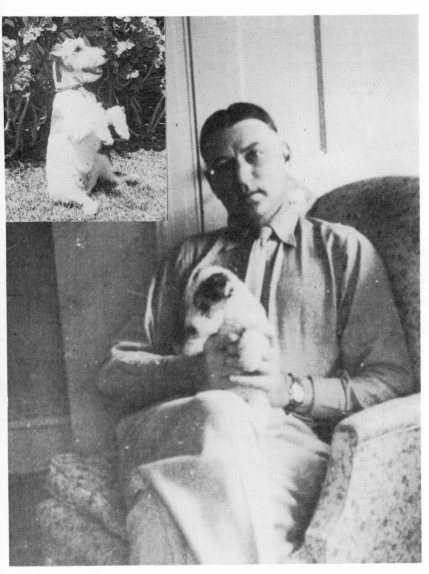

Thomason and Winkie during his Washington tour of duty as aide to Colonel Roosevelt. A man of many moods, Thomason loved dogs and was rarely without one. The death of the family pet Winkie had a tremendous impact on him. (Note inset of Winkie performing manual of arms routine.)

— Courtesy Sam Houston State Library

On June 6, 1938, Southwestern University of Georgetown, Texas, conferred upon Thomason the honorary Doctor of Letters degree. Pictured here is Leda Thomason congratulating her husband after the ceremony.

*   — Courtesy Thomason Collection, SHSU Library*

Another Southwestern University scene. From left, Dr. Thomas Herbert Thomason, John's brother; Thomason (center in academic regalia); and Dr. J. W. Thomason, his father.
                              — Courtesy Emily Thomason Petersen

Members of the Thomason family present for the ceremonies accompanying the hanging of Colonel Thomason's portrait in Austin. From left, Mary Thomason Stafford, James J. Thomason, Margaret Thomason Cole, Dr. Thomas Herbert Thomason, Mrs. J. W. Thomason, John's mother; Dr. Robert H. Thomason, Elizabeth Thomason Johnson, and Emily Thomason Petersen.

— Official US Marine Corps Photograph,
courtesy Emily Thomason Petersen

Governor Allan Shivers accepts the oil portrait of Colonel Thomason to hang in the state capitol at Austin. Artist Suzanne Atkinson, daughter of Dr. Thomas Herbert Thomason and painter of the portrait, stands to the right of painting. The ceremony took place on April 20, 1960.

> — *Official US Marine Corps Photograph,*
> *courtesy Emily Thomason Petersen*

The Thomasons in front of their Washington home.

The first home of Major and Mrs. Thomason in Washington, D.C. at 4920 Indian Lane.
— Courtesy Sam Houston State Lib.

Leda Thomason in the Thomason home in Washington, D.C.
— Courtesy Leda Thomason

Dr. J. W. Thomason, John's father.
— Courtesy Sue Thomason Noordberg

John William Thomason's maternal grandparents, Eliza Nolley Goree and Major Thomas Jewett Goree. Before her marriage to Major Goree, Miss Nolley—a poet and intellectual—was a member of the faculty of Andrew Female College in Huntsville, Texas. Major Goree, who was a Texas prison superintendent in Huntsville, served in the Civil War on the staff of General James Longstreet. Called affectionately Manda and Dad, both had a profound influence in the shaping of Thomason's character.

— Photographs courtesy of Leda Thomason

Birthplace of John William Thomason on Avenue J, Huntsville, Texas. The two-story Victorian mansion built in 1891 has been restored and is now occupied by Thomason's nephew, Dr. Thomas C. Cole and Mrs. Cole.

— *Courtesy Colonel Thomason Room, SHSU Library*

Four generations. From left, John's maternal grandmother, Mrs. Thomas J. Goree; Mrs. J. W. Thomason, John's mother; John William Thomason, and son Jack.

— Courtesy Emily Thomason Petersen

Thomason and Leda before their marriage in 1917.
— Courtesy Sam Houston State Library

Jack Thomason as a teenager.
— Courtesy Sam Houston
State Library

John William Thomason III, who
was called Jack to distinguish him
from his father, and his wirehaired
fox terrier Winkie at Christmas-
time in Washington, D.C. Circa
1925. Jack was six.
— Courtesy Leda Thomason

Sue Hayes Goree before her marriage to Dr. J. W. Thomason in 1892.
Miss Goree was a graceful horsewoman.
— Courtesy Leda Thomason

Dr. J. W. Thomason, John's father, relaxing in his library.
— Courtesy Sue Thomason Noordberg

Mrs. J. W. Thomason, John's mother, on her ninetieth birthday. The library held for the grand Southern lady many wonderful family memories.

— Author's collection

Sue Thomason Noordberg, Thomason's oldest sister, when she and her husband, Henri Noordberg lived in New York in 1962.

Emily Thomason Petersen, Thomason's sister, at Mrs. Petersen's home in Houston in 1975.

— Courtesy Emily Thomason Petersen

Austin College building. Dating from 1853, the structure was donated by the citizens of Huntsville to the state as the nucleus for a teacher's college in 1879.

— Courtesy Sam Houston State University

Old Main. Erected in 1890, historic Old Main was destroyed by fire on February 12, 1982, in its 92nd year.

"Tilley's Tap" The seven-mile spur to the I&GN Railroad was familiarly known as "Tilley's Tap" for its conductor J. Bob Tilley, because he operated it erratically to suit himself. Note its proximity to prison buildings in the background.

— *Author's special collection*

Huntsville's Unknown Soldiers. The seven unidentified soldiers buried in Huntsville typify one of the town's most memorable legends. This is an exceedingly rare photograph.

— *Author's special collection*

The USS John W. Thomason, *DD 760, a destroyer, was launched on September 30, 1944, at the Bethlehem Steel Company shipyard in San Francisco. The destroyer, a ship of the* Sumner *class, saw action in the Far East and earned seven battle stars and other awards during the Korean War.*

Today the proud old ship has been rechristened the Nan Yang *(Southern Seas) and is a part of the Navy of the Republic of China (Taiwan). Houston Post columnist Donald Morris, a former seaman who served three years on the* USS John W. Thomason, *revisited it in Kashiung in 1981 and wrote a moving account of the experience. The Chinese, whom John Thomason loved, have taken excellent care of the 39-year-old vessel now facing the end of its noble history.*

— Official Marine Corps Photograph,
courtesy Emily Thomason Petersen

The USS John W. Thomason, resplendent with colors flying and red, white, and blue decoration, awaits its launching.
— Official Marine Corps Photograph, courtesy Emily Thomason Petersen

Leda Thomason and her party. Leda, at center holding flowers, is flanked by Dr. Herbert Thomason, Ruth Wynne Thomason, General Paul Wakefield, left, and Mrs. J. W. Thomason, Emily Thomason Petersen, Major Jack Thomason, and Katharine Hart.
— Official Marine Corps Photograph, courtesy Emily Thomason Petersen

The Lone Star flag of Texas was presented to Leda Thomason as a part of the ceremony. Here, flanked by her son Major Thomason, left, and General Paul Wakefield, lifelong friend of Colonel Thomason, and others, she examines the state's official symbol.

— Official Marine Corps Photograph, courtesy Emily Thomason Petersen

HENDERSON YOAKUM   *SAM HOUSTON*

Henderson Yoakum and Sam Houston were Huntsville's most distinguished citizens of the nineteenth century and the town's most revered heroes. Henderson Yoakum photograph is from an oil portrait by the artist George E Allen. Circa 1846. The original painting hangs in the home of Mrs. Florine Robinson of Huntsville.

*John Thomason, left, and J. Frank Dobie, who was a senior at South-
western University when John was a freshman in 1910. The two remained fast friends and saw each other infrequently as their professional schedules and travels would permit. This is a rare photograph
heretofore unpublished.*
                           — *Courtesy Thomason Collection, SHSU Library*

J. Frank Dobie in his study at home in Austin.

Critic and playwright Laurence Stallings, who served with Thomason
in World War I and later introduced him to Scribner's; Assistant Secretary of the Navy Roosevelt, and Thomason. Stallings entertained
Thomason and Roosevelt while they were on the West Coast en route
to inspect the Fleet Air Base at Pearl Harbor in 1935. Laurence, co-
author of What Price Glory, was employed at one of the major motion
picture studios at the time.

— Courtesy Thomason Collection, SHSU Library

Thomason on duty as aide to Assistant Secretary of the Navy Roosevelt. Thomason, left, and Colonel Roosevelt are in civilian clothes.
— *Courtesy Thomason Collection, SHSU Library*

Assistant Secretary of the Navy Henry L. Roosevelt. As aide to Colonel Roosevelt, Thomason became a close friend.
— *Courtesy Thomason Collection, SHSU Library*

Assistant Secretary of the Navy Roosevelt and his staff inspect the fleet Air Base at Pearl Harbor in 1935. Thomason stands to the left of Roosevelt (center in civilian attire).

Author Ernest Hemingway, *left*, publisher Charles Scribner III, *and* editor Maxwell Perkins. Hemingway considered Thomason the greatest authority on warfare of his time. Thomason and Perkins collaborated with Hemingway on his anthology Men at War. *(1942)*
— *Robert Disraeli Films*

Novelist James Boyd and his wife Kathryn. Jim, as John called Boyd, was his best friend. The Boyds and Thomasons took vacations together and visited each other often. The two men carried on a lifelong correspondence.
— *Courtesy Thomason Collection, SHSU Library*

Captain John W. Thomason commanded a Marine contingent on the USS Rochester in 1925.

— Courtesy Thomason Collection, SHSU Library

Officers of the Legation Guard in 1932. Thomason is seated to the extreme right in the front row.

— Courtesy Sam Houston State Library

Horse Marine on duty at the Legation Guard in 1932.
— Courtesy Sam Houston State Library

Jack Thomason models his sergeant's uniform at the Legation Christmas party. Thomason had his tailor make the green uniform for Jack's Christmas present.

— *Courtesy Sam Houston State Library*

The Marine Guard was organized as a battalion. Captain Thomason commanded the Thirty-eighth Marine Gun Company.
— *Courtesy Sam Houston State Library*

Polo players and their mounts. Thomason is second from right.
— *Courtesy Sam Houston State Library*

Captain Thomason accepts the All Arms Trophy presented by Dr. John C. Ferguson of the Legation Guard in 1931. The award was made to the best drilled company in the battalion.
— Courtesy Sam Houston State Library

Thomason and his favorite race horse Temujin, whom he named for Genghis Khan.
— Courtesy Sam Houston State Library

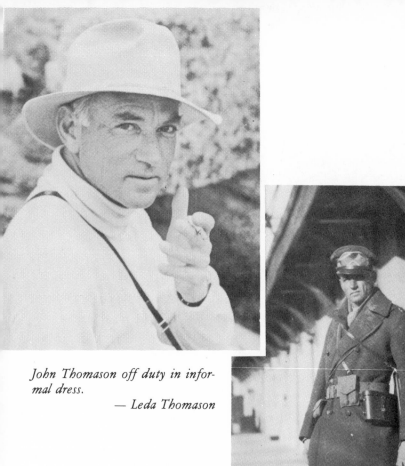

John Thomason off duty in infor-
mal dress.
— Leda Thomason

Thomason at his stables in Peking ready to ride. He and scientist Roy
Chapman Andrews made many exploratory trips around the Chinese
capital.
— Courtesy, Sue Thomason Noordberg

*Leda Thomason leads Temujin in after a spectacular race in 1932, in which he won first place.
Temujin represented the Thomason-Brown stables.*

— *Courtesy Sam Houston State Library*

Bust of scientist and explorer Roy Chapman Andrews sculpted by Thomason during the tour of duty with the Legation Guard in Peking. Friends pronounced the work a remarkable likeness of the scientist.
                                    — Courtesy Sam Houston State Library

Leda Thomason and Jack enjoy the scenic shoreline at Peitaho.
— Courtesy Sam Houston State Library

Leda Thomason got to know the ricksha coolies quite well and became fond of them. Note as the coolies rest here, one of them (R) takes the opportunity to show off.

— Sue Thomason Noordberg

Thomason and his Number 1 Boy. The servant was a sort of maitre d'
who supervised the entire domestic staff and also served as a liaison.
                        — Courtesy Sam Houston State Library

Scribner's window display for Thomason's Lone Star Preacher. *The display was the handiwork of Thomason's editor, Maxwell Perkins, who sent him the photograph.*
                    — *Courtesy Thomason Collection, SHSU Library*

Fix Bayonets! *based on World War I was Thomason's first book published in 1926.*

Jeb Stuart, *biography of the Civil general, was Thomason's fourth b published in 1930.*

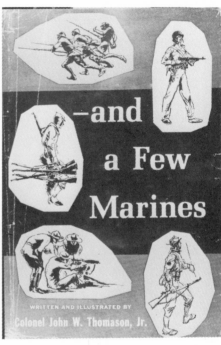

...ie Star Preacher, *now conceded by
...ny to be the greatest novel written on
...Civil War from the viewpoint of the
...thern soldier actually engaged in
...nbat. The protagonist Praxiteles
...inn was the portrait of John Stevens, a
...thodist minister, who fought in
...od's Texas Brigade. The book was
...blished in 1941.*

— and a Few Marines *was Thomason's
final book published in 1943. The book
was dedicated to Colonel Thomason's
son, Lieutenant John William Thomason,
III. Jack, as he was called to differentiate
him from his father, wore his father's
mantle in the Marine Corps proudly.*

Captain John W. Thomason in full dress uniform, 1930.
    — Courtesy Emily Thomason Petersen

9 A Ship Is a Man's World . . .

When John Thomason was detailed to the guard of the
USS Rochester, flagship of the Special Service Squadron, based
at Balboa in the Panama Canal Zone, he inquired of another
Marine, who had ostensibly served the same position, what it
was like. "Why it's just like shore duty," the friend told him.
"Got any family? Sure — take 'em down on an Army transport.
Fine place. Sleep ashore every night. Golf. Tennis. Swimming.
Panama City just across the street, a happy place —

"Ship lies in Balboa most of the time — go out occasionally
on short cruises around the more interestin' an' historic ports of
the Caribbean Sea — visit briefly an' pleasantly the beautiful
capitals in Central America — best sea job in the Marine Corps
— feller."

With this glowing introduction to his new assignment in
the tropics, Captain Thomason reported for duty aboard the
USS Rochester in the spring of 1925. When he boarded ship the
vessel was flying the two-star flag of Rear Admiral Julian L. Latimer, commander of the Special Service Squadron. Since Admi-

ral Latimer had served as judge advocate general of the navy on
the staff at Hampton Roads, the two men knew each other.

The trouble-fixer of the State Department in Central America, the squadron, in addition to the flagship, consisted of the
Denver, the *Cleveland,* the *Galveston,* and the *Tulsa,* all gun
boats mounting five-inch firearms. There had also been the *USS
Tacoma,* but she ran aground on Blanquilla Reef off Vera Cruz in
January of 1922, with a norther blowing. Now, when the tide was
out, you saw her bones bleaching in the coral fangs of Blanquilla.

The oldest armored warship on the active lists, the *Rochester* had been a focal part of United States naval history. She was
Sampson's flagship in Santiago in 1898 — the *USS New York.* As
a lad of five, John had gone aboard the *USS New York* at Galveston with his father right after the Spanish-American War, but
he did not even dream of commanding her Marines one day.

After 1911 she was flagship for the Asiatic station — the
USS Saratoga; and when the later *Saratoga* airplane carrier was
authorized, her name was changed to the *USS Rochester.* By
1917 they added 14 feet to her stacks, gave her a general overhaul, and assigned her to convoy service. At the outset of World
War I her crew claimed she had sunk a submarine.

After World War I, when she was flagship of the destroyer
flotillas, Charleston and Hampton Roads knew her. She had relieved the old *Birmingham* on the Caribbean station when that
grand lady faced retirement. To most of the ports of all of the
oceans in the old days, her white and spar-color were familiar.

Then in 1925, with her name changed once more and already in her thirty-fifth year of duty, the *USS Rochester* — with
her patrician forehead, three towering stacks, four eight-inch
guns and eight fifty-one caliber fives, and her formidable ram
bow — was destined to add more renown to her chronicle.

To Admiral Latimer, Captain Thomason, and the officers
of her deck and gunnery divisions, the *Rochester* was more than
a ship. She was a symbol of naval tradition. While at one time
the *Rochester* was the proud mistress of the seas, her chief claim
to distinction when Captain Thomason took command of the
Marine Guard was that she was the only steam-driven and coal-
fired armored cruiser afloat in the United States Navy.

Since the *Rochester*'s guard was really a major's command
and Thomason was a junior captain, he was fully cognizant of
the honor and faith reposed in him. But as proud as the 32-year-
old Marine was, he faced his first tour of sea duty with mixed
emotions on that spring day of 1925. The farewells, though perfunctory on the surface, were the opposite. The tremor of Leda's
kiss and the glowing eyes of the boy he idolized were engraved
on his heart.

In the Special Service Squadron Marines learned the sea
phase of the profession. The largest guard in the Navy, 103 enlisted men and two officers, staffed the flagship. Guards on the
other ships numbered 50. Thomason's duties, as commanding
officer of the Marine detachment, as the Guard was called, consisted of manning one of the gunnery divisions and spearhead-
ing the ship's landing party. There were other routine duties
such as quarterdeck honors, informal guard mounts, morning
and evening colors in port, instructing the ship's personnel in
the use of small arms and the supervision of range and target
practice ashore, as well as participation in the "Full Guard and
Band."

But gunnery and landing force duty were the principal
functions of the Squadron. There was always something about
the landing force activity that gave the Marines the feeling of
being on parade. At any foreign capital, regardless of the race or
color of the ruler or whether his cabinet were accustomed to shoe
leather, he got the full guard and the guns and his national colors at the foretruck. Not only that, the Marines went ashore in
these remote places proud that they were the representatives of
all their Corps. It really made a difference how the Leathernecks
wore their uniforms and how they carried their liquor.

Most of the officers' families lived in government quarters
or privately rented bungalows at Balboa, where the shops and
the docks of the Fifteenth Naval District and the long concrete
piers of the Zone shipping were located, along with the anchorage of the Special Service Squadron.

Between the docks and Ancon hill, about a mile from Panama City in the southeast section of the Zone, Balboa sat liter-

ally at the crossroads of the world. A procession of ships from every conceivable port, with all of the maritime flags, frequented Balboa: diesel-powered cargo boats from Norway and Sweden — trim, neat, and coughing — barnacled Britishers, sailing at venture, loaded to their plimsol lines; and sophisticated, highsided Britishers cruising under established houseflags, both most punctilious in dipping the Red Ensign to the American colors.

There were French ships from Nantes and Bordeaux and Le Havre pushing the South American trade; Italians from Genoa and Naples; unclassified Greeks from Piraeus; Peruvians with clipper bows and raking stacks and sleazy top-hamper; taut, red-stacked Chileños, always bringing mail, and Japanese and Germans. Infrequently tall white liners on world cruises docked at Pier 18 to flood the base with tourists.

There were all varieties of American ships — fruiters, freighters, tramps; West Coast merchant vessels with cargoes of yellow lumber, and long oil-tankers with overlapping bow and stern. Liberty parties from the United States Fleet anchored there and Scouting Fleet destroyers tied up at the Marine base. Foreign warships cruised by to visit.

Not only was Balboa a pleasant and exciting place, it was also historic and picturesque. Ten miles or so ashore a paved road led to Old Panama, where the jungle went down to the sea and where the rich town was situated before the advent of Sir Henry Morgan, buccaneer and deputy governor of Jamaica. In 1671 Morgan and his thousand buccaneers captured Porto Bello and Panama on the Isthmus. So total was the destruction of Panama — his most notable victory — that a new city — Panama City — was built nearby.

On the site of Old Panama, buffeted by the surf, there remained the crumbling masonry of a seawall on which the cordovan boot heels of those conquistadores left their devastating imprints. There in the matted vegetation were visible the high gray ruins of the once flourishing town . . . the walls of the *Intendencia* and the remnants of the convent once patronized by the daughters of wealthy Spanish grandees. There was the Cathedral of the Golden Altar — a marvel of the New World — in whose tower grew a slender cieba tree. Inland stood what was once a bridge of massive stone, glutted with weeds but with its graceful arch still hanging clear. It was over this bridge that the broken Spanish garrison retreated from the incursion of Morgan's corsairs on the savannah where the concrete road ran.

In 1925 New Panama was a swirling admixture of white and black and tan and yellow races so polyglot that its population communicated in many languages as well as in a jumbled patois common to the area. It was a place where you could purchase almost anything or do almost anything. Marines on shore patrol familiarized themselves with its intricacies. They had to.

From Amador on the mouth of the Canal, army posts ran inland — Corazal and Clayton and Gailliard — and provided pleasant evening drives. Balboa was clean and well kept with green grass throughout the dry season and with tall palms growing in ranks. On the whole, there was no place in the tropics so livable as the Canal Zone.

However the multiple duties of the *Rochester* kept her away from the Panamanian base for months at a time. Moreover, as Thomason became more deeply entrenched in the tour and discovered what the nature of his assignment actually was, he learned that the Marine who had painted such a rosy picture of it had gone only through the Panama base on the *USS Henderson,* had danced at the Union Club, and stopped at Jimmy Dean's on the way back to Pier 18.

Having been two weeks at sea engaged in long range battle practice, Thomason wrote his mother on May 17, 1925: "I miss Leda and Jack cruelly and wish they were down here; but chances are we are going to Peru. If our plans should change . . . I will cable Leda to take the next United fruit boat from New Orleans."

By July 1, 1925, John was writing his father from the Canal Zone about Jack. He expressed appreciation for the kindness of both parents to his son and felt that Jack had benefitted medically by being under his father's professional care. Neither John nor Leda gave their five-year-old son the high rating in deportment that his grandparents did. "I can hardly imagine him as good as you all report him," John wrote.

John Thomason had been in the Canal Zone a month when
the first combat article, retitled *Fix Bayonets!*, ran in *Scribner's
Magazine* in June. But he was soon aware of its overwhelming
reception and the fact that the literati of New York had named
him one of the greatest writing discoveries since the World War.
He was informed of these facts in a long cable from the *New
York World* on July 12, 1925. John Thomason replied to the cable characteristically:

> I follow the profession of arms because I like it. I would
> be very happy if material of mine added to the reputation of
> my corps, but I hear no call to go outside of my professional
> duties to act as press agent or that sort of thing.
>
> My stories were written without ulterior motive and my
> drawings were made the same way. I wished to record my im-
> pressions of certain interesting events, and I was more con-
> cerned with the men who took part in them than in the events
> themselves. The stories were written in the West Indies dur-
> ing 1919 and 1920 from letters and notes I had made in the
> war. My drawings were made in France or from material I had
> collected there. I did not think of publication when I made
> them.
>
> I did some newspaper work on the *Houston Chronicle* in
> 1916 and have written tactical studies for service publications.
> I am naturally pleased that my stories . . . were well received,
> but I was assured by Captain Stallings and Miss McMein that
> they were good. . . .
>
> I am flattered by your cable, but I reply principally to ex-
> press publicly my obligation for the courtesies and friendly
> interest of Captain Stallings, Miss McMein, Joseph H. Chapin
> and others of that circle without whose efforts the stories and
> things referred to would probably still blush unseen.

No sooner was the magazine off press than a flood of letters
began to reach Scribner's editorial rooms. Almost overnight a
captain of the Marines had achieved the extraordinary success for
which thousands of young writers in America had been striving.
In due course letters from Scribner's editors containing
specimens of the kudos Thomason's article evoked caught up
with him in the tropics. If he had entertained any doubts about

the *New York World*'s seemingly extravagant cable, they soon vanished.

An excerpt from a four-page letter from W. C. Linderman of Holland, Michigan, read: "Captain Thomason, I salute you with all the devotion a man of the ranks has for a gallant, sympathetic officer. Mr. Woollcott, I give full assent to your critical gratitude. Such are the sentiments prompted by a reading of *Fix Bayonets!*.

"Please, Mr. Editor, don't let anyone debase this gem by calling it a 'picture' or 'portrayal' of the Marine Corps. It's far more embracing than that; it's the very essence of every combatant soldier's experience, be he Marine or artilleryman. Corporal Tritt belongs as much to my 'b' Battery of the 118th F. A. as he does to the 49th Company of 1st Marines. And Captain Thomason embodies the confidence-inspiring gallantry that I admired so much in my own captain."

Heyworth Campbell of the editorial staff of Conde Nast Publications wrote Art Editor Joseph Chapin:
"Dear Joe

"The June lead *Fixed* [sic] *Bayonets* is a sensation. A number of attention-callers have mentioned it. Frederick T. Chapman, whom I consider one of America's best draftsmen, has just been raving about The Captin's [sic] illustrations."

William Stuart of the United States Post Office of Canister, New York, joined in the applause:

> This letter may be entirely uncalled for, yet I can not refrain from complimenting you on the article in your June issue. I refer to "Fix Bayonets!" by Captain John W. Thomason, Jr. I had never heard of Captain Thomason, but I assume he is no novice at writing; for, in my opinion, he has produced the greatest piece of descriptive writing along military lines since Hugo wrote of Waterloo. It is realism raised to the n'th power . . . Scarcely any real literature has thus far been produced. However, I should unhesitatingly class "Fix Bayonets!" as literature. That it will live I have no doubt.
>
> You have a large corps of readers to satisfy, and you doubtless have a better idea than I do as to what type of reading the majority like; but for myself nothing would be more pleasing than to hear that you intend to use more of Captain Thomason's material.

Two days later Chapin wrote Thomason again enclosing additional letters of acclamation — from veterans. Dr. C. Burns Craig of New York City wrote:

> I have just read *Fix Bayonets* and got such a thrill from the capacity of Capt. Thomason to breathe the scorching, blasting, spirit of battle into his description that I hope you will tell him so.
>
> His description of the conduct, attitude and speech of the American soldier in France, both behind the lines and in battle is the best I have read. The art with which he has conveyed to the reader, the atmosphere of the entire affair, is truly remarkable.
>
> I served during the recent rumpus with the 77th Division so that I know something whereof I speak.
>
> Eventually probably the inside story of the war will be told and patched together by fighting men who can write instead of literary men and journalists "at the front."

Alexander Mackenzie Watson, Major U.S. Marine Corps (retired) had this to say:

Mr. Robert Bridges
Scribner's Magazine

Dear Sir:

> I very much want to tell you with what interest (intensified perhaps because of having been a Marine for twenty-one years) and admiration I have read Capt. Thomason's *Fix Bayonets* in your June number. I can never recollect having read quite such a pen picture of war either ancient or modern. During the war and always since, I have been lost in admiration of what American troops accomplished in France. The Villers-Cotterel-Soissons fight (the actual turning point of the war) I believe has a never-to-be-forgotten place in my memory . . . Please accept my congratulations on having given to the world such a superlatively fine piece of war literature and do let us all have something more from Captain Thomason's gifted pen.

Chapin's letter to John also stated that payment would be made in a lump sum on the second war article as soon as the staff could get it into galley proof and determine what illustrations that they had would go with it. He added in longhand an interesting postscript: "I forgot to say that the drawings in our window at the time of publication attracted much attention. I was interested in watching men stop and look at them."

Meanwhile, back in New York, Scribner's realized the pertinence of its discovery. The August issue of the magazine feature "Behind the Scenes with Scribner's Authors" apologized to the *Dallas News* for overlooking the fact (in the June issue) that Thomason was a Texan born at Huntsville; announced that *Marines at Blanc Mont* would be the lead article in the forthcoming September issue; and devoted over a page (captioned "What you think about it") to letters praising Thomason.

The editorial lead stated that "Captain John W. Thomason, Jr., stirred our readers up to a pitch of unanimity rarely reached since this department has been in existence. From service and non-service men, from all sections of the country, they come." Douglas Maxwell of 250 Park Avenue, New York City, was quoted: "Of all the war stories that I have read this is . . . by far the best; true to life and well written. I hope that you will see fit to publish more articles by the author."

The article concluded with a longer and more sophisticated letter from Grant Shepherd of New York, the commander of Company E of the 23rd Infantry, who took part in the Soissons fight.

> I wish to express to you the feeling which has come to me after reading "Fix Bayonets!" It is one of very considerable gratitude to Captain Thomason in the first place, and for SCRIBNER'S MAGAZINE for having been the means by which a certain number of our fellow citizens are accorded the privilege of viewing a true picture of a part of the first two days of a battle which is acknowledged by all those best informed as the turning point of the war.
>
> I will always agree with Thomason when he says that his memory of the two nights and days we experienced in getting into position will be the most vivid recollection in connection with that attack.
>
> The 23rd Infantry held the extreme right of the line for the division — E Company having the right flank. . . .

In the same issue of *Scribner's Magazine* appeared a navy story *An Uncharted Course,* by Harriett Welles, the wife of Vice Admiral Welles, and illustrated by Thomason.

In the September issue of the magazine Thomason again dominates "Behind the Scenes with Scribner's Authors." As a preface to *Marines at Blanc Mont,* the column carried a photograph of Captain Thomason, together with additional biographical detail, and quoted him from Alexander Woollcott's article "Introducing Captain Thomason of the Marines," which had appeared in the June, 1925, issue of *Vanity Fair.* Thomason had contributed illustrations for the article and had written an open letter to Laurence Stallings commending him on his realistic portrayal of Flagg and Quirt in *What Price Glory.*

The editor of "Behind the Scenes . . ." reminds his readers that Thomason is with the *USS Rochester* in the Canal Zone and also quotes him on his reaction to his recent success: "It is, I think, a good thing that I am down here at the ends of the earth living on a battleship with six 5-inch 51-calibre guns to take care of. Otherwise I would probably get such a delusion of grandeur as to be quite impossible." Those close to Thomason, however, would have been the first to deny any such probability.

As the newspaper comments and letters of praise continued and queries about the possibility of purchasing Thomason's drawings reached Scribner's, the November issue of the magazine quoted Alexander Woollcott in his department, "The Stage," in the *New York World* for September 21:

> Except, then, for this picture and the three plays hereinbefore cheered for, this department has no ardent recommendations to make, unless you wish to buy the September *Scribner's* and read the incomparable feat in word and line therein achieved by Captain John W. Thomason, Jr.

The Scribner's editor took the opportunity to explain that *Monkey Meat,* in the current issue, was Thomason's first short story and promised that *The Conquest of Mike* would be published in an early number of the magazine.

The state press reechoed the national media and Thomason's family took notice. "I am glad you all are pleased with the vicarious publicity that has come along," John wrote his father, assuming his customary low key stance. "The things were well received. I will have to scratch gravel to keep up now . . . They [Scribner's] are also discussing a book with me. . . ."

Maxwell Perkins, who had joined Scribner's in 1910 and spent four and a half years in the advertising department before stepping up to the editorial staff, had been a protege of the venerable and formidable William Crary Brownell, editor-in-chief and one of America's foremost literary critics. By 1919 Perkins, whose primary duty had been the proofreading of galleys, had become a promising young editor.

He earned his editorial spurs when he discovered F. Scott Fitzgerald and published his *This Side of Paradise* in 1920. Still considered a junior editor in the early twenties, Perkins advanced steadily to the status of Scribner's editorial right arm and was moving closer to the legend of the twentieth-century publishing world he became.

By the time Scribner's began to publish Thomason in 1925, Perkins's place in the hierarchy was fixed, and Chapin and Bridges were of the opinion that the Marine captain's work was of such quality as to merit their editorial genius's attention. From then on all subsequent dealings involving Thomason were handled by Maxwell Perkins. The experience resulted in an editor-author relationship that was artistically satisfying to both and to a warm friendship that ended only with Thomason's death.

After all the fuss and furor, a man with a less level head might have required a bigger hat. But not John Thomason. The *Rochester's* first major trip was a state visit to the Republic of Costa Rica. A phase of the visit was Thomason's mission as shore patrol officer of a selected detail of 100-odd seamen, who accompanied the admiral and his entourage on the six-hour train ride from the coast to the capital, San Jose. Thomason anticipated the event with the excitement of an adventurous youth, and his introduction to the country took precedence over everything else. His description of the climb, to his mother, reflects an enthusiasm akin to that of a schoolboy, instead of a man who had just become a name.

. . . you go through infinite banana plantations and set-
tlements of Jamaican Negroes and jungles unbelievably lush
and green. Buzzards, parrots, pigs, snakes, Jamaicans with
machetes, goats, palm-leafed shacks. (Jamaicans do the work
of the tropics. Nobody else will stand the heat and general
misery attendant upon heavy manual labor in this climate.
Fever and snakes take a lot of them. You see graves around
every hut. But there are lots of babies rolling around the dirt
— nobody seems to mind.) For a while you get glimpses of
the Caribbean; surf breaking on white beaches. Then the
train begins to climb. It's a narrow-guage road, very bumpy.
The vegetation changes. The air gets cooler. After about 3
hours you come out on the side of a great valley. A river runs
3,000 feet below you. Banana plantations are down there and
a dense nest of jungle green. Another 1,000 feet up and you
are in the high hills—mountains with clouds around the tops
and trailing down in the folds of them. You are in the north
temperate zone. Coffee grows around — you pass that. It's
really cool, cool as the Catskills. Fine country — hedges —
stone fences — orchards — cattle — white men.

Still the starry-eyed tourist, Thomason found the city of
San Jose more pleasing than Camaguey or Panama. Its isolation
had saved it from being Americanized as were Cuba and Panama. What foreign influence evident there was French. John felt
that America ruined her dependencies. "They . . . take on all
our unpleasant qualities and few, if any, of our good points.
They learn to drink hard likker [sic] standing up in bars; their
picturesque and individual native clothing is discarded for the
shameless crimes of the mailorder houses, their laborious hand-
tooled furniture is thrown aside for the golden oak from Grand
Rapids. They scrap their leisurely manners . . . for 'Yankee
snap' and 'pep.' In the end they are neither Cubans, Panamani-
ans . . . as the case may be, but something wholly awful.'' John
found the town of San Jose to be incredibly innocent and the
liberty party to be virtuous beyond comprehension. The town
rolled up the carpet around 10:00 p.m.

The second trip, after the return to Panama, was to Key
West, Florida, to provide General Pershing and his staff with

transportation to the Republic of Peru. President Coolidge, who had been requested to serve as arbitrator by contending factions, named Pershing chairman of the Chile-Peru Commission to conduct a plebiscite to settle the Tacna-Arica discord between Peru and Chile.

The *Rochester* landed at Callao, Peru, in August. Optimists believed the mediation could be consummated in a few weeks. However, the situation was so complex and the disparity between the factions so great that the conference held at Lima extended to six months.

Thomason and the Marine Guard served ashore and at the capital and provided security forces at the residence where Pershing was quartered and the sites where the conference was held. Adverse reaction to the Yankee negotiators by an element of the population complicated the mission. With their experience in World War I, Pershing and Thomason whiled away much time in stimulating conversation.

When the second article in the combat series — *Marines at Blanc Mont* — was featured in the September issue of *Scribner's,* John Thomason, aboard the *Rochester,* was off the coast of Arica, Chile, instead of being north of the Virginia Capes — off the Jersey Sands — ready to dock at the Brooklyn Navy Yard, on October 1, as the Marine contingent had been promised. The date of the return to New York had been postponed to December. Again the impact of the article and incisive illustrations was tremendous. Former Marines, who had served in trench warfare, once more inundated Scribner's office with praise for the authenticity of both the text and the drawings.

In November, when the third segment — *Monkey Meat* — appeared in *Scribner's,* John was in Arica, where it was evident that an impasse had been reached in the proposed negotiations between the two countries. Thomason had found the Chilean city less than interesting and was only too glad to vacate it. "The sweetest sight that human eyes ever beheld is the Morro [precipitous headland overlooking the town] of Arica receding over the stern," he wrote his father.

Encouraged by his recent success, Thomason became increasingly prolific. The tour of duty in Peru netted him three stories:

The Conquest of Mike, Crossing the Line with Pershing, and *Mail
Day,* all of which he illustrated with pen-and-ink sketches. The
first, scheduled for publication by *Scribner's Magazine* in January
of 1926, is the delightful account of the Marine canine mascot's
mutiny until a new captain proves his fortitude and measures
up to Marine tradition. *Crossing the Line with Pershing,* which
would be featured in the August, 1926, issue of *Scribner's Magazine,* is a facetious tale based on the visit of "King Neptune" and
his retinue to the *USS Rochester* to celebrate the ship's crossing
the equator.

Mail Day, scheduled for inclusion in the April, 1926, edition
of *Scribner's Magazine,* is actually a nostalgic sketch in which
Thomason incorporates a wealth of Marine folklore involving the
arrival of a mail boat and the various reactions of the crew to the
thrice-welcome event. There were — somewhere around the
world, for most of the Marines—women; and on this day for a little while, according to Thomason, "they come aboard with the
letters — mothers and sweethearts and wives. . . ."

After the captain's inspection, he goes aft "and the bugles
sing 'Carry on' — and 'Mail O'." The shock-headed company
clerk comes on the double from the detachment office and
climbs on a mess bench while one hundred Marines crowd eagerly around him. Invariably there are those who get no mail. As always they wait until the last, then sadly lounge off—forward —
by themselves.

The captain inspects his own mail left on his desk by the orderly. There are ten letters not counting two long official envelopes. . . . What a luxury it is to sort out seven addressed to him
in that familiar angular handwriting . . . so peculiar to the lady
who wrote them!

> . . . How her pen, you remember, flies across the page.
> Impetuous. And unless the nib is perfectly new, scratchy . . .
> It is a long time ago since that raw forenoon in late winter, a
> nasty gray day,.with a wet sea-wind flailing East River, when
> you said appropriate things and came up the gangplank. She
> —game and all that. So was Jack, valiant in his five years, and
> not unaccustomed to partings, and not quite sure what it was
> all about . . . No tears, but her mouth was soft and quivery

when you kissed it, and unshed tears are bright in the eyes
and fall like rain upon the heart — Man's a fool to go to sea!
And he always does . . . A ship is a man's world quite. No
place for women in it. . . .

By the end of November of 1925 the *USS Rochester* was relieved on station by the *USS Denver* so that she could go into
dry dock in the Brooklyn Navy Yard for repairs. Pershing, whose
health declined, meanwhile, turned his duties over to his successor, Major General William Lassiter, and returned to the United
States. As it transpired, the litigation over the disputed areas of
Tacna and Arica continued for several months. In fact, the problem would not reach final resolution until 1929, long after the
arbiters would have abandoned the mission. In 1929 the factions would settle their own difficulty, awarding Tacna to Peru
and Arica to Chile.

Before proceeding to New York, the *USS Rochester* returned to the base at Balboa for partial removal of barnacles and
refueling. In the brief interim Captain Thomason went ashore
to do a little Christmas shopping. He was looking for a sword
suitable for an admiral of five seasoned summers and a necklace
for a girl with hazel-green eyes.

On December 17, once more at sea, John Thomason headed
a long Christmas letter to his father: "—En route New York,
running up — to the Windward Passage, with Haiti on the star-
board hand like a cloud. . . ."

On December 23, 1925, two days before the anniversary of
the Savior's birth, the barnacle-encrusted *Rochester* docked at
the Brooklyn Navy Yard; and the crew descended the gangplank
in a dramatic snowstorm. Walking tall among them was 32-year-
old Captain John William Thomason whose eyes searched for the
face of that special person awaiting his arrival. Leda had come by
train from Texas to join him. Since he would be busy with writing
and drawing and conferring with publishers, arrangements had
been made to leave Jack in Huntsville with his grandparents.

The couple scarcely had time to register in one of Brooklyn's
better hotels than Thomason's return to the United States from
the tropics was discovered. Since the publication of the three Ma-

rine Brigade articles in *Scribner's Magazine* had made of the author-artist's name a magic phrase in New York, the elite of the literary world converged upon the couple and showered them with invitations and social courtesies.

"I appreciated for the first time that I was in some small degree famous . . . ," John wrote his mother timidly on January 12, 1926. "I took leave from the day after we got in and finished Sunday, the last writing and drawings for a book to be called *Fix Bayonets!* I have a very liberal contract (experts tell me, better than ordinary under the circumstances) and if the thing sells, we will make a little money."

Then he plays it down: "Nothing exciting, for it is not that kind of a book. But some . . . Anyway, I'm out nothing since the magazine has already paid me for the stuff it published — about half." Now the wonder of it takes hold and he reverts to the boy in his father's library fascinated by large books with pictures in color . . . "It will make a large book with a great many pictures and a colored jacket — the same drawing that was the frontispiece of the September *Scribner's* . . . I'll send you a copy — though it will not come out until March, and I leave in February around the 20th."

Scribner's was taking everything it could get from Thomason and *Liberty* magazine had been "a fine meal ticket." But now the William Randolph Hearst International Magazine Corporation, which included *Cosmopolitan, Good Housekeeping,* etc., was competing for his services. The editor Frazier Hunt contracted with Thomason for twelve stories or articles, together with illustrations, for 1926 and 1927. According to the agreement, he was to be paid $1500 each for the first six; $1750 each for the next three; and $2000 each for the subsequent contributions. He agreed to do six a year. Few writers of the time were commanding higher fees.

Hearst tried to put Thomason under exclusive contract for everything he would produce for a number of years, but he declined as he wished to remain independent. "As I am now," he told Hunt, "there's nobody over me but my major general commandant and God, and I like it that way." The contract permitted Thomason to write on any subject he chose and at any length — "the shorter the better."

But fame did not rest easily on the brow of John William Thomason. "People give teas and dinners, etc., just to meet me," he wrote his father a few days later. "And I do not like that part of it at all . . . I've done a lot of work and had to do a lot of going, and I'll not be sorry when we rig ship for sea and I get away with my own people again."

The last week, terminating the two-month's stay in New York, was exceedingly hectic and crowded. "People were lovely to us," he wrote his mother from aboard ship on February 28 . . . "To tell the truth, though, I was quite ready to leave New York — Leda's remaining behind being the only sad feature . . . there are a lot of things about what you might call fame that I do not care for at all. You get to feeling rushed, and I do not like to feel that way. . . ."

Before leaving New York, John invested in an etching outfit and had made a few plates with better success than he had expected. The thing that impressed him was that you could make as many prints from the intagliated surface of the metal as you chose.

A storm delayed his arrival at Guantanamo Bay by one day, but Thomason still hoped to reach Panama about the same time as Leda and Jack would arrive by commercial transportation.

When the final installment of the Marine Brigade articles appeared in March of 1926 and the subsequent book *Fix Bayonets!* was released, Captain Thomason was on Deer Point at Guantanamo Bay. As range officer for the *USS Rochester,* he was in charge of 500 men engaged in small arms practice. These included Navy blue jackets who had joined the contingent for the purpose.

Routine was strict. Reveille was at 5:30; range shooting began at 6:30; "dinner" at camp was at 11:45; resumption of range practice was from 1:00 to 4:50; then taps were sounded at 9:00. The Marines, who were trained to shoot, gave no trouble. But a sailor and a rifle were, in Thomason's opinion, "rather hopeless when combined."

In a letter to Dr. Thomason, under date of March 5, 1926, John describes his work at length and looks forward to a resumption of family life when Leda and Jack arrive at the end of the month. "Life is reduced to a fine simplicity," he observes. "We are dirty, happy, and pleasantly weary." But he makes no mention of his forthcoming book. He was either too busy or too tired.

Fix Bayonets! made publishing history. Unlike many first books, it typified an auspicious beginning of a career. The author-artist's ability to integrate so effectively the two forms of artistic media — a feature that was to be demonstrated in all of his subsequent books — became a distinctive Thomason colophon.

By June, the time of Leda's and Jack's arrival in the Canal Zone, Thomason was receiving news of the publication. Within less than three months *Fix Bayonets!* had gone through a third printing of 15,000 copies. "Maxwell Perkins of Scribner's writes me that *Fix Bayonets!* is selling," John wrote his mother, May 17, 1926 . . . "He sent me some reviews; all of them are very generous . . . Certainly people have received it very well."

Stallings, among the first to proclaim Thomason's talent, said: "His battle accounts, better than Crane's, better than Hugo's, as good as Tolstoy's, are due not only to his superb ability to write and to draw but chiefly to his amazing feeling for war." High praise from the man who helped to launch Thomason came as no surprise.

However, other critics were uniformly laudatory. The *New York World* pronounced *Fix Bayonets!* "the finest monument of the American Expeditionary Force and a notable volume of prose with drawings that are of permanent interest to American history."

The *New York Evening Post* was ecstatic: "Here is a book! Here is war and here is the soldier man as he is, was, and always will be, in times of stress and strain and battle and in his times of ease. Now that the hysterical brethren have popped off their chattering and shell-shocked little impressions of the war, along comes a really great book. It runs straight as a cleaning rod. it is as keen as a newly-ground sword-bayonet. Splendid as the tale itself is, the illustrations all but tell the story themselves."

Even the London *Times* took note: "No book which we can recall that has for subject the actual fighting of the Great War, has appeared to us to equal this. The drawings match the prose."

The review that Thomason read with the most interest, but not without mixed feelings, was one by Thomas Boyd, author of *Through the Wheat,* a book the artist had illustrated. Boyd's review appeared under the caption "Over There" in the *Saturday Review of Literature,* April 3, 1926.

John had considered Boyd's *Through the Wheat* to be "the first meritorious book about our part in the war." Despite the book's merit, it did not have good sales. Scribner's, who published the book, followed it with a volume of short stories by Boyd [not related to James Boyd], involving the war—*Points of Honor.* Nor did Boyd's second book on the war theme sell well.

"Yet I thought them good," John wrote his mother. "He [Boyd] was a private in the 6th Marines. Now he reviews *Fix Bayonets!* in a tone that drips green. He was very kind about the pictures, and he joined conservative-like in the general opinion of the writing. But it came hard to him. And I remember at Norfolk, when *Through the Wheat* came out, I wrote and congratulated him on it."

The first stricture Boyd cites is the omission of any references to his regiment in the book. "Telling of his own experiences in the thirty-eight days of fighting at Belleau Wood, Captain Thomason does not mention a single act from which a member of the Sixth regiment could orient himself; yet Belleau Wood is small and soldiers of the Sixth regiment fought there close by soldiers of the Fifth. Captain Thomason's accounts of these attacks seldom concern more than his own battalion."

Boyd accuses the battalion, or at least Thomason's company, of being more warlike and bloodthirsty than most outfits. He contends further that Thomason's Marines seldom took prisoners and preferred the bayonet with which to disembowel German machine gunners to the Springfield rifle or the Colt automatic, with which to shoot them, which seemed more civilized. Moreover, at too close quarters they used their rifle butts "after the drill manual manner."

As "green" as the review seemed to the author, it concludes on a positive note: "Captain Thomason's account of the attack at Soissons on the 18th of July is as good a piece of description of that bright and dramatic scene as any yet written."

Meanwhile Frazier Hunt had introduced Thomason in the May, 1926, issue of *Cosmopolitan* in a provocative article captioned "What a Fighter! What a Writer!" and illustrated by a full-length cut of the Marine in uniform. The author-artist's photograph demonstrated his favorite stance with his right foot forward, knee slightly bent, thumbs tucked into his belt, and a swagger stick in his right hand.

"When you first talk to him it's hard to believe that he had lived and fought through the years of hell that he has," Hunt states. "The Marines were only carrying out their great tradition . . . that stretched from the heights of Chapultepec to the sands of Tripoli and through the tragic glory of Belleau Wood, Soissons, the Champagne, and the Argonne. Captain Thomason had fought through all this last. . . .

"For seven years he dreamed of those nightmare days and nights. Then suddenly he started writing about them and illustrating his tales with a pen that had been dipped in tears and blood . . . America has never had anyone quite like him. . . .

"But first of all he's a fighting man . . . He can draw as well as he can write and he can write as well as he can fight.

"And man how he can fight!"

From the date of that issue throughout 1927 such Thomason stories and sketches as *A Dog Worth Fighting For* (August, 1926), *Luck* (September, 1926), *The Drama of a Poor Dub* (November, 1926), *Jungle War* (May, 1927), *Tell It to the Marines* (July, 1927), and *The Killer* (November, 1927), all illustrated by the author, appeared in *Cosmopolitan*. In subsequent book publication some of the titles were altered. For example, *The Drama of a Poor Dub* became *Kupid's Konfidential Klub* and *The Killer,* became *Before the Rain.*

Not only did the stories stem from reality, some were written immediately after certain incidents occurred. For instance, *The Drama of a Poor Dub* was based upon the accidental death at Guantanamo Bay of a lonely Marine who had difficulty adjusting to the service.

Thomason was reunited with Leda and Jack at Hotel Tivoli in Ancón in June. But he had to report for sea duty almost immediately. "Leda was not quite shaken down here when we left last month," he wrote his mother after rejoining her, "and I only heard once from her during the cruise. So I didn't know how she and Jack were liking it. Jack, indeed, had been almost mutinous, wanted to go back to Huntsville. . . ."

But, happily, John found the two contented and delighted with life in the Canal Zone when he returned. Jack had found congenial playmates, he and his mother were enjoying swimming in the ocean off Fort Amador in the afternoons, and she was playing golf at the Country Club almost every day.

The following August the ship and crew spent a week at Port Limon, Costa Rica. When John arrived at Colon on August 13, Leda and Jack came over that evening and stayed at the Washington. They came aboard Friday morning to go through the canal with John. The event was especially interesting to Jack as his father detailed a corporal to show him around the ship. He crawled all over the vessel from fighting tops to the engine room. At the end of the inspection the six-year-old said: "All right, corporal, you can go now. That's all I want with you. Thank you."

The corporal, a big German, told Captain Thomason about it with excessive pride. "He iss one fine boy, sir. Already he has the habit of command, sir."

Thomason's visit with his family was short-lived, however, as political conditions in Nicaragua deteriorated. Asked to intervene in the revolution led by Juan Bautista Sacasa and General José Maria Moncada, the State Department turned the request over to the navy for action. The navy passed it on to the Special Service Squadron with Admiral Latimer assuming local responsibility.

At the end of October, 1926, John himself explained his presence at Bluefields thus: "We came to this Mosquito Gulf the last of August in response to screams for aid from American capital at Puerto Cabezas — the north corner of Nicaragua, which was being shot over.''

Admiral Latimer's mission was precarious. While under orders to protect American lives and interests, essentially along the seaports threatened by the warring factions, he was at the same time instructed to observe a strict neutral attitude. As part of his strategy, he established a system of neutral zones, or restricted areas at the principal ports, under Marine control. In these zones fighting by the factions was prohibited under a penalty of forfeiture of weapons and ammunition. Then, if the contending factions could not maintain law and order in their own occupied territory, the Marines obligated themselves to discharge this responsibility.

To cope with the accelerated revolutionary activity and to curb rioting and looting, the Special Service Squadron occupied several sites. Seamen from the *Cleveland* and the *Galveston* also concentrated their efforts at Bluefields. The *Rochester* Marine Guard, commanded by Thomason, joined the landing parties of the two ships. From September to December his composite force successfully maintained a neutral zone at Bluefields in conjunction with units that patrolled waters adjacent to the port. With its strategic location on the coast, Bluefields — the source of mahogany and fruit — was of enormous economic importance. A key to the coast, Bluefields collected 90 percent of the country's total revenues. Heretofore all fighting had been for the possession of Bluefields. As the Marines held it, it benefitted neither side.

Although the United States government had leaned toward the support of Chamarro, the conservative strong man of Nicaragua, the liberals were winning the revolution. Realizing that he had supported a lost cause, President Chamarro withdrew in favor of Adolfo Diaz. The liberals refused to recognize Diaz and continued to fight.

When the Marines declared the vicinity of the Rio Grande, midway between Bluefields and Puerta Cabezas, a neutral zone, the liberals concentrated troops at Pearl Lagoon, south of the Rio Grande. On Christmas Day the liberals won a major victory over the conservatives and came into power. Bringing pressure to bear in Washington, they influenced a partial reversal of United States policy and regained substantial arms previously seized by the Marine landing parties.

Thomason, aware that the United States government "had backed the wrong horse" and had, in a measure, tied the Marines' hands behind them, became disenchanted. He did not participate in the intervention at Rio Grande, however. He remained ashore in command of a detachment of 130 men until January 3. He led a detail on a reconnaissance of the river and its banks. In the meantime the liberals avoided the American patrols and focused their efforts on Puerto Cabezas, eighty miles north of the Rio Grande.

Christmas Day was particularly dismal for Thomason. "I really didn't notice the day—spent it in the rain, reconnoitering the swamps around the mouth of the Rio Grande," he wrote his father in January of 1927. "It was bad to be jerked out by sudden orders when we'd all expected to be together . . . and Leda left with all the packing to do alone. We'll try to make up for it to ourselves and everybody this year."

Still the United States Marines carried on as best they could under the circumstances. To counteract the liberals' concentration at Puerta Cabezas, the *Cleveland* and *Denver* landed seamen there to set up a neutral zone. During the first week in January they were replaced by Thomason's company from the Rio Grande. By this time almost all ports on the east coast of Nicaragua were patrolled by landing parties from various units of the Special Service Squadron. The liberals protested American interference and Latimer was forced to call for reinforcements. A division of light cruisers from the Scouting Fleet was dispatched to his aid in January, and by midspring three additional vessels were serving in Nicaraguan waters. Finally the number of vessels patrolling along both east and west coasts of the republic during the spring and summer of 1927 totaled thirty-six.

Despite this demonstration of strength, the revolutionary movement gained in momentum and in popularity. Against all odds, the American government continued to support the losing Diaz regime. In addition to supplying Diaz with arms, America sent in the remainder of the Fifth Regiment of Marines and a Marine aviation squadron. By the middle of March approximately 2,000 men were engaged in patrolling activities.

Since most of the action at this time was in western Nicaragua, the flagship of the Special Service Squadron was shifted from the Caribbean to the Pacific. Because of the emergency in Nicaraguan waters, the *Rochester* did not take time to return for her annual overhaul. She steamed to the Canal Zone in February for such hasty repairs as could be made locally.

Undoubtedly Thomason, in view of the preceding events, was looking forward to reassignment when his tour of duty aboard the *Rochester* was up on February 28, 1927, and Captain Franklin A. Hart would release him. Leda and Jack had left on December 19. It had not been easy for her to make the move from Panama by herself.

"*F*[ix] *B*[ayonets], by the way, is still selling," John wrote his mother on January 7, 1927. "But I'll have another book out in March if I ever get north to settle the details. It's being made up now. It's the *Scribner's* and the *Cosmopolitan* stories of the past year — Not, I think, very good, but they want to print them. I don't mean they are carelessly done. I don't work carelessly, but they are not in *F. B.*'s class . . . I do not think I will ever do anything that good again—and I'll probably never have such a subject again. . . ." Despite the nature and increased scope of his duties during the second year aboard the *Rochester* Thomason had produced a vast quantity of material and had advanced his career considerably.

Representative stories based on his Nicaraguan detail included *One Razor-Strop — Sixty-five Cents,* published in *Scribner's Magazine* in the January, 1927, issue; and *Marines See the Revolution* in the edition of July, 1927. *One Razor-Strop — Sixty-five Cents* narrates how Marine John Paul Jones, who — despite the promise of being N.C.O. material—sacrifices everything because of the petty theft of a cheap razor-strap from the mail. None the less dramatic, but obviously less fictional, *Marines See the Revolution* presents an intimate version of the Marines' contact with one of the leaders of the factions and discloses minute details that would scarcely make the newspapers or be included in official records.

Both stories were later published in book form, together with others involving incidents related to Thomason's tour with the Special Service Squadron. The first appeared in *Red Pants* (1927) and the second in the subsequent volume, *Marines and Others* (1929).

The publication of *Red Pants* in 1927 was a fitting conclusion to the Nicaraguan tour. Dedicated to Leda Thomason, the volume is comprised of ten selections beginning with the titular story and ending with *Mail Day*.

The story *Red Pants* goes back to the battle of Soissons in World War I, when the Senegalese and North Africans of the Moroccan Divisions were fighting with the Fifth Regiment of Marines. The Marines had not eaten for three days except for what food they could cadge off the French outfits and could forage from the knapsacks of Boche casualties.

When the men of the galley detail finally arrive, they have only rice and a few cans of corn bill with which to cook up a "slum." While the food is in preparation, a soldier wearing the uniform of the Moroccan Division is caught with his musette bag full of the precious corn bill and a can in each hand.

Apprehended and brought before the officer in charge — Thomason — the Senegalese proves to be a former stevedore of Galveston, Texas, who had joined the Senegalese in Marseille because of his fascination for the red pants of the uniform.

The meeting of the two fighting men — one black and one white and both winners of decorations for bravery — with the Southern background is interesting and gives the author the opportunity to record the old folk rhythms of a Negro dialect that is no longer a part of the culture.

The reception of the book was comparable to that of the preceding *Fix Bayonets!* The *Philadelphia Record* was quite voluble: "Excellent stuff — a pair of war stories, sketches of life among the Nicaraguan insurrection, a tale of Marines on liberty and lady friends, a dog story, and an impression of mail day aboard a battleship somewhere on the rainless coast of South America. The war episodes have all the dash and feeling of au-

thenticity . . . in Captain Thomason's earlier book . . . and the
Thomason drawings, as in *Fix Bayonets!* would be worth the
price of the book without a word of writing." Other critics were
equally generous in their praise.

During the Nicaraguan tour Thomason also submitted to
the *Marine Corps Gazette* an article titled *With the Special Service Squadron,* which ran in the June, 1927, issue. The article
recounts details of the Marines' experiences in the squadron and
analyzes problems faced by the detachment, together with its
methods of resolution. The author's summation provides an interesting epilogue:

> Finally, a tour in the Special Service Squadron, while
> some of it drags interminably, will be over much more quick-
> ly than you'd suppose . . . Lazy days off the South Coast of
> Central America, rocking in the long Pacific swell . . . when
> only routine gets you through the hours . . . Hot nights in
> the windless Gulf of Yucatan, when you sleep on deck and
> the stars are low and soft and bright . . . Rainy season on the
> Mosquito Coast, where your shoes and your belt will show
> green mould every morning . . . White and gold uniforms,
> pretty women and champagne and moonlight on the terrace
> of the Union Club in Panama . . . and at least, bucketing
> through Western Ocean storms to . . . the lines over the Bol-
> lards at Pier 8 in New York Navy Yard, and no more sea. . . .

10 Potomac Potpourri

Following his draconian experience in the tropics, Thomason drew a desk job in the nation's capital. Specifically he was detailed to the United States Army War College at Fort Humphreys, Washington, to assist in the compilation of a history of the Second Division.

Thomason, whose *Fix Bayonets!* recommended him, was handpicked for the assignment. After first consulting him, General John A. Lejeune had approved Thomason personally for membership on the panel of writers. The general, who had commanded the Second Infantry Division, American Expeditionary Force, in which Thomason had served in World War I, was not only impressed with his excellent combat record, he admired him for his literary and artistic talents.

"I would rather read your books on military events and careers than of any other author I know of," General Lejeune wrote Thomason later.

A writer himself, General Lejeune was empathetic with Thomason's need for leisure time to devote to his own work and hoped that the Washington station would permit it. Admiration between the two Marine officers was reciprocal.

As a preliminary measure to the assignment, Thomason, who had sufficient leave remaining from his previous tour of duty, requested permission to spend six weeks in Germany and France at his expense collecting data for the project. Permission was granted.

The couple left their son in the care of his paternal grandparents in Huntsville and sailed from New York in August. Two letters documenting this period of Thomason biography are pertinent. The first, written on the date of the departure from Washington, July 30, 1927, is Thomason's farewell to his son. Frequently Thomason compared persons to birds and animals. Conspicuous at the top righthand space is a sketch of two birds typifying himself and Leda.

> Dear Jack:
>
> Your mother and I are lightly perched on the bough, just lifting our wings to fly. The trunks are packed and gone. The bags are packed and at the door. We were going to phone [for] a taxi, but it rained and we're waiting for the rain to slack before we go. [Yesterday they had taken the family pet Badge to Mrs. Johnston's to board.] The car is up on blocks in the garage, with the radiator drained and the air out of the tires. The curtains are all down and put away and so is everything else. The house was empty after you left. Now it's desolate. We wish you were going with us, but you'll enjoy Europe more when you are older. Texas and your gallant steed is more fun now. Don't ride him too hard and look out for cars. Be courteous to your attendants and even your friends. I am glad to hear of your enjoying everything. I wish that you would manage to write us a letter sometime. [Here John lists two addresses in Care of American Express, one in Berlin, the other, in Paris.] With all our love to you and Grandfather and Grandmother and the rest —
>
> Your Daddy
> JWT

The second letter, under date of August 8, was penned aboard ship two days before it docked at Antwerp. Characteristically, in the upper left-hand corner is a sketch of the vessel. Although Thomason employed the terms "Daddy" or "Your Daddy" as a complimentary close in such early letters to his son, he eschewed emphasizing the paternal relationship and wrote to Jack as an individual.

Dear Jack—This afternoon we saw on the port hand Bishop's Rock light, which is the first English land you come to as you go East. It's in the Scilly Isles . . . Tomorrow morning early we will be in Plymouth, which is the place the Pilgrim Fathers sailed from on the *SS Mayflower*—and that afternoon we come across the channel which the French call *La Mancha* . . . Then we go on to Antwerp. There your mother and I get off. That will be Wednesday about noon. This is a slow boat. We have been watching the white cliffs of the Cornish Coast this afternoon. Land looks very good to us. Somewhere over yonder is Tintagal, which you will find mentioned in the King Arthur stories if Grandfather reads them to you. There are lots of boats around pitching and tossing in the sea. While this *Belgenland* is so big that she sails very steadily. She's a nice boat — very pretty inside — and lots of room. There's been only one day when it was really rough. Your mother has, I think, enjoyed all her trip. . . .

I've drawn you a picture of the *Belgenland*. She has three stacks and flies the British flag. Do you remember what it's like? We'll write again—meantime be good, and try writing a letter to us yourself. . . .

John and Leda disembarked at Antwerp, Belgium, on schedule, August 10.

In Berlin and Potsdam Thomason devoted a month to the inspection of official German records and documents pertaining to the war. He pursued a strenuous regimen from 8:00 in the morning until 3:00 in the afternoon. "It is very interesting," he wrote his father. "But my ignorance of German is an almost insuperable handicap. I'm getting something done, however."

Thomason's fame had preceded him to Europe. The American ambassador and prominent authors entertained him in Berlin. Notably among the latter was a Dr. F. Schoenemann, who had been an exchange professor at Harvard for seven years and at the time of the Thomasons' visit was head of the American

Institute at Berlin. John also met some interesting American editors who were touring Europe together.

Before settling down to routine John and Leda enjoyed
touring and sightseeing. They also rented a car and spent weekends visiting places of interest and journeying through much of
the Rhineland, with which Thomason had become familiar from
his service with the American Army of Occupation at the end of
the war.

In Antwerp they visited the zoological gardens and inspected several Rubens, Rembrandts, and Hals in the art galleries. They spent an afternoon browsing around in Brussels. In
Berlin palaces, museums, and the old armory, where were displayed memorabilia of Frederick the Great and Bismarck, drew
them. They found the Royal Palace in Berlin, the table on which
the Kaiser signed the declaration of war and where the mobilization orders were displayed, and the balcony from which he addressed the German people, intriguing.

In Potsdam they visited Sans Souci (Without Worry) and
the Neues Palast (the New Palace), both edifices built by Frederick the Great. One of the cities they found to be most enchant-
ing was Dresden, the capital of Saxony. It was exciting to inspect
Raphael's *Sistine Madonna* and other treasures at one of the galleries there.

"The best thing in France is Paris," Thomason had written
Elise in 1922. This was his first visit to the city of matchless architecture, great painters, expansive boulevards, and exquisite gardens since his contact with Paris in 1918. After working hours,
John took pride in showing the city to Leda.

The French capital, which John and Leda visited in 1927,
was the same Paris Ernest Hemingway found to be a "moveable
feast" in the early twenties. And, interestingly, both writers
pursued comparable routines. Just as Hemingway had carried
his notebooks and pencils with him to the sidewalk cafes and art
galleries he frequented, so did Thomason take along his sketchpad and pens wherever he went. When materials played out, he
drew on travel posters, menus, theatrical programs, or whatever
came to hand. He alternated between pen-and-ink drawings
and watercolors, according to his mood, the kind of light the

day brought, and the life peculiar to the quarter he found himself in at the moment.

Undoubtedly he retraced many of the steps of his friend Hemingway as he captured the magic of Paris in line and color. He and Leda appraised the lights of Paris at night from the roof of Notre Dame, reviewed military parades on the Champ Elysées, noted the everlasting flame burning at the Arc de Triomphe.

They strolled along the Left Bank congested with antique dealers, bookstalls, and picture vendors; tarried at the Sorbonne in the heart of the Latin Quarter, patronized its cafes famous for illustrious clientele and superb cuisine. They wined and dined at Lipp's, where Hemingway struggled over his writing. They descended the stairway to the small park at the edge of the Seine at Pont Neuf to watch the native fishermen take *goujon* with their long caned poles.

They climbed the cobblestone hill to Montmartre to get a glimpse of French nightlife before the quarter was supplanted by Montparnasse. They lingered at Place du Tertre to observe the smocked and beretted artists working before their canvasses.

They dropped by Sylvia Beach's rental library and bookstore at 12 rue de L'Odeon — Shakespeare and Company — where the literary elite of the world gravitated to exchange international gossip. They spent hours in the Louvre, where Thomason's favorite painting Goya's *Dona Rita of Barraneches* held them longest. When time permitted, they attended the *Odeon* and the *Opéra*.

As always, the zoos and botanical gardens lured the artist. He found the birds in the vicinity of the Ile Saint-Louis fascinating. At another park he discovered his beloved dogs and horses among the lions, tigers, and elephants.

After he returned to Washington in September, Thomason began immediately the task of compiling the results of his research.

While John began his work, Leda traveled to Texas to retrieve Jack. The vacation away from his parents had not affected him adversely. He had grown tall and wiry and his muscles had hardened and he was more active. Soon after their return to

Washington, Jack was enrolled in school. "He seems to endure it well enough," his father wrote, October 20, 1927, "although he does not find the pursuit of knowledge stimulating, I gather. He reads some but not very well." The truth was that the lad who could command a Marine corporal with competence at the age of six and who had distinguished himself in the Canal Zone by trimming the sails of the community bully in a fair fight, could not digest the pabulum that the teacher at school was employing. The adventures of Fluff, the white kitten and the chickens of farmer Brown who lived in the white house by the road held no appeal for the young sophisticate. On the other hand, reading that interested adults interested Jack. "I do not think that he . . . will ever be a good student," John wrote his parents, "but he will go after the things that he cares about and get them."

The first year in Washington was pleasant enough and productive. John worked pretty much on his own schedule and managed time for his literary and artistic endeavor, even though he conceded that he was busier than he liked to be. "I really have more in the writing and the drawing line than I can well do," he wrote his father May 25, 1927. "Not knowing how long my vogue will last, I must take advantage of it. I do not think *Red Pants* will sell as many copies as *Fix Bayonets!* did. The stories are not very good stories . . . However, the magazines take everything I write and pay me well for them."

Up to this time Thomason had produced two books — *Fix Bayonets!* and *Red Pants,* for which he had drawn on his combat experience and his tour with the Special Service Squadron on the *USS Rochester.* During the Washington tour he began *Marines and Others,* which Scribner's would publish two years later. In addition, he wrote and illustrated two short stories — *The Killer* and *Distinguished Service Cross. The Killer,* which ran in the November, 1927, issue of *Hearst's International* and *Cosmopolitan,* focused on the hanging of a black murderer at the state penitentiary in Huntsville, Texas. Thomason and a cousin had witnessed the execution.

Distinguished Service Cross is another story that recreates an incident of trench warfare in France. Both stories would appear in *Marines and Others,* with the caption of *The Killer* being altered to *Before the Rain.* During this period commissions for illustrating books by contemporaries included Frazier Hunt's *Custer, The Last Cavalier* and Theodore Roosevelt's *Rank and File.* Moreover, Thomason wrote and illustrated an article entitled *The Marine Brigade,* which was scheduled for publication in the *United States Naval Institute Proceedings* in the November, 1928, issue.

With their improved economy at this time, the Thomasons were able to live more comfortably and enjoy luxuries heretofore denied them. They purchased a new home at 3503 Quebec Street in northwest Washington on a pleasantly wooded site. The charming residence cost $18,500 and Thomason paid the sum of $2,500 down and agreed to terms of paying "$125 per month for the rest of our lives." He would have made a larger down payment, but was advised against it. Inasmuch as he disliked being in debt, he bought a Buick coupe, with seating capacity for four, and paid $2,180 cash for it.

At Thanksgiving, John took inventory. The year before at the same time he was on the bluff at Bluefields. The year before that he was having dinner with a British magnate in Tacna. Then here in November of 1927 he was in Washington with his family. "I have to be thankful for a life that moves and has color in it," he wrote his father, "and a moderate amount of fortune; love; and perhaps some useful work. And we've saved six or seven thousand dollars, though we should have saved more."

As Christmas of 1927 approached, Jack, in the opinion of his father, continued to be "bright, beautiful, and undisciplined." He had three presents for his father, but John could not be sure that he would receive any one of them. Each time he attempted to inculcate "Some of those principles of conduct which have made such a splendid man of me, he becomes enraged and announces that he'll give me only one or maybe two and fling the rest to the poor," John confided to his sister Sue. One night Jack became so piqued at his father that he decided not to give him anything. Still John was consoled by the fact that his son's anger, while not as hot as John's, dissipated as quickly as Leda's. This being true, there was the chance that he might get something after all.

Meanwhile, work was going forward on the Second Division project at the Army War College and John took pride in his accomplishment. "We are getting into the history. It's interesting," he wrote his father on January 21, 1928. "But I have no idea how it's coming out. We want to take this mass of military facts and make them coherent, intelligent, and interesting. Facts, especially military facts, are stubborn things. Whatever I get out of it, it will be useful experience, and I am certainly getting a vacation from the military services."

The second year of duty at the Army War College was much like the first except that it was almost disrupted. By mid-1928 the United States had taken a more aggressive political stance in Nicaragua. Not only did the nation commit itself to disarming the rebellious elements within the country and the suppression of banditry, it also addressed itself to the establishment and training of a native constabulary. Confronted with the prospect of an extended occupation and pacification, the Corps vitally needed all of its officers for field operations in the South American republic, with the exception of those on duty in Haiti.

In January Lieutenant Colonel Elias R. Beedle requested that Thomason be assigned to his staff. However, General Lejeune denied the request. In his opinion the completion of the history of the Second Division was of equal importance. The commander's decision pleased Thomason who had had enough of the tropics and was enjoying the domesticity of family life. "I don't pine for tropic duty any more," he wrote his father. "It's uncomfortable, full of chances to get into trouble — under our system of handling things — and sometimes dangerous. Further, Leda makes me more comfortable here than I've ever been in my life. . . ."

Another thing, Thomason was opposed to interrupting Jack's schooling. With improved motivation, Jack was making rapid progress in his studies. He was reading with his father now, showed an aptitude for drawing, and a feeling for words.

Valentine's Day was a special event for 8-year-old Jack Thomason. He set up a large cardboard box appropriately labeled to accommodate the seasonal overflow of special messages. Two or three days in advance colorful bulky envelopes rattled importantly through the mail slot all addressed in the childish scribble of his schoolmates to Jack Thomason. Meanwhile, he was adding considerably to the family's postage bill himself.

Jack impressed upon his father that he too was supposed "to come through" with some kind of "seasonal observance." Dutifully John sat up late on the night of February 13 painting in tempera a cupid in a shrapnel helmet on a large red heart! It proved to be an experiment in which Captain Thomason of the Marine Corps and successful author and artist learned his limitations. He could not paint cupids. But the colors were sufficiently violent to please the ardent young admirer of such ephemera. "Jack, like his mother," John reflected, "makes much of all occasions."

The Thomasons led an active social life in the nation's capital. They enjoyed entertaining in their gracious home on Quebec Street and moved in social circles that crossed several professional lines. The main event of the season was, of course, a White House reception. President and Mrs. Coolidge tendered four such functions annually: to members of Congress, the diplomatic service, the judicial branch of government, and the Army and the Navy. Guest lists often overlapped because of numbers and for the sake of convenience. In February of 1928 the Thomasons attended the congressional reception on Pennsylvania Avenue.

As Thomason had not worn his "mess dress" in two years, he tried it on and discovered that he had increased in an east-and-west direction so that it required "overhauling" in the hands of an expert tailor. Thomason did his own button shining since he had no mess boy and Leda did not polish buttons. Leda, slender as a flower and beautifully gowned, was her usual impressive self.

On the evening of the event the Thomasons and another couple drove their car to the Roosevelt Hotel and parked it. For half an hour they tried to obtain a taxi. Snow covered the ground and it was bitter cold. When they finally got a taxi traffic was so congested that it took forty minutes to drive the last two blocks to the White House.

The two couples alighted at the east entrance and joined the crush to check their wraps. Then they were assimilated by the mob that formed four abreast in the east corridor to start the line to meet the president and his lady. The line proceeded so slowly that there was ample time to observe the portraits of the presidents that lined the walls. One of President and Mrs. Coolidge by Howard Chandler Christy was prominent. "Very pretty. Pretty is the word," John later described it.

Tediously the guests mounted the stairs and wound their way through various rooms — the red, the green and the blue, herded expertly by aides. Flowers were everywhere but in well ordered arrangements. The artist in Thomason made a mental note of the harmony of the decoration, together with proportion, as the procession inched its way along.

The procession finally narrowed to columns of two abreast, until an aide shuffled them into single file through a narrow doorway. Inside they found themselves in the presence of the president of the United States and his lady. The president and Mrs. Coolidge awaited their guests in the recess of bay windows in a small room. A Marine, two aides, and a sailor stood at attention before them. Another aide, standing beside the host and hostess, took the name of each couple as they approached and repeated it to the president and his lady. The president extended his hand and the guests moved along to acknowledge Mrs. Coolidge. Mrs. Coolidge shook hands more warmly than her husband and tried to vary her greeting to each guest.

The ceremonial affair ended almost before the guests were aware of it. Again the Thomasons found themselves a part of the milling mob of three thousand, through which they made their way, departing the same way they came.

Meeting President and Mrs. Coolidge for the first time was to Thomason an unforgettable experience. He had seen the president at a distance before, but that had not prepared him for the face-to-face meeting. He was "fatter than you expected him to be filling his evening attire without a wrinkle," Thomason wrote his mother. His face did not look sour, as if he had a dill pickle in his mouth, as Thomason had heard Mrs. Alice Longworth say. " — it looks sad," John wrote Mrs. Thomason. "It is the face of a man under almost overwhelming responsibility. For lack of a better word, I'd say, his eyes are tragic . . . Mrs. Coolidge is more vibrant and more vivid."

To Thomason, Coolidge had as much distinction as any man he had met recently and more than most. John concluded that the president's sad expression resulted from his having to shake hands with 3,000 persons in a single evening.

At Easter time in Washington fifty thousand visitors converged upon the capital to enjoy the cherry blossoms. Leda drove the family to the site of the Japanese gift, and because of the influx of people, it took an hour and twenty-five minutes to get around Potomac Park — a distance of only a mile and a half. The profuse flowers, which completely surrounded the Tidal Basin, were spectacular. The sun had come out to heighten the scene. But a nip in the air and Washington's windiness made wraps comfortable.

Recently the War Department had restored to its pedestal in front of the War College barracks the statue of Frederick the Great, a gift of the Kaiser in the days when Roosevelt was consul. "When we entered the war, the authorities, yielding to popular clamor, removed it to a cellar," John wrote his father. "Now after eleven years it emerges." The incident raised a question. What would the authorities do with the cherry trees in case America and Japan went to war?

In the meantime, while his parents exuded with the masses over the beauty of the cherry blossoms, young Jack ws more excited about the sailboat his grandparents in Huntsville had donated at Christmas. He sailed it in the Lincoln Pool and it rode beautifully.

By April of 1928 work on the history project had settled down to a grind, and pressure built up to the extent that Thomason was granted two months' sick leave to recover from exhaustion.

Accordingly, he and Leda made a leisurely overland trip into Virginia and North and South Carolina the following month. By telephone and letter they kept in touch with Jack, who remained in Washington to attend school. At this time Jack had begun to write his own letters.

The couple combined business with pleasure as they visited historic museums and Thomason continued to work at illustrating and writing as the trip progressed. By this light work he was able to defray expenses of the trip that covered more than a month.

The first point on their itinerary was Richmond, where they visited the Confederate Abbey and the Confederate White House. The Abbey yielded fine murals and many portraits of Confederate generals. On display at the Confederate White House were such rarities as the plumed hat of Jeb Stuart, the uniform Lee wore at Appomattox and similar relics of Stonewall Jackson, Jefferson Davis, and A. P. Hill, and in addition a quantity of prints, drawings, and papers, all of which held special interest for Thomason.

After spending a night en route at Raleigh, John and Leda arrived at Southern Pines for a visit with the James Boyds and Struthers and Katherine Newlin Burt. Boyd and the Burts, like Thomason, were successful writers on Scribner's lists. Boyd had reserved a quiet and private cottage—Highland Pines Farm— for the comfort of the visitors. Later after the vacation cottage closed for the season, the Thomason stayed over a few days as house guests of the Boyds.

On their return to Washington, John and Leda stopped for a visit with Elliott White Springs, author of "scandalous tales" (Thomason's phrase) and operator of two lumber mills, who lived at Fort Mills, South Carolina. The visitors stopped for tea and found their host so congenial that they spent the night in his ancestral ante-bellum home. Not only was the residence a rare specimen of pre-Civil War architecture and reminiscent of life in the Deep South, it had figured prominently in Confederate history. The last Confederate cabinet meeting was held under the big live-oak tree in front of Springs' mansion, and Confederate President Davis was captured two days' march from the site. On the grounds stood an extraordinary statue erected by Springs' grandfather — a monument commemorating the faithful slaves of his plantation during the war years.

Upon his return to Washington, Thomason resumed work briefly. Then, with accumulated leave, he and his family took a cottage at Sherwood Forest, Maryland, for July and August. Besides the rest and relaxation in a wholesome rural atmosphere, which provided swimming for Jack and golf for Leda, it gave Thomason leisure time in which to enjoy the coming presidential election, already waxing hot, and the opportunity to make future plans for his career. Even though John was prohibited from voting because of his service connection, he maintained close contact with political activity by radio. He favored Smith, the Democratic nominee, over Hoover, the Republican. While he felt that a nation that could survive Harding could survive anybody, he was convinced that Smith would represent the country's best interests.

During his vacation John paid more attention to correspondence as his leisure time permitted. Sporadically he exchanged letters with Sam Houston's youngest son, Colonel Andrew Jackson Houston. Colonel Houston's communications were invariably lively and replete with spicy information anent current events. For instance, he informed Thomason that the real reason for the striking monument erected to his father on South Main Street in Houston was that the sculptor owed a member of the Fine Arts Commission a debt and told him frankly that he could not pay it unless he got the job.

Another correspondent of several years was Professor Joe Pritchett, whom Thomason had known in his early days at Sam Houston Normal Institute. Pritchett requested a favor of his friend. He asked Thomason to design a lettered plaque for the hospital Bible class room. Thomason was forced to decline because he didn't do lettering. As he explained it to his father, ". . . I can't draw anything that doesn't move."

The greatest dividend accruing from the Sherwood Forest retreat, aside from benefits to Thomason's health, was his decision to write the Jeb Stuart biography. Both of the author-artist's published books had been autobiographic, as his third — *Marines and Others,* based largely on the Nicaraguan station —

would be. No one realized better than Thomason that his stories did not conform to the structural techniques usually followed by professional authors. He readily conceded that he was lacking in what is called plot sense.

However, the very uniqueness of the Corps was in itself a determining factor in the writer's treatment of material. To give a story a technical beginning, a middle that advanced to a climax, and a proper resolution would have risked misrepresentation of life in the Marine Corps—a thing that the author, dedicated Leatherneck that he was, declined to do. Thomason had achieved, nevertheless, a singular realism without stooping to obscenities or cheap sensationalism. Furthermore, nobody could match him in the portrayal of the soldier under fire.

But the author-artist was not content to work in one genre. Despite his extraordinary success and monetary returns, he felt that it was time to experiment with other literary forms and extend his scope . . . time to attempt something more sustained and creative. The Civil War theme represented his second area of interest. Since his boyhood days he had stored up a wealth of stories and reminiscenses from his grandfather, Major Goree, and his uncles. Throughout the years he had found the subject of Lee the soldier stimulating and admired Douglas S. Freeman, who was writing a biography of the Confederate general. He had also toyed with the writing of a biography of his grandfather Goree's friend Longstreet. But in later years Longstreet had published his own memoirs, and there was at least a record of his involvement in the war between the North and the South.

Soon after Thomason's *The Killer* had appeared in *Cosmopolitan*, the fabled Maxwell Perkins, who had already become something of a legend in the publishing world himself, reminded Thomason that a definitive biography of the dynamic cavalry leader James Ewell Brown Stuart remained to be written. In an earlier letter he had made a specific proposal:

> What would you think of this idea? — To take some Southern figure of the Civil War who is not too well known in general, and yet played a significant part . . . and simply write the story of his career with plentiful illustrations. Even so well known a figure as Stuart . . . This would give you a

chance . . . to write highly interesting military history . . .
and for character drawing, and for showing the old South —
all things that you can do so well.

So, after serious consideration, Thomason abandoned the
idea of the Longstreet biography in favor of Stuart, who had not
lived long enough to publish his own story. He plunged immediately into an intensive program of research in preparation for
the project. He took advantage of his ready access to files of the
National Archives and to the Library of Congress, as well as
those of the Army War College. He sifted through the voluminous collections of the official records of the Union and Confederate armies, along with unit histories, periodicals, and newspapers, innumerable letters, and unpublished manuscripts. As
soon as he compiled this data, he initiated a search for more intimate detail.

After returning from the two-months' vacation at Sherwood Forest in September, Thomason resumed work on the Second Division history with a fresh outlook. Even so, he was forced
to face some unpleasant facts. For one thing, he had learned
that the work was not the simple undertaking that he anticipated at the outset.

For another, he was convinced that it was vastly easier to
make history than to write it — "assuming that you want to
write what actually occurred," he explained to his father in October of 1928. Furthermore, "when Napoleon characterized history as 'lies, agreed upon,' he spoke more from sound data than
from cynicism."

Nor did Thomason expect his work to achieve publication
in the form in which he had painstakingly written it. Since his
adherence to truth would point up certain errors made by the
officials in charge, he rather expected that considerable censor-
ship would prevail. At this stage Thomason had finished the statistics involving the first forty-four days "except for a little re-
touching and cross-checking of events." The job was more than
half done. "Actually writing it will not take too long," he said,
"and will be the easiest and pleasantest part of the job."

In the fall of 1928 Thomason was able to resume fishing and hunting with which his confining routine at the Army War college had interfered. He and Captain Oates, another Marine officer, spent a few weekends at Solomons Island on the Chesapeake Bay, where they took some nice sea-trout and great numbers of pan fish. Occasionally, Leda and Jack and Oates' wife and son went along; and to the admiration of John Leda caught more and bigger trout than anyone else. She had also taken the biggest pickerel from Picatenny Lake during the tour at Dover. She and Jack, however, did not view fishing with the same excitement that John did.

John and Dr. Broaddus had leased a point on the Potomac near Dahlgren, where they enjoyed good duck-hunting. Since the minute examination of thousands of pages of fading records and yellowing documents had affected his vision making new glasses necessary, Thomason was relieved to find that his shooting eye had not suffered irreparably.

Thomason's third year in Washington was busier than ever but most fruitful. To make up for time lost on sick leave and vacation, he worked longer hours seldom getting home in the afternoons before dark. Moreover, except for the reappearance of a stomach ulcer that bothered him toward the end of the year, he had completely regained his health.

"Regarding my historical work, it quite possibly approaches an end," he wrote his father in December. "The developments of the last month or so have somewhat changed the look of things, and I believe that I can finish up here by spring and get back to service again." Once more he reiterated that he did not expect his work to be published in the form in which it was written.

". . . my work on the battles around Belleau Woods has stood up under all criticism, and the war lords, my masters, are beginning . . . to wish that they had left me in Nicaragua . . . What I have done is the plain, simple narrative, sufficiently non-technical to be intelligible to any person with patience and interest enough to read through it . . . and the narrative discloses that our officers were not always wise, prudent, successful, and adequate. No officers are . . . But it is not customary to admit it. . . .''

Meanwhile, in the spring and winter of 1929 Thomason made trips throughout Northern Virginia, Northeastern Maryland, and points adjacent to Gettysburg, Pennsylvania, to visit the battle-sites and attempt to visualize the engagements in which Jeb Stuart had participated.

The museums of Richmond, with which he was familiar, and files of various southern historical societies also yielded valuable information. In fact, no possible source was overlooked. But documentary evidence was not enough. Thomason made many pilgrimages into the Virginia countryside to meet and talk to people who lived along the roads where Stuart's squadrons had marched in the war zone, including at least one who was a trooper of the Black Horse, in the Fourth Virginia Cavalry — an old soldier who lost an arm marching to Jeb Stuart's battle music.

"My own work has progressed well enough," John wrote Dr. Thomason . . . "the biography of Jeb Stuart is doing as well as could be expected; some of it has gone to Scribner's and they like it; and I am adding to it every day . . . I have sold a story to *Liberty* for enough to carry us through the winter. . . .''

Thomason devoted as much time as possible to the Stuart biography despite other commitments. For an intimate insight into the man himself, he interviewed Stuart's nephew and three granddaughters, who made the general's private correspondence and papers (heretofore unread except by members of the family) available to him. The nephew, Henry Carter Stuart of Elk Garden, Virginia — the present head of the family, who had known the cavalry leader personally as his Uncle James, was particularly helpful. From memory and a wealth of experience he was able to provide Thomason with much material otherwise unobtainable and with inimitable descriptions of the period and the society in which Stuart moved. The three granddaughters — Mrs. Marrow Stuart Smith, Mrs. Flora Stuart Old, and Mrs. Virginia Stuart Waller Davis, all of Norfolk — provided Thomason with intimate material that became an integral part of the story behind the scenes.

As he proceeded, Thomason found his work increasingly interesting but not easy. "It is difficult, for some reason," he wrote his father, "to produce in writing my impression of the man and of his character. Imagine a person with the glitter and panache and dash of Prince Rupert, of King Murat—who is also in his private life, like Stonewall Jackson, in his uncompromising piety. Though I think he was a better Christian . . . than Stonewall Jackson. Old Stonewall . . . was a mighty man out of the Old Testament. Joshua—Joab—Abner—was his prototype. In the military sense, Stuart takes his importance from the fact that he was the eyes and ears of Lee. . . ."

By December of 1929 Thomason's third book, *Marines and Others,* was released by Scribner's. Invariably the perfectionist, Thomason felt that it was eclipsed by its predecessors. "My new book is out," he wrote on December 7, 1929. "Somehow I have not been interested in it and I do not imagine that it will have a large sale. All the stories except one have previously appeared in magazines, and I do not think highly of them . . . it amounts to this at the age of 36, along with quite a fair amount of routine work, I have written and published three books—one good one, one fair one, and one indifferent. [*Fix Bayonets!, Red Pants,* and *Marines and Others* in that order.] I have some hope for my Stuart. It won't be, at any rate, written in sand—like magazine stories."

Notwithstanding the author's lack of optimism, *Marines and Others* was accorded a reception by both literary and art critics equally enthusiastic to that given Thomason's previous books. The *New York Evening Post*'s comment was typical: "That uncanny knowledge of economy of line which makes the Thomason sketches mind-searing, permanent things, is carried into the leatherneck's writing. He has a mighty gift of saying the most in the least words. . . ." Before the month expired *Marines and Others* had exceeded a sale of 2,500 copies and would top 5,000 before the end of January.

Also in December of 1929 Thomason received additional recognition as an authority on World War I. As one of the four most articulate writers of the war who had actually served in the conflict, he was invited by *McCall's Magazine* to submit to a comprehensive article titled *Four Soldiers from Four Countries.*

Thomason's collaborators were Erich Maria Remarque — the German private who wrote the bestseller *All Quiet on the Western Front;* R. C. Sheriff — the English officer and author of the play *Journey's End;* and Henri Barbusse — the French *poilu* who wrote *Under Fire.* Thomason himself was identified in the article as "the captain of American Marines who wrote *Fix Bayonets!*"

The commentary, published eleven years after the war, bore the consensus that war testifies to the brotherhood of man and that, while it kills in combat, it does not destroy ideals. Remarque believed that one could be proud of his nationality without going to war to prove it. A person could confirm the premise by seeking to understand the kinship that unites the world.

To the Englishman, war brought gratitude for life. The nearer the soldier drew toward death, the finer his conception of living became. The Frenchman felt that no new ideals were born of war. Rather he viewed war as a catalyst that strengthened the old ideals and sharpened man's sense of reality.

In his commentary, *The Hope of the World,* Thomason is both realist and philosopher. The soldier went to war, served obscurely, and "endured for four years . . . withdrawn from the high places where the statesman and the generals ordered events." In the meantime, intervening years had dimmed the memory, even of what the war was all about or whether the rewards of victory justified the sacrifice. To Thomason, the American, the battles revealed "the universal decency . . . and the worthiness of the common man." No longer was the enemy the dangerous creature spawned by propaganda. "He is an individual crumpled," with the same expression on his face you saw on that of your comrade, "who fell back yonder." To Thomason the hope of the world was "that the lessons of decency and tolerance which one generation learns from its war may be transmitted to the next."

The year 1929 was not without its sadness. On September 15 of that year Thomason's maternal grandmother, to whom he had given the affectionate name of Manda, died. Major Goree had died twenty-five years before, when John was a boy of eleven; and Mrs. Goree had made her home in Huntsville since his death.

"It will not seem the same in Huntsville without her," John wrote his mother. "She was one of the landmarks of my life. Besides a very warm affection, I have always had the most genuine admiration for her qualities of mind and spirit. In her way she was a great person. My own aptitude for writing and drawing, I think, comes through you from her. . . ."

As Thomason's research for the Jeb Stuart biography progressed and the history of the Second Division was winding down to its conclusion, he continued other work. Among the subsidiary benefits of his Civil War research was an article entitled *The Capture of John Brown,* an account of the surrender of the abolitionist at Harpers Ferry, which appeared in the September, 1929, issue of the *Marine Corps Gazette.* Jeb Stuart had been present at the surrender.

Two of his most significant short stories produced at this time were *Special Cases,* a study of two officers of disparate character in action on the Western Front, which was published in *Liberty Magazine* in October of 1930; and *Born on an Iceberg,* a narrative based on the Nicaraguan Revolution. Appraised as one of the selections ranking highest, *Born on an Iceberg* was included in the *O. Henry Memorial Award Prize Stories of 1930* by Blanche Colton Williams.

The story, which originally appeared in *Liberty Magazine* in March of 1929, was the one that brought in enough money "to carry the family through the winter." It concerns a Norwegian medical student, who is said to have been born on an iceberg because she does not allow men to interfere with her professional life. Caught in the throes of the Nicaraguan Revolution, in the practice of her profession, she is forced to make a startling decision. Her action demonstrates a courage born of extraordinary strength and deep compassion that belie the stigma of being "born on an iceberg."

Thomason's illustrations contribute to the effectiveness of the story. There are five: three portraying the central figure Karen at different stages of the plot development; one of the revolutionary general, Miron; and one of a dead soldier, all indicating pertinent action. The story itself is reminiscent of O. Henry technique, particularly the aspect of the surprise ending.

Parallels between the two writers are remarkable, even though John Thomason was only seventeen when William Sidney Porter died in 1910. Draftsmen and illustrators, both writers drew material from experience. Porter, who took the pseudonym of O. Henry, produced his first serious work while incarcerated in a federal prison at Columbus, Ohio. Thomason found his identity as an artist and writer through the ordeal of trench warfare in France during World War I.

In youth both authors went through periods of drifting and experimentation. Porter tried ranching, worked in a drug and cigar store, kept books, served as a draftsman, and as a paying teller in an Austin bank. Thomason tried teaching school. Both underwent an internship through newspaper work: O. Henry for his own weekly, *The Rolling Stone,* and later the *Houston Post;* Thomason for the *Houston Chronicle.*

Neither writer cared enough for the academic atmosphere to earn a university degree. Both either broke or ignored the conventional canons of writing yet produced masterpieces. The stories of both reflect a peculiar quality of realism tinged with romance. Both were addicted to humor and exploited the surprise-ending technique. Both achieved their first recognition from New York publishers and wrote for the big magazines of their time.

It has been said of O. Henry that he *humanized* the short story. The appraisal is equally true of John Thomason.

An enjoyable interlude in the spring of 1930 — and a welcome escape from the gruelling routine of the Army War College — was a hurried visit with Jim and Katherine Boyd at Southern Pines when they were celebrating the release by Scribner's of Boyd's latest book — *Long Hunt.* As busy as Thomason was completing the final chapters of *Jeb Stuart* before the expiration of his Washington tour and concluding the Second Division history, Thomason read *Long Hunt* through before laying the novel down.

"Your Long Hunter remarks that each man has the right to be his own kind of fool," he wrote Katherine on April 5, 1930. "He has much to say, this Long Hunter, for the bruised but enduring spirit of man — Long Hunter makes articulate in homely universal phrase many truths that the rest of us aren't free to say. Herein he serves the race."

To Jim he wrote: "Your women have the soft greedy hands, the adamantine defenselessness, and the flame that draws us like a light draws the June bugs on a warm summer evening.

"Excellent as is your background — pure craftsmanship, all excellent — it remains entirely incidental, and of no consequence to that striving between the fundamental impulses wherein your story lies. It is any man and any woman."

Thomason's Washington tour of duty ended on July 1, 1930. Despite some unpleasantness and strain from overwork, Thomason and his assistants accomplished a stupendous piece of work, and upon its completion, tactical and technical data were intricately indexed and catalogued. The information compiled provided the basis for the publication of *The United States Army in the World War, 1917–1919,* by the Historical Division of the Army in 1948.

From a personal viewpoint the tour was doubly rewarding. It gave Thomason the opportunity to do serious research and to travel. It proved conclusively that he was more than an autobiographical writer, more than a Boswell for the United States Marine Corps. Certainly, Thomason would never abandon the Leatherneck theme but that he was equally articulate in other areas was important to him as a serious author and artist.

In the summer and fall of 1930, *Jeb Stuart* appeared in a series of six segments in *Scribner's Magazine.* The book that followed added new dimension to Thomason's stature.

Critical acclaim was unanimous. The *New York Times* declared that *Jeb Stuart* was "Not merely competent or excellent, it is literature. Everything he [Thomason] tells about starts out vividly from the pages, and, once told, is there to stay with the reader forever." The *Boston Herald* categorized it as "one of the great military biographies in many years."

The *Philadelphia Public Ledger* proclaimed it "A book that has all the earmarks of greatness. His *Jeb Stuart* lives, walks, talks, rides, fights and leads his men with song. He gallops through . . . momentous events that transpire before the reader's eyes. The book is a gallery of unforgettable portraits that do everything but walk right out of the pages."

The *New York Herald Tribune* concurred that it was "Spirited and eloquent, decidedly one of the best military biographies that has appeared recently. His account of the ride around McClellan is as fine a piece of description as you are likely to meet, and his accounts of Seven Days, Antietam, Chambersburg, Fredericksburg, and Chancellorsville are both full and brilliant."

At the expiration of his Army War College duty, Thomason was ordered to the Asiatic Station for reassignment. When he learned that he was to be posted to the Marine detachment at the American Legation in Peking, China, he arranged for a month's leave to visit with his parents in Huntsville. Before leaving Washington, he received a letter of commendation from Dr. Thomason, who was reading the serialized version of *Jeb Stuart* in *Scribner's Magazine*.

"He [Stuart] was not one of the great worthies but he was very high in the 2nd classification, and he was a gorgeous human soul," John wrote in reply. He added a postscript: "I never evoked from you before such a note of appreciation. I am very proud of it indeed."

Although the book would not be released until after John's departure, he read his first proofs before leaving Texas. The Thomasons of Huntsville took the occasion to celebrate the forth-coming publication and John's new station in the Orient by calling the clan together for a family reunion. In a special letter to his mother dispatched from Terrell on July 31, 1930, en route to the West Coast for embarkation, John wrote:

> Huntsville was delightful, and it was such a privilege to see you all together and at such ease as was possible under the circumstances. My respect for your ability, as a quartermaster and supply officer, is extravagant. Also I depart full of admiration for my family, my tall brothers and my lovely sisters,

and the pleasant and fortunate people they have brought into the family with them. Herbert, James, and Robert are all distinguished and able gentlemen destined . . . to good and useful lives. Elizabeth has iron in her . . . Mary has every appearance of being the most excellent of mothers. Emily is engaged in reproducing herself, and by and large, the world would be better off with more Emilies. In Margaret you have bred a beauty. God knows what life has in store for her; she is too pretty for her path to ever be dull. Sue I consider the best of the lot. Handsome, cultivated, of genial, active mind, and of an unselfishness perfectly sublime (and therefore a little deplorable, for she will always do herself less than justice). I wish that she would not spend that golden character of hers so lavishly upon others, but that she might save some of it for herself. I kiss her hands and am expressing myself to her perhaps more eloquently elsewhere. As for me, the oldest, you all seem to have the kindest of opinions. . . , far too kind, as I know better than anybody.

All the foregoing, of course, comes back to you and father, the authors of whatever good is in us. . . .

11   *With the Legation Guard in Peking* [*]

In 1930 there were three main approaches to Peking. You could enter the ancient Chinese capital by the Imperial high-way, from the southwest, over flagstones rutted by the cart wheels of ten centuries. You could descend upon the city from the north, through the Kalgan gate and Nankow Pass as Tartar conquerors did, mounted on shaggy ponies behind yak-tail standards. Or you could enter Peking by railway — after crossing the vast Pacific Ocean.

The Thomasons came by the latter, arriving at Peking on September 3, 1930. They had embarked from San Francisco on the *SS President Adams,* August 8, in order to visit Honolulu and Japan en route. After spending a day exploring the island of Oahu, they arrived at Kobe on the 28th. From Kobe they went

---

[*] In 1928, when Chiang Kai-shek transferred the seat of the government to Nanking, the name of the ancient capital of Peking (Northern Capital) was changed by edict to Peiping (Northern Peace). But to the residents and foreigners who visited it, the name remained Peking. The name of Peking was officially restored under the Communist regime in 1949.

to Kyoto, the ancient capital of Japan, from where they sailed two days later through the picturesque Inland Sea. The last nine-day leg of their journey took them to Shanghai, where they took a train for Peking. It had been a pedestrian journey. But they had loved every minute of it from the swaying hula hula girls of the Honolulu beaches in mid-afternoon to the goose-winged fishing junks that beat down out of the burning Inland Seacoasts at sunset.

Nothing warned the Thomasons of what to expect in the world's oldest living civilization. They came to China totally un-prepared for what they were to encounter. When they arrived, the flat part of northeastern China had already begun to exhibit the khaki-colored appearance of winter and looked the same in all cardinal points of the compass. Every foot of arable soil was under cultivation and blue-coated coolies swarmed like insects upon it.

Interspersing the rows in the fields were mounds of assorted sizes and unusual architectural designs. These were the burial places of the dead, among which were commemorative tablets and upright plinths of carved marble. Monotonous shrines to gods and princes rose austerely from the furrows, cluttering the landscape. In the south and east the great sky bordered the hollow land. To the north and west the hills circled, their contours sharp and remote like an ancient etching viewed from a distance.

Then suddenly there loomed before the Thomasons the Great Wall of China! Once man's most formidable rampart and later to become the only man-made object visible from outer space, the 3,333-mile Wall, with its unfortified bastions, was a peaceful relic of ancient Chinese history.

Colonel James C. Breckenridge, commanding officer of the Legation Guard, and others gave the Thomasons a hearty welcome and they settled down temporarily at the Hotel de Peking. The China station for Marines of Thomason's rank and experience was a coveted assignment. In spite of the jocular treatment to which the mounted detachment was subjected in musical comedy, the Legation Guard at Peking — the parent organization of the Horse Marines — was comprised of carefully selected and well-trained officers and enlisted men who were skilled horsemen and whose mounts were the finest of thoroughbred Mongolian ponies.

The Thomasons took an apartment on Rue Gambil in the Legation Quarter on October 15 and set up housekeeping. Their car had preceded them to the Orient, but they had had to wait for their household effects. Later they planned to find a suitable house. Although the place—Culty Chambers—was on the third floor, it was capacious. There was some central heating of steam, and each room, even the bath, was equipped with a fireplace. The 20 by 30-foot living room had two. To offset the absence of closets and shelves for books, the Thomasons purchased huge Chinese camphor wood chests and wardrobes and had shelving installed.

With these added conveniences and a competent household staff, the apartment was livable. The servants consisted of a number 1 boy, a coolie, one amah, two maids, a number 1 cook, a second cook, and a chauffeur. These did not include the stablemen who looked after the horses. Actually there were five servants in the apartment proper, each of whom was responsible for one particular duty. For instance, the coolie lighted the fires but the number 2 cook laid them and removed the ashes. While the coolie waxed the floors and polished the brasses, the amah swept and dusted. The number 1 boy took care of John's clothes and served as a coordinator and interpreter, as none of the others spoke English. The amah took care of Leda's clothes.

The chauffeur drove the car and kept it in good repair. The number 1 cook seemed to occupy an unusual place in the household organization. He addressed himself exclusively to the cooking and the Thomasons rarely saw him. All negotiations with him were conducted through the number 1 boy. The cook received a selary of $145 Mex a month for providing meals for the family of three, received 20 cents extra for each tea guest, $1.00 extra for dinner guests, 75 cents extra for luncheon guests, and $2.00 a day extra for house guests. The cook did the buying of the food and submitted daily menus for Leda's approval.

The Legation Quarter itself occupied a unique place in the City of Peking. Colorful flags of many nations identified the site as an international community. The combined strength of the garrison was 2,000 officers and enlisted men. Thomason's detail was commanding officer of the machine gun company. Over and above the 500-man American Marine Detachment, there were a Japanese and British battalion of corresponding size, 300 French troops, and 200 Italian Marines serving under naval officers. Except for emergencies, the different legation guards acted independently, and each was responsible for the security of his own installation and for control of the nationals residing in the Quarter and in Peking and its environs.

Independent of Chinese control, the Legation Quarter approximated a defended military zone equipped with its own security forces, police and fire departments, electric power, and even reserve food supplies. Part of standard equipment was a naval radio and receiving station. As a result of the Boxer attack in 1900, foreign emissaries took extra precautions for defense. Not only was the Quarter protected on three sides by strong loopholed walls and steel gates surrounded by a dry moat, it also maintained control of the fifty-foot high Tartar Wall, or south elevation of the adjoining Inner City.

A narrow rectangle, with dimensions of about a mile by three-eighths, the Quarter lay along the south Tartar Wall from Chien Men to Hata Men and north to the Tung Chang an Chieh. In addition to the legations of the various foreign powers, the Quarter contained foreign banks, a hotel or two, theaters, a few department stores and shops, the compounds of the Customs, Salt, and Postal administrations, residences and apartment houses, and the foreign clubs.

Though the community was crowded and many were forced to find housing elsewhere because of the infiltration of other nationals, living at the Legation Quarter was extremely pleasant. Buglers from the American, British, Italian, and Japanese marked the time by the hour musically—a custom which added to the pleasant atmosphere.

A special feature of the Quarter that added substantially to the community's enjoyment was the outlying Glacis—an area devoted to international sport. The United States Marines' part was a baseball diamond. The British had a gridiron for rugby; the

Italians, a space for a game played with a rubber ball. The Japanese, invariably militant, covered their section with barbed wire and practice trenches. The French devoted their area to polo, which everybody played. The whole area was surrounded by a bridle path where everyone could exercise his ponies and, as Thomason phrased it, "condition his liver against the assaults of food and drink sustained in the hospitable houses in the Quarter."

Clean and well-paved streets added convenience, and there was always a feeling of security. Occasionally, however, when tensions flared up, the Quarter became a refuge. The first to take advantage of it were the wealthy Chinese themselves. They rushed to the foreign hotels and crammed the vaults of the Quarter's banks with their valuables. At such times servants of the Legation families would smuggle their relatives and friends into their sleeping quarters. Moreover, if danger seemed imminent, ministers would order their nationals to come in — teachers, missionaries, doctors, and the people living on the edge of the city. Quarters were assigned according to available floor space.

Life in Peking, with its strange sights and sounds and smells, converged in the streets. By night and day peddlers and venders hawked their commodities and wares in the streets, some enticing trade by their melodious cries and others by striking the gong at intervals or by brandishing hollow wooden ducks which made a resonant sound.

Foremost among these were the food vendors. Equipped with their mobile kitchens, cooking pots and braziers, trestles for counters, and benches, they seemed ubiquitous. You could watch the food being prepared and you might consume it on the spot or take it home as you desired. Small broilers split in half looked as if they had been laquered. Fried cakes, the staple of the coolies, were stacked in high piles. There was always a wide variety of edibles and each vender was a specialist. But, regardless of what he specialized in — fowl, fish, meat, or vegetables — over everything there clung the odor of bean sauce.

Most ingenious among these venders was the noodle man. Noodles were indispensable to the Chinese diet. You could have your noodles in various colors and shapes. An artist at his craft, the noodle man could roll and shape the dough magically to your exact specifications — round, square, flat, hexagonal. Expert noodle men had been known to demonstrate their skill at parties for the edification of foreigners.

Competing favorably with the noodle man for ingenuity was the candy man. Like the others, he transported his equipment on his barrow: melting pots and braziers, jars of bright-colored sugars, blowing-reeds in assorted sizes, and a light cane frame for the display of his art. Invariably the idol of children, the candy man blew and spun melted sugar into fantastic shapes with the dexterity of a skilled glass blower—an ornamental vase, a lotus blossom, even a dragon replete with scales, horns, and claws.

A most extraordinary peddler was the fan and featherbrush salesman who resembled a glamorous bird with his colorful stock attached to a frame across one shoulder. When a customer approached him, the peddler set his display rack on the ground in order to conduct his business leisurely. The fans were made of paper, silk, and dried palm leaves. At the time in China the fan was considered an essential part of a lady's or gentleman's personal equipment. Fans were popular with all classes, and people used them for many purposes: to dust the furniture, blow up fires, to cool the food and tea, and to shade one's eyes from the sun. There were special styles for festive occasions and a fan for each season — spring, summer, and autumn.

Then there were the sidewalk merchants who lined the streets, a square of blue coolie cloth spread before them in the dust to accommodate their merchandise. They sold curios, gewgaws, imitation jade and glass, cheap jewelry, etc. Yet you could sometimes find a bargain or purchase accidentally the real thing. Such incidents had happened.

There were also the peanut venders seated by their baskets with the nuts spread out in front of them. As often as not you might stumble over them outside the massive studded gates of the Temple of Heaven or another location equally as important. Sometimes you encountered peddlers of camel bells, pipes, good-luck charms, and trinkets plying their trade at one of the watch-towers along the Great Wall.

But for greater variety and authenticity, the Thomasons and other members of the Quarter patronized the reputable bazaars and shops. One off Morrison Street, near the Quarter, which had hundreds of little stalls and shops — partly covered and partly open — offered everything for sale: food, drink, wearing apparel, toys, books, and ornaments. The place was crowded night and day by people buying walking canes, riding crops, porcelains and bronzes and jades, antique vases, scrolls, paintings, even decorative snuff bottles.

Although the Thomasons were not the avid collectors that some of their friends were, they did accumulate a store of treasures. Leda assembled a modest collection of small jade articles including some snuff bottles. John — animal lover that he was — picked up a few porcelain horses. Leda's tastes ran from fine fabrics — tribute silks — to antique vases; John's from decorative metals to other art objects. They both shared an interest in exquisite furniture and books.

An integral part of the Peking street scene was the coolie with his ricksha behind him. Since life in Peking in the early thirties was relatively unhurried, many people preferred the ricksha to the motorized taxi. The vehicles, examples of perfect balance, ran smoothly and fares were cheap. After sundown, with their little spirit lamps lighted, the coolies and their rickshas made a fascinating sight along the boulevards. The Thomasons remembered the pad-pad of the coolies' feet as one of the most distinctive street sounds of Peking.

With 20-odd commissioned officers and four companies, the Marine Guard was organized as a battalion. The four companies consisted of Headquarters and Headquarters Company, which included the Mounted and Signal platoons and the band; the Sixty-second Company, a rifle unit with a mortar platoon; the Thirty-eighth Company, a machine gun component; and the Thirty-ninth Company, which was equipped with four light artillery field pieces. Ordinarily considered an infantry organization, the battalion was equipped with supporting arms for defense. It was routine for the battalion, with the exception of the Headquarters Company, to provide a guard of the day and fur-

nish sentries, on a rotating basis, not only at the American Legation and at the Legation Quarter gates but also on the height of
the Tartar Wall overlooking the sector. Still another duty was
that of roving patrols throughout the city for the security of diplomats, families of the Marine Guard, and residences and places
of business of American nationals.

Furthermore, the Legation Guard, as indicated, was responsible for the protection of the lives and property of all Americans, irrespective of status, in the entire province of Hopei, of
which Peking was the geographical center. This included missionaries and others scattered in small communities of North
China. Rescue plans for evacuation and transportation under escort to the Legation Quarter were carefully detailed so as to be
expedited promptly in the event of emergency.

Upon arrival in Peking, every American was required to
register with the Legation, to state the nature of his business,
give his address, and report his movements. Commanding officers of the Guard and officials of Peking and the immediate
environs of the mounted detachment acted upon the data thus
collected. They made periodic inspections to ascertain the locations of residences and the whereabouts of American nationals,
engaged in frequent investigative and reconnaissance details,
and provided occasional escorts for officials and others who traveled into remote areas of the province.

As commanding officer of the Thirty-eighth Marine Gun
Company, Thomason had multiple duties. In addition to the
training and administration of his men, he participated in troop
formations, inspections, weekly battalion parades, marches and
hikes into the surrounding country, field maneuvers, and terrain exercises. He also took part in simulated-combat problems
and in tactical situations.

Twice a week Thomason's company furnished the guard of
the day. As officer of the day, he served in the formal guard
mounts at the beginning and close of each tour of duty. Thomason was likewise responsible for the posting of sentries and the
inspection of their posts and those of the Marine compound. He
was available for immediate contact within the city as well as the

Legation Quarter. In the event of unforeseen developments, he made investigations and took remedial action.

Thomason's performance of duty was invariably excellent. In April of 1931 his company was awarded the All Arms Trophy for being the best drilled and the most military in appearance of all the units in the Legation Guard.

Dr. John C. Ferguson, who commissioned the trophy, presented it in a special ceremony. Designed by Thomason, the trophy was further evidence of the Marine officer's ability to combine his feeling for artistry with his duties in the Corps. In the shape of a winged globe surrounded by the emblems of the Marine Corps, the memento reflected the ancient Egyptian symbolism typified by the victory of the principle of light and concept of virtue over darkness and evil.

An out-of-doors man, Thomason especially enjoyed the three-week summer encampment at Peitaho. Located on the Gulf of Chichli, about 100 miles from Peking, Peitaho Beach was the summer resort of North China. During the summer three companies of the battalion, in rotation, proceeded by rail to the site for rest and combat training. Simultaneously they used the machine gun and artillery ranges maintained by the Fifteenth Infantry encamped at Chinwangtao, a treaty port and transport anchorage in the area.

The camp under canvas not only provided relief from the monotony of drills and guard duty, it offered water sports for recreation. Marine officers' families frequently accompanied them. At the height of the season some 10,000 sought escape from the oppressive summer heat, half of them consisting of missionaries.

An incidental meeting at Peitaho with a 13-year-old girl gave Thomason his story *Missionary's Daughter,* a study of the harsh life of an American schoolgirl in the Orient and the enforced maturity that deprived her of the natural joys of childhood. First published in the *New Yorker,* the story was later included in Thomason's fifth book, *Salt Winds and Gobi Dust,* issued by Scribner's in 1934.

Although the Horse Marines were obsolescent, the unit was well suited to the narrow streets and roads of Peking, which were originally constructed to accommodate wheeled carts and rickshas. As Thomason was to write later in his story titled *Sergeant Bridoon of the Horse Marines:* ". . . Our Mounted Detachment was an anachronism. It dated back to the Boxer times, and in the years before the motorcars it served a useful tactical purpose in the way of patrols and communications." Moreover, for sheer pomp and panoply demonstrated at parades and reviews, the Mounted Marines were indispensable. Indeed the Horse Marines were the reminder of a bygone era of military pageantry.

For that matter, the City of Peking itself was an anachronism of sorts. The northern capital presented a constantly shifting population encompassing most of the reputable professions — diplomats, officials, and celebrities — along with the less known and disreputable. Visitors to Peking, for instance, ran the gamut of diversity from the really important personages, including renowned scientists, scholars, artists, writers, sculptors, stage and screen luminaries, commerical tycoons, and missionaries, to the inveterate adventurers, social sycophants, hangers on, and freeloaders, not to mention those ubiquitous ladies and gentlemen with no visible means of support who inhabited the best hotels.

That the City of Peking, as crowded as it was and without adequate modern transportation and other conveniences, should draw this heterogeneity — like the proverbial moth to the flame — was one of many Oriental enigmas. But to John Thomason it soon became a kaleidoscope that nourished his artistry. In his story titled *The Sergeant and the Bandits* — a narrative that begins as a hunting expedition in the vicinity of the Great Wall and the Yellow River and develops into a tale of daring heroism — he categorizes these conglomerates of humanity as ". . . the many odd fish who come and go about Peking, providing an unfailing interest in the North China scene." They were also to him " — a cosmopolitan gumbo, possible only in deep Asia."

Perhaps Thomason's most unusual story pertaining to these weird specimens that regularly infested the capital was *The Collector.* In this instance the protagonist — a doctor from the Middle Western United States — had come to the Chinese capital seeking a decapitation. He needed the decapitation to complete his universal collection of executions, which he photographed himself with a fine movie camera and showed to his friends. He had just collected a strangulation, of which he was proud because of the lighting and timing.

The Marines' occupation of a diplomatic station in China involves international history. Their development paralleled both Chinese domestic and foreign affairs. The Manchu capital of Peking was not a treaty port per se. However, since the Treaties of Tientsin of 1858 and the Peking Convention of 1860, the United States, Great Britain, France, and Russia had sent diplomatic representatives to the imperial capital and provided residences for them.

By the end of the nineteenth century, eleven foreign powers had installed chancelleries within the Legation Quarter. In comparison with the quarters of British and French envoys, the size of the American diplomatic mission was negligible. But in 1898 anti-foreign sentiment and unrest became so acute that a small Legation Guard was established at Peking as a protective measure for Americans living in North China. The unit was comprised of only 20 Marines drawn from the three ships of the Asiatic Squadron. Following this action, a larger complement of Marines was made available for the protection of the American Consulate at Tientsin, the nearest seaport to the capital. When conditions improved, both guards were returned to their duties at sea.

Then in 1900, when the Boxers surrounded Peking and animosity toward foreigners reached new heights, the Legation guard was reestablished. Throughout the summer of 1900, the United States Marines, assisted by contingents of European troops, successfully defended the Legation Quarter against repeated Boxer attacks. The Marines held out until the Allied Relief Expedition of 18,500 Americans, Europeans, and Japanese armed forces came to their assistance.

At the cessation of hostilities in September the Legation Guard was reinforced by a company of the United States Ninth Infantry. By September of 1905 Marines relieved the army unit. Moreover, from that time until 1941, when Japanese forces overran North China, the American Legation Guard became an ex-

clusive Marine Corps obligation. During that period the strength
of the Marine Guard varied in proportion to the necessity dictated
by Chinese internal and external affairs.

By 1929, the year before Thomason took up his station at
Peking, Chiang Kai-shek, who occupied the new capital he had
established at Nanking, was in nominal control. In the autumn
of 1927 he defeated Communist opposition by evicting the Soviet advisers from Hankow and by liquidating great numbers of
the Communist dissidents. To complicate Chiang Kai-shek's difficulties, however, the Japanese occupied part of Shantung soon
afterward.

Since 1928 Chinese domestic policies had been stormy. Despite the fact, Chiang Kai-shek made some progress toward a
stable government and retained control over the Nationalist
army. The fact remained that the South and West had capitu-
lated to Nationalist rule only to present a common front against
the aggressive Japanese. Following the purges of 1927, the Communist party armed itself and posed an even greater threat to
Chiang Kai-shek's government.

By 1930, the year of Thomason's arrival, the Communist
army had expanded into a formidable force and Soviet influence
was spreading to large areas. Between December, 1930, and October, 1933, the Nanking government mounted five campaigns
in an attempt to wipe out the Communist army and seize the
Soviet bases. By October of 1934 the main Communist forces
had been driven from their southern base of Kiangsi.

Express treaty rights and general principles of international
law of more recent date further justified the presence of the Marines in China. According to international law, a government
had the right to land armed forces in another country to protect
its citizens, if the foreign power was unable to do so, regardless
of capability or willingness. In addition, the system of extraterritoriality, which prohibited the Chinese government from exer-
cising jurisdiction over foreign nationals in civil and criminal
cases, was still in effect. As late as 1939, the law of extraterritoriality in China was retained by Great Britain, France, Japan, and
the United States.

As time-consuming as military duties were at the Legation, they did not interfere with social activity. There were the customary diplomatic receptions and ceremonial functions, along with dinners and cocktail parties, which were a focal part of Legation life. The Thomasons contributed greatly to the social life of the Quarter. Leda mastered the art of the small elegant dinner party and the couple were noted for the success of their informal luncheons and cocktail parties.

Of the Legation crowd, Thomason said that they were "a slick, highly polished lot, — very much on the social side, and they discuss international politics and the menace of the moment and their neighbor's wife with equal freedom and gusto."

The Thomasons often played golf at a course near Paopashan, only ten miles away. While Leda excelled at bridge, Thomason indulged himself in a variety of equestrian sports — polo, steeple-chase, and point-to-point. As an active member of the Peking Hunt Club, he took part in its scheduled riding events.

A subsidiary of the Peking Club was the Race Club, in which Thomason took an enthusiastic interest. The annual spring and fall races sponsored by the organization and held at "Running Horse Village" in Paomachang permitted Thomason to race his string of native ponies. He took pride in the animals and trained them himself but entrusted the riding in the competition to native jockeys. His racing ventures paid off handsomely and he spent much time at the tracks working with the animals. His favorite of the string, and a consistent winner, was a gray gelding, which he called Temujin for Genghis Khan, one of his heroes from Oriental history. In one of his best Sergeant Houston stories — *The Sergeant and the Siren* — a horse by the name of Temujin, "whose gray coat shone like new silk," wins the third race for the Marine with a sweep of twenty-odd hundred dollars.

Among Thomason's intimate circle of friends at this time were two horse enthusiasts and ardent racing companions. The first, Captain Julian Brown, had been transferred from Shanghai to Peking in the fall of 1931 for duty at the Legation as a student of the Chinese language. Thomason also shared the language interest. The men became extremely close friends and entered into a partnership in racing ventures.

A mutual interest in both horses and writing led to Thomason's friendship with the other—the United States explorer and naturalist, Roy Chapman Andrews. Famous for his books on his central Asiatic field trips, Andrews had lived in Peking for fifteen years when Thomason arrived. He sold Thomason two polo ponies and the men spent much time training the animals and participating in the sport. Andrews, to whom the Orient had become commonplace, rediscovered its marvels through the impressionistic eyes of Thomason the artist as the two explored it together.

During the Peking tour Andrews sat for a portrait which Thomason modelled from clay. The naturalist's friends considered the work an outstanding piece of sculpture and a remarkable likeness of the subject.

One of the most popular books in Andrews' library was *Fix Bayonets!* Since the writing read so smoothly, he felt that Thomason had written it with little effort and no revision. He wondered if the book did not, in a manner of speaking, almost write itself.

"You couldn't be more wrong," Thomason told him. "I don't know how many times I rewrote each paragraph and each sentence. I almost literally took each word out, thought about it critically, and put it back or found a better one."

In Peking the favorite pastime of the Thomasons, like others of the Legation Guard, was promenading on the Walls after evening colors. They never failed to exult over the sharp outline of the Wall's bastions against the east and the interminable series of watch-towers that dotted its borders.

"When the weather's pleasant, everybody walks on the Wall in the evening," Thomason wrote in *Love Story of a Marine.* "It's one of the wonders of the world and a fine place to watch the sunset." Again in *The Sergeant and the Spy* it is ". . . one of those rare evenings with no dust blowing, when the North China air has the tang and sparkle of approaching winter, and is like wine to breathe, and crystal clear, so that the Western Hills . . . look near enough to touch."

Like other inhabitants of the diplomatic community, the Thomasons were familiar with the Wall's history. "They built it to keep out the Mongols and the Tartars from the north. Built it for bandits on ponies to look up to," Thorkildsen tells Sergeant Houston, squinting his good eye, in *The Sergeant and the Bandits*. Then refreshing himself with sips of brandy, as the two travel near the Wall at Kilgan, the one-eyed Thorkildsen volunteers that the Wall had never stopped a major invasion because the generals sold out to "any worthwhile customer coming along," but that "It had saved the small villages and farms behind it from two thousand years of raids." Not only did Thomason preserve the Wall's grandeur in stories, he captured it in sketches.

Other areas of the northern capital attracted pedestrians. There were the three cities, one within another, and a fourth — the Chinese city, toward the south — which drew sightseers. The four-mile-square line of the Tartar Wall identified the Tartar city, to which the oblong-shaped Chinese city, with its fourteen miles of walls, was adjacent.

There was the Imperial city with its reddish walls and great streets running east and west. In it were the palaces of the court officials and imperial princes. Within the Imperial city was the Forbidden city, the Violet town and the residences of the dragon emperors. An enclosure somewhat longer than it was broad, it lay behind a wide moat and a double wall. In summer the Thomasons found it especially intriguing when glowing lotus filled the moat and white cranes stalked among the rose-pink blooms. An ornamented tower graced each corner of the wall: East Gate Glorious, West Gate Glorious, Gate of Divine Military Progress, and the Meridian Gate.

Perhaps most interesting was the Forbidden city — the quarters of the former Ming and Manchu emperors — with the roofs of its pavilions tiled in imperial yellow. The pavilions included audience halls, council halls, halls devoted to ancestry veneration, as well as the imperial living quarters. Smaller buildings housed the concubines and eunuchs and provided storage. Each pavilion had its own courtyard and formal entrance. Small conventional moats with white marble balustrades threaded the courts. Terraces and ceremonial flights of steps were also balustraded. Some of the buildings had been converted into museums. Ancient works of art brought visitors especially to the outer throne halls known as the Hall of Supreme Harmony and the Hall of Preserving Harmony.

Two places the Thomasons liked to visit for leisurely contemplation were the Temple of Confucius and the Temple of Heaven. The Temple of Confucius was in the northern section of the Tartar city. To get to it you traversed noisy alleys infested with scavenger dogs and naked children. You went through a passage under dragon cypresses between ranks of memorial tablets commemorating the patronage of emperors and princes.

The passage led to a terrace, from which you descended to the main court by marble steps that flanked a spirit stairway. The temple was so thickly shaded by the interlacing branches of ancient trees that your first impression was one of gloom. The sun, however, penetrated the trees to reach the red walls of the pavilions and the painted patterns of the overhanging eaves of brilliant blues, purples, greens, reds, and yellows.

No noises of the city obtruded here. No statues graced the shrine — the High Place of an Idea. Only tablets richly engraved appeared above the altar. Ashes of joss sticks in the incense burners testified to the many worshippers. You found here a meaningful tranquillity and departed with the feeling that you had made contact with an Elder Wisdom.

By contrast the Temple of Heaven, which was located toward the south in the so-called Chinese city, was sun-drenched and its walls enclosed a park larger than the Forbidden city itself. You entered it from a highway along a large avenue to the center of a terraced line of pavilions. The round Hall of the Happy Year, to the north with its blue tiles and triple roof, was one of the distinctive features of the Peking skyline.

In the opposite direction, through open pavilions and archways, was the somber altar of white carved marble. The altar was comprised of three round terraces of varying dimensions, the top one being the smallest. Steps leading to the altar were in arrangements of nine — the mystical number — with the flagstones of the pavement laid in concentric patterns repeating the nine. The roof of the altar typified the vault of heaven.

On weekends the Thomasons enjoyed visiting the public parks, once reserved as private gardens for the imperial family and as ceremonial spaces of the temples. In the west-central part of the Tartar city, within the Imperial Wall, and west of the Forbidden city, they visited the grounds of the Sea Palaces, bordering the South, Middle, and North seas. Another favorite was the Summer Palace. Built by the Empress Dowager Tzu Hsi, "Old Buddha," who was virtual ruler of China for half a century until her death in 1908, the Summer Palace was situated in the vicinity of the magnificent Jade Fountain, which fed the lake near the site. The grounds, including some of the most beautiful gardens in the orient, consisted of seven hundred acres.

A place the family frequented most was Central Park — Peking's most popular playground — opening off the Tung Chang an Chief. In the spring, when the plum trees and the cherry trees were in bloom, it was at the height of its season. With the brilliant reds and greens of its graceful double-roofed pavilions, its grotesquely shaped, water-worn rocks, and avenues of cypress trees, it was one of the most delightful garden areas in the city.

Besides its ornamental waterways and winding walks through the rock gardens and blossoming trees, there were elegant restaurants and pleasant tea gardens. Since the small admission fee excluded the beggar and coolie class, the park was the haunt of Chinese gentlefolk as well as foreigners. Often three generations of a family sat together with pleasure as poets and philosophers conversed lengthily over tea and watermelon seeds. Here you were sure to see Chinese aristocrats of both sexes arrayed in the finest of Oriental silks walking in the sunshine. Many of the native girls were quite lovely "with skin like magnolia petals, and slim, exquisite figures, and narrow black-fringed eyes aware of spring."

When their schedules permitted, the Thomasons found diversion in travel. By rail, only forty miles away, they could reach Nankou Pass, another segment of the Great Wall. At Kalgan, farther up the line, they enjoyed exploring the outer perimeter of the Wall that crowned a majestic elevation of mountains. Beyond was the Province of the Suiyuan extending to the Gobi Desert and the Mongolian border. Thomason found splendid hunting in the vicinity of the Yellow River, where such quarry as mountain goats, pheasant, geese, and bustard — a species of wild turkey — were plentiful.

Then a train trip "down country" to Shanghai for shopping, entertainment, and visiting with officers of the Fourth Marines and their families was always pleasant.

In spite of its exotic atmosphere and opportunities for diversion, the capital of Northern China had its debit side. Situated ninety miles inland from the coast with an elevation of 125 feet above sea level, the city was subject to sudden seasonal changes and extremes of temperature, to which Occidentals adjusted with difficulty. From the flat coastal plains, adjacent to the Yellow and White rivers, winter winds shrouded the city with a film of gray-white dust. In summer the sea winds transported clouds of hot moist air that seemed like a gridiron.

Two months of freezing underscored the winters. Northerly winds gusted fierce dust storms, which frequently lasted almost a month and deposited a coating of yellow powder. Not the least infinitesimal crevice escaped it. "A Peking dust storm is no light matter," John wrote his father. "The air turns windy, and the fine Gobi dust permeates everything." To offset the effect of the severe winters, the Legation inhabitants wore heavily padded clothing and burned immense fires in their private quarters.

Another major problem closely related to the climate was the prevalence of disease. Since sanitation in the centuries-old republic was substandard, such diseases as amoebic dysentary, malaria, and pneumonia were common. In addition, there were less frequent outbreaks of bubonic plague and typhoid fever. The Thomasons were not immune to these health hazards. It was the grave illness of Jack in 1931 that gave the Thomasons serious concern. Eleven-year-old Jack contracted scarlet fever following a slight chill resulting from overexertion on a scout hike. Jack was a member of the Dragon Patrol, a boy scout organization. The assorted members — American, English, Japanese,

Chinese, French, and German — were Jack's friends and class-mates in the American school in East City.

On this particular Saturday the scoutmaster, a young American missionary, was hiking the troop through Chien Men and the Chinese City to the open spaces around the Temple of Heaven; and Jack felt that, if he did not join them, he would be called a sissy and would lose face. Although susceptible to respiratory afflictions, he appeared to be well, free of sniffles at the time.

His parents insisted, however, that he dress warmly. Instead of the regulation shorts and wool stockings, they had him don britches and puttees. After breakfast Jack passed his dad's formal inspection: service kit, canteen of chow-water, knife and coil of rope, sweater and muffler, all weighing no more than his capacity to handle. For sheer swank he carried a curved Mongol bow and a quiver of arrows slung across his back.

The family car, with Yang the chauffeur at the wheel, conveyed Jack and his gear to the appointed place of meeting. It was just above freezing with the clouds threatening snow and an unaccustomed dampness in the air — an unusual development as Peking was ordinarily hot and cold but rarely damp. Over lunch the solicitous parents hoped that their son was under cover for the noon meal, which inevitably included outdoor cooking. Anxious, Leda had driven out in the forenoon and observed the troop doing evolutions in a system of Chinese practice trenches and she obtained from the scoutmaster the hour of the return march. She told the scout leader that she would send the car for Jack if the weather became more inclement.

At three o'clock, when the Oriental day was settling down to twilight and the wind had shifted to the northeast and turned raw, she sent Yang with the car. Yang returned alone. He explained that to save face, his young master had declined the ride home.

Later around teatime Jack straggled in. While he sat by the sea-coal fire, a little tired from the pleasant activity, the parents restored him with all the food he could eat. He had been cold, he said, only once when he sat down in the trenches for an hour and listened to a lecture with demonstrations on an important phase of scoutcraft. His mother hoped that he had sat on his poncho — not on the bare ground. Of course, he had sat on the ground, he informed her testily, like everybody else.

When his mother looked in on Jack that night, she thought he appeared somewhat restless and his head seemed a little hot but his breathing was normal.

The Thomasons had guests for the weekend from Shanghai, and the next day, with snow on the ground, they took them to see the Summer Palace. The sky was clear, despite the bitter cold, and the Western Hills were blue and silver in the sun.

Scarlet fever struck soon afterwards. Then suddenly Jack had a dangerously high temperature. The medical officer of the Guard came and remained. A nurse was summoned and other doctors; specialists were consulted. Meanwhile, Jack complained that his head hurt and that he had an earache.

Through the brown gloom of a dust storm they took Jack to the hospital. For the next three weeks his life hung by an invisible thread. The major trouble was diagnosed as a mastoid in the right ear. The chief surgeon in the eye, ear, nose, and throat department was a Chinese surgeon by the name of Lieu who had a worldwide reputation for his successful operations on mastoids.

Virginia Broaddus, whose husband and son had both suffered from mastoids and who was with the Thomasons during Jack's illness was a consolation to Leda and a great help to the family.

The renowned surgeon operated first on the right ear. In a week a mastoid in the left ear required surgery. In the third week the right ear had to be reopened. Soon the infection extended to the kidneys and other complications developed.

With his only son facing death, John Thomason walked in the hospital corridors alone trying to adjust himself to the idea. His service in the Marine Corps had been extensive and he had observed human suffering, but nothing to prepare him for this.

When Thomason returned to the room, where Leda waited with the doctors, he expected to see the cold waxen image of what had been his son. Instead, John Thomason witnessed a miracle. He saw the life come back into Jack, as the doctors by his bed arose and nodded affirmatively to each other. The crisis had passed.

But Jack's recovery was slow and his parents became habituated to that magnificent hospital facility that served the rich and the poor alike. People paid according to their means; and if they had nothing, they paid nothing. Ricksha coolies took you there if you said simply, "The *Fu*." However, it was more accurately known as the Rockefeller Foundation.

(In May of 1937 John Davison Rockefeller died, having attained the age of 98. His biography by B. F. Winkleman, released soon afterward, inspired Thomason, who by that time had become literary editor of the *American Mercury,* to write the moving account of his son's illness and his indebtedness to the philanthropist. "The century through which he was to live has been perhaps the most eventful in recorded history," Thomason commented, "and he set his impress large upon it." His summation at the end of the article merits scrutiny: "It is the fashion nowadays to regard with cold suspicion the ethics and morals of those individuals of us who accumulate wealth. But, at the risk of being outmoded, I consider the world to be a better place because John Davison Rockefeller lived in it." The article, as it was originally published in the October, 1937, issue of the *Mercury* was captioned *Notes on an Economic Royalist.* Retitled *My Debt to Rockefeller,* it was reprinted in an abridged form in the *Reader's Digest* in January of 1939.)

By December 31, 1930, sales of *Jeb Stuart* reached 6,000 copies and by the ensuing June the book went through four editions with interest still increasing. "Max Perkins writes me that *Jeb Stuart* sold 7,000 copies up to January, which is no bad sale for that type of book in such hard times," John wrote his mother in March of 1931. "He thinks it will double that sale in the year and perhaps continue to sell a little as *Fix Bayonets!* continues to do. It has received more attention . . . than anything I've written and attention of a more intelligent kind."

Whether the success of *Jeb Stuart* had anything to do with it or not, the Army War College was dissatisfied with the results of the collation of the information collected by the panel and tried to persuade Thomason to return to Washington and re-write it. If ironic under the circumstances, it was likewise highly interesting. John wrote his father about it on March 12, 1931:

> The last few weeks I have been pestered with a great deal of radio correspondence from the War College and 2nd Division people. They want me back. The general staff mastermind . . . who was brought in to collate the stuff we did has finished his job and apparently pleased nobody. They want me to return, with a free hand, take charge of the Section, and write the history in its final form myself, according to my own ideas, which is, of course, the only way I would do it.
>
> This is flattering and indicates a sweeping change of heart towards me. They always regarded me with distrust and suspicion because (a) I am a Marine and so not subject to army discipline; (b) I am very young; (c) I have never been to the General Staff Schools. But I have no intention of tying myself up with them again. I am perfectly well here, and my work and surroundings are entirely congenial. I want no more relations with the army.

Meanwhile, Thomason had resumed the writing of short stories with renewed interest. "They are not important," he wrote his father. "But I get a lot of money for them." At the time Thomason was commanding as much as $3,000 for a story.

By June of 1931 Jack had recovered his health to the extent that he had adopted a new hobby inspired by his fondness for the author of *Cowboys North and South.* As usual his father observed from the sidelines with special interest. "Through reading the works of Mr. Will James he [Jack] has decided to go in for roping, throwing the lasso — in a big way" —John wrote his mother, "and has today provided himself with a suitable line. As soon as he gets the kinks out of it, he is going to start serious work with it."

So far the redoubtable pony with which John had provided Jack had been cooperative. John was doubtful, however, that the animal would accept the rope without a struggle. "But I am very curious as to his reaction to the rope . . . I think he will go sideways out from under. But he's built very close to the ground, so it won't matter."

By Christmas Jack had progressed to another special interest — a Marine sergeant's uniform with chevrons on the sleeve. The desire for the uniform was implanted by Colonel Breckenridge, who presented Jack with a sergeant's warrant which authorized him to wear the chevrons on his sleeve.

Jack began his drive in time to have the uniform for Christmas Day. Thomason had his Chinese tailor Men Him create such a uniform in forester green, and Jack modeled it at the Christmas party tendered the captains and their families. Not only did Jack initiate his beautiful uniform with all the swank and swagger that an eleven-year-old could muster, he accoutred it with an old Krag-Jorgenson nickel-plated bayonet that someone's attic had yielded.

Thomason's tour of Asiatic service was extended to a third year because of the government's need to economize and the ostensible Japanese threat to North China. Japan had invaded Manchuria in the summer of 1931, and by the end of January, 1932, had launched attacks on Shanghai. Succeeding events provided Thomason with one of the most exciting experiences of his career.

Still under forty at the time, Thomason was feeling the effects of the fast-paced social life common to the quarter. Innocuously as he had entered into it two years before as the accepted cultural pattern in the Orient, he now had second thoughts.

"I have a year to spend in this romantic land. I hope to weather it out. But there's too much eating, drinking, and dancing for a man of my quiet tastes," he prefaced his journal of the Japanese war to Jim Boyd, January 28, 1932.

"And as I write, the Japanese are barging around with fleets and field armies, looking for trouble which they are sure to find if they persevere." The Japanese had shelled the Woosong forts the day before and had landed in Shanghai. Fighting had persisted for twenty-four hours, and the international forces in Peking were placed on the alert.

"I think the Japanese had sound reason for going into Manchuria," John pointed out, "but their conduct since . . .

convinces me that they have an idea they can lick the world, and it doesn't matter where or when they start . . . They appear to have worked themselves into the same *Weltmacht oder Niedergang* [world domination or downfall] spirit that animated the Germans in 1914. But there has never been a time in the history of the world when there was so much combustible material lying around, as there is now. There could be a new world war tomorrow. . . .''

In his next entry, dated February 4, he states that the Japanese landing force suffered a defeat from the Cantonese battalion in China's 19th Route Army and had to send for reinforcements. "The perambulant Chinese government is fled to Yoyang, the very ancient capital of the middle kingdom, down in Honan below the Yellow River,'' he explained. "It was the Shia capital of the Emperor Wu in the days when Pharoah was a great name in the world. Say 2000 B.C. and the last Chin Emperor ruled there in 1230 before the Mongols took Peking. At any rate, the Japanese can't shell it; no transportation, too far to walk. Meantime . . . we are prepared here [Peking] as well as we can be . . . which may mean much or little . . . I don't believe Peking is important enough to draw serious Japanese aggression. There's nothing here except the ministers and the moribund machinery . . . of . . . the viceregency of the north.''

By February 15 Thomason was able to report that the Japanese had 20,000 regulars and 7,000 Marines ashore since the preceding week in Shanghai and that China was proud of the 19th Route Army's defeat of the Japanese in the Champei district. The 19th Route Army had resorted to guerrilla warfare to stop 3,000 Japanese yellowjackets. The Champei district, congested with mud-walled tenements, masonry, and narrow lanes, was conducive to this type combat and the Japanese had been trained for formal fighting in the so-called grand manner, out in the open.

But Thomason could contain himself no longer. His next entry to the journal dated "Around the 12th April" was made after his return from an observation tour of Shanghai, where he watched the action. "Shortly after the last entry in this journal, I got entirely fed up with Peking, took my life in my hands, and asked the commanding officer for leave to go to Shanghai and observe the events taking place . . . So I got there to see the end of it and had the opportunity to study the field of operations . . . Your letter [his letter to Boyd] was written after the event. But I offer these notes:

"(1) There is a legend of Japanese invincibility which has been accepted in China — and in California — since 1894.

"(2) In Manchuria, 1931, 350,000 Chinese troops organized better than anything else in China fled the hell out of the three eastern provinces before 35,000 Japanese as fast as God would let them. . . .

"(3) The Chinese 19th Route Army — 3 divisions — about 35,000 men — has been fighting somebody for the last twelve years. South Chinese fight. North Chinese don't. The 19th RA came to Shanghai in December as escorts to the Canton government of Sun-Fo and Eugene Chen, which succeeded Chiang Kai-shek. By simply being hardboiled they gradually occupied all the stations around Shanghai, which were formerly garrisoned by the inoffensive North Chinese troops of the Nanking government."

Even though the Japanese, after three attacks, were finally successful in forcing the Chinese to retreat to the Yangtze River, they met with stubborn resistance and lost prestige. First to last, the Japanese engaged 35,000 men and lost 3,500. The Chinese engaged 75,000 and lost 12,000, not counting civilians.

Thomason also described each operation in the most minute detail in a lengthy letter to his father and drew maps to illustrate. "I got down to Shanghai through the kindness of General Breckenridge who gave me 15 days leave toward the end of the fight there and was able to study the field of operations thoroughly immediately after it was over," he wrote the doctor in March. ". . . It is too near now to see results or where it leads. The Japanese myth of invincibility has been shattered . . . The Chinese — at least the Cantonese army — stood and fought and still exists. It may awaken the Chinese to a sense of nationalism."

As an observer attached to the Japanese 11th Division, which pursued the 19th Route Army to the Yangtze River, Thomason got a close view of the Japanese soldier in action.

Whereas he considered the officers in the Japanese army charming companions and good "cup-companions," he appraised the soldiers as inferior. Their regulars were vastly overrated as fighting men in the field. Their ideas on liaison, communication, and supply were confused. They did not understand their weapons. "And all this stuff about *Bushido* to the contrary, notwithstanding," they were no more anxious to die for the Sublime Emperor than was Thomason himself.

Thomason declined to write a story on the Japanese army for the *North American Newspaper Alliance* since his impressions of the Japanese soldier were antithetical to the myth of Japanese invincibility. He honestly felt that from his vantage point he stood to lose more than he would gain by trying to explode the old credo that America must keep herself armed against the terrible Japanese.

In August the Thomasons spent three weeks at Iron Wood Point, the campsite of the Legation Guard at Peitaho Beach. The comfortable quarters for the officers and their families consisted of spacious tents with wooden decks, each equipped with a private shower in a separate compartment in the rear.

The scenic shoreline punctuated by rocky points and headlands, reminiscent of the Catskills, attracted a conglomeration of society. Certainly the Marines held no monopoly on it. "You see every variety of person and of costume from us in beach pajamas and shorts — on men and women — to the sleeved and bloomered bathing suits of the '90's," John wrote his mother, ". . . Among the women you really see more pajamas and shorts than dresses." John himself had become converted to shorts only recently and regretted the years his "legs had suffered unnecessarily."

Always present were the missionaries, who leased houses in the area; the affluent Chinese and foreigners, from Shanghai and other treaty ports, who maintained palatial summer residences at Peitaho. There were invariably the great hordes of Russians — "a dispersed and wretched people" — who dressed in any way possible.

From the point on a clear day the Thomasons could look across the bay at Chinwangtao — the army's summer camp, eight miles away — and watch the transports come in. When the air was clear enough they viewed the eastern tip of the Great Wall, where it was anchored to the sea. It was strange to think of the other end on the border near Tibet, 1800 miles to the west.

Not even five days of bad weather — a windy northeaster and rain — interfered too much with the fun of bathing, fishing, and riding. Although swimming was forbidden to Jack, he had his own boat and his pony. The three returned to Peking on September 2 much refreshed and well.

Before leaving camp, John learned that he would replace the present post adjutant who would be leaving in a few days. The manner in which he came to be chosen was remarkable. The captain in line for the post, as John explained it, was passed over because "he has a young son, who is perhaps the worst boy that ever lived, and the colonel can't bear to have him around. Therefore poor old — — — who wants to be adjutant . . . stays with his company; and I . . . must take over."

The Communist troubles in the vicinity of Hankou were becoming increasingly serious and the nationalist government was still at war with Japan. Yet the average Chinese accepted the unrest stoically. "The Chinese pursue their way with calm," John wrote his father, "while murder and rapine rage in the next street."

A distinguished Chinese gentleman conceded that the times were bad but that the nation had witnessed such times before and they had passed. "It is, in all respects, similar to a period in the Sung Dynasty," he stated. "That was bad, but it passed and tranquillity was restored." The Sung Dynasty exemplified the cultural period from 960 to 1279 and its accomplishments resembled those of Europe in the Renaissance. Aware of this, John asked his friend how long the bad period endured.

"Oh," the Chinese gentleman answered politely, "five hundred years or so."

As post adjutant, Thomason took the additional duties in stride. Moreover, with the Japanese still occupying portions of China, the job demanded substantial responsibility. Arrange-

ments and recommendations for both the defense of the Legation and evacuation, if necessary, were routine duties of the post
adjutant, even though final decisions were in the hands of the
commanding officer.

While his friends in the field of journalism were maximiz-
ing the Japanese war in China, even misrepresenting the overall
situation, Thomason refused to compromise integrity. When
the *North American Newspaper Alliance* cabled him to "Rush
800 words panic siege riots fighting in Peking," he cabled back
"No panic no siege no story in Peking." On the same day his
friends among the newspaper correspondents sent their papers
dispatches about plans to evacuate all of the Americans. "It's
true. There are plans," John wrote. "They were last revised in
1927, and are a part of our routine here."

However, in May of 1933, when the Chinese northern front
at Kubeiken Pass, 60 miles from Peking, and the eastern front at
Tuan Kou, 12 miles from the town, collapsed, tension in Peking
grew in proportion. Three divisions of retreating Chinese troops
entered the city and occupied the east wall and east section.
other divisions settled at the perimeter of Peking to cover the
roads over which the Japanese were expected to advance.

Thomason had been convinced all along that the Japanese
would not penetrate Peking because it had neither tactical nor
strategic value and its occupation would involve international
complications. The situation became extremely sensitive in view
of two circumstances. The area in the east city, around the ob-
servatory, which the troops occupied, was the district where
most of the American residents lived and where the Japanese
colony was quartered. If fighting began there, the people would
have to be brought into the Legation, possibly under unfavorable circumstances, for their evacuation. One third of the command occupied a rifle range outside of the city to the east, which
could not escape involvement if fighting started. The guard
kept roughly one third of its people, together with important
material set up in the area, throughout the summer. Although
to have brought the personnel in would have been prudent, it
would have disarranged the training schedule for the year. Furthermore, the action, more than likely, would have precipitated
panic in the city.

Consequently — since it was his duty — to assess the situation and make recommendations, Thomason insisted that the Americans pursue their routine occupation as though nothing was happening. Thus the Legation Guard maintained an "attitude of outward ease." It necessitated the careful observation of developments so that the guard would have at least a two-hour start in case of an emergency. "We did more actual soldiering in three days," Thomason wrote his father, "than I have done since I left Nicaragua." Just as the tension rose to a breaking point, the two sides agreed on a truce and things eased down. By keeping quiet and refusing to get excited, Thomason felt that they had prevented regrettable incidents from taking shape.

The Japanese took a position twenty-one miles north and about fifteen miles east of Peking. They had control of the railroads and strategic control of China north of the Yellow River, which was probably all they wanted for the present.

Throughout April and May the Chinese fought at Jehol. Although they were defeated, many of them fought admirably with what they had. Thomason admired their stamina. They had poor officers and no modern equipment. They faced Japanese tanks, artillery, and bombing planes with only rifles and bayonets. At no time and no point had the Japanese infantry, unsupported by artillery and bombing, succeeded in driving the Chinese from a position. Not only was the Chinese soldier as brave and enduring as the Japanese, he was more intelligent. Every Chinese was an individual. Thomason concluded that the Chinese soldier was fine military material: "Give him competent leaders, decent training, and adequate weapons, and he will do as well as anybody."

The Thomasons' enjoyment of their three-year stay in the Orient was increased by the presence of visitors from various parts of the world. Their spacious guest quarters, staffed by efficient domestics, were seldom vacant. Among their guests were such interesting people as Alexander Woollcott, Will Rogers, the Frazier Hunts, and Roy Howard.

Woollcott, acerbic critic and radio commentator, who had known Thomason since World War I, when he wrote for the

Stars and Stripes, came to Peking in 1930. A gourmet, said to have been eating his way around the world, Woollcott came to test the famous Peking duck as well as to visit Thomason. "John Thomason never published a sloppy or careless piece of writing," Woollcott said of his friend. "I don't know of one whose output has been more consistently good."

In 1925 Woollcott joined Franklin P. Adams, Heywood Broun, and Laurence Stallings in the newspaper field in New York. A capricious man of widely emulated urbanity, he would later add acting to his repertoire.

Will Rogers — humorist, motion picture actor, and home-spun philosopher, who started his career as a rope-twirling cow-boy — came to Peking in December of 1931. The columnist, who was proud of his American Indian heritage and who bragged that he never met a man he did not like, addressed the Marines for nearly two hours and, as Thomason described it, "put on a gorgeous show." Rogers concurred with Thomason that condi-tions in the United States would not improve until the Demo-crats put a man in the presidential chair. An inveterate traveler and unofficial ambassador of good will, Rogers would die in a plane crash over Alaska with pilot Wiley Post only four years later — August 15, 1935.

The Frazier Hunts arrived in Peking shortly before the Thomasons left for their vacation in Peitaho in 1932 and ac-cepted the invitation to occupy the house while their hosts were away. Hunt — better known as Spike to his intimates — and Thomason had been close friends since Thomason began to write for *Cosmopolitan* in 1926. A representative of the Hearst magazine syndicate, Hunt was interviewing important person-ages as he circled the globe. The next celebrity on his agenda was Chiang Kai-shek at Hankow. He and Mrs. Hunt had just come from Mukden, the chief city in Manchuria. Prior to that they had covered much of Japan and Hunt had interviewed its leaders. No doubt he was also collecting material at this stage for his later book, *MacArthur and the War of Japan,* which Scribner's would bring out in 1944.

Roy Wilson Howard, head of the Scripps-Howard newspa-per chain, visited Thomason in the final year of his tour, 1933.

Howard, a friend of Thomason for over a decade, had been chairman of the newspaper chain since 1922 and was likewise a longtime senior editor of the *New York World-Telegram and Sun*. He had spent two months — April and May of 1933 — observing conditions in the Pacific Ocean. For years a conservative and consistent pacifist in favor of disarmament, Howard was influenced by his observations to reverse his policy.

He told John that the editorial policy of the Scripps-Howard papers on disarmament would be adjusted and that the position had been a mistake. Upon his return to America, he planned to editorialize strongly for a United States Navy measuring up to treaty limits and for the establishment of an adequate army. Undoubtedly Thomason exerted influence on Howard's reversal but would have disclaimed credit.

Despite extra duty and added responsibilities, Thomason managed to devote much time to sketching and writing. He was also able to accept commissions to illustrate books by contemporaries. In 1932 he illustrated Thomas Nelson Page's *Two Little Confederates* and a volume of war verse compiled by Theodore Roosevelt and Grantland Rice — *Taps, Selected Poems of the Great War*. He began editing and illustrating *The Adventures of Davy Crockett*, which Scribner's would release in 1934.

But Thomason's most important work accruing from the Asiatic tour was the volume of short stories titled *Salt Winds and Gobi Dust*, which Scribner's released soon after his return to America. *Salt Winds and Gobi Dust* reflects a seasoned maturity as it explores the intricacies of Oriental culture and its impact on the American Legation Guard. Typical selections include *Mixed Marriage* and *The Story of a Princess*, both of which appeared in *Scribner's Magazine* in 1933; the aforementioned *The Collector* and *Note on Justice*, which originally appeared in *The New Yorker;* the Sergeant Houston story, *The Marine and the Emerald Sweeps;* and the extraordinary *With a Dust Storm Blowing*.

An unusual feature of the work is the individual dedication of some of the thirteen selections. Most of them are inscribed to a particular person by name. But two are exceptions. *With a Dust Storm Blowing* is dedicated "To a Courteous Tipstaff

Whom I Have Never Met," and *Advance Guard,* "To Marine
Detachment *USS Rochester.*"

On August 21, 1933, Thomason received his orders to report to the Department of the Pacific at San Francisco. Four days
later the family took passage on the *USS Chaumont* at Chinwangtao.

In 1936, three years after his return, Thomason would write
an additional half dozen stories depicting life in North China.
These first appeared in the *Saturday Evening Post* and eventually in his final work—*And a Few Marines.* Also in February of
1936 his article entitled *Approach to Peiping,* which was illustrated by twenty-five staff photographs, appeared in the *National Geographic Magazine.* Among the author-artist's personal files were four other stories in holograph relating to the
Orient and to the Legation Guard, which he undoubtedly intended to submit later for publication. With these and other
manuscript were notes and sketches of symbols testifying to
Thomason's absorption in Chinese art and culture.

In Peking Thomason had added sculpture to his media of
artistic expression with exceptional success. Reference has been
made to the bust of Roy Chapman Andrews. In all, Thomason
created perhaps a dozen sculptures that included a portrait of
his son, which he had cast in bronze.

Thus Thomason's tour in Peking represented one of his
richest from the standpoint of creativity despite Jack's illness
and the unsettled state of affairs. Besides, his tour was peculiarly
timely inasmuch as only five years later the mounted detachment was dissolved and the Occidental's place in the Orient was
approaching its inevitable end.

12 Horse-and-Buggy Man

After disembarking at San Francisco on October 4, 1933, Thomason returned to Texas with the understanding that he would report to Washington for reassignment not later than November 28, 1933. To make the trip to Texas he purchased an Auborn car and drove across the country.

Since affairs in Cuba were unsettled, Thomason expected to be recalled for expeditionary duty on short notice. President de facto Grau San Martin's unsatisfactory control of Cuban affairs was grounds for intervention by the United States. The Seventh Marines were reactivated for the emergency and during the fall of 1933 the Second Battalion of that regiment and several ships of the Training Squadron were dispatched to Cuban waters to be ready for the protection of American lives and property ashore if necessary.

But the cautious diplomacy of Ambassador Sumner Welles avoided trouble; and by 1934, upon the assumption of the presidency by Carlos Mendieta, the Platt Amendment, giving the United States the right of intervention, was nullified. While awaiting orders Thomason kept busy. His famous essay *Hunts-*

ville, which John McGinnis, his former freshman English instructor at Southwestern University and later editor of *Southwest Review,* prevailed upon him to write, appeared in the journal in the spring of 1934. Thomason had been collecting material for the essay as he began his Asiatic tour, but the essential charm of the piece is its autobiographic nature — the self-portrait of a groping artist. In August Thomason's story titled *The Mating of a Stamp Collector* appeared in *Scribner's Magazine.*

Thomason received no emergency orders, however. Upon reporting to headquarters at the end of his leave, he was assigned the detail of junior Marine aide to Assistant Secretary of the Navy Henry L. Roosevelt. Although Thomason and Roosevelt had known each other socially prior to the appointment, the former reacted to the post at the outset with mixed feelings. In line for promotion, Thomason was eager to undergo training for field grade officers.

On the other hand, the return to Washington was a kind of homecoming. It put the Thomasons into closer touch with their families in Texas than they had been in the three years in the Orient and reunited them with former friends including the Broadduses, James and Margaret Sykes, and Senator Morris Sheppard, along with close friends attached to the Corps. Robert Thomason, who was studying medicine at Duke University, visited them as often as his academic schedule would permit and Sue, Elizabeth, and Margaret were in and out.

Their place in Cleveland Park was leased. After living temporarily in the Martinique family hotel on Sixteenth Street, the family installed themselves in a comfortable house on December 13 in time to settle down before Christmas. The house was located in Spring Valley on the western edge of the District of Columbia in a wooded sylvan setting. It was a two-story residence witement. The first story consisted of an oversized living room, a central entrance hall running the depth of the house, a large dining room and adjoining kitchen and pantry, and a spacious study and library. The second floor was comprised of five bedrooms and two baths. The garage was in the basement under the study.

As soon as they were settled, the Thomasons enrolled 13-year-old Jack in the cathedral school of St. Albans. He was placed in a form which was equivalent to the high seventh grade. The scholastic standards of the capital schools were higher than those of the English school in Peking. Jack liked the school and began to make real progress.

Although the family missed the luxurious domestic service they enjoyed in Peking, John found himself a black houseboy in a free lunch line downtown and Leda eventually employed two maids who proved to be almost satisfactory. It was also at this time that they acquired the wire-haired terrior Winkie to whom they became attached.

Once the house was running smoothly, the Thomasons had a continual flow of guests from Texas in addition to members of their own families. Mrs. Sarah Gibbs of Huntsville never failed to visit when she came to the national capital to attend the conventions of the Daughters of the American Revolution.

One of the Thomasons' most frequent visitors from the Lone Star State was Paul Wakefield, a friend dating from John's *Chronicle* days in 1917, when the two subsisted essentially off buttered popcorn. Wakefield frequently came alone but at times brought someone with him to the capital, usually a politician, with an axe to grind.

Another Texas visitor was Paul Jones, who was then living in New York and had become an officer in the Institute of Physical Science. It was the first time John had seen or heard of Jones in nine years.

Social demands in Washington seemed at times excessive. For instance, it was not unusual for two affairs to be scheduled for the same evening. Colonel and Mrs. Roosevelt were at home one evening at 5:30 to the foreign naval attachés. Then at 9:00 o'clock they and their aides and wives attended a reception at the White House. The fact that each event necessitated a different uniform further complicated the timing. To Thomason these occasions were more or less perfunctory. Leda seemed to enjoy them more than he.

However, both enjoyed informal weekends spent with friends more than the grand functions. One such affair was a four-day weekend visit at Roosevelt Hall in Skaneateles, New York. "We have had people in our house continually since May, but last week . . . we went on the 20 of July for a weekend with Colonel Ted Roosevelt at Oyster Bay," John wrote the doctor. "He lives very simply in an old house, but his friends and play-mates are the Long Island nobility, and I have never seen such pleasures and palaces."

Roosevelt Hall, the old colonial mansion built around 1830, near the head of Skaneateles Lake — a fifteen-mile-long body of water — provided a delightful place for both bathing and fishing. Skaneateles is one of the largest and the easternmost of a series of elongated streams comprising the scenic Finger Lakes. As always John and Leda enjoyed the beautiful surroundings and welcomed the relief from the scorching capital heat.

As the tour progressed, Thomason and the assistant secretary of the navy enjoyed the sports activities available at Skaneateles.

Since Senator Claude A. Swanson, the secretary of the navy, was seriously ill, the total responsibility of directing naval affairs devolved upon the shoulders of Colonel Roosevelt. Inasmuch as Colonel Roosevelt was an exceedingly active official — entertaining frequently, attending luncheons and formal dinners, making endless inspection trips, participating in ceremonies, and delivering speeches — the work as aide was demanding. Lieutenant Commander Jerauld Wright, a line officer from the navy, was appointed senior aide. Duties of the two assistants included everything from liaison between the diverse bureaus and branches of the naval establishment and the office of the assistant secretary to affairs of a purely social nature. Moreover, the aides accompanied the secretary on his agenda of engagements, served as secretaries and personal confidantes, prepared Colonel Roosevelt's official reports, drafted his speeches, and routed incoming mail.

Despite his time-consuming duties, Thomason found Roosevelt to be an able official and a man of infinite charisma. The two made their local inspections in a converted seventy-five-foot Coast Guard cutter and frequently got in hunting and fishing on the side. Not only did Roosevelt share Thomason's absorption in these sports, he encouraged him to write and sketch. The fact was that he had handpicked Thomason for the detail over a long list of qualified candidates. Soon the two became close friends, their families exchanged visits, and Thomason's experience in Roosevelt's employ was both personally and professionally rewarding. Six months after beginning the assignment Thomason's promotion to the rank of major became effective. "My commission will be along in a few days," he wrote his father, "and then I may with propriety be addressed as major." On December 14, 1933, Colonel Roosevelt awarded Thomason a Silver Star Medal to replace the citation dating from March 17, 1923, in recognition of gallantry demonstrated at Soissons in 1918. The new decoration was authorized by both the army and the navy.

Thomason maintained close contact with his publishers in New York. During the first year of his service as aide to Colonel Roosevelt he toyed with Lee as a possible subject for a biography. The extent to which he was obsessed with the subject of the Confederate general is revealed in a letter he wrote in February of 1934 to James Boyd:

> I have been working intensively on the Lee (when I should have been doing something else). . .
>
> Of course the significant years of Lee's life were the last ten — 1860, say, to 1870. Up to that time the record has only one or two high spots: he was a capable officer, who performed his details with monotonous devotion and wrote pleasant inconsequential letters to a very wide variety of kinsfolks and friends. His family connections, his handsome person, his uniformly high standard of performance in his routine missions, all combine to mold for him the consistent favor of old General Scott. General Scott was a terrific snob, who dearly loved well-connected gentlemen; and when he found a person who was not only of good family and correct address, but also competent, he took excellent care of that man . . . Lee's family and personality got him his early opportunities and his abilities made him equal to them . . . I most preeminently concern myself with *Lee, the Soldier.* It is the fashion to adore him for his greatness in defeat, for his quiet application to pedagogy in Lexington after the war. But without those flaming battles in his background, there would have been nothing particularly arresting in sight of the elderly gen-

tleman. Teaching school, after his professional career, was closed to him. . . .

Now here's my point. None of his letters, none of his reports, none of his recorded conversations, nothing of his well-attested sanctity, piety, and humility, are consistent with the savage and reckless conceptions he brought to his practice of the art of war. Of course, there is historical example for headstrong and furious recklessness in war where great considerations are involved. Frederick the Great's last battle with the Russians — I think Zorndorf is a case in point. But Lee did such things time after time, did them when there was no apparent reason for doing them. . . .

— My mind keeps going back to the fact that Uncle Philip Lee gambled away Stratford — the birthplace — that Father Light Horse Harry was a wild speculator who went to jail for debt. That Lee was only two or three generations away from the gaming, wenching bloods of the Restoration — and that country gentlemen in England never grew to plaster saints. He, the General, was a man of undoubted masculinity, and in every normally equipped male there is just so much hell that has to get out. And all those reckless ancestors, and the repression of forty years of rectitude, found release at Gaines' Mill and 2nd Manassas, at Sharpsburg — oh, particularly at Sharpsburg — at Gettysburg — and at the Bloody Angle. . . . A man is not that man as he stands in his boots; he is also that man's ancestors and all the things that man has wanted to do and didn't.

— Again it looks as though Lee, when he wrote resigning the U.S. service, that he would never again draw his sword except in defense of Virginia, meant almost literally that. He never appeared to have taken much interest in the war outside of Virginia.

I can't escape the conclusion that his personal, carnal love . . . of fighting for fighting's sake was a motivating influence in all his decisions — and also that he was essentially a provincial in his outlook.

— Against all this are arrayed certain imponderables. Millions of men and women believed in him like they believed in God . . . As to his actions, he was on the ground with the tools in his hands — the men under his eye. How far, then, can you honestly judge him . . . If you ever write a bi-

ography, you will see how insidious is the temptation to speculate on what might have been.

    For instance, Jackson. I have recently dug out a statement
. . . that at the time of the Battle of Chancellorsville orders
had been drafted for Jackson to assume command of the Confederate armies in the West. The possibilities behind that order are tremendous. Jackson was the most purely intellectual
type of soldier. There is no way of knowing because he died so
soon, but the probabilities are that he would have been as
outstanding with an army as he was with a corps. . . .

    As indicated James Boyd, another writer on Scribner's list,
and his wife Katherine, of Southern Pines, North Carolina, were
close friends of the Thomasons. A newspaperman and novelist,
whose first work *Drums* published by Scribner's in 1925 had
been a best-seller, Boyd, like Thomason, was a veteran of World
War I. His branch of the service was the American Ambulance
Corps. Besides having the editor Max Perkins in common, the
friends shared similar views on literature, writing, politics, and
world affairs with an absorbing interest in the Civil War theme.
Not only did the couples enjoy visiting each other, for most of
their adult lives the men engaged in a lively and informative
correspondence, which they facetiously categorized as their
"Socratic Dialogues."

    As Colonel Roosevelt's aide, Thomason came in close con-
tact with President Franklin Delano Roosevelt, to whom he
sometimes referred in his letters as the Great White Father and
not always favorably. "I have seen the president at close range
several times," John wrote Dr. Thomason. "He is a compelling
figure. Whether he is right or not, I do not know and I doubt if
he does . . . Colonel Roosevelt says he has known him all of his
life, never thought much of him before, and that his only explanation of it is the man's inspired." The two Roosevelts were
cousins.

    Regardless of his assessment of the president's foreign and
New Deal policies, Thomason was impressed with Roosevelt's
exact and intimate knowledge of all naval affairs. Having served
ably as assistant secretary of the navy during the two terms of
Woodrow Wilson, Roosevelt had come by his knowledge hon-

estly. It was also Thomason's pleasure to learn that President Roosevelt admired him as a writer and kept one of his books on his night table.

Colonel Roosevelt inspected naval and Marine Corps installations on the Atlantic and Pacific coasts and in the West Indies and Hawaiian Islands. In the summer of 1934 he visited the naval shipyards at Charleston (Boston) and Portsmouth (Kittery) and toured the shipbuilding of Bethlehem Steel Company at Quincy, Massachusetts. Thomason accompanied Roosevelt on all of these tours. In December of 1934 the two inspected the naval base at Hampton Roads and the Portsmouth (Norfolk) shipyards, as well as the Newport News Shipbuilding and Drydock Corporation.

In January of 1935, they toured the naval shipyard at Charleston, South Carolina, and the Marine Corps Recruit Depot at Parris Island. While Colonel Roosevelt went on to observe the first of a series of annual fleet landing maneuvers at Culebra Island, Thomason returned to the base at Washington to compile the inspection reports.

The ambitious program of the assistant secretary of the navy concerned the West Indian Islands as a possible future defense of the Western Hemisphere, including the Panama Canal Zone. He planned to improve the naval facilities at Guantanamo Bay, Cuba; the Tenth Naval District at San Juan, Puerto Rico; and the Naval Fuel Depot at Charlotte Amalie (St. Thomas) in the Virgin Islands.

Colonel Roosevelt's plans projected beyond the Eastern Seaboard to the Pacific Ocean. Accordingly, in May and June of the year, he and both aides conducted a series of inspection tours to naval shipyards and shore installations on the West Coast and in Honolulu. After concentrating on anchorages and bases in California on the West Coast, he included in his itinerary a trip to Pearl Harbor.

In California, Colonel Roosevelt and his entourage were guests at the Hearst Ranch at San Simeon, from where John sent Mrs. Thomason of Huntsville a Mother's Day message. ''. . . and it may interest you to know that Miss Marion Davies, early that

Sunday morning, was the one who reminded the party that it was Mother's Day," he wrote her on June 29, 1935.

"To summarize events we left here 2 May, via Chicago, to Seattle; hence to San Francisco; thence to Los Angeles; then to San Diego . . . thence aboard *USS Houston,* to Honolulu, where the Colonel got sick — largely from overexertion — and curtailed our program thereby, thence to Los Angeles returning, and so by train to Chicago and Washington, having been about 5 weeks . . . the colonel departed this morning for a two weeks' vacation at his Skaneateles place, and I look forward to a breathing spell."

Thomason enclosed in his letter a speech he had written for Colonel Roosevelt, who delivered it over NBC hookup on May 9, 1935, Eastern Standard Time, 8:15-8:45. The address defining the American spirit and designed to stimulate patriotism was well received and widely circulated. Thomason had mastered the techniques of speech writing with crisp short sentences and the employment of the apt phrase and carefully chosen quotations to illustrate his points.

Members of the inspection detail took along their rods and reels and tackle, shotguns, and golf clubs, and, depending upon the time and places of visitation, enjoyed their favorite sports. Invariably Thomason took along his notebooks and sketchpads and paints. Furthermore, in spite of irregular hours and constant demands on his time, he managed to do considerable sketching and writing.

Meanwhile, Roosevelt's illness was complicated by high blood pressure, and for the remainder of his term of office he had to content himself with the supervision of those shipyards then employed in rebuilding the United States Navy to comply with treaty limits. Thus, for the first time since 1916, the navy underwent major renovation in the interest of national preparedness and as a vital aspect of President Roosevelt's attempts to combat the depression.

By October 8, 1935, with Congress out of the capital and the speechmaking season for resident officials in full swing, Thomason's duties increased. Much in demand, the colonel had "been on the radio and trumpeting around otherwise." On top of speechwriting at this time, part of Thomason's routine consisted of making digests of long-winded documents dealing with public affairs and reducing ideas and directives to the level of human speech.

At this time Jack Thomason's emergence into young manhood was an infinite source of pleasure to his parents. At fifteen and mature for his age, he had taken his first plane trip to Texas by himself. "Jack returned on schedule time," John wrote his mother. "His trip down placed a great strain on us. Of course, he loved every minute of it . . . and it's silly to be nervous . . . I don't like flying and don't enjoy airplanes, conceding freely that such sentiment brands me as an old fogey. Jack, if he lives, will probably own and operate his own plane, just as I have my little personal Ford roadster. Let him. I'm really a horse-and-buggy man."

(Thomason could not know, ironically, that his son, with his enthusiasm for flying, would be the victim of a plane crash only a few years hence.)

Spending the summer in Texas with his two sets of doting grandparents had agreed with Jack, who declared it was his best vacation ever. He had returned to Washington tanned and taller and with hands and feet so big that he could no longer wear his father's socks, shoes, and gloves, for which Thomason was grateful. But what was particularly gratifying to his father was that his son professed to love Texas. "Living the nomad life we lead, I have been afraid that he would fail to get his roots into something," John confided to his mother. Not only had young Thomason grown up to girls at this tender age, he was already manifesting an interest in foreign service and an aptitude for writing — which propensities were pleasing to both parents.

For years Thomason had been fascinated by one of Napoleon's most flamboyant officers—Jean Baptiste Antoine Marcellin Marbot — a colonel of hussars in 1815, whom the French general had promoted on the eve of Waterloo. Thomason's admiration for the dynamic officer was such that he had carried a copy of the original of Marbot's *Memoirs* around in his Marine gear during World War I with the intention of working on the theme. The editing and illustrating of the work became one of Thomason's major projects during the tour with Colonel Roosevelt.

In preparation he collected several books containing photographs and illustrations of the Napoleonic campaigns in Russia. Published by Scribner's in 1935, *The Adventures of General Marbot* attests further to the author-artist's ability to treat war with zest and humor without sacrificing fidelity to truth.

Actually the work was scheduled for publication in 1934 in time for Christmas. ''. . . but when they sent me the proofs of the drawings, I would not approve the size of some of the reproductions,'' John wrote his mother on February 15, 1935. He protested and, much to his surprise, Scribner's consented to his suggestions. The alteration in size of the illustrations made the book too late for the Christmas list. Then they decided to wait until the next Christmas ''to get a better sale.'' Consequently Scribner's released the work in late summer.

After releasing the book, Editor Perkins, who considered Thomason's illustrations the best he had done up to that time, recommended it to Ernest Hemingway. ''I haven't been able,'' he said, ''to find much of anything worthwhile yet, except the *General Marbot* . . . It is really a grand book. It is a man's book. . . .'' Later it was said that *The Adventures of General Marbot* became for Hemingway a lifelong favorite.

James Boyd also liked the Marbot and gave it a good review in his newspaper, the *Southern Pines Pilot*. John wrote Boyd that Scribner's had paid him for the drawings and that was about all that he expected to get out of it. He himself was tremendously satisfied with the handsome job his publishers had made of the production.

Meanwhile, *''Lee's Men* are marching slowly for me,''John reported. ''And what with one thing and another, both I and the Army of Northern Virginia are a little tired. I'm going to take 30 days' leave in November and December, and hope to get the first two chapters in shape to send Max — who grows impatient. They should be done now, but the last three weeks I had to take time out to write some stories.'' It is of interest that at this point Thomason has shifted his interest to Lee's men instead of Lee, the Soldier as he had originally planned.

By the end of October he was writing again to Boyd, who had invited him to come to Southern Pines to work on the Lee project. "... I'd like nothing better — as I need not tell you. Later this year I may take advantage of it, for I do not think I will be able to launch my Confederate book here. I had no luck with Stuart until I went into retreat there at Southern Pines." Still he was sidetracked again: "I am doing some blood-and-thunder stuff — to specifications — for the Sat. Eve. Post . . . This keeps my liquor dealers in the style to which they are accustomed." The truth was that Thomason and his family had moved up to a more expensive lifestyle that required the additional income that the big slicks paid him for work on short notice.

However the author-artist's productivity, in addition to the Marbot project, was enormous. He contributed *Note on the Employment Situation, Shanghai Racket,* and *Service with a Smile* to *The New Yorker* in 1935, and *Washington Racket* in 1936, together with illustrations. He published *Our Disappearing Ducks,* an appeal for the conservation of wildlife, in the May, 1935, issue of the *Saturday Evening Post.* In subsequent issues of the *Post* he introduced his famous Marine character, Sergeant Houston, in *The Sergeant and the Spy* and *The Sergeant and the Bandits.* Rough-hewn and romantic, Sergeant Houston—an actual Marine Thomason knew—bore the stamp of Leatherneck tradition and even resembled Thomason himself. In 1936 Thomason wrote the foreword to *The Romantic Flags of Texas* by Mamie Wynne Cox of Huntsville.

Nor had he abandoned the Lee study at this time despite the appearance of the four-volume, definitive Freeman biography of the "General of the lost cause" in 1935. As a matter of fact, Thomason's review of the work in approximately 2,500 words was featured in the *Dallas Morning News,* March 10, 1935. Since Thomason did nothing carelessly, his sustained review of the Lee biography is in itself a worthy piece of literary criticism. Proclaiming the book, which took Freeman twenty years to write, the "best American biography of his time," John sent his father a set.

"The first chapter of the book I am now writing is all on Lee," he wrote his father. "I am trying to get his vital essence into 8,000 words . . . There is no difficulty in ascertaining the facts of Lee's career . . . But the difficulty of the biographers has been, not to find out where he was, whom he saw, and what he did, but to reconcile the flaming things he did with his character as the memoirs and his own writings show him. No biographer of his has ever said so, and my friend Dr. Freeman would repudiate the idea with as much violence as he could muster, but it is my conviction, from more than ten years' professional study, that Lee the soldier loved being a soldier and loved to fight. . . .

"Lee should not have failed. But no great captain has ever been successful, who was not in combination with some great political head . . . Molte and Bismarck, for example. War, except as a politic instrument, is sterile. The soldier's achievements become significant when applied to the broad political situation by the statesman . . . Frederick and Napoleon were exceptions, but they combined in themselves both the head of the army and the head of the state. Wellington was a lesser captain than Napoleon, but he had behind him Castlereagh and Metternich . . . Grant had Lincoln. Lee, unquestionably one of the great commanders, was backed by no statesman of equal stature. . . ."

While Colonel Roosevelt had curtailed his activities for the sake of his health, Thomason secured a month's leave in November of 1935 and he and his family returned to Texas for a vacation.

By this time Thomason had achieved celebrity status in his native state and was eagerly sought out and interviewed by the press. Still somewhat shy, he nevertheless met the reporters with surprising equanimity and fielded their questions skilfully. He was particularly well received in Houston, where he had begun his writing career on the *Houston Chronicle* before World War I. The fact that he had completed a three-year tour in the Orient before assuming his present post with Colonel Roosevelt, assistant secretary of the navy, added to his stature.

The newsmen sounded him out on being indigenous to Texas. He informed them that no matter where his Marine duties called him, he would never forget that he was a Texan. "I always will remain a Texan," he said. "I love the state and I love its people. They are different. Texas is not a mere geographical or political division — it's a race of people. They look and act in a different way."

At the time Thomason was still working on Lee and the Army of Northern Virginia — a work tentatively called *Lee's Men.* "The more I study Lee, the more I discover that he did not have a broad conception of war and its objectives," he told newsmen. "In his philosophy and approach to war Lee was in a real sense feudal and medieval. His main idea was just to fight the enemy. . . ."

"The man in the war between the states who best knew the objective of war and how to reach it was General [William Tecumseh] Sherman of the Northern forces. He was a modern soldier — far, far ahead of his time.

"The big trouble with the South was that there was no one who knew what war was all about. The South had good generals and gallant soldiers — better fighters than the North had, but in Secretary of War [Edwin M.] Stanton, hated and despicable as he was in many respects, the North had a war minister who knew the objective and the ways to reach it. I think the three greatest ministers of war in modern times have been Napoleon's Carnot, Stanton, and Newton D. Baker."

"Major, if you go back to foreign service, where would you like to go this time — you have been in Europe, Asia, and South America — ?"

"Oh, anywhere with the troops," Thomason replied without hesitation.

"China was a wonderful land in which to live — and take things easy," he admitted. He had had three years in Peking. "But three years is all you ought to live in China, . . . If you stay longer you will be lulled to sleep, you'll be corroded!"

Asked which of his writings gave him the most pleasure, Thomason named the Stuart biography, which had been exceedingly popular with the Texas audience. "He [General Stuart] was a gorgeous character! It was a joy digging into his colorful career."

The last two services Major Thomason performed for Colonel Roosevelt were to plan his funeral and assist in his burial. When Thomason returned to Washington he found that Colonel Roosevelt's condition had worsened. The assistant secretary's role in building up the United States Navy had exacted its penalty.

On the morning of February 22, 1936, the United States Naval Hospital staff had called in the best cardiologists and heart surgeons in the area. The doctors consulted through the forenoon, and the colonel seemed to be improved. John took his family home, feeling that a shadow had lifted. But Dr. Carl Broaddus, the navy doctor, called John back from the car. He said that he was just a country doctor, but that things didn't look good to him.

Half an hour later Colonel Roosevelt died, "like a man dies shot through the heart," as Thomason described it to Dr. Thomason. "It was at least quick and merciful. He had suffered some, but at the end, it was all done in three breaths."

Earlier that day Thomason had visited the colonel. Roosevelt had made a few jokes, asked about Leda and Jack. He rallied remarkably, showed an interest in all the people around him . . . insisted that as soon as he was up, he would take John and Carl Broaddus to Key West for a real vacation.

The impact of Roosevelt's death is further reflected in the letter Thomason wrote to his father: ". . . He was a very gracious gentleman . . . a splendid public servant . . . He was young, only fifty-six, and he should have been good for another twenty years. But his energy drove him to tasks beyond reason. He worked us all hard, but he worked himself hardest of all. He was a driving, dynamic person; but with all that he never lost the human touch. Seeing large things and handling large affairs, he could always realize the individual.

"Most of his life he served the Republic. As assistant secretary of the navy, in a critical time . . . he has carried the whole load, taken all the criticism, and except for a few people close to him, had none of the credit. He was genial and kind and loved all the good things of life. His relation with his family was beautiful. I shall not know his like again."

Leda, who had been called to Texas because of illness in her family, returned to Washington in time to help select the gravesite of Roosevelt in Arlington. She was a favorite of the Roosevelt family and would miss the colonel. From the hour of the colonel's passing on Saturday, the 22nd, to the day of his interment on the 25th, Aides Wright and Thomason literally worked around the clock to perfect details. With the concurrence of the family, they turned down President Roosevelt's offer of the White House as the place for the memorial service. Instead they chose the little church of St. John's from which to hold the religious ceremonies.

Still, as Thomason described it, ''They gave him a grand funeral, the kind of funeral given to the most distinguished men . . . It was a very general recognition, which was never expressed in his lifetime, of the place he filled in the government . . . with the President, the Vice President, the cabinet, and the little cabinet, and the diplomatic corps attending. There were seven ambassadors . . . and the high ranking officers of the services [armed forces]. There were also rough-hewed delegations from labor unions and shop committees out of the shipyards, to whose representatives he [Roosevelt] never failed to listen with patience and reason.'' Thomason, knowing that the colonel would have wished it, saw that these latter were seated where they could see. There were also in attendance the shipbuilders and two elderly black menservants who had revered the deceased.

The admirals of the navy and the commandant of the Marines were pallbearers. A mile and a quarter of Marines and sailors preceded the cortege to Arlington. Thomason and Wright marched in front of the casket bearing Colonel Roosevelt's flag.

As tired as the two were on the evening of February 25, after Roosevelt's burial in Arlington, both could very well be proud of their ''last job for him.'' Finally, ''I've been greatly privileged in my duty here,'' John confided to Dr. Thomason, ''I feel as though I had come to the end of a trajectory. An aide serves in a position, both personally and officially, of a peculiar intimacy. I do not think that I can ever give such service again.''

Immediately Thomason set about clearing up unfinished

business and attending to such details as were necessary to insure a smooth transfer of the office to Roosevelt's successor, Admiral Standley, acting assistant secretary of the navy, under whom he served for the remaining months of the tour. Secretary of the Navy Swanson was still confined to the hospital.

Much of Thomason's work was tedious and undoubtedly painful. In the midst of it Mrs. Roosevelt insisted that he select from the deceased's personal effects a keepsake. John, who had a predilection for walking sticks, chose Colonel Roosevelt's birch cane to which the assistant secretary had been attached.

Before leaving the office on Constitution Avenue, Thomason was notified by the University of Texas at Austin, which he had attended one year, that it had elected him to honorary membership to the Phi Beta Kappa Society. In January of 1937 President Roosevelt named Charles Edison of New Jersey as assistant secretary of the navy.

At the termination of his duty and before reporting to the Army War College at Fort Humphreys in September for his next assignment, Thomason and Leda vacationed in Canada. They stayed at a place on the St. Lawrence River called Chamard's Lorne House. "Chamard's is a long wooden barn of a place," John wrote his mother, " — a little different from anything I know and it's on the quiet side, which I like. The meals are simple and adequate. We have one of the few rooms with bath. It's not expensive. There's a good golf course right below it and a very fine one over beyond the Manor Richelieu. . . ."

John had found a good library in the vicinity and any number of interesting people to converse with while Leda enjoyed bridge nearly every day. Before returning to Washington, John and Leda joined Jim and Katherine Boyd in Toronto, Canada, for a brief visit.

In compliance with his request, Jack was permitted to spend the time with his grandparents in Huntsville. At sixteen Jack had excelled in school, he was gregarious, and handled himself well whether he was with young people or adults. Besides he was popular with the younger set of Huntsville and had a job. He served as chauffeur for Dr. Thomason just as his father, before him, had held the reins from the driver's seat of a buggy.

Colonel John W. Thomason, 1942. This was thought to be Colonel Thomason's last formal photograph. Made by Harris and Ewing, Washington, D.C.

— Courtesy Sue Thomason Noordberg

13 Literary Editor of the American Mercury

Controversial Henry L. Mencken, co-founder of the *American Mercury,* with George Jean Nathan, and its longtime editor, is best remembered for his criticism of American life and championship of the American language. But it was neither as a critic nor as a linguistic scholar that he made one of his foremost contributions to American letters — namely, the recognition of the genius of John W. Thomason. His offer of the literary editorship of the magazine to Thomason resulted not only in a literary profile of the late thirties in itself unique, it also provided a compelling psychological portrait of the author.

> Why don't you review some books for us? [Mencken wrote Thomason.] We'll send you your choice of all the books published in the United States every month. What you'll do will be to select a book that interests you, and write us a little article on it, say, two thousand words or so. Anything that comes into your head. Then give us a sentence or two on the others, for the Check List. And we'll pay you such-and-such. How about it?

Almost immediately after Thomason reported for duty at the Army War College at Fort Humphreys in the summer of 1936, he assumed the chair of literary editor of the *American Mercury.* As a result what could have developed into a monotonous ten-month grind became an exciting experience as Thomason submitted his monthly contribution to the magazine in addition to performing his duties at the post. The very nature of the assignment accounts in some degree for Thomason's originality in the articles. Moreover, it gave the writer a latitude that allowed him to voice his individual views on subjects of his selection and, at the same time, explore another genre of writing — the informal essay as a vehicle of literary criticism.

He had reviewed books for the magazine for several years, and certainly he did not accept the post without serious thought: "This summer when the magazine was reorganized," he wrote to his father, on November 16, 1936, "they requested me to serve as literary editor and backed the offer up with enough money to pay my rent. I placed the proposition before the Secretary of the Navy, through the Major General Commandant and the Chief of Naval Operations, officially and in writing. They gave their official approval to my so serving."

Thomason had nothing to do with policy. The *Mercury's* idea was to maintain a sort of open forum, to which anyone could contribute who desired a hearing and could frame his thoughts in acceptable English. "If the magazine should turn sour on me, I can always resign . . ." he explained, ". . . In my own writings, I am entirely non-political . . . But if we achieve a fascist state, and they measure us for muzzlers, I can always retire to the country west of Huntsville, where I think I would not starve." His reference to "the country west of Huntsville" was to Oakland, the ancestral Thomason home.

At the inception of his editorship Thomason's subjects played the scale of diversity from titans of world history to a contemporary black deity of Harlem and included afflictions of the great, the subject of war, and current fiction. The essays began with Genghis Khan, Temujin, who opened up the East and the West.

Although centuries separated them, Julius Caesar, Christopher Columbus, and Peter Romanof had in common dissatisfaction with their respective worlds and each succeeded in changing it. Caesar established the Roman Empire, Columbus expanded the world's frontiers by a couple of continents, and Peter the Great forcibly modernized Russia. Father Divine — who was not born but "combusted in 1900 on the corner of Broadway and 134th Street," was chiefly distinguished by the orchid Rolls-Royce and red monoplane in which he contacted his converts.

Through the years readers have been aware that Julius Caesar was subject to epileptic seizures, that eighteenth-century Samuel Johnson was scrofulous and bloated with indigestion, and that nineteenth-century Byron was breeched with a clubfoot. Fewer probably knew that Columbus was plagued with syphilis, that Montaigne's gravel affected his essays, or that Pepys, the diarist, underwent gall stone surgery without benefit of anesthesia.

It was Thomason's deduction that James Kemble in *Idols and Invalids,* reviewed in the October, 1936, issue of the *Mercury,* was not interested so much in exposing the irregularities of the famous but "the whimsical and tragic halter ropes by which the flesh checks the vaulting spirit . . . and the way in which a royal spirochete has . . . altered national destiny."

Since the world in the late 1930s was girding itself for the second global holocaust, many books appeared on the subject of war. Thomason considers three in a single article: one by former Secretary of War Newton D. Baker, one by the socialist Norman Thomas, and one by author T. H. Wintringham. Both war and love, Thomason philosophizes, have functioned as institutions for a long time, but not one has been able to mitigate either.

Baker, in *War in the Modern World,* investigates the inherent causes and objects of war as an institution. His only hope for the prevention of war is by international agreement. While Thomason concurs in part with Baker's major premise, he is more objective and defines war as "the weapon of decision which men take up when their milder arguments fail of accomplishment. Men have used the weapon for a long time and," says Thomason, "will continue to use it until self-interest, no less than altruism, impels them to a better way."

Thomas's book — *War: No Profit, No Glory, No Need* — is, in the reviewer's opinion, as emotional as its frantic title indicates. To prove that no glory attaches to war Thomas quotes poetry and discredits "the poor professional soldiers" who only fight a war "after their masters, the politicos, have brought it about." The author devotes considerable space to the question of Why Men Fight without giving the obvious answer, which, according to Thomason, is "because they want to fight."

Thomason rebuts Thomas's plea for disarmament, as the nation's arms race progressed, with the observation that altruistic experiment is a lonesome road. "There can be no compromise in national security."

With patience he answers Thomas's proposal of a *defensive navy* as a solution to war. Although the American navy may employ lines of defensive strategy, that is not enough. "In a war offensive tactics (not defensive) are the only tactics" that win. "There is no second prize in battle. A second best navy never wins."

Thomason categorizes Wintringham's *The Coming World War* as "a calm book without exclamation points." He agrees with the writer that the next war would be more mechanized than the first World War with the air force playing a greater part than it did in 1918. Altogether Thomason finds Wintringham's arguments thoughtful and sound. Interestingly enough, both Thomason and the author proved to be correct in their predictions about World War II. Thomason's summation on the subject of war as an institution is relevant. "Before war can be abolished, it must be controlled . . . But it is by data, rather than denunciation, and through proper deduction from data assembled, rather than in hysteria, that men will find their way to the solution of the problem."

Thomason approaches the criticism of fiction gingerly, because — unlike writers of biography and history who deal with known facts — the novelist relies upon himself to create his own material. Of the six novels reviewed in 1936, two involving the American scene and one the South Seas are characteristic.

The first is *The Lorenzo Bunch* by Booth Tarkington. Although the winner of the Pulitzer Prize in 1922 and the author of *Monsieur Beaucaire* and *The Magnificent Ambersons* had passed his heyday, Thomason remains loyal. Tarkington's *The Lorenzo Bunch* is further proof to Thomason that no one of the time equalled the novelist in the portrayal of contemporary American life. The novelist writes "as Franz Hals painted, with a swaggering simplicity." Thomason concludes that ". . . you feel with him [Tarkington] that the garden-variety American, for all his defects, is still pretty decent under pressure. . . ."

The second novel, *Honey in the Horn,* by H. L. Davis, takes its title from the ribald ballad, which begins:

. . . He met her in the lane and he laid her on a board,
But he played her up a tune called Sugar in the Gourd.
Sugar in the gourd, honey in the horn.
Balance to your pardners, honey in the horn —

Set in Oregon and relating the experiences of the orphan Clay Calvert, the Pulitzer Prize-winning novel reminds Thomason of another classic dealing with a wanderer, *Huckleberry Finn,* and another talented reporter of the American scene, his favorite — Mark Twain.

Thomason finds *The Hurricane,* by Charles Nordhoff and James Norman Hall, to be "a fine workmanlike piece of writing with no foolishness about it." Moreover, it compares favorably with such masters of the hurricane story as Joseph Conrad and Lafcadio Hearn. The collaborators Nordoff and Hall also treat effectively the aspects of loneliness and mystery of the South Seas.

Since Thomason had spent almost three years at the Army War College while he worked on the history of the Second Division, he was aware of the excellent research facilities at the post's library and archival materials essential for special study. These sources of material, combined with those of the Library of Congress and the National Archives, provided ample data for his military research as well as grist for the mill of his editorial commitment.

That Thomason could discharge his editorial chores simultaneously with his military duties without neglecting either was

confirmed by his Certificate of Completion, signed by the commandant at the end of the tour: "His [Thomason's] presence has
been of material assistance to us in advancing our instruction here
and has contributed greatly to the better understanding of the
mutual cooperation that must exist between the two services."

But that he found time to engage in other important creative pursuits at the same time is incredible. In November of
1936 he began the publication of his first novel in a six-part serial in the *Saturday Evening Post*. The magazine announced the
series on the editorial page as a publishing event in an article titled "Meet the Major." After identifying Thomason as the creator of the Sergeant John Houston stories and the man who was
equally at home on the China Coast or the Rio Grande, the article quoted a capsulated autobiography of the author-artist.

Thomason never failed to give credit to those who had
helped him along the way. After summarizing his education, he
stated: "Later I reported for the *Houston Chronicle* under M. E.
Foster and C. B. Gillespie, who between them, taught me whatever I learned about writing."

Then following a resume of his military career, he described
his family: "Married a Texas girl who is still patient with me.
Have one son, sixteen, now two inches taller than I am, to my
chagrin. . . ." Undoubtedly a man of Thomason's multi-faceted
personality and achievements was not an easy man to live with,
but Leda Thomason herself was no ordinary woman.

About himself personally, Thomason wrote: ". . . Not
much on games; a little polo . . . very bad golf. Have ridden a
lot of horses and shot a lot of guns. As much shooting and fishing as I can get. Enjoy food, drink, open country, conversation,
and the profession of arms. No particular ambition outside the
last, except that I have one more book on the Southern Confederacy in my system."

If Thomason was feeling the strain of overwork at this time,
he was uncomplaining and retained his forthright sense of
humor. He was forty-three that year, he said, and knew of nothing he could do about it. "But I still have all my teeth." The
sketch was accompanied by a photograph of Thomason in uniform reflecting his customary stance with thumbs tucked inside
his belt.

John Thomason received a large volume of fan mail. The appearance of the story in the *Post* prompted an unusual one. It was from Margaret Reese Potter, a former citizen of his hometown and friend of the Thomason family. "I was delighted to see in the *Saturday Evening Post* of November 14, not only one of your inimitable stories, but a personal sketch of the author," the lady wrote. "It came as a distinct shock to learn that you had attained the venerable age of forty-three, for when I saw you last you were in your early twenties. There is still a striking resemblance in this picture of the typical military man who has ridden a lot of horses and shot a lot of guns, to the meticulous young captain who had just taken unto himself a bride, 'a Texas girl' who played the violin. The slim waist and the thin face are the same, but that nonchalant air comes only from years of practice. . . .

". . . I remember you in a way that should be gratifying, not to say flattering. My husband was pastor of the Methodist Church in Huntsville during the fateful years of 1914–1918, and you were one of our first World War heroes . . . It was quite an event for us to go over to the home and hear one of your letters read. How proud your mother was of those letters! They were her *Croix de Guerre,* her Victoria Cross, her own D.S. medal . . . I gloried in the magic of your words. Your pen-and-ink sketches, however clever, were really not necessary, so vivid were your pen pictures. I used to sit wide-eyed and breathless through the reading of the letters. . . .

"Out of the maze of memories of those tragic years certain incidents stand out clear-cut as a cameo. Do you recall the story your father used to tell of a certain cleaning and pressing bill presented by you shortly after you entered Southwestern University? To him the bill seemed unnecessarily large, and he mildly suggested that he hadn't had that much pressing done in a decade . . . Your retort courteous was, 'Yes, but look at the difference between your trousers and mine!'

"I have read all your short stories and enjoyed them immensely (What pals you and Mark Twain would have been!). This last one . . . swept a nostalgic wave across my heart. I have lived outside of Texas for ten years, and have just moved to Jonesboro, Arkansas." She equated Texas with Dixie: "But whenever I am asked, 'Is it true what they say about Dixie?' I invariably reply, 'Every word of it's true, but the half has never been told. . . .' "

The novel published by Scribner's in 1937 at the conclusion of the series in the *Post* was entitled *Gone to Texas*. It is concerned with the romance of a swashbuckling Yankee officer who is tamed by a Rebel spitfire against the backdrop of intrigue and hell-for-leather gunplay on both sides of the Rio Grande. Set in the immediate post-Civil War era in Texas, the book's profuse illustrations are so faithful to the theme that you can almost hear the characters' inflections of the Southern drawl, for which Thomason had a keen ear.

Although Thomason conceded that he was talked into writing the novel and felt that it was not one of his best works, *Gone to Texas* was well received. "Since I last saw you, I have all unwittingly wandered into writing a novel," John wrote to Jim Boyd. "I may have mentioned at Bar Harbor Max Perkins's ordering a series laid in Texas. 1868. Short stories. But they didn't jell . . . Max discerned a novel in them at once and I said I'd deliver the manuscript by 1 July. Now God help me, I have two more stories to do. I have got these damn people into messes that I can't possibly get them out of. . . . On top of which I labor diligently at the Army War College and have other responsibilities . . . What shall I do with Lt. Ed Cantrell, Miss Brandon Hawkes, and Miss Vashti Silver? God knows, I don't."

True enough Thomason maneuvers the three principal characters into an almost untenable predicament: in a fit of temper Brandon Hawkes shoots Ed Cantrell; they fall madly in love while she supervises his recovery in her home as her guardian secessionist uncle opposes the match; and Miss Vashti Silver faces a streak of bad luck. Her wagon train freighting a cargo of 100 bales of cotton is robbed by a gang on the Laredo road, the wagon-master slain, and the best mules driven off. And now with an order for 277 head of horses on a government contract, and a sizable gun-running deal in progress, her main agent quite inopportunely gets himself wanted for murder.

The success of the series both as separate short stories and as Thomason's first novel confirms his uncontested ability to resolve the plotting. An interesting sidelight on the publishing of *Gone to Texas* is the respective assessments of two of the greatest editors of the time. While Perkins of Scribner's felt the stories did not stand alone but would publish them as a novel, George Horace Lorimer, popular editor in chief of the *Saturday Evening Post,* hailed their exposure as a series of short stories to be a breakthrough in publishing history.

Thomason's prodigious output for 1937 also included the story *Scow-Gun Marriage,* which was featured in the December 4 issue of the *Post* and illustrated by the author. *Scow-Gun Marriage* is a game conservation tale with a novel twist. The inbred inhabitants of Drowned Island are employing the expensive and illegal scow-guns to kill migratory birds — specifically ducks — their main source of economy. To stop the violation the Federal Bureau for Game Conservation sends a young agent to locate the guns and get the identities of the perpetrators. The story is an excellent example of Thomason's ability to follow the conventional structural principles of writing when it suited his purpose.

At the close of his tour with the Army War College in June of 1937, Thomason was assigned to the Naval War College at Newport, Rhode Island. By the month of July he was one of nine Marine officers and sixty-one line officers enrolled in the nation's oldest service institutions of its kind.

Two important events marked the new assignment. In October, Thomason was notified of his promotion to the rank of lieutenant colonel. "By the way," he informed his mother, "I make my number as lieutenant colonel on the 1 November." Somewhat later he was awarded the Navy Cross. Having seen a notice of it in the local Huntsville newspaper, the *Item,* which was misleading, he explained the true conditions under which the award was — or would be — made. His letter dated March 8, 1937, states:

> I was recommended for that affair in July, 1918. The Army gave me a decoration which I have worn for years: it is the Silver Star . . . A recommendation was turned in, in process of time, to the Navy, along with a number of others. The Navy Board of Awards sat on them. They were listed in alpha-

betical order, and when the board was about in the middle of
the alphabet, they were ordered to desist. I don't know the circumstances; it was in Daniels' time. Last year the decorations,
or rather, the recommendations for the same were brought up
for reconsideration, and very much against my advice and
wishes, they framed mine in a special bill and put it in the way
of legislation. I understand it is a sort of test case, and if it is
granted, it opens the way for reconsideration of the whole list. I
have declined to be interested in it, and sincerely wish that it
had not come up this way. What I did is noted on my military
record; and I have seen so much chicanery and politics in the
matter of decorations that I have no respect for them at all. Besides, I want no decoration from the Congress. I have seen the
Congress at close range. They may, collectively and individual-
ly, be high authority on many important matters, but I have
never heard anything that makes me to believe them competent to judge "gallantry above and beyond the call of duty."
The present status is that the Senate has passed the bill making
the award, and it is now on the House calendar, but I don't
know when it comes up before that august body. I had not
known until I saw the *Item* today that Senator Sheppard was in
any way connected with the business. If that is true, I shall have
to go and make my manners to him, however it turns out, and
I dislike such things. I think I have from you my unwillingness
to be under obligations to anybody.

Soon the family of three were ensconced in a cottage on
Washington Street convenient to both the business section of the
city and the beach. "Our house is small, but has everything we
need in it," John wrote his mother, "and our servant, an Irish
woman, is about the best cook we ever had." The only drawback
to the small house was that they had no room for guests.

"Newport is a quaint little old town, a curious mixture of
old and new," John wrote. "Our street is on the Bay and the
houses bear markers indicating the various generals and admirals
of Rochambeau and De Grasse who were quartered in them when
the French Expeditionary Force lay here during the Revolution.
There are still some respectable people on the shores and the old
cemetery is close behind us. Also the stores. The modern town
has grown up inland. But on the point, south of us, are the great

houses of the very rich and their estates. The streets of the various parts are crooked and narrow like Charleston, S.C. — most of them are one way, and all of them ought to be."

The family took to Newport from the very start. "We have been here no more than six weeks, and I have never known the time to pass so quickly," John declared. "We both like Newport very much and Jack, in spite of his gloomy predictions, is having what appears to be a wonderful time. There are any number of young gentlemen and young ladies about his age, and they lie on the beach all afternoon, dance all night, and sleep all morning. At least that appears to be their routine."

The new tour of duty had several advantages. The first was the location of the base. Not only was Newport the site of the navy's most important shore installation, it was the most fashionable resort of the Atlantic seaboard providing unusual entertainment and sports which were open to the officers of Fort Adams and the staff and student body of the Naval War College. Besides the stimulating social life and entertainment there were other assets. Among these were the so-called Reading Room — an exclusive men's club — and its quiet gardens at 29 Bellevue, where Thomason did much of his work. One of the Marine's watercolors, *The Rebel Yell,* adorns a wall of one of the club rooms.

Still another asset was the scenery of Newport. It was conducive to the early morning walks and afternoon drives and excursions to which Thomason and his family had accustomed themselves. The Marine officer, accompanied by his dog and usually his tall son, enjoyed regular morning hikes along Cliff Walk, which followed the northern shoreline to Bailey's Beach, where they could take a dip if they chose. The family took afternoon rides along lovely Ocean Drive beyond the showplace homes of the summer colony and the golf club. They enjoyed the cup races and regattas, and when his schedule permitted, Thomason put in time at the golf club and the race track and engaged in water sports.

The chief advantage of the Newport tour was that it permitted Thomason's literary editorship of the *American Mercury* to continue uninterrupted. By this time his articles had begun to attract much favorable attention, some of it from readers who found it difficult to believe that such wisdom and widespread knowledge belonged to a man who was primarily a career officer in the United States Marine Corps.

From January 1937 to January 1939, Thomason produced more than two dozen essays that progressed from the lives of such international figures as Lincoln, Napoleon, John D. Rockefeller, Henry Adams, John J. Audubon, and Rudyard Kipling to world affairs and major issues confronting American life. The literary profile for which Thomason was responsible included the unsettled conditions of Europe, the Japanese threat to the Orient, the nature of the coming global conflict, along with topics as divergent as the Bible, the Southern viewpoint, personal reflections on book reviewing, the cure for alcoholism, the conquest of pain, and the impact of Puritanism on American culture. Nor did Thomason ignore his native state of Texas.

The essay entitled *The Best Best-Seller,* prompted by *The Bible Designed To Be Read As Living Literature,* edited by Ernest Sutherland Bates, was the literary editor's first offering for 1937. To introduce it, Thomason meticulously traces the antecedents of the King James version of the Bible and shows the publication's impact upon religious freedom and printing.

Citing the King James version as the most important book in the English language, Thomason notes that institutions as antithetical as slavery and foreign missions may be justified on Biblical sanction. Moreover, whole generations have found in the scriptures a way of life. As a case in point, he cites the style of Kipling, Pearl Buck and Ernest Hemingway:

> As to Kipling, read his *Collected Verse* with the Old Testament at your elbow. He owes much to the minor prophets and to Kings and Chronicles. Mme. Buck's narrative is the method of the Old Testament, unmistakeable in its rhythm and balance . . . Hemingway, who, if he ever sees this comment, will probably be annoyed, has the hard lapidary verbiage of the Book of Joshua.

For one who read the Bible through three times by the age of ten and admitted that he himself owed the force of his own style of writing to it, Thomason speaks with authority.

The Bible, says Thomason, is the most convincing and comprehensive record of human experience and aspiration existing in the world. In the edition edited by Bates, the books are arranged chronologically and by classification: histories, stories, drama, and poetry — with a brief preface orientating each book to the overall arrangement. Thomason also notes that Bates is considerably indebted to the King James version as a source.

Thomason finds the living parallels between Biblical happenings and the contemporary scene provocative. There is, for example, the general and administrator who brought the Israelites into the Promised Land — Joshua, whose modern counterpart is the professional staff officer, impersonal in war, in statesmanship, and in government. The apprehension of the Canaanites as the Chosen People on the Southern horizon finds an interesting analogue in representations before the League of Nations as one of the principal powers begins to pursue its Manifest Destiny.

Of particular interest are the living parallels between the Biblical situations and the American political scene of the thirties. For instance, "Not even the Old Guard have devised such mouth-filling curses against the New Deal as lurk in the chapters of Jeremiah and Lamentations." Despite the proponents of Roosevelt's New Deal policy, vocal opponents were convinced that it was undermining the foundations of American freedom, and Thomason was well aware of this.

Among the short stories, *Ruth* is "a lovely tale for any time and land . . ." The character Daniel is "a man of talent" and the woman Esther, "a clever Jewish young lady who . . . saved her people from an early Persian pogrom . . ." Finally, there is *Ecclesiastes*, "as cynically wise, and as utterly pagan, as anything that ever proceeded from Grecian groves."

In *Reflections on Book Reviewing* you get a second glimpse of the impressionable boy lying on the rug in his father's library. You observe him there feasting upon the rich illustrations of books like *Idylls of the King*, the Doré Bibles, and others. But you get more. You follow the boy's reading regimen up to the time that he entered college.

Dr. Thomason began his son's reading of fiction with Dickens' *David Copperfield*, too early to generate enthusiasm. Thom-

ason remembered *David Copperfield* as the one book by the author of *The Pickwick Papers* and *Oliver Twist* that he did not like.
But he enjoyed the rest of Dickens and recalled finding a cheap
dog-eared copy of *Dombey and Son* in the Champagne in 1918,
which he read with much pleasure under fire.

After Dickens, Dr. Thomason prescribed the reading of
Thackeray. Having had the tough, uphill Dickensenian initiation
to fiction, Thomason became a Thackeray convert almost immediately. Henry Esmond, Major Pendennis, and Colonel New-
comes soon became intimate friends. Later Thomason came to
think of *Vanity Fair* as one of the three great novels, along with
Les Miserables and *War and Peace,* and reread them annually. In
time he raced through the delightful pages of Washington Irving,
James Fenimore Cooper, Nathaniel Hawthorne, and Mark Twain.
He had all of the Henty books, but the Horatio Algers and the so-
called dime novels were conspicuously absent from the physician's
book shelves.

For an introduction to poetry Thomason was fed Tennyson
and Longfellow, obviously the doctor's favorites. In time he advanced to Shakespeare, whom he relished; to Byron, whom he
found exciting; and to Wordsworth, whom he considered obtuse.

Thomason recalled those early years happily as the horse-
and-buggy days, when he accompanied his father out to the
farm, first to open the gates, then later to do the driving. "When
our people progressed beyond the kindly two-horse team and the
pleasant country roads . . . they lost something." By the time he
was fifteen Thomason felt that he had done his most important
reading.

Paul Palmer was the editor to whom Thomason submitted
his monthly contribution in 1938. After his essay anent book-re-
viewing ran, Palmer quoted to John a statement made by Albert
Jay Nock: "For Gawd's sake make sure Thomason sticks with
you; put it to him as a matter of public service, if necessary. You
can never replace him." To the reader's praise Palmer added his
own: "Echo! Your work gets better and better — there is nothing
in the magazine which I am prouder to publish."

Thomason enjoyed his work as literary editor. When the
books arrived he kept files on them writing down the title,

author, publisher, price, etc. Then, as he read, he made notes under each separate listing. A rapid reader, he read whenever his duties on the post permitted and at odd moments snatched at random. It was sometimes possible to get through a chapter while Leda dressed before the couple went out of an evening. Frequently Thomason read himself to sleep at night.

The editorial experience taught Thomason that "to meet a date-line runs the days together like beads on a string" and that the reviewer is obligated to inform himself on a given subject to be able to appraise a writer's work in terms of his purpose. The procedure required much collateral reading and consumed a great deal of time.

Regardless of commitments and crowded schedules, Thomason was never too busy to answer letters from amateurs seeking advice and assistance. Moreover, whenever he could grant a favor, he did so without reservation. A letter addressed to Miss Katherine B. People of New York, dated April 13, 1937, and dispatched from Washington, D.C., is typical:

Dear Miss People:

Your letter and my mother's, forwarding your note to her, arrived in the same mail. It is a pleasure to hear from you.

As to the illustration job, even if it were possible for me to take on any additional work at this time which it isn't — I would not undertake it, because I don't think I could do New York street scenes well. I am not sufficiently familiar with either the backgrounds or the people.

As to Max Perkins, he is the easiest man in the world to see, if you have anything to show him — and one of the kindest gentlemen. A letter isn't necessary. I will mention you in the next letter I write him.

With best wishes for the success of your book.

Sincerely,
John Thomason

Miss Katherine B. People
New York

Perhaps the most perceptive essay ever written on the Southern viewpoint — and one of the finest of the series — is *The*

Old South Myth. The essay appeared in the *Mercury* in July of
1938 and was subsequently anthologized in university text-
books. Although the article is expository, it is not a rationale,
strictly speaking, for Southern culture. Rather, Thomason
equates the Old South Myth with that of the Lost Atlantis and
explores the multiple facets of its constituency with ''a demon-
strable basis in fact.''

One of the principal facets is the belief that the Southern
colonies were settled by the gentry, younger sons of the nobility,
gay cavaliers, ''while behind every Southerner stand blue blood,
bright steel, and good red wine.'' Despite the gracefulness and
attractiveness of pre-war society in the South, it was founded
upon two factors that had outlived their usefulness: slavery and
agrarianism. With or without the Civil War, both were doomed.

Another facet of the myth is the idea that the South was
stratified into aristocrats, poor white trash, and Negroes. This is
as preposterous as the white-porticoed mansions of romance.
Still there is no denying that the myth emphasizes plantation
life, mammy-singers, the fields of cotton bursting in bloom,
and the slicked-up black stereotypes singing spirituals at the
foot of the steps of impressive mansion entrances.

That the South was fighting to preserve the institution of
slavery per se is another major phase of the myth. Robert E. Lee
manumitted the slaves his wife inherited from the Custisses. Jeb
Stuart, the dynamic Confederate cavalry leader, owned no slaves.
Indeed, many of the rank and file, who fought for the South,
owned no slaves.

Another facet of the myth relates to the Confederate soldier himself—the stigma that he was undisciplined. It has been
said that, except for his lack of discipline, the Confederate soldier was probably the finest in the world. This statement requires clarification. The incompetence of the Confederate sub-
sistence and supply departments was notorious. The Confederate soldier was neither fed, clothed, nor shod as he had a right to
expect. He appeared to be undisciplined because he had to fend
for himself. He left the ranks to forage for food (straggled) in order to return to fight.

This deplorable situation prevailed despite the fact that adequate quantities of food and clothing existed in the South. At the end of the war warehouses were bursting with supplies of food and clothing that had not been distributed.

Still another vital aspect of the myth was that the South was united behind the boys in grey. The very principle of states' rights upon which the Confederacy was created made a united front impossible. Still many Southerners faced the war with courage befitting the Age of Chivalry. There were simply not enough of them and their code was outmoded.

In concluding, Thomason returns to the Lost Atlantis analogue:

> Once down there in the South and West there was a fabulous country, where all the men were radiant and all the women lovely, and people went singing at their toil . . . On them the sun shone . . . and the birds made music. . . .
> For you will never kill that Myth. Too much of it is true.

Texas is represented in four essays based upon a biography of Santa Anna, an autobiography of Congressman Maury Maverick, and accounts of the winning of Texas independence and of the Galveston storm of 1900.

Santa Anna is to Thomason *History's Perfect Rascal.* The essay is a condensation of the major events outlined by Wilfred Hardy Callcot in his biography of the Mexican general who was defeated at San Jacinto on April 21, 1836. Thomason recommends the book for instruction and entertainment to those persons who plan to vacation in Mexico. He finds his subject constant in only one respect — treachery.

Under the heading of *The Story of Texas,* Thomason reviews *Texas Independence* by the last surviving son of General Sam Houston — Andrew Jackson Houston. Published by the Anson Jones Press of Texas, the book presents a sequence of events beginning with Stephen F. Austin's colonization of Texas in 1822 and extending to the establishment of the Republic of Texas in 1836, with focus on the fight for independence.

The book is not among the most valid accounts of this period of Texas history despite its documentation from the extensive papers from the old warrior's files. At best the work is a curious compilation and the author "is not an historian after the academic mode." Again Santa Anna is portrayed as the leader of the Mexican army that invaded Texas.

Thomason discusses Congressman Maury Maverick's autobiography *Maverick American* with tongue-in-cheek. You gather that he is amazed that the book achieved publication. The only conventional chapter is the first. But while the book is without form, "it is by no means void. One of the charms of such a book is that you need not worry about the place you leave off; you can pick it up anywhere."

In the second chapter entitled "The Stork Tells a Story" Maverick "gets himself born" and then ignores the stork to tell his own story. While he states that ancestor worship is the bunk. . . , "he traces out relationships to the sixth great-grandfather."

As he skips around from one unrelated topic to another, he manages to explode the accepted dictionary origin of the term *Maverick*. ". . . His family . . . were never cattle barons at all; they went into lumber." Rather appropriately captioned *Maverick on Parade*, the article is a gem of its kind revealing a rare aspect of Thomasoniana.

Catastrophe in Galveston, Thomason's version of the storm of 1900, is a moving blow-by-blow report. It reads as if Thomason witnessed the storm. The fact that his grandfather, Major Goree, was living in Galveston when the disaster occurred contributes a personal note.

Galveston, across the bay where the Trinity River empties into the Gulf of Mexico, was in 1900 the most popular resort on the coast. In the summer afternoons everybody bathed, promenaded, or drove his carriage over the smooth, crisp sands of the beaches. Murdock's Restaurant, extending over the surf, was the place to eat in those seemingly innocuous days; Bettison's Pier on the north jetty was the main fishing establishment; and the Beach Hotel was the most luxurious place to stay on the Gulf Coast.

With its flat white buildings rising from the sea, its oleander-lined streets, lawns shaded with palm trees, and its vine-covered, breeze-swept verandas, Galveston was crowded with tourists until the summer season closed at the end of August. The

Thomasons, vacationing with Major Goree, left on September 1, seven days before the cyclone struck the island.

Three days later the United States Weather Bureau at Galveston posted a bulletin to the effect that a tropical cyclone was moving westward to the Gulf. But at first no one paid any attention to it. Citizens recalled that there had not been a major storm since the old port of Indianola had been destroyed in 1872, nearly thirty years ago. In the nineties there had been some talk of building a seawall for the island, which was thirty miles long and a little over a mile across at its widest point and only twelve feet above the tide marks at its high spots. But those who proposed the seawall were branded as visionaries or alarmists.

Then on Saturday, September 8, a great wind blew and the surf boomed on the beach, each tremendous breaker lapping a little further upon the sand. From fifty miles an hour the velocity of the wind went to ninety-six, then escalated from 110 to 120. Hauling from east to southeast, the wind "raised the Gulf in its arms and hurled it on the island." From one to five feet in depth the water rose to twelve. Major Goree did what he could to help his neighbors, then battened down his own doors and windows. By the light of a kerosene lamp he observed the water rise through the floor from the basement inch by inch to a depth of over twelve feet. Sometime after midnight the water stopped rising and Major Goree, alone in his home on Twenty-first Street, considered the storm was over and went to bed.

Sunday, the ninth, the bay and gulf were bland. But the seaward side of the island was devastated with hugh windrows of wreckage. High water had gutted the bayside. The living searched for remembered possessions and intimates and failed to find them. Looters appeared on the scene. Soldiers from Fort Crockett and citizens' companies were armed to patrol the island.

Food and water became scarce. For days communications with the mainland were cut off. Estimates of the dead were from 3,000 to 5,000. Since it was impossible to inter bodies in the fluid sand, they tried to burn them. Burning proved to be too slow; so they stacked the dead on barges and sent them out to sea. The next morning the tides returned the barges. No lists were kept; identifications were impossible.

The courage with which the people of Galveston met the tragedy, rehabilitated themselves, and raised the level of their island seventeen feet and built a seawall around it — all without federal aid or kindred benefaction — is without precedent. In 1915 they weathered a worse storm with minimum damage. But from the storm of 1900 Galveston would never completely recover.

Thomason wrote the essay partly from memory and from what he read in Sam Acheson's *35,000 Days in Texas: A History of the Dallas News and Its Forebears*. Forerunner to the *Dallas News* were the *Daily Galvestonian*, founded in 1839; and the *Galveston News*, founded in 1842. In 1843 the paper changed hands and was subsequently issued as the *Dallas News*. The story of the evolution of the *Dallas News* was neither new nor especially popular, but the paper had interpreted and helped to shape a hundred years of history in the Southwest.

"The reporter writes in sand; his enthusiasm of today is dead as Hannibal tomorrow. But the reporter's medium is as enduring as life itself because it is the record of life." Thomason's observation was based in part upon his own experience with the *Chronicle* before World War I.

It was inevitable that Thomason would have to choose sooner or later between the literary editorship and other creative activities of more significance to his career. However, he devoted two and a half years to the position as he pursued other enervating, but gratifying, projects.

14 Into This Peace ...

Thomason's next station took him to the Pacific Coast. As was his custom during the interim between the close of one tour of duty and the beginning of another, he and his family vacationed in Texas. While he was on his brief holiday, two events of note occurred—one pleasant, the other tragic. The first, involving Southwestern University at Georgetown, was totally unexpected. In recognition of his literary achievement the university conferred upon John Thomason the honorary Doctor of Letters degree on 6 June 1930. Since he had not distinguished himself as a student at the institution and recalled his final semester with some misgivings, he valued the award doubly.

The other occurrence was the death of John's favorite dog —the wirehaired fox terrier Winkie. From Terrell, the home of Leda's parents, John wrote after leaving the family in Huntsville:

> Going through Dallas, we took Winkie to a dog hospital — one of those recommended by Dr. Smotherman — and they found by microscopic examination that Winkie had hookworms. . . .

> We left him there, and he will be through his treatment
> — if alive — on Sunday morning, when we pick him up. . . .
> — I could add that we greatly appreciate your kindness
> to him at home, all of you. After all, a dog is part of one's in-
> formalities (in our case anyway) and to bear with the same is
> to assume a care.
> And when he's himself he's really great to be with and
> great company. . . .
> — I add a sad postscript: Winkie died about 6:35. The
> vets were most considerate, called up about 5:30 to say his
> heart was not responding to adrenalin, that the feces were
> alive with hookworms, that the prospects were bad . . . They
> kept up a stream of bulletins which was all they could do — or
> we either — which indicates a human spirit on their part . . .
> and will probably be reflected in the bill.
> He was a happy little dog all his life. We had him more
> than four years and shared what we had with him. We will re-
> member him.

John's sparse signature "J," without the customary complimentary close, is almost indecipherable. The family was devoted
to Winkie. Frequently John referred to him in his letters. Leda
was distressed that Winkie had sustained a black eye in a fight.
Winkie missed Jack during school and would not leave his side
in the evenings when he returned home. Thomason enjoyed a
special relationship with the terrier, whom he had taught to
stand at attention and salute in the manner of any good soldier.

Thomason's affinity for animals, particularly dogs and
horses, was innate. Two of his best dog stories are *The Conquest
of Mike* and *The Odyssey of a Little Dog*.

Arriving on June 18, 1938, Thomason reported for duty on
the twentieth. At the outset he was assigned duty at San Diego
as officer in charge of the West Coast Platoon Leaders' Class,
which convened on July 5. John was particularly pleased to work
with the West Coast Platoon Leaders. "The WPLC is a special
reserve stunt of the corps, now in its 3rd year," he wrote his
mother soon after his arrival. "The young gentlemen are recruited from the top flights of the junior and senior classes of
distinguished universities which have not ROTC units of the

army or navy. They are assembled in Quantico, for the most part, and out here, and receive 6 weeks intensive training. Under certain conditions, a percentage of them are granted commissions, and the others are enrolled in our reserve. It is a very important assignment, in full lime-light; and very nice if you do well, but extremely damaging if you don't. . . ."

Thus through the month of July and part of August, Thomason supervised the instruction of over a hundred students seeking commissions as reserve officers. At the end of the six-week encampment, he assumed command of the Second Battalion, Sixth Marines — a rifle regiment and one of the principal elements of the Second Marine Brigade, Fleet Marine Force. "The battalion will be no trouble," he said. "I've been doing that sort of things for twenty years."

At this time the Thomasons were trying to adjust to the absence of Jack, who had remained East to finish preparatory school at St. Albans. "We miss you very much," John wrote his son. "The house is so empty without you that your mother spends as little time as possible in it. I, as you know, am still occupied with professional exercises at Kearney. End of second week — haven't killed anybody yet, but our fingers are still crossed." Interestingly, Thomason, who had been reared strictly under the father-knows-best dictum, signed letters to his son at this time simply as "John" or "John Thomason."

To his father John reported on December 6, 1938: "Out here matters go along so smoothly that it's hard to realize another year is almost gone. My duties are congenial and not too exacting, although a battalion command is one which requires constant attention and thought. I have a good battalion — about 500 officers and men — and we get on well together. They handle to satisfaction under all demands . . . and I believe they would fight. But soldiering is vastly more complicated than it used to be."

When Thomason began his career in the Marines, a company consisted of 250 men, a battalion, 1000, who were nearly all riflemen. There were, he said, no machine guns, no automatic rifles, no other weapons. In his present setup there were

300 rifles with no more than 36 automatic rifles, eight to twelve heavy machine guns, and two 81-millimeter mortars.

"So with half as many men, we have more than twice as much firepower," he pointed out. "The trend is further in the same direction. There is now being manufactured and issued a new automatic 10-shot rifle to replace our old triple-shot, bolt-action Springfield. It will be a long time before there are enough of the new ones to go around, even in the regular establishment, but the firepower they confer will be incredible. In fact they will burn ammunition up so much faster than it can be supplied in combat, of any system we have, that I feel some doubt of the practicability of the weapon. But I'm just an old-style soldier, who knows from experience how difficult combat supply can be and our staffs are more forward-looking than the chaps like me."

Meanwhile Thomason kept up his enormous correspondence, manifested an interest in affairs pertaining to his own family, things related to friends, and world conditions. There was the recent marriage of his youngest sister, Margaret, of whom he was exceedingly fond. Unable to attend the wedding, he was eager for all the details. Margaret had married Dr. Thomas C. Cole, whom John had met the preceding summer. "We note from the *Item* that the family was duly assembled," he wrote Dr. Thomason, "and that you gave away the bride. . . ."

Thomason expected his friend Jim Boyd to come out to California to arrange for the motion-picture version of his latest novel, *Long Hunt.* John himself had had offers from Hollywood. The Leland Hayward Agency saw cinema possibilities in *Gone to Texas* and in September of 1937 sought an exclusive ninety-day motion-picture option over the rights. The agency even enlisted the assistance of Maxwell Perkins to try to convince Thomason he would be wise to do it. But Thomason declined, "But all their [Hollywood's] propositions have strings that I would not risk," he told Jim. "I rape too easy."

Neysa McMein had written that the new wife of Laurence Stallings, who was then employed at the movie capital, was very nice. Max Perkins kept prodding John in "his courteous but determined way" to submit the Lee manuscript. Max had sent him the Tom Wolfe *Memorial Bulletin* issued by the University of

North Carolina. It prompted him to take note of Wolfe's passing
(on the preceding September 15) in his Christmas letter to Boyd:

> What a queer genius Tom Wolfe was! I spent a Dutch
> Treat club night in his company. I did not like him. But you
> felt his force. He had something few of us had — He felt he
> had a message to deliver that was important. I envied him
> that — the faculty of believing that things are important.
> After forty-five years of living, I see very few important
> things. Well, he was terrifically alive and is dead. If there's an
> answer, Ecclesiasticus had it.
>
> A hell of a thought for Christmas!

Jack had spent the holidays at home. "He's grown into a
fine, grave young man, courteous, assured, and I think intelligent. He'll go to Princeton. And be a better man than the
tough old mercenary, who fathered him," John could not resist
boasting to Boyd.

It was a strategic period in the history of the Corps, and
Thomason's extensive tour of line duty at the San Diego base
proved to be one of the most active and satisfactory periods in
his military career. The intensive training program in 1938 and
1939, under his direction, included field exercises, small-arms
firing and musketry, conditioning marches, and ship-to-shore
landing maneuvers. Highlights of the tour were the participation of his battalion in landing exercises and other maneuvers
ashore at San Clemente, off the coast of Southern California.

> San Clemente passed as all things passed — [John con-
> fided to Jim] — my people performed the indicated evolu-
> tions in spite of our accomplished starts. Every landing exer-
> cise I see goes further to convince me that such a project,
> against organized resistance, is the most delicate and difficult
> problem that can beset us. I'd want local control of the air,
> local and strategic control of the sea, a superiority of at least 6
> to 1 in troops — and on top of that, a hell of a lot of luck, to
> attempt it. As to your theoretical soldiering, what we learn
> from it is that we don't learn much. But it's far less exacting
> than the other. Even so, I seriously doubt that I see another
> war in any active time. I concede that the opening moves have

been made for the Second World War of the century. But the
great powers are now in that stage which, in the old days of
limited war, was the phase of maneuvering for position. . . .
Incidentally the Far Eastern pot is boiling again. Events out
there are always unpredictable in implication. . . .

Having barely survived the crucial Hoover administration,
the Corps emerged from the depression years in better condition
than it had been at the beginning of that lean period. Among
its recent achievements, over and above the adoption of newer
concepts and techniques of conducting warfare, were a new promotion system and a new type of organization purported to develop into a carefully integrated Marine air-ground task force.

Thus the late 1930s witnessed the decline of the "Old System," as effective as it once had been. One of the chief reasons
for its obsolescence involved responsibility. Under the "Old System" responsibility was not restricted to an individual but rested
on the shoulders of many men in the Corps. It was accepted as a
Corps obligation.

For example, if one Marine officer failed to perform his duty effectively or proved to be incapable of solving a problem, the
system took control. That is, the system acted as a sort of plural
surrogate in providing assistance. It was a kind of "big brother"
policy at work.

The system represented the finest, the most professionally
capable, of the noncommissioned officers of the Corps: the company first sergeant, the gunnery sergeant, the platoon sergeant,
and the section leader, all bound by their own individual ethical
codes. To them the Corps meant more than a military organization. It was quite literally a lifestyle with the Marine uniform
typifying their badge of honor.

Excellent marksmen and preternaturally disciplined, the
Leathernecks were equally dedicated to their specific duties as
they were to the organization with which they identified. These
were the regulars, familiarly known as the "Old Breed." These
were the regulars, who despite the seeming insignificance of any
Marine's role, were supportive of him as a part of the system.

Consequently, the "Old Breed" subscribed to a dual concept of responsibility. While their main objective was to enforce

the orders of their superior officers, they felt compelled to monitor the welfare of those men under their immediate command—the fresh recruits, the apparently weak, the disoriented. Disciplining an incorrigible or controversial private was only one aspect of their job. Guiding a naive and inexperienced young officer through a difficult field problem or a complicated tactical maneuver was likewise a part of the "Old Breed's" military obligation.

Much admiration and tradition attached to the "Old Breed." For that matter, Thomason's treatment of Sergeant John Houston in his series of stories was, in large measure, a salute to the "Old Breed" and its role in the Corps. Thomason himself was in many respects both a proponent and exponent of the "Old Breed."

Understandably the old system worked well with a Corps of only 20,000. But the emergency legislation prior to America's entrance into World War II, plus the Marine Corps' expansion to 400,000, rendered it ineffectual. Moreover, the "Old Breed" suffered irrevocably from the attrition of promotions and casualties, and the few who remained were greatly outnumbered by the wartime overflow of volunteers. Then, in time, technicians and bureaucrats, armed with machines and statistics, moved in to replace the old system completely.

Still the inevitable end was a decade away, and in the interim while Thomason discharged his duties at San Diego, he stressed the effectiveness of the rifle and the bayonet, the light machine gun, and the hand grenade as employed by capable soldiers. After all, it was as a practical soldier that he had made his finest contribution in World War I and in the tropics.

Furthermore, it was as an instructor in the Fleet Marine Force that Thomason excelled. The man who once found himself temperamentally unsuited to the teaching profession became one of the most successful and highly respected instructors in the history of the Marine Corps. The young men under his instruction especially appreciated his down-to-earth approach and personal interest. They also admired him for his infinite patience, for his wise counsel, and for the example he set. There was no doubt about it. Men under the command of Colonel John Thomason considered him "a hell of a good C.O."

Thomason's Wednesday afternoon sessions held informally over a pipe and a bottle of beer in the corner of a mess tent were exceedingly popular at Camp Elliott. At these sessions he encouraged some, corrected a minor error of another, suggested an increase at one point, a discontinuation of another, gave endorsement where it was warranted, and made himself available for private counseling when it was needed. No topic of current interest was rejected at these meetings, and Thomason would talk on any subject for hours as he invited students' questions and answered them. He was likewise a good listener.

Though he himself was individualistic, Thomason stressed teamwork. A case in point was that he preferred company musketry firing and scouting to individual rifle practice and competitive shooting on the range. And though he gave individual instruction whenever he deemed it necessary, he preferred team competition as opposed to a demonstration of the superior skills of one man over another.

The part of Thomason's legend that he made the Marines because of his portrayal of the Corps in his books was likewise true because of his influence upon the young Marines during this period of the late thirties. Even two decades later officers and men of the Corps, on active or reserve status, recalled their service under Thomason's command with the conviction that they were superior Marines as a result of the relationship. Moreover, just as he had set high standards for them, so did they project the same to the men who later came under their command.

Forty-six on February 28, 1939, Thomason took inventory. "I can still march a battalion twenty miles a day," he wrote Dr. Thomason, "and do it now about once a week. But I'm already too old for the strain modern war imposes on a regimental officer."

It was in the following April that he, realizing that he was overworking and had to curtail activities, resigned from the literary editorship of the *American Mercury*.

In June, Leda went East to attend Jack's graduation exercises at St. Alban's. At that time the Thomasons learned that Jack did not want to attend Princeton, but preferred to enroll in the fall at the University of Virginia. Although Princeton had accepted Jack and John had hoped that he would matriculate there, he did not inflict his will upon his son.

Stallings and Thomason took advantage of their geographical proximity to renew acquaintance. "I still look back with pleasure to seeing you and Leta [sic] and the old General [Von Boetticher]," Stallings wrote John from Culver City, where he was employed by Metro-Goldwyn-Mayer Pictures. "In about three weeks Louise and I will have some guest quarters fitted up. I pray you and Leta will visit us then. I have some choice spirits, both wine and flesh, ready to tangle with you — and Louise would like to give Leta a hand-tailored tour of the film camps."

John detected marked changes in his friend. "He [Stallings] appears grown up now," John wrote Boyd later. "The bloom is off the butterfly's wings. [He is] much graver and much quieter. All geese, no longer swans. Though some occur, of course. Too bad about Helen [Stallings' first wife]. She shouldn't be through yet."

Literary and artistic projects, along with his duties at the station, occupied Thomason. In July of 1939 his story entitled *The Wicked Do Not Always Prosper*—a follow up of the material in *Gone to Texas*—appeared in the *Saturday Evening Post*. In December of 1939 *Sergeant Bridoon of the Horse Marines*, a piece evolving from his experience of observing the Japanese attack on Shanghai and the final story relating to the American Legation Guard in North China, ran in the *Post*.

Thomason abandoned temporarily his customary metier of watercolor to do an oil portrait. The work was a portrait of a Marine executed by order for the commissioned officers' mess at the San Diego Marine Base, for which Jack posed. The enormous canvas, four by six feet in dimension, excited much admiration. Thomason, however, perfectionist that he was and pressed for time, was not pleased with it. "I'm not satisfied with it," he wrote Sue, "but perhaps it's like Dr. Johnson's Dancing Dog. Question is not how well the dog dances, but that the dog dances at all."

Even though John had not expected war so soon, its imminence added impetus to his work at the base. When the conflict began officially on September 3, 1939, after Hitler's invasion of Poland two days before, the Thomasons were enjoying a Labor Day weekend at Ensenada, Baja California. John's reaction expressed in a letter to General Friedrich Von Boetticher is pertinent.

As if to underscore the time and seriousness of the event, he wrote: "This morning about seven o'clock . . . we heard over the radio in the car the announcements from London, Paris, and Berlin which indicated that Europe has embarked upon the Second World War. It is a lovely morning at 0700. The night mist was clearing off, the sun was breaking through the clouds, over the mountains of Mexico, and the water was beautifully blue. The *Todos Santos* islands, off the bay, were silhouetted in pale amethyst. Half a dozen fishing boats were pulling out, and strings of pelicans were going along with them. The wind was soft and cool from the southwest. There was a murmur of surf on the rocks and a thin crying of gulls and no other sounds at all. Into this peace comes news of the world gone mad."

Thomason felt that he and his former opponent in combat shared similar convictions: "You and I have spent our lives in arms, and I think it an honorable profession. We have fought in one great war. We will fight in another one. We have met also on the common ground of history and art. And I think this morning you regret, as I do, that men cannot live in peace . . . Wars can no longer be localized or limited. Our lives will be different from this day, and the end of it we cannot foretell, but we know that what our duty is, we will do.

"Wherever those duties lead us, I will hold you in my heart, my dear friend as a respected colleague and a good companion. I hope that you will so remember me. . . ."

General Von Boetticher was the military and air attaché of the German Embassy in Washington, D.C. Thomason met the German officer in 1927, when he did research in Germany in preparation for the writing of the history of the Second Division. Years later, after Boetticher came to Washington, he renewed contact and the two became friends. Because of their mutual interest in history, Thomason invited General Boetticher to accompany him on a visit to the Gettysburg campaign routes— Fredericksburg, Virginia, and Harrisburg, Pennsylvania. Boetticher left the country after the United States entered the war in 1941.

The Thomason family concern at this time was for the safety of Sue in war-torn Europe. Sue, who had gone abroad for special study at Oxford and who had met and married Henri G. Noordberg, was living in Amsterdam. John attempted to console his mother. "I know you're awfully worried about Sue, and I wish I could say something to ease your mind," he wrote September 8, 1939. "But I took in my signs as a prophet when the war started . . . I still think that Hitler was surprised by the firmness the French and British showed and that he believed that his bluff would work one more time, as it did a year ago. Even now, I think it quite probable that, when he has pulverized Poland . . . he will offer to negotiate. . . .

"Holland ought to be as secure as any place in Europe. Invasion of Holland, with the British navy controlling the sea, offers small compensation in comparison with the obvious disadvantages. Such a step was considered by the Germans in 1914–1918 and rejected. Her neutrality, in fact, is highly desirable to Germany becuase it gives the Germans an outlet, even under restrictions. In the land war no party . . . wanted Holland involved, because she was available as a sort of clearing house for intelligence activities and had important commercial and administrative facilities as well, which were used by all belligerants. It may well be the same way this time.

"Should it come to war, unquestionably the Dutch will be evacuated to England first and then elsewhere. The German army could be bottled indefinitely by inundations. Of course, there are the airplanes, but all the data we have indicate that actual damages caused to life and property by aerial bombing is negligible. . . ."

Whether he convinced his mother or not, John Thomason was proud of Sue's electing not to run. "Sue's decision to remain is just what I'd expect of Dad's [Major Goree's] granddaughter — your child — my sister."

Now that the die was cast, Thomason hoped he would be permitted to continue his service at San Diego as a regimental officer or that he would draw a staff assignment with the Brigade in the active field.

As early as February, 1940, he had been aware of the threat of war in the Pacific and of the measures taken by the United States for the defense in that area. ". . . We are quietly but definitely mobilizing in the Pacific right now. The cruiser force that went to Honolulu last year is being about doubled by detachments from the Fleet, and Honolulu is named — for the first time — as the permanent base of important increments of the fleet," Maxwell Perkins quoted him in a letter to Ernest Hemingway. ". . . Our new Defense Battalions—they are really very powerful artillery regiments—are designed for service in the Pacific Islands, and the first of them has its preliminary orders. We'll be garrisoning Midway, Wake, Johnson Island, French Frigate Shoals very soon. In all of which lies the seeds of war."

Having accumulated twenty-three years of service in the Marine Corps in 1940, Thomason was toying with the idea of retirement. ". . . unless there is a war, I shan't stay much longer in the service," he wrote Perkins. "I'm 47 this month, and I have put in 23 years. That's nearly enough."

A pleasant departure from camp routine came in March of 1940, when Thomason had the opportunity of a visit with his extraordinary friend Alexander Woollcott. Woollcott was starring in George S. Kaufman's new play, *The Man Who Came to Dinner,* which was based on the most waspish aspects of his personality. The play's run in San Diego was spectacular. "We saw Alex Woollcott last night in *The Man Who Came to Dinner,*" Thomason wrote his father. "As Woollcott playing Woollcott, he was super, and the whole show was screamingly funny. Should one of the other road companies — there are three — come to Houston, by all means see it . . . I borrowed the general's barge and am taking Alex for a ride around the harbor this afternoon. He sends his compliments and regards to you and mother, and insists that he will return to Huntsville when he can. A curious and entertaining fellow."

Lieutenant Colonel Thomason was relieved of duty in the Fleet Marine Force on June 10, 1940. Because of the war situation in Europe his leave to visit Texas was revoked, and he was granted fourteen days in which to report to the Naval Department in Washington for reassignment. Without knowing the precise nature of his Washington detail, even though he had heard that three offices were competing for his services, Thomason set out in his car, with Leda, on a pilgrimage across the continent.

Jack, who had made the dean's list at the end of his first year at the University of Virginia, was visiting in Huntsville with his grandparents. He had expected his parents to join him there until he learned that his father's leave had been cancelled.

The peripatetic couple reached Fort Wayne, Indiana, on June 19. Their itinerary had taken them from California across the states of Nevada, Wyoming, Nebraska, and Iowa. They had been traveling an average of 400 miles a day with the exception of the day before their arrival in Fort Wayne, when their mileage totaled 500 miles. Also, except for the last two nights, they had stopped at "tourist camps," which John preferred to hotels because of the convenience of handling his own luggage. But the camps thinned out and deteriorated as they came east.

It seemed to be the opportune time to enjoy the scenery and appraise the country as the couple viewed it from direct contact. "This is a great country of ours," John wrote from Fort Wayne. "California has a variety of terrain and produce comparable to that of Texas. Nevada is all grey green cups and naked mountains. Utah is mountains of the texture and color of wrinkled elephant hide interspersed with perfect gems of cultivated land and white salt deserts. Wyoming is best of all — green upland pastures, swift running streams and always a line of mountains, snow-capped, marching majestic on one hand or the other. Nebraska looked like grazing, solid and assured. It was surprising to see so few cattle on their ranges. Iowa — Illinois — half a day to each, and now Indiana — are magnificent farming lands. I have never seen such fields. They will make bumper crops this year and get poor prices for them."

The next day the couple encountered a heat-wave and beat a terrific storm of rain and thunder that night by about ten minutes as they reached Burlington, Iowa. "— And in all this 2500 miles of travel, we have seen no soldiers — except one or two thumbing rides — and hardly a highway policeman," he wrote. "A great, fat, peaceful country of decent, kindly people intent on their own affairs and resentful of anything distracting them from the same."

But invariably when the service station attendants spied the Marine Corps tag on John's car, they asked: "When (not *if* or *maybe*) are we going to get into the war?" It seemed to John that they tore themselves reluctantly away from their radios "to give you gas." When? John Thomason only hoped that America would have a year, or better, a year and a half in which to prepare for the ordeal ahead.

The nearer John and Leda came to the District of Columbia, the thicker grew the gloom diffused over the radio. France buckled under Hitler's steel. Even the voice of Winston Churchill over the airwaves sounded like a defeated Englishman facing his country's annihilation.

15 Pearl Harbor and Lone Star Preacher

The Thomasons arrived in Washington with two days to spare after their 3,021-mile odyssey and no worse mechanical trouble than a faulty fuel pump and an overheated engine. To his utter amazement, John Thomason relieved Colonel Robert Blake at the Latin American desk in the Office of Naval Intelligence.

Since he was hoping for a billet in the active field, his disappointment was apparent. Another factor contributing to his disenchantment was that at this strategic time regimental and divisional commands, obviously the stairways to promotion, were being awarded to his contemporaries, the very men with whom he had served since 1917. Thomason rated such a command and no more dedicated Marine existed than he.

Why, then, was he being overlooked? With the Corps it was apparently not a matter of overlooking Thomason. It was the same type of preferential treatment the Corps had extended him before when it had assigned him to a desk job or station that required extensive paperwork or writing. It is reasonable to think that the Corps considered Thomason irreplaceable. Singularly handsome, dynamic, talented, Thomason occupied a special place in the United States Marine Corps. He had become its symbol as well as the Corps' Boswell. The Marines could replace other casualties less gifted. Men like Thomason, they could not. He was much more valuable to the Corps in a public relations post than in serving as an expendable officer in the field. Besides it was important to the Corps to keep Thomason functioning as an artist.

Also his superiors knew that he was well qualified for the post from previous experience and would do a creditable job, as he always had. Although Thomason's superior officers had frequently consulted him before giving him an assignment, they had not contacted him this time. However, realizing the significance of the station in view of world events, Thomason accepted the appointment gracefully and settled down to routine. After all, the war was merely beginning. Perhaps the opportunity for duty in the field of operations would come yet. Certainly he intended to renew his efforts to get into the action.

During the first few months of 1940 President Roosevelt asked Congress to appropriate $4 billion for national defense. To strengthen national unity he named Henry L. Stinson, secretary of war, and Frank Knox, secretary of the navy. Stinson and Knox had assumed their new posts about the same time as Thomason had in the summer of 1940.

When France fell, Hitler tried to bomb and starve the British into submission. Since the British Royal Navy could not cope with German submarine attacks on shipping, Prime Minister Winston Churchill, in May, 1940, asked Roosevelt for fifty old American destroyers in exchange for six naval bases in the Caribbean. In addition, Great Britain leased bases in Bermuda and Newfoundland to the United States. A string of vital island bastions along the Atlantic frontier increased the operations of the American navy substantially.

In September, Congress enacted the first peacetime draft in American history. In the midst of these events the presidential election took place in November, and Roosevelt won a third term but by a much smaller majority than in 1932 or 1936. Then in the following January of 1941, the president asked Congress to appropriate $7 billion for lend-lease to support the war.

With the enactment of lend-lease, America's chances of entering the war were increased. As a measure of defense, the American navy rapidly expanded its activities to the North Atlantic in search of German submarines and radioed their locations to Allied warships and planes. In April of 1941 the United States occupied Greenland, and in May the president declared a state of national emergency. Hitler successfully invaded Russia in June, and in November the United States granted $1 billion in lend-lease to that country. Meanwhile, Iceland was occupied in July of 1941 and the draft law extended in August.

After the Germans attacked the American destroyer *Greer* in the North Atlantic in September, Roosevelt ordered the navy to "shoot on sight" any German craft found cruising in the vicinity of Iceland. Then, following the sinking of the destroyer *Reuben James* on October 30, Congress voted to arm American merchantmen and allow them to transport cargoes to Allied ports. Thus by December, 1941, America was actually at war with the United States navy playing a significant role, and while Thomason was occupying a desk job, he was making a vital contribution to it.

Meanwhile, Japanese-American relations had steadily deteriorated after Japan resumed war against China in 1937. With Japanese troops threatening French Indochina, Congress placed exports of certain war materials under a licensing system. Later in answer to the creation of the Rome-Berlin-Tokyo axis, Roosevelt extended the embargo in September of 1940. Shortly afterward he froze Japanese assets in the United States and clamped an embargo on oil when Japan occupied Indochina.

When the United States demanded the complete withdrawal of Japanese troops from China and Indochina, Japan retaliated by attacking the naval base at Pearl Harbor, Hawaii, on December 7, 1941. Although the commanders at the garrison had been alerted, they believed an attack was impossible and took precautions only against sabotage. In less than two hours the United States lost a major portion of its Pacific Fleet; two battleships sunk, six others battered, approximately a dozen lesser vessels immobilized; more than 150 airplanes wrecked; and over 2,300 servicemen killed and 1,100 wounded. Japanese casualties were minor.

The United States Pacific Fleet had been stationed at Pearl Harbor since April of 1940. Even though the attack left the nation almost impotent in the Pacific, it helped to unify a country bitterly divided over the reelection of Roosevelt. Congress declared war on Japan the next day, December 8, 1941.

All these circumstances, and especially the Pearl Harbor debacle, affected the Office of the Chief of Naval Operations and the Office of Naval Intelligence. The attack on Pearl Harbor also increased the responsibilities of the chief of the American Republics section.

It was common knowledge that Marine officers of German and Italian vessels had surveyed the major and minor ports and the coastal waters of the entire Caribbean littoral and its islands. After the information thus obtained was evaluated and coded, it was of incalculable importance to the Axis submarine commanders. Furthermore, the presence of colonies of German and Italian nationals in Central and South American republics, loyal to their homelands and capable of inciting animosity in their localities against Pan-American solidarity, posed a major problem. As if to compound the situation, there were several of the Latin American republics that had contracted for the services of German and Italian naval, military, and aviation missions.

Not only were Thomason and his staff required to deal with this unsavory situation, he himself handled much of the intelligence paper work personally and screened applicants to fill various naval posts attached to American embassies and legations at Latin American capitals.

In the summer of 1941 the Marine Corps commissioned Thomason to paint a recruiting poster. Announced in the *Dallas Morning News* and other papers October 5, 1941, two months before Pearl Harbor, the poster was particularly significant in view of the explosive global situation and the prominent role the Corps had played in World War I.

The composition depicted a striding Leatherneck in full color who seemed to be saying, "Let's go!" It is noteworthy that the Marine so portrayed wears the pre-World War II uniform with the characteristic flat helmet and gaiter-like leggings, rather than puttees, and carries a Springfield rifle, cartridge clips attached to his belt, and his musette bag containing his gas mask.

Copies of the poster were displayed in Marine bases and recruiting centers throughout the nation and the Marine Corps also issued miniature impressions of it in the form of a stamp to give additional impetus to Marine recruitment. The creation of the poster was another demonstration of the special service that Thomason rendered the Corps with so much pleasure and satisfaction.

Thomason solved his problem of an ever-increasing work load by reporting to his office fully an hour and forty-five minutes before his associates. Promptly at six o'clock, if not a few minutes before, he began his day. By the time members of his staff began to arrive, he was well underway.

At times when official matters were not urgent, he devoted the extra hour and forty-five minutes to writing and sketching. After lunch, he worked until early evening.

An important part of his duty was attending diplomatic functions at the Latin American embassies. Thomason attended these events religiously but usually left in time to spend an hour or two at home preparing for the next day's work. Rarely did he get to bed before midnight.

Thomason reserved weekends for his family and friends. A dedicated family man, he spent as much time with his wife and son, enrolled at the University of Virginia, as his crowded schedule would permit. On Sundays the family enjoyed taking walks in the parks near their apartment on Massachusetts Avenue and sometimes entertained their friends at lunchtime.

As the war progressed, Thomason's duties continued to increase. He familiarized himself with the machinery of the Navy Department, especially the complex operation of the Office of the Chief of Naval Operations. He was equally conversant with the work and problems of his contemporaries in both the State and War departments, along with the officers of the Foreign

Service and the Military Intelligence Divisions of the Army similarly engaged in intelligence work.

But not all Thomason's work was confined to a desk. In the
fall of 1941 he spent two and a half months touring all of Latin
America. During the 25,000-mile trip he visited every naval attaché office and observer post in operation.

On the flight, which extended from the last of August until mid-November, Thomason, as representative of the Navy
Department, headed a team of Army officers of the Engineer
and Air Corps. An overall purpose of the mission was to choose
airport sites for the defense of the Panama Canal and coastal patrol aircraft engaged in convoy operations. Another objective
was to establish closer communications with the officials and
diplomatic representatives of the Latin American republics.

Flying in two Army Air Corps B-18 bombers, the aggrega-
tion touched down in Mexico City and visited five Central
American capitals before landing at Albrook in the Canal Zone.
From there the flight proceeded down the west coast of South
America with a few days spent at Bogota, Quito, La Paz, and
Santiago en route. Next the team flew the length of the Andes,
stopping at Buenos Aires.

Behind his desk in Washington Thomason realized that his
duties had more than doubled, but he had not taken into account his declining capacity to absorb concomitant pressures and
frustration that were part of it. Not until the aggregation
reached Buenos Aires did he become aware of it, when exhaustion forced him to surrender himself for medical treatment and
rest at the Hospital of the Little Company of Mary for a few days
while the team continued the tour without him.

At 48, Thomason, who had never adjusted well to flying,
to begin with, discovered the unalterable fact that in an extended period of demanding duty and routine his body was becoming increasingly susceptible to the stress and strain of debilitating air travel, going without sleep and proper food, and even
the perturbation over the aspects of Latin American protocol
and diplomacy, much of which was alien to him. He rejoined his
contingent at Rio de Janeiro.

After the trip to Rio de Janeiro, the group made stops at Salvador, Recife, Portaleza, and Belin. The itinerary also included Cayenne, Paramarilbo, and Georgetown in the Guianas, Port-of-Spain at Trinidad, and Caracas in Venezuela. The team inspected Havana and the principal Cuban ports, along with those of Haiti and the Dominican Republic. Nor did the aggregation overlook the British base sites from Jamaica eastward to the Leeward and Windward Islands chain.

The lengthy aerial tour of Latin America and the Caribbean gave Thomason the added pleasure of many hours of sketching and making notes for prospective stories. Upon his return to Washington, he wrote Sister Peters, one of the nuns who attended him at the hospital in Buenos Aires, a charming thank-you note in which he sketched a page-length self-portrait designed to show that he had completely recovered.

For the success of the mission Thomason was later awarded the Air Medal by the War Department, under date of May, 1943. As gratified as he was at the achievement of the activity, he was glad enough to return to his sedentary post at Washington and to be relieved from the rigors of air travel.

Thomason was aware that he occupied an unusual place in the Corps. He had succeeded in convincing his superiors that his primary concern was his duty as a Marine officer, not the arts. But at the same time he was appreciative of the pride that Brigadier General Sherman Miles of the Army and General Lejeune and other commandants of the Corps took in his creative activities. On the other hand, he realized that there were a few in the Corps who felt that a Marine officer should not have outside interests and resented the lifestyle that Thomason's writing and art made possible.

A significant occurrence that marked Thomason's return to the base in Washington was the publication of the Civil War masterpiece — *Lone Star Preacher.* The publishing event of 1941, the novel was released by Scribner's in January, after the final segment had run in the *Saturday Evening Post* the preceding December. Thomason had contemplated the writing of such a book since early manhood. "I would like to write a great book," he confided to his father during his teaching days, "or paint a great picture that would live on that war."

He had investigated Robert E. Lee and had accumulated considerable manuscript on the Confederate general. Nor did the definitive four-volume Freeman biography of Lee discourage him. But, after that publication in 1935, when he learned that his friend was also writing another voluminous Lee study on the specific aspect of the material as he [Thomason] was, he deferred to him. Freeman's three-volume *Lee's Lieutenants: A Study in Command* was published in 1942.

Although Thomason could have submitted his manuscript for *Lee's Men* a year before Freeman's work was ready and Perkins urged him to do so, he chivalrously laid it aside leaving Freeman an open field. At any rate, his research of Lee had contributed to *Lone Star Preacher,* and with the release of *Gone to Texas* in 1937, Thomason had served his internship in the genre of the novel and had found the category challenging.

Furthermore, his publishers had wanted another book of the magnitude of *Jeb Stuart.* Even before the manuscript of *Gone to Texas* was finished, Maxwell Perkins was urging Thomason to write a Civil War book based upon the battlefields — a vehicle to show both the magnificence and sordidness of warfare. Perkins envisioned the hypothetical volume as a parallel to *Don Quixote* in its presentation of the diverse viewpoints of the realist and the idealist.

He suggested for a hero an elderly man whom life had deprived of combat experience but who had read about war and romanticized it. For the story line he proposed a soldier, or veteran friend, who would accompany the old gentleman on a tour of the battlefields. The conversation of the two would give expression to the contrasting points of view. Another phase of the plotting would deal with the adventures of the two on the road. "It could be a truly great book," Perkins said, "to be called *Tour of the Battlefields.*"

Instead of the aging romanticist who glamorized war, Thomason modeled his protagonist, Praxiteles Swan, upon John Stevens, the former Methodist chaplain of the Confederate Army — the fighting octogenarian he had known during his

Penn City days. Stevens's accounts of his experiences in Hood's Texas Brigade, coupled with the Civil War lore the author had stored up since boyhood, enriched the novel. Along with the earlier investigation of Lee, the extensive research for *Jeb Stuart* also paid dividends.

Rather than write about the battlefields passively after the war, Thomason chose to recreate the action of the engagements and to portray the men who fought in them. While he adhered to strict historic fact, he combined with it his feelings for war and powers of creativity. Although the central figure is the red-headed fighting minister, who takes his religion to the battle-fields with him, such Confederate officers as General Lee himself, Stonewall Jackson, Longstreet, and Hood weave in and out of the scenes with unerring dispatch.

Thomason was equally meticulous in creating the illustrations for the volume. He made as many as a dozen preliminary drawings of figures and scenes before he was satisfied with the final sketches he used. Particularly in *Lone Star Preacher* are the illustrations literary, rather than decorative. They are brutally realistic, even to the point of ugliness, as they help to tell the story and reveal character. No reader confuses a sketch of Lee with that of Jackson or mistakes Longstreet for Hood, so flawlessly accurate are the illustrations right down to their minute physical and psychical characteristics. Ingeniously the two arts of illustration and writing combine in *Lone Star Preacher* to make a single cogent statement.

Coming less than two months after Pearl Harbor, as America officially entered World War II, the novel burst on the national scene like a bomb. Critics generally agreed that the novel not only compared favorably with *Jeb Stuart*, it was of similar excellence. Typical of Eastern opinion was that of Stanley Walker in the *New York Herald:* "Few if any living writers can match Thomason in handling the military man in fierce action. He knows these men. They are among his ancestors."

Most vocal of the Texans was Thomason's former fellow student at Southwestern University — J. Frank Dobie. In a review in the *Houston Post,* Dobie hailed *Lone Star Preacher* as the supreme Civil War novel and cited it as "the mellow fruit of

generations of lives in Huntsville and of the career Thomason
has lived away from it.'' He stated further that ''His [Thoma-
son's] birth and rearing in this place are of more importance to
the town and of more significance to Texas than Sam Houston
dying there.''

Thomason's cousin W. H. (Will) Kittrell, Jr., of Dallas sent
him a copy of Dobie's review and informed him of his friends'
interest in the book. ''Night before last Frank Dobie, Walter
Prescott Webb, Harry Crozier, Lt. Governor Coke Stevenson, a
man you should know; Colonel Paul Wakefield of Lovelady,
Texas, and the writer held a lengthy discussion of *Lone Star
Preacher* . . . and it would have done your heart good to hear
their comments on your book . . . you have written a really
great book, John. I agree with *Pancho* Dobie's estimate that it is
'the finest flowering of Texas literature that has yet been published.' ''

Despite the fact that Thomason declined Perkins's suggestions, the editor recognized at once that there was greatness in
the story of Praxiteles Swan. He particularly liked the Sharpsburg chapter, felt the impact of its character.

While *Lone Star Preacher* does not overemphasize the sor-
did side of warfare, neither does it ignore it. This aspect also excited Perkins's enthusiasm. Asked about ''the awfullest sight''
he encountered in the whole Civil War, Elder Swan recalls a
scene on the night following the battle of Sharpsburg. After setting his pickets in the edge of the east wood, he returns to camp
traversing the site of the day's fighting still befouled with the
battle's carnage. In the midst of it he sees a flickering light — a
light which seen that far forward could draw enemy fire.

Captain Swan investigates and discovers a poker game in
progress. ''. . . There was a big buck-Yankee, stripped naked,
and spread-eagled on his back . . . The light I saw was from a
candle, stuck firm between his teeth. An' there were four of . . .
the command the boys called the Louisiana Tigers . . . sitting
around him . . . a-throwing their cards down on the dead Yankee's chest. He was a big Yankee. His eyes were open and sort of
gleamed.''

One of the most compelling episodes concludes Chapter VII, the penultimate segment of the book. When Captain Swan returns from an inspection of the Brigade lines, he is confronted by a captive Yankee medical officer, who demands to know what the Southerners are fighting for.

Almost exhausted, Swan leans heavily on his saber. "Young man," he measures his words carefully, "when I came up here in '61, I had States Rights in mind. I never gave much thought to the politics of it. I'm a minister of the gospel when I'm home. Now, I don't know. I hear the boys talk. Reckon, if we're fighting for anything, we're fighting for General Lee."

Then he straightens up and places both hands on the hilt of his saber. His voice grows big in the shadow of the Wilderness. "A man's bound to fight," he declares, "for what he believes in. He's bound to keep on fighting — that part of it's with him. But whether he wins or not — that's with God."

Charles Scribner's Sons — Publishers and Booksellers, which occupied a ten-story edifice of classical design crowned with two obelisks and distinguished by graceful pilasters, was located on Forty-eighth Street. The ground floor — a large oblong room with vaulted ceiling — served as the bookstore. By the architectural standards of the time the storefront flanked by huge display cases was elegant.

The more ingenious of Scribner's staff had arranged for a special display of *Lone Star Preacher* in one of the spacious showcases with the colorful Confederate flag providing the backdrop and the original illustrations framing the sides. Max Perkins put his own stamp upon it and took a photograph to send John.

Among Thomason's personal effects in the Thomason Collection is a picture of the showcase display with Max Perkins's note clipped to it. The note consists of one sentence: "I thought this, from our best window, might please you," and was signed "Always Yours, Max."

Apparently it did.

In subsequent years several chapters from *Lone Star Preacher* would be reprinted by other writers. Examples during Thomason's lifetime are Alexander Woollcott in *As You Were,* F. Van wyck Mason in *The Fighting American,* both published in 1942; and George S. Perry in *Roundup Time* in 1943. In later years William Peery, editor of *Twenty-One Texas Short Stories* (1954), and Gordon Carroll, editor of *The Post Reader of Civil War Stories* (1958), would reprint chapters.

Presumably the novel influenced Ernest Hemingway to bring out in 1942 the anthology titled *Men at War: The Best War Stories of All Time.* Not only did Hemingway include three chapters from *Lone Star Preacher,* two from *The Adventure of General Marbot,* and one from *Fix Bayonets!,* he also had the editorial assistance of Thomason. As an authority on war and critic of classic literature involving it, Thomason was a viable choice. Hemingway regretted that it was not possible to use his friend's drawings. A tome of over a thousand pages leaves no room for illustrations.

Later Dobie would write in *A Texan in England* (1946) that: ". . . In Praxiteles Swan, 'the Lone Star Preacher,' and his comrades, all the memories of the Texas men in grey are gathered up. They are saturated with whatever it is that the pines and the prairies of their soil infuse into human nature and with a belief in 'something' that will make their lost, and perhaps wrong, cause forever noble . . . For those men *'believed in something.'* "

As the national spotlight focused on Thomason, his legend continued to expand and the image he projected in the Marine Corps became an integral part of it. Whether Thomason cultivated his own legend, as some of his contemporaries believed, was immaterial. The popular profile of the hard-fighting, hard-drinking, terrifically talented Marine existed nonetheless.

The fact that the author incorporated facets of the Marine image in his books supported it. Moreover, it occasionally gave rise to exaggerated stories and gossip disparaging to Thomason. Whether the stories had any factual basis or not, the impulse to dramatize them in constant retelling tended to displace fact with fiction.

A typical example of such apocryphal tales is one involving Thomason's "writing discipline." Attributed to a fellow officer of his Peking days, the story is likewise a commentary on Thomason's drinking habits. The anecdote is quoted here from the Introduction by Robert Leckie in the edition of *Fix Bayonets!* published by Scribner's in 1970:

> He was always fighting a deadline . . . Sometimes he'd get a check in the mail . . . and an order to write a story in six weeks. He'd call his houseboy and tell him to load up with whisky. His wife would leave the apartment for a few days and we'd all come in and drink John's whisky. We'd ask him when he planned to write the story and he'd show us a calendar with a date encircled. He'd chuckle and say, 'The whisky ought to run out about then,' and we'd laugh and go on with the party. Sure enough, a day or so before the deadline the whisky'd be gone, and once John got over his hangover, he'd sit down and write and draw like hell. He never missed a mailboat to Frisco.

Undoubtedly the yarn originated from the fact that Thomason often wrote under contract or on commission, receiving his fee in advance, because of the tremendous demand for his work. But in its present form the anecdote cries for rebuttal. In the first place, writing did not come easy for Thomason. Writing for the Marine officer was a slow, agonizing, time-consuming procedure. As a matter of fact, he would have rejected such a cavalier performance as unworthy of his standards.

By his own admission, Thomason never wrote anything carelessly. For much of his work he prepared thoroughly in advance, conducting extensive research for both his short stories and books. The author's notebooks, ledgers in which he wrote, annotated sources, and original manuscripts in the Thomason Collection confirm that Thomason wrote painstakingly, revising tediously as the work progressed. Sometimes he revised only certain paragraphs, but frequently he reworked a specimen of writing from the beginning.

In some instances there are as many as three versions of the same story or article in the collection, one of which bears the label "not final copy." Other specimens of his writing techniques reveal that he worked on a single story at odd times employing whatever materials — letterhead stationery, ledgers, notebooks, sheets ripped from tablets — that were convenient at the moment.

Sketching came more natural to the artist. True, he drew hastily in the heat of combat, sketched beginnings of scenes only to capture an instant impression and lay aside to finish later. But frequently he immersed himself in research to achieve authenticity in his illustrations, and his sketchbooks show he executed a progression of studies before he was satisfied with the results. Witness the care he expended on the illustrations for the Stuart biography and the Marbot memoirs.

The most convincing evidence that John Thomason did not drink to excess is the work he did. His spectacular record of achievement and productivity is the strongest disproof of any allegation that he was guilty of overindulgence.

Thomason's record in the Marine Corps was impeccable. From the time of his induction in 1917 until the end of his career in 1944, he served his country with distinction. His World War I record speaks for itself: the Aisne-Marne (Château-Thierry) Defensive, June 6 to July 5, 1918; the Aisne-Marne Offensive (Soissons), July 17 to July 21, 1918; the Marbache Sector (Pont-a-Mousson), August 7 to August 16, 1918; the San Mihiel offensive in September; and the Meuse-Argonne Offensive (Champagne) in October.

An exemplary officer, Thomason was twice decorated for the same act of gallantry in action, first with the Army's Silver Star and later with the Navy Cross. The Navy citation reads in part:

> For gallantry in action at Soissons, July 18, 1918. While attacking through the Forest de Retz his company was stopped by heavy casualties from violent machine gun fire. The enemy machine gun nest was discovered to be under brush about fifty yards distant from the company's position. To prevent further severe casualties he, together with one enlisted man, advanced on the enemy machine gun nest from a flank, and with great gallantry, captured the nest containing two heavy machine guns, and killed the crew of thirteen.

In fifteen years, discounting the three he spent on the history of the Second Division, Thomason produced and illustrated eleven books, five of which dealt with the Marine Corps, two of which concerned the Civil War, and one of which involved Texas after the War Between The States. Furthermore, he wrote and illustrated a vast number of short stories and articles, including thirty-odd essays for the *American Mercury,* while simultaneously illustrating books and stories for other writers. His connection with the *North American News Alliance* permitted him to cable stories to the *New York Times* and other daily papers from his tours of duty over the world. Invariably he was writing at the request of a friend: an introduction to a book, a memorial to a fallen comrade, and articles for the yearbooks of the schools he attended.

He published his final book—*and a Few Marines*—and illustrated Robert S. Henry's *'First With The Most' Forrest* in the last year of his life. His byline reappeared in the *Saturday Evening Post* the month after his death.

Thomason's place in the literary world was secure before the 1930s. By the 1940s his reputation as an author had skyrocketed to new heights. The number of times Thomason's material was reprinted during his life probably exceeded that of any other writer of his day.

All Thomason's books were successful. Not only did he immortalize the United States Marines and humanize the tragedy of the Civil War, his treatment of the two themes culminated in three masterpieces: *Fix Bayonets!, Jeb Stuart,* and *Lone Star Preacher.* Although he declined to take an academic degree, Thomason had the satisfaction of seeing his essay *The Old South Myth* anthologized in university texts one year after its publication in *American Mercury* in 1938.

Thomason's artistic production, comprising some 5,000 separate items, includes such wide range of media as pencil drawings, pen-and-ink sketches, charcoals, watercolors, etchings, and oils. The artist also experimented successfully with modelling, and in addition to the portrait of his son at the age of eleven and the bust of his friend Roy Chapman Andrews, he created a self-portrait and sculptures of Chinese characters that intrigued him. His Marine poster is still admired.

Not only did Thomason produce his famous poster and publish his third masterpiece in 1941, he added new and refreshing stimulus to his Marine figure by writing another of the popular Sergeant Houston stories. Entitled *The Sergeant and the Ship*, the narrative was based on an actual incident connected with Thomason's intelligence work. As indicated, a major concern of the American Republics section was the surveillance of Axis vessels which sought escape in the Caribbean and Pacific Coast ports from British cruisers. German and Italian tankers and cargo carriers transported concealed armaments and sometimes strategic materials to be delivered to Axis submarines at some prearranged place of contact. In the story Gunnery Sergeant Houston, in the capacity of a United States naval shipping officer, thwarts an enemy ship's appointed rendezvous.

The year 1941 was memorable to Thomason for still another reason. His son, having withdrawn from the University of Virginia to enter the armed forces, had secured a commission as second lieutenant in the Marine Corps Reserve. A profound admirer of his father, with whom he maintained a close relationship, Jack was unhesitatingly interested in preserving the paternal image. Like his father, he had not cared to take a university degree. Moreover, he shared his father's enthusiasm for the Marine Corps and gave it his best effort. It was Jack's own decision to join the Corps, but his father could not have been more pleased with his son's choice of a career.

The acceleration of the war by the Axis powers affected Thomason's section of the Office of Naval Intelligence markedly. It brought almost instantly a virtual avalanche of applicants for jobs in Latin America — easy berths in a land of abundance and far-removed from the fighting front. To sift out the undesirables and incompetents in favor of the conscientious and qualified would have taxed the knowledge of human nature and diplomacy of a lesser man than Thomason.

Throughout the German submarine offensive of 1942, while the good neighbor policy was being exploited to the utmost, naval attaches and observers in the American republics were more efficient in the operational field than in the diplomatic. They worked almost around the clock with naval officers of some of the more strategic republics in the organization and training of naval defense forces.

There was also the imminent possibility of a surprise attack on the Panama Canal Zone locks because of the Canal's proximity to the Latin American republics. A suicide strike on one of the essential canal installations was not ruled out. Furthermore, the very lifestyle of some of the people and the nature of the terrain were favorable to such attacks. As a consequence, banana clearings, goat pastures, along with miles of beaches and acres of sandpits, were placed under constant surveillance. Attaches and observers devoted much time to land and sea patrols and making frequent reconnaissance flights over potentially dangerous areas.

In the summer of 1942 Thomason's section had increased from a mere dozen on his staff to fifty commissioned officers and enlisted men, with more than a sprinkling of WAVES serving in his Washington office and over twice that number on duty abroad. His reaction to the WAVES, in fact to all women in the various branches of the armed forces during the war, is interesting, if not amusing.

As his department became increasingly staffed with WAVES, he wrote his mother about it facetiously. "Eventually, says our truthful and patriotic secretary, 'WAVES will replace all enlisted men and junior officers who can serve at sea.' "

The prospect of receiving a WAVE ensign and fourteen ratings in February inspired further comment. ". . . It is all good clean fun. The Bureau of Personnel has issued a solemn ukase about saluting in relation to the WAVES. Regulations . . . note that the junior will salute first, regardless of sex classification, but adds our gallant Bureau, naval officers are gentlemen before they are naval officers and will doubtless act accordingly."

Thomason was not always certain whether the saluting WAVES were showing respect for the uniform or merely making a play for a pickup. "The gals . . . accompany their arm motions with such sweet smiles that more than one old curmudgeon (such as I am) is thrown into doubt," he wrote his mother. "It is perhaps fortunate that all the WAVES I have seen are downright unattractive . . . and neither the hardboiled hat they wear nor the uniform is entirely kind to a female with too much there and not enough yonder . . . The Army . . . enjoys the services of more talented casting directors. I have seen some very pretty WACS. . . .

"We have also the British and Canadian WACS, WAAFS, WRENS, and what you will. They don't run to beauty . . . but they are more military than Life Guardsmen. They don't smile when they salute and when they salute, believe me, you stay saluted!"

With the exception of Bolivia, naval attaché posts were operating at all of the South American capitals and an average of three naval observer offices in each republic. Organizations of corresponding size were maintained in Cuba, Haiti, and the Dominican Republic. In Central America attaché posts operated in Mexico City and Guatemala City. Approximately all the major Mexican ports on both coasts had observer posts. To augment the set up, eleven naval missions devoted to training activities were based in the major Latin American republics. Under the supervision of Pan-American Division of the Office of the Chief of Naval Operations, these ports depended, nevertheless, upon the naval attachés residing in American embassies for assistance in matters pertaining to salary and transportation.

In January of 1942 Thomason was elevated to the rank of colonel, first on a temporary basis, then on a permanent basis in the spring.

Thomason returned to Texas to attend the funeral of his father, whose death occurred on March 4, 1942. The doctor's death came within a week after the Thomasons' golden wedding anniversary. Because of Dr. Thomason's illness, the couple did not celebrate the occasion, even though a number of their children honored them with their presence.

His father's death came as no surprise to John. In 1936, when he and his family made their annual visit to Texas, he noticed with corresponding anxiety his father's declining health.

> Of all the men I know, he has come nearest to living and ordering his life the way he wants it [John wrote Sue shortly afterwards]. He is still the autocrat of his own world. The past holds for him no reproaches and the future no terrors . . . But in any case, he is entirely the master of his own destiny and the captain of his soul.

Dr. Thomason's demise was noted in the state press. He was eulogized, not as the father of the famous author-artist and Marine officer, but as a prominent Methodist layman and a man of science who had made a notable contribution to the field of medicine. He was also acclaimed for his humanitarian and philanthropic activities.

In spite of Dr. Thomason's seemingly autocratic tendencies, he possessed a gentle, sensitive nature that was known only to his immediate family. He kept a record of birthdays, deaths, and other important anniversaries, accompanied by personal comments, photographs, and clippings. The diminutive booklet in which he preserved this memorabilia also included biblical quotations underneath each printed date opposite the entry page.

The first inscription read: "J. W. Thomason and Sue Hayes Goree married February 24, 1892, at Rusk, Texas." Inserted loosely with the entry was a card inscribed "My Own Precious Darling with the request that she wear some of the flowers at the wedding tomorrow."

The second entry recorded that the couple's first child "John W. Thomason, Jr., [was] born February 28, 1893." The remainder of the page was filled with five capsule-sized photographs of John as a boy. No other page in the little volume contained as many photographs and some pages had none.

Diminutive photographs adorned all records of the Thomason daughters' birthday anniversaries. None of the pictures were made during the children's infancy. At a later date the doctor had attached photographs taken during their girlhood and had written underneath the record of birth a word or phrase which described the character of each.

For instance, the first, Sue Goree, whose birthday was April 5, 1896, was characterized as "Wise, sane, loving, dutiful;" the fourth, Elizabeth — born August 17, 1907 — was categorized as "Sweet Song Bird;" and the fifth, and last daughter, was identified simply as "Our Darling Baby Margaret Thomason born May 15, 1912." Other daughters were identified similarly in accordance with their personalities or character traits.

As a specialist in the treatment of diseases of the eye, ear, nose and throat, Dr. Thomason had acquired stature in the medical profession. But he took more satisfaction in the success of his children than he did in his own attainments. At seventy-eight he had lived long enough to see two of his sons pursue the family tradition of medicine — Herbert and Robert, whose wife Betty was also a doctor; and two daughters choose husbands in the profession — Emily, Dr. Henry A. Petersen of Houston and Margaret, Dr. Thomas C. Cole of Huntsville.

Dr. Thomason had seen all nine of his children well established professionally. In his later years he manifested great pride in John's multiple talents and fame.

The demise of Dr. Thomason, for whom John had been named and who had a major influence on his formative years, marked for his oldest son the end of an era. Shortly after his father's death, John wrote Sue: "The Doctor's funeral was a family, a tribal, a regional occasion . . . When he went, an era went with him and a circle was broken . . . I find the world a poorer place now that he is gone. . . ."

Colonel Thomason made his second tour of Latin America in the fall of 1942. In a measure it provided an antidote to sorrow occasioned by his father's death and came as a welcome change from the routine in Washington. Although it was shorter and less debilitating, the tour was in many ways a repetition of the first. Again Thomason inspected naval attachés and observer posts, focusing on those along the Pacific Coast of South America. The aggregation visited the country's capitals as it had before, with the same degree of success.

Upon his return to Washington in November, Thomason renewed his attempts to secure an active assignment or a command. The Solomon Islands Campaign had started and Guadalcanal was the center of much activity. These facts, along with Thomason's two-year moratorium from fleet duty, only increased his eagerness to participate in combat.

In his final year in Washington he had been forced to curtail his creative activity so drastically that he had published only two stories, neither of which he had illustrated. The first, *Dog Eat Dog*, appeared in the *Saturday Evening Post* in May of 1942;

the other, *And So He Went Along,* ran in the magazine in January of 1943.

It was gratifying to Thomason that Jack had obtained a transfer in January of 1943 to the First Marine Division then stationed in Australia following its great success in the Solomons. "You have all the news about Jack that we have," Thomason wrote the boy's grandmother, who worshipped him. "He's now in Vandegrift's First Division, somewhere in Australia . . . That division came away from Guadalcanal much exhausted and full of malaria and it will probably be some time before they are employed again. General Denig, his boss, tells me that they plan to bring him home for special duties, after he has some combat experience. Many of my friends from out there have seen him, and they all speak highly of him."

Thomason's relief arrived in March, and by the fifteenth he was on his way to California to join the staff of the Amphibious Training Command of the Pacific Fleet, based at Camp Elliott in the vicinity of San Diego.

16 *Semper Fidelis*

When John Thomason joined the staff of the Amphibious Training Command at Camp Elliott on the West Coast in March of 1943, he was optimistic. His work in the Office of Naval Intelligence had been officially classified as *outstanding*. Consequently he expected assignment either to a command or a combat post corresponding to his rank of colonel and high rating.

Meanwhile sales of *Lone Star Preacher* continued to soar, and his latest book, *and a Few Marines,* was well received. Dedicated to his son, Lieutenant John William Thomason, III — "a young Marine of this war" — the anthology of thirty-seven stories captured the true spirit of the United States Marines in peace and at war. The selections, ranging in scene from battlesites in France to South America, the Caribbean, and North China, brought forth once more the acclamation that Thomason was the Kipling of the Marine Corps.

The *New York Herald Tribune* led the way: "Colonel Thomason could well be called the Kipling of the Marine Corps. Observant, intuitive, witty, and sympathetic, he has gathered up innumerable threads with which to weave a glowing tapestry, a variegated scene peopled with men in uniform as they really are.''

Undoubtedly Thomason's realistic portrayal of the Marine molded the attitudes and spirit of the Corps during his lifetime and projected an example for young officers and noncommissioned men just as Kipling's depiction of the British Tommies in his stories and poems set the pattern for their inferior counterparts in Queen Victoria's regiments.

However, except for the semi-autobiographic nature of Thomason's work and the influence of the Bible, the analogy with Kipling ends here. Invariably the standard-bearer for British imperialism, Kipling, who always wrote down to the preservers of *Pax Brittanica,* could not cope with its decline after the Boer War. Even though he continued to write until his death in 1936, much of Kipling's work lacked substance. Thomason, on the other hand, who venerated the United States Marine and wrote with all of the pain that only a perfectionist exacts from himself, remained articulate. As late as 1970, when *Fix Bayonets!* was reissued, Robert Leckie wrote in the Introduction:

> Here in muscular, evocative prose and spare, stark pictures was the Marine Corps family: cocksure colonels, swaggering captains, shy shavetails, and most vivid and lifelike of all, our NCO's . . . Here also were the places these men had been — Belleau Wood, the Rhine, Peking, the Gobi Desert, the Banana Republics of the Caribbean, the wide oceans and most of the capital cities of the civilized world. . . .

With so much going for him and apparently free of worries, Thomason plunged enthusiastically into his work as assistant area inspector attached to the staff of the Amphibious Training Pacific Fleet. Within a month his expectations of an overseas assignment were realized when Admiral Chester W. Nimitz offered him the post of war plans officer and inspector of Marine bases. It was an impressive billet, a post tailormade for Thomason. Few men in the Corps were so well equipped to fill it as he from his previous experience dating back to his tour of duty with Assistant Secretary of the Navy Roosevelt.

"It is the very best appointment a Marine officer could have," John wrote his mother. "The Admiral is a friend of many years' standing. He asked for me in January, 1942, when he went to the Pacific command, but the Office of Naval Intelligence would not release me." Thomason assumed his new duty on April 23, 1943, with headquarters at Pearl Harbor.

Meanwhile, critics were seriously reappraising Thomason's art. They noted similarities between his art and that of the French military painters of the 1870s, who recorded graphically both the desperation and the glory of the Franco-Prussian War. Thomason may have surpassed his precursors — Alphonse de Neuville and Edouard Detaille — in his clarity of line, eye for precise detail, and grasp of the immediacy of battle.

Certainly there is no denying that Thomason holds an immediate place as the latest, and possibly the greatest, in the galaxy of military artists exemplified by Frederick Remington, Thore de Thulstrip, and Charles Schreyvogel — famed for his depiction of the United States regulars of the nineteenth century and of Zogbaum and Reuterdahl, who were famous for portraying the ships and men of the New Navy, brilliant in its success in the War with Spain.

Thomason's incisive pen-and-ink sketches did for the Marine Corps of World War I, and the two decades following, what Remington and his contemporaries had done for the American Army and Navy a century earlier. Thomason had more in common with Remington himself than with the latter's contemporaries. Both artists took their formal training at the Art Students League of New York. Both recorded the image of a thing as they saw it, were known for depicting swift action and intimate detail. Both had an exceptionally wide range of subject matter. Remington had also illustrated a number of articles and books of his own, and during the Spanish-American War had served as a war correspondent and artist.

But it was the Spanish painter Francisco Goya, from whom Thomason drew major inspiration and subconciously identified. To Thomason — Goya, whose paintings, drawings, and engravings covered every aspect of the life of his time — was ". . . one of the greatest painters who ever lived." Goya's *Los Desastres de la Guerra,* a series of etchings published in 1863, which recorded the French atrocities committed in Spain during the Peninsula War, had a remarkable influence on Thomason's art.

". . . and Goya was so much more than a painter!" Thomason wrote to a young officer in the Marine Corps. "I think the important thing about him was that he was so thoroughly alive, and he lived in every way right up to the limit of his large capacities. . . ."

Thomason could very well have been talking about himself. Few people of his time lived as fully or extracted comparable gratification from life. It is no exaggeration to say that Thomason's prodigious achievements in both the literary and artistic fields, as well as in the Marine Corps, would have reflected credit upon half a dozen men. Much of his success was due to his enormous vitality that characterized all of his activities and his determination to excel.

Moreover, Thomason lived life "right up to the limit of his large capacities" until his time ran out. Thomason's ardor for living became even more evident when he joined the staff of Admiral Nimitz at Pearl Harbor.

Almost immediately after reporting on April 23rd, Thomason toured the entire theater of operations, inspecting installations in the New Hebrides, New Caledonia, and in the Central and Southern Solomons, including Guadalcanal. In early July he was hospitalized briefly at Melbourne, Australia. Despite his weakened condition he completed his rigid inspection tour. By mid-July it was necessary for him to seek further medical treatment at Pearl Harbor.

"I was up at Guadalcanal . . . last week," he wrote Jim Boyd on July 27, 1943. "The boys are all bedded down . . . I went there and bowed my head. It's rather a nice place under palm trees . . . In Melbourne I was taken with double pneumonia, which should have killed me but didn't."

Thomason exposed himself to extreme danger when he observed the seizure of Munda, the Japanese airfield on New Georgia Island, in a joint operation involving the Marine Corps and the United States Army.

"I went on and finished the circuit, including a nice fight now going on in the Northern Solomons, at New Georgia — Munda — Rendova — Buka . . . I was in a 90 mm gunpit when a dive bomber came in on us — we had 6 of his planes burning in the air at that time. This bastard came right through everything we had and put a 290 kilo bomb right on the breech of the gun — and I was the only one who survived . . . I was on an LSC [Landing Ship Cargo] — the 343 that was divebombed the next day. They killed the staff sergeant . . . I was up with the 43rd Division — the most incredible bunch of Indian Tamers you ever saw in your life — and I have never been in so much danger as I was then. They shoot from 2000 yards back at everything that moves. . . ."

(It is of passing interest that Thomason had been forced to alter his opinion of the Japanese as fighters since the attack on Shanghai in 1932.)

But as much as Thomason desired to serve his country actively in World War II, the custom of putting duty before self, the grueling hours of desk work, the additional time he devoted to his creative activities, and the fact that he refused to compromise either profession — all conspired to prevent him.

In addition, there were his close calls with death in the major battles of 1918, when he was gassed — a thing he tried to forget but which his friend Woollcott kept remembering; the rigorous life of the tropics; enervating hours of air travel and concomitant inconveniences, all of which had left their impact. Thus at only fifty John Thomason had lived with such zest that he had undermined his health.

His condition deteriorated so rapidly that with less time in the South Pacific than four months, it was considered in the best interest of his health that he return for state-side duty.

"I am returning to our shores sooner than I thought I would," he wrote his mother on August 7 from aboard ship. "They made up their minds in Washington that, in view of my pneumonia, my health was too precarious for foreign duty . . . Admiral Nimitz held up my orders while a reconsideration was requested. But General Holcomb's solicitude for my health could not be shaken, and I'll be in San Francisco tomorrow . . .

In San Diego the next day . . . the pneumonia pulled me down some . . . But I did some very hard traveling in my convalescent period. . . .''

Two weeks later Thomason assumed the post of operations and training officer of the Amphibious Training Command at Camp Elliott, determined to discharge his duties to the extent of his capabilities.

Detachment from the Pacific Fleet was naturally a blow to Thomason's ego. His final tour of duty could have been the most difficult of his career, had his philosophy and determination to make the most of an unfortunate situation not sustained him.

Max Perkins wrote John soon after his return: ''. . . Anyhow, it was a great chance for you to see it all'' [seizure of Munda] . . . ''And one can't help but be glad that you are back even though knowing that you prefer not to be. . . .

''— *and a Few Marines* goes along and I think the outcome will please you . . . I hope everything goes well with all of you.''

John Thomason was not a person to mope over misfortune. On the contrary, he could accept it at face value and rise above it.

''There's a lot of the war left,'' he wrote his mother, ''and anything may happen before it's over . . . I propose to spend the rest of it as comfortably as possible, do what they tell me to do, and come home [Huntsville] for good when it's over.'' Whatever his losses, there remained always the recompense of home.

In one sense John W. Thomason never really left Huntsville. In another, and a very real sense, Huntsville never left John Thomason. He removed himself physically from the familiar scenes of his boyhood and youth, but he retained those lasting impressions of home and solid values that Huntsville had transmitted to him.

For in those remaining months at Camp Elliott — Thomas Wolfe to the contrary — John Thomason went home again. As he had begun his artistic career with the drawing and painting of wildlife around his father's farm so did he return to the sketching and painting of the feathered creatures native to the West Coast — the same symbols of home and everything home meant, transferred to another locale. As time permitted, he also hunted in the unusual terrain near the base as he had done as a boy in the fields and woods of East Texas.

Thomason had said his valedictory to the Corps in — *and a Few Marines*. Now it was his privilege to reappraise those basic values to which he related in boyhood. Furthermore, he went about it with a dignity and intensity that astonished those close to him.

As if these activities were not enough to attest to his living life to the "limit of his large capacities," John Thomason wrote a last short story which appeared posthumously in the *Saturday Evening Post* in April of 1944. "I'm glad to tell you that we are buying THE COLLABORATOR, which we all like very much indeed," the editor wrote him on February 2, 1944. "It is too long, but I will use a sympathetic pencil on it. You will, of course, see galleys and can smooth any rough spots that I may leave. It is needless for me to tell you how glad we are to have you back in the book."

It is of more than parenthetical import that the author's final utterance was a story of love, warfare, and heroic death set in the Pacific island of Arawate during World War II. Like most of Thomason's stories involving the Marine Corps, it stemmed from truth. One Fred Krautz — a Marine with an unblemished record, who came to the Legation Guard in Peking in the early 1930s and was detailed to the machine gun company Thomason commanded — had remained in China when United States citizens were advised to leave in 1941. Unable to obtain a passport for his White Russian wife, the Marine had gone into business in the Orient.

Later, under the pressure of the Japanese, he was forced to become a collaborator with his wife and son as pawns. It was during Thomason's service with the Office of Naval Intelligence that he picked up the trail of Krautz and learned of the Japanese connection.

Krautz's mission was to penetrate the American formation at Arawate, wearing a Marine combat suit and carrying United States web equipment and helmet and a Garand rifle, and ascertain the strength of the operation. He had been promised the privilege of reuniting with his wife and son in Shanghai upon the completion of his mission.

In the interim, however, Krautz learns that the Japanese have already liquidated his family. With nothing to lose, then, but his life, he undertakes the mission as a means of retrieving his honor. Before his death, he succeeds in alerting the Marines and helps them to defeat the Japanese in a decisive action.

Generally an encore is not expected to measure up to an artist's usual performance. *The Collaborator* is an exception. In its preservation of Marine Corps tradition, it is one of Thomason's most compelling epics of the Leatherneck.

It is an interesting coincidence that the last book to which Thomason directed his artistic talents dealt with the Civil War theme. It was Henry's *'First With the Most' Forrest,* a biography of the Confederate cavalry leader, Nathan Bedford Forrest, published by Bobbs-Merrill in 1944. When General Forrest, a military genius, was asked to explain his success in winning battles, he said that the way he won was "to get there first with the most men." Today Forrest's military maxim has become one of the most misquoted in American history: "I git thar fustest with the mostest men."

Thomason created the striking design for the dust jacket in five colors against a blue-gray background. The composition is a portrait of the general in resplendent Confederate uniform astride his horse. Titled "Forrest in Action," the design is repeated in a black and white photograph as the frontispiece.

A pleasant interlude during the Marine officer's respite came at Thanksgiving when Jack returned to La Jolla to spend the holiday with his family. The occasion gave Jack the opportunity to rejoin his lovely bride, the former Ruth Wynne of Huntsville, whom he had recently married and who had been living in California with Jack's parents. While their husbands served the country in the armed forces, Leda and Ruth had engaged in hospital work at home. It was Lieutenant John W. Thomason, III's first visit home from his tour of combat duty in the Pacific, and no doubt he and his father enjoyed man-to-man discussions of the progress of the war in that theater of operations.

Thomason spent Christmas of 1943 in the Naval Hospital at San Diego. "We have not had the details of your Christmas yet," he wrote his mother on December 29th, "but you must have had a quorum of the outfit [the Thomason family] present . . . I write from the Naval Hospital in which I was admitted on 19 December with a recurrence of my stomach affliction [ulcer] . . . and I expect to be out and back at work shortly. . . .

"The Southern California winter has started and it's raining every day. Everything is sort of bleak. . . ." As if to emphasize the discouraging atmosphere and add graphic documentation to his letter, Thomason includes a pen-and-ink sketch of a sick soldier wearing fatigues. At the top is the notation "Shell shock (W.W. II neurosis), Munda, July '43." It is interesting to note that he employs the phrase in common use in World War I instead of the expression "battle fatigue" current at the time.

Released from the hospital in January, Thomason was readmitted the following month. On February 28, his birthday, he began his final letter — to his mother — and finished it on March 1. As usual Thomason's thoughts were multifaceted: the family, the war, his illness, the future, his birthday, and the death of a close friend.

"I'm not particularly uncomfortable," he wrote. "Before I came in I merely felt low." On March 1, he continued: "meanwhile, your kind birthday letter arrived with check which I'll spend foolishly as you wish. Fifty-one years is fifty-one years, and I have outlived a lot of them. Jim Boyd, perhaps my best friend, died at Princeton day before yesterday. He was making a lecture . . . collapsed at a reception afterwards, and never regained consciousness. I will never look upon his like again."

The expression of tribute Thomason had reserved for only two men. The first time he used it ("I shall not know his like again") was when his friend Henry L. Roosevelt died. Both friends who predeceased him left the scene young. Roosevelt was 56, Boyd 55.

James Boyd — John's intimate friend for more than two decades — succumbed to a heart attack at Princeton, New Jersey, February 26, 1944. A native of Pennsylvania, Boyd had graduated from Princeton in 1910. He had served in the St. Mihiel and Meuse-Argonne offensives as had Thomason.

"As soon as it's [the war's] over, I'll retire and live in Texas," John wrote. "I have still a lot of hunting and fishing to do, and I want to learn to paint." For Thomason to make the statement about his art was characteristic of his innate modesty.

Leda and Jack were in his thoughts: "Leda continues at her good works . . . I'm sure Robert [Dr. Robert Thomason] hated to miss his regiment's attack on Eniwetok and Jack missed New Gloucester, too —"

On March 12, 1944, a few minutes after noon, death retired Colonel John William Thomason from the United States Marine Corps after a distinguished career spanning twenty-seven years. It was the Marine officer's belief that his Supreme Commanding Officer would "discharge" him only after he had earned the right to immortality.

Thomason's untimely death shocked the literary and military worlds. Within the fewest hours all Marine Corps posts and stations in the United States knew of the tragedy. The national press conveyed the news as quickly as wire services and air waves could transmit it. Professional magazines and periodicals followed with voluminous tributes.

Among the most notable eulogies from Thomason's literary peers were those by William Rose Benet and J. Frank Dobie. In the *Saturday Review of Literature* (March 18, 1944) Benet, whose *The Dust Which Is God* won a Pulitzer Prize in 1942, said:

> . . . Colonel Thomason of the Marines was a true artist. In pen, pencil, or watercolor, the free stroke conveying movement and life, which is the mark of the artist born, was always his. As he drew, so he wrote, from his first *Fix Bayonets!* James Norman Hall ranked him with Barbusse and the Masefield who was prose writer in the last war . . . How well he would have written of their [the Marines'] great exploits had he lived . . . He seemed born with the crafts of writing and drawing both at his fingertips.

Some months before, Thomason had written to Dobie, who had just completed a year of lecturing at Cambridge. "The Empire's [England's] impact on you gives me no concern," he had stated in part, "for I am also a fairly wide-travelled Texican [sic]. Cities and dreams and Powers simply remind us of something better that we know ourselves . . . when this [World War II] is over, I shall return to Texas, and I look forward to seeing you there."

Since their student days at Southwestern University the two authors had maintained contact. Thomason's mellowness is mirrored in his words. Few people of the time were better qualified to speak with authority on "Cities and dreams and Powers." It was typical of Thomason to identify Dobie, whom he considered to be the salt of the earth and a typical Texan, with that "something better" peculiar to the state.

Before Dobie got around to answering the letter, he learned of Thomason's death. In the *Southwest Review* (Summer of 1944) the author of *A Texan in England* says goodbye:

> Well I had looked forward also. I imagined a cool place in the shade along in the evening, with perhaps something else cool befitting the time of day, and talk until long after the dusk had blurred the shadows . . . Now we won't sit in the shadow made by a great elm tree, but the gracious shadow he cast upon the land of his birth and of his imagination's play will never be entirely blurred out . . . In the name of people who, because of what you have written, are richer . . . and live more abundantly on the soil they belong to, I salute you, John W. Thomason, soldier in the old gallant tradition, fine Southern gentleman, and patriot who made your own corner of the earth more beautiful.

Another friend who was deeply bereft at Thomason's death was Roy Chapman Andrews. When Dr. Andrews learned of John's demise he got in touch with the family and wrote for them a tribute that is classic for its simplicity. The version quoted here is slightly excerpted:

> A ripple of excitement went through the American colony of Peking, China, when we heard that John W. Thomason, Jr., had been assigned to the Marine Corps detachment of the Legation Guard. We were accustomed to the great and the near great, and to interesting people of many nationalities, but John's arrival was something special. Before he came

I knew him only through his writings, but to others in Peking he was a comrade in the Corps or a personal friend.

When we met I liked him instantly. He had a warm smile and the soft voice, quiet dignity and innate courtesy of a Southern gentleman. He became my friend. We spent many hours together and none were ever dull.

John was proud of and passionately devoted to the Marine Corps. Even his interest in art and literature never superceded his love for the United States Marines. No company was more thoroughly trained than his, and in none did the men have higher respect for their commander. . . .

John Thomason was richly endowed with many talents. As I knew him, he was a lover of peace and the cultural side of life but, paradoxically, in his own profession he was a man of war. If he had to make war, knowing the waste and horror and pity of it, it was a job to do and he would do it well. John never did anything poorly.

They buried John Thomason in the family plot in Oakwood Cemetery in Huntsville following a simple service held from the family residence on Avenue J, his place of birth. He had recorded in *Sergeant Bridoon of the Horse Marines* his wish to be interred at home: ". . . my friends would never walk past my grave in Arlington, where a retired Marine rates being buried . . . No, my bones would not be there."

The body was transferred to Huntsville from San Diego under military escort with Colonel Gilder G. Jackson, Jr., of the Marine Corps performing the courtesy. Brigadier General Paul Wakefield, a friend who had followed Thomason's career from the outset, attended the funeral as an official representative of Governor Coke Stevenson. At the graveside rites another Marine, Lieutenant John William Thomason, III, delivered the brief oration.

Spring comes early to East Texas. Green grass carpeted the path from the iron gate facing west at Houston's monument to the Thomason plot. Through the interlacing branches of oak and magnolia trees the sun's gold and the blue of the sky filtered down. They left John there. They left John where above, the wild geese he loved to paint fly south against the muted tones of autumn sunsets. . . .

Postscript

In February, only a month before John's death, American bombing raids on the continent had been stepped up on a gigantic scale. By May the *Luftwaffe* conceded failure to beat off the air cover for invasion. John had missed D-day, which had been delayed by a storm until June 6, by less than three months.

In the war in the Pacific, he had been able to check off Guadalcanal in February of '43 and victories in the Marshall Islands a month before he died—February of '44. It was regrettable that he could not wait for the taking of the volcanic island of Iwo Jima by the Marines in February of '45—the bloodiest battle in the history of the Corps—in which his son Jack's demonstration of courage won him the Silver Star.

Much of the bitterest fighting any the dropping of the bombs on Hiroshima and Nagasaki, the inevitable fall of Japan, and the signing of the articles of surrender aboard the battleship *Missouri* in Tokyo Bay on September 2, 1945, all occurred after Thomason's death.

Had John Thomason lived until the end of the war, he would have felt relieved, but saddened, at the wholesale destruction and the tremendous sacrifice of human life. Despite his acceptance of arms as a profession, his superior knowledge of military tactics, and his successful experience in combat—as well as his earlier sense of drama in relation to war—Thomason became a pacifist as he matured. Again and again he professed his love of peace in his letters, in his articles, and in his books.

Years before, John Thomason had become insensitive to commendation. But his death was the occasion for many honors. An oil portrait of Colonel Thomason hangs in the state capitol at Austin—a distinction reserved only for the Valhalla of Texas immortals. Painted by Susanne Atkinson, daughter of Dr. Herbert

Thomason, the portrait was accepted by Governor Allan Shivers on April 29, 1960, in appropriate ceremonies.

In 1955 a medal authorized by the 84th Congress and signed by President Dwight D. Eisenhower was struck in Thomason's honor as a commemoration of the one hundred twentieth anniversary of the signing of the Texas Declaration of Independence. The Texas Heritage Foundation, which held the medal in trust, presented it as the Distinguished Service Medal to the Thomason family February 28, 1959, acclaiming Colonel Thomason as "Soldier, Writer, Artist, Sculptor, Poet, and Texan."

The graphic arts building at Sam Houston State University bears his name and carries an impressive testimonial plaque in its foyer. The elegant centerpiece of the Sam Houston State University Library, which houses rare documents and books and special collections, including the magnificent Thomason Collection of over 5,000 items, is a memorial called the Colonel John W. Thomason Room. A Section of the Marine Corps Development and Education Command at Quantico, Virginia, has been named Thomason Park in memory of the young Marine who once trained there.

On November 4, 1961, when the magnificent three-panel Texas monument of native red granite was unveiled at the Vicksburg National Military Park, the inscription of the center panel read:

> Texas remembers the valor and devotion of her sons who served at Vicksburg and in other theaters of the War Between the States. "For those men believed in something. They counted life a light thing to lay down in the faith they bore. They were terrible in battle. They were generous in victory. They rose up from defeat to fight again, and while they lived, they were formidable. The heritage they left of valor and devotion, is treasured by a united country."
> — John W. Thomason, Jr.

If John Thomason could ascend those eleven steps, emblematic of the eleven states of the Confederacy and serving as the base of the monument, he would be pleased at the recognition accorded the classic *Lone Star Preacher*. However, he would probably spend more time before the smaller right panel of the monument reading the names of the Texas Units that engaged in the Vicksburg Campaign and their officers — the real heroes of whom he wrote.

As recently as February 4, 1979, when Chinese Vice Premier Teng Hsaio-ping made an official visit to the United States, after a normalization of relations between the two countries, a specimen of Thomason's art executed during his tour of duty in the Orient was presented to the dignitary. The work, a watercolor gousche, was the original for Thomason's Christmas card mailed from Peking in 1932. Appropriately the composition was centered by a Mongolian peasant feeding a camel.

The presentation was made by Lieutenant Governor of Texas William P. Hobby when the vice premier included Houston in his itinerary. Sam Houston State University provided the painting.

The gesture had more significance than many people realized. Thomason's enthusiasm for Oriental culture was a vital part of him. He developed a deep appreciation for the Chinese people themselves and spent many hours in recording the Oriental life patterns with his brush and pen. He anticipated with pleasure that time when the immense province would become a unified nation. In one sense the gesture was tantamount to a posthumous recognition of the Peoples Republic of China thirty-five years after Thomason's demise and forty-six after the artist's tour of the Orient.

In recent years Thomason's sketches and paintings have been exhibited in many parts of the United States and never fail to inspire admiration.

But the recognition that John W. Thomason would have appreciated most came on September 29, 1944, within six months after his death. On that date the United States Navy Department christened a destroyer the USS John W. Thomason (DD 760) in his honor. The warship was later pressed into service in the Far East and earned seven battle stars and other awards for its contribution to the Korean Campaign. A Marine to the last, John Thomason, who had lived by a ship's bells at sea, would have treasured this honor above all others.

John William Thomason III — who died in an airplane crash near Calcutta, India — survived his father by five years. He was 28. Today, side by side, their resting places marked by identical gray granite headstones bearing *Semper Fidelis* and the Marine emblem, the dust of the two Marines mingles with that of Houston and Yoakum. Besides the Marine insignia and name on the younger Thomason's monument, the inscription reads: "Major, USMC Res . . . Born Camaguey, Cuba, June 14, 1920, Died Calcutta, India, March 27, 1949."

If but briefly, the traditional Thomason mantle had rested gracefully on the young Marine officer's shoulders. His service record in Guadalcanal, New Guinea, Saipan, and Iwo Jima during World War II was brilliant. A decorated Marine officer on reserve status, Thomason had entered the diplomatic service in 1946. At the time of his death Major Thomason had served as the American vice consul of public affairs in Calcutta for three years.

On Colonel John W. Thomason's marker, in addition to the insignia, dates, and name, is the phrase "Soldier — Artist — Writer" and the last two lines of the final quatrain of Stevenson's "Requiem."

> [*This be the verse you 'grave for me:*
> *Here he lies where he longed to be;*]
> *Home is the sailor, home from the sea,*
> *And the hunter home from the hill.*

Confederate soldier on horseback   *Idealization of a Southern officer*

Illustrations from Lone Star Preacher.
    — *Courtesy Sam Houston State Library*

Illustration from Lone Star Preacher.
        — Courtesy Sam Houston State Library

Illustration from Lone Star Preacher.
— *Courtesy Sam Houston State Library*

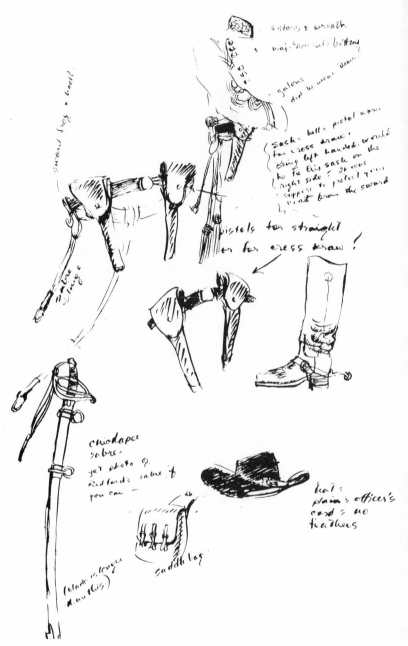

Illustration from Lone Star Preacher.
— *Courtesy Sam Houston State Library*

Drawings from Fix Bayonets! *Many of the sketches were done under fire.*

German and Marine in hand-to-hand combat.
— Courtesy Thomason Collection, SHSU Library

Red Pants

Gone to Texas

Adventures of General Marbot

Colonel 1st Virginia Cavalry
1861

Jeb Stuart

Born on an Iceberg

Boy with gun

Characteristic Southwestern Birds. One of the artist's last sketches.

Mallards, 1916

UNITED STATES MARINE CORPS

MARINE BARRACKS

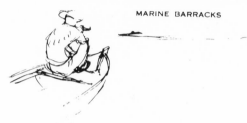

Target 'gator at 12 o'clock

Captain John W. Thomason, 1925. Thomason was exceedingly proud of the cut and fit of his uniform.

— Courtesy Leda Thomason

Letter from France to Dr. and Mrs. Thomason. This was one of Thomason's first letters.

Self-Portrait which Colonel Thomason enclosed in a letter in 1941. This is a first publication of the sketch.

— Courtesy Thomason Collection, SHSU Library

Page from a Thomason letter to Boyd, October 30, 1935: "The sketch is a tongue-in-cheek portrayal of the two authors at work. Although their editor and close friend Maxwell Perkins grew impatient for manuscript at times, the two were quite productive and gave him no problem. Thomason's inscription reads: Max Perkins' conception of two of his first-string writers hard at work on their forthcoming novels. And the hell of it is, that old Egyptian overseer Max is quite correct in his judgments. . . . I'm sorry your visit must be expended locally. I can't come. See you in Newport this summer. I'm wearing my usual hat, by God. John."

— James Boyd Papers, Southern Historical Collection,
University of North Carolina Library,
Chapel Hill, North Carolina

FLEET ADMIRAL CHESTER W. NIMITZ, U. S. NAVY
728 SANTA BARBARA ROAD
BERKELEY 7, CALIFORNIA

10 October 1958.

Dear General Wakefield:—

Every so often in the armed forces of our country we find a gifted person who is not only an efficient and courageous fighting man — but a capable writer and author as well.

Such a one was the late Colonel John W. Thomason Jr., USMC - who coupled with his writing talent the rare ability to make vivid drawings of the characters and scenes he wrote about.

On top of that he was a fighting marine who served most satisfactorily on my staff in the Pacific during World War II. Before that we had worked together on the Board of Control of the U.S. Naval Institute in Annapolis Maryland.

It was a valued privilege to have known and worked with Colonel Thomason.

Sincerely
C. W. Nimitz

Letter from Fleet Admiral Chester W. Nimitz, U.S. Navy to General Paul Wakefield, 10 October 1958, recalling Colonel Thomason's service in the Pacific during World War II. General Wakefield passed the letter on to Thomason's family.

— Courtesy Emily Thomason Petersen

*A specimen of Thomason's lusty humor, "All a Soldier Needs Is . . ."
was made during a discussion on essential equipment for field service
at the Army War College in 1937. Quantity reproduction by offset
lithography followed to satisfy the requests for copies by Thomason's
classmates. Lost for several years, the sketch resurfaced and was published for the first time in* Fortitudine, Newsletter of the Marine Corps
Historical Program, Washington, D.C., Vol. III, Fall 1973.

Bibliography and Thomason Checklist

Barns, Florence E. *Texas Writers of Today*. Dallas: Tardy Publishing Company, 1935.

Barretto, Larry. "Of the Marines: Review of *Red Pants*." *Herald Tribune Books*, May 15, 1927.

"Beau Sabreur," *New York Times*, July 22, 1940.

"Behind the Scenes with Scribner's Authors," *Scribner's Magazine*, 78 (June 1925), 2; 78 (August, 1925), 2; 78 (September, 1925), 2-3; 78 (November, 1925), 3.

Benét, William Rose. "Immortality in Writers," *Saturday Review of Literature*, XXVII (March 18, 1944), 14.

_____. "Round about Parnassus," *Saturday Review of Literature*, November 26, 1932. Salutes Thomason's fine illustrations in the World War I anthology of verse *Taps* by Roosevelt and Rice.

Bolton, Theodore. *American Book Illustrators, Bibliographic Check Lists of 121 Artists*. New York: R. R. Bowker Company, 1938.

"The Book of the Day: The Lively Career of Jeb Stuart, Most Romantic Figure of the Civil War," *The New York Sun*, November 19, 1930. Illustrated with dust jacket design.

"The Book of the Week." Review of *Adventures of General Marbot*, *New York News*, October 6, 1935.

"Book of the Week: John Thomason Writes Biography of *Jeb Stuart*," *Dallas Journal*, November 16, 1930.

Boyd, Thomas. "Over There," *Saturday Review of Literature*, II (April 3, 1926), 680.

Burlingame, Roger. *Of Making Many Books*. New York: Scribner's Sons, 1946.

Byrd, Sigman. "Byrd's-Eye View: Huntsville's Famous Marine," *Houston Chronicle*, July 26, 1955.

Campbell, Walter S. *The Book Lover's Southwest*. Norman, Oklahoma: University of Oklahoma Press, 1955.

Carroll, H. Bailey. "Texas Collections," *Southwestern Historical Quarterly*, 56 (July, 1952), 131-132.

Clicquennol, Ralph N., First Lieutenant, Cavalry Reserves, U.S. Army. "Stuart Forrest, Daring Cavalrymen, Figure in New Books; Captain Thomason Writes of Stuart; Englishman Immortalizes Forrest," *The Knickerbocker Press*, Sunday, January 18, 1931. Copy in Thomason Collection is annotated by Thomason.

Commager, Henry Steele. "In Turbulent Texas's Romantic Youth: A Richly Illustrated Novel of Days When Wild Dreams of Mexico and Indians

Came True." Review of *Gone to Texas, New York Herald Tribune Books,*
Sunday, October 24, 1937. Illustrated by three sketches from the novel.

_____. "Ruperts of the Confederacy." Review and comparison of Thomason's
Jeb Stuart with Erick William Sheppard's *Bedford Forrest, New York
Herald Tribune,* November 16, 1930. Illustrated with sketches from *Jeb
Stuart.*

Dedication of Texas Monument Vicksburg National Military Park, Vicksburg,
Mississippi, November 4, 1961, Program Sponsored by United Daughters
of the Confederacy, Texas Division, State Building Commission, Texas
State Historical Survey Committee.

Dobie, J. Frank. "Dobie Praises 'Lone Star Preacher,' Traces the Background
of Thomason," *Houston Post,* Sunday, February 2, 1941.

_____. "Jeb Stuart: And Another Soldier and Gentleman," *Houston Post,*
February 6, 1944.

_____. *A Texan in England.* Boston: Little Brown & Company, 1946.

_____. "John W. Thomason," *Southwest Review,* XXIX (Summer, 1944), x.

Dwyer, Charles Lee. "An Appreciation of Colonel John W. Thomason, Jr.: An
Address Made To The East Texas Historical Association," Henderson,
Texas, February 26, 1976. Typescript in Thomason Collection.

Dykes, Jeff C. "Tentative Check Lists of Western Illustrators, XXV, John W.
Thomason, Jr.," *American Book Collector,* April, 1967.

Erskine, John. "Rare Tales of Daredevil Leathernecks." Review of — *and a Few
Marines, Chicago Sun Book Week,* June, 13, 1943. Illustrated by jacket
design.

"Fame," *The New Yorker,* January 23, 1926, 11-12.

" 'Fix Bayonets' War Classic; Volume By Texas Officer Is Remarkable Story Of
Conflict," *Dallas Times Herald,* April 4, 1926. Illustrated by pen-and-
ink sketch entitled "Automatic Rifle Man" made by the author in the
heat of combat.

Freeman, Douglas Southall. "A Glorious Book on Stuart Reviewed by Doug-·
las Freeman," *Richmond News-Leader,* November 11, 1930.

Gaston, Edwin W. *The Early Novel of the Southwest.* Albuquerque, New Mexico: University of New Mexico Press, 1961.

Gelder, Robert Van. "John W. Thomason Writes of Turmoil in Texas."
Review of *Gone to Texas, New York Times,* October 24, 1957.

Giesmer, Maxwell. "Latest Works of Fiction," *New York Times Book Review,*
May 9, 1941.

_____. "Latest Works of Fiction: The Devil Dogs." Review of — *and a Few Ma-
rines, New York Times Book Review,* March 9, 1943. Illustrated with
jacket design and six pen-and-ink sketches by Thomason.

Graves, John. "The Old Breed: A Note on John W. Thomason, Jr.," *Southwest Review,* LIV (Winter, 1969), 36-46.

Griffith, B. S. "The Army in the Grand Manner: The Major Goes to Texas."
Review of *Gone to Texas, Charlotte, N.C., News,* November 7, 1937.

"God's Will Be Done," *Knoxville (Tennessee) Journal,* October 20, 1930.

Goree, Major Thomas J. Papers. Archives, Louisiana State University Library, Baton Rouge, Louisiana.

Gould, John. "Fix Bayonets! Marines' Story of World War." *The Wichita Falls Times,* May 9, 1926.

Guerard, Albert. "Memoirs of a Gallant Hussar." Review of *Adventures of General Marbot,* " edited and illustrated by Thomason. *New York Herald Tribune Books,* November 10, 1935. Illustrated with drawings from the book.

Hale, Leon. "The Brief, Productive Life of a Marine," *Houston Post,* Sunday, January 20, 1980.

Heinl, R. D. Colonel, U.S. Marine Corps. "Preface" to —*and a Few Marines.* New York: Charles Scribner's Sons, 1943.

Hunt, Frazier. "What a Fighter! What a Writer!" *Hearst's International & Cosmopolitan,* May, 1926, 17.

"Huntsville's Famous Marine," *Houston Chronicle,* July 26, 1955.

The Indian Head, VI, 19 (Washington, D.C., October, 1931), Second Division Army War College. Features a photograph of Captain John W. Thomason and his Chinese chauffeur standing beside Thomason's sedan automobile near the Temple of Agriculture in Peking. Of special interest is an Indian Head (insignia of the Second Division) on the cross bar in front of the radiator of the car. The report was that the Oriental chauffeur considered the Indian Head an amulet.

Jackson, Joseph H. "Major Thomason Presents General Marbot, Lively Napoleonic Adventurer," *San Francisco Chronicle,* November 3, 1935.

"Jeb Stuart," *The Post* (Vicksburg, Mississippi), October 24, 1930.

Johnson, Robert V. (ed.). "John W. Thomason Jr. Depicts Fighting Parson in Civil War Story 'Lone Star Preacher,' " *Houston Post,* January 20, 1941.

Johnston, Ben B. "Today's Book:" Review of *Salt Winds and Gobi Dust, Macon Telegraph,* May 8, 1934.

Kuest, Frank. "The Battle of Belleau Wood," *The American Legion Magazine,* 105 (October, 1978), 14-15, 62.

Kunitz, Stanley J., and Howard Haycraft (eds.). *Twentieth Century Authors: A Biographical Dictionary of Modern Literature.* New York: The H. W. Wilson Company, 1942.

Leckie, Robert, USMC. "Introduction" to *Fix Bayonets!* New York: Charles Scribner's Sons, 1970.

Leisy, Ernest K. *The American Historical Novel.* Norman, Oklahoma: University of Oklahoma Press, 1950.

"Letters: Readers Say November 1979 *Gazette* Was Best Ever," *Marine Corps Gazette,* 64 (February, 1980), 14-16.

"Literature and Letters," *The Times-Picayune,* December 28, 1930. Compares Nathan Bedford Forrest (*Bedford Forrest* by Captain Eric William Sheppard, Dial Press) and *Jeb Stuart.*

"The Lord Helps Those Who Help Themselves," *New York Daily News*, March 9, 1933. Editorial comment on Thomason's cable to the *New York Times*, March 6, 1933, in which he details a firsthand account of the Japanese invasion of China.

Major, Mabel, Rebecca W. Smith, and T. M. Pearce. *Southwest Heritage: A Literary History*. Albuquerque, New Mexico: University of New Mexico Press, 1948.

"Marine Captain Told By Cable He Is Famous," *Houston Chronicle*, July 13, 1925.

Morrison, C. M. "Captain Thomason Describes World War as Leathernecks Saw It in 'Fix Bayonets!' No Cant and No Simpering in Finest Account Yet Written of Americans in Action in France," *Minneapolis Tribune*, May 2, 1926.

MSC Arts Committee and the Wildlife & Fisheries Sciences Department in conjunction with the 97th Meeting of the American Ornithologists' Union presents: TEXAS ART IN ORNITHOLOGY, MSC Gallery, Texas A&M, August 6-26, 1979 Program. Thomason exhibit included books and brochures, photographs, and twenty-four paintings and sketches of wildlife.

McGill, Ralph. "A Rugged Marine Views His Wars And His Peace." Review of — *and a Few Marines*, *The Atlanta Constitution*, Sunday, May 9, 1943. Illustrated with jacket design and other sketches.

McGinnis, John H. (ed.) "Ten of Captain Thomason's Tales Rescued From Cosmopolitan Files." Review of *Red Pants*, *Dallas Morning News*, Sunday, May 1, 1927. Illustrated by sketches from the book.

_____. "Captain John W. Thomason Collects His War Sketches." Review of *Fix Bayonets*, *Dallas Morning News*, April 4, 1926. Lead article, five columns, approximately half-page and illustrated with three of Thomason's sketches made under intense machine gun fire.

_____. "John Thomason Writes Life of General Stuart," *Dallas Morning News*, November 16, 1930.

_____ and Alice Kizer Bennett. "Brave Tale of Old Texas Pictures Reconstruction." Review of *Gone to Texas* by John W. Thomason, Jr., *Dallas Morning News*, October 24, 1937.

Norwood, W. D., Jr. *John W. Thomason, Jr.* Austin: Southwest Writers Series, No. 25. Austin, Texas: Steck-Vaughn Company, 1969. Contains four Thomason illustrations.

O'Brien, Esse Forester. *Art And Artists Of Texas*. Dallas: Tardy Publishing Company, 1935.

Past, Ray. "John W. Thomason, Jr., Artist-Writer: An Exhibit" in *The Library Chronicle* of the University of Texas at Austin, iv, No. 2, Summer, 1941.

Past, Raymond E. " 'Illustrated By The Author' A Study of Six Western-American Writer-Artists." A doctoral dissertation, the University of Texas at Austin, June, 1950. A comparative study of Thomason with

Frederick Remington, Charles Marion Russell, Will James, Ross Santee, and Tom Lea. Contains six Thomason illustrations.

Reid, Don, Jr. "Throng Pays Tribute: Thomason Funeral Held at Huntsville," *Houston Post,* April 22, 1949.

Robinson, George. "He Made His Mark," *Houston Post,* March 23, 1944. Tribute.

"Romance in Texas." Review of *Gone to Texas, New Orleans Picayune,* October 31, 1937.

Ruggles, William B. "John Thomason Depicts Dashing French Officer. . . ." Review of *Adventures of General Marbot, Dallas Morning News,* Sunday, October 6, 1935. Illustrated with sketches from the book.

Smith, Rebecca W. "The Southwest in Fiction," *Saturday Review of Literature,* XXV (May 16, 1942), 12-13, 37. Reprinted in Pearce, T. M. and A. P. Thomason. *Southwesterners Write.* Albuquerque, N.M.: The Univesity of New Mexico Press, 1947.

Stallings, Laurence. "Books Of The Day: Captain Thomason's Christmas Gifts —His Artful Devices of Two Wars," *Ft. Worth Star Telegram,* December 11, 1932. Commentary on Thomason's illustrations in Thomas Nelson Page's *Two Little Confederates* and in *Taps,* the anthology of war verse compiled by Theodore Roosevelt, Jr. and Grantland Rice.

_____. "The Soldier, the Artist, and the Writer in *Fix Bayonets!*", New York World, April 4, 1926. Illustrated with four of Thomason's combat sketches.

Stuart, Henry Logan. "In the Mad Maze at Belleau Wood: Captain Thomason and Hervey Allen Write Two War Books That Were Worth Waiting For," *New York Times Book Review,* April 11, 1926. Includes three illustrations from *Fix Bayonets!*

"Teng Ends Tour of Houston," *Houston Post,* February 4, 1979.

"Texan's Work Adorns Poster; United States Marines; U.S. Terminal Annex Building, Dallas, Texas," *Dallas Morning News,* October 5, 1941. Illustration accompanying the article is a photograph of a striding Leatherneck who seems to be saying, "Let's go!" Thomason did the poster which was announced two months before Pearl Harbor.

"38th Company Activities," *The Legation Guard News,* Vol. 1, No. 89 (Peiping, December 1, 1931); *The Legation Guard News Annual,* Vol. 1, No. 5, 1931, pp. 16-17.

Thomason Collection. Yellow filing case containing correspondence from readers, letters from publishers and contemporaries; filing case of clippings and memoranda pertaining to career; filing case of reviews of Thomason's books; case of maps; filing case of material pertaining to Huntsville, Texas; filing case of material involving the United States Marine Corps per se; scrapbooks, notebooks, sketchbooks; photographs and other ephemera.

"Thomason Collection Moved," *The Houstonian,* Sam Houston State University, Huntsville, Texas November 22, 1963.

"Dr. and Mrs. Thomason Have Golden Wedding Anniversary on Tuesday," *Huntsville Item*, February 26, 1942.

"Colonel John W. Thomason," *Houston Post*, March 14, 1944. Editorial.

Thomason, John William, 1893-1944. [A Collection of Original Drawings of Colonel John W. Thomason Presented to the University of Texas by Mrs. John W. Thomason, n. p.], 1911-1918. Most of the drawings are pen-and-ink sketches and are not dated.

"Colonel John W. Thomason Dies in Naval Hospital," *Houston Post*, March 14, 1944.

"Colonel John Thomason, Famed Author and Soldier, Succumbs," *Houston Chronicle*, March 13, 1944. Also *New York Times*, same date.

"Colonel John W. Thomason, Jr., 51, Marine, Painter, Author, Dead," *New York Times*, March 12, 1944.

"Colonel Thomason, Fighting Writer of U.S. Marines, Dies," *Fort Worth Star Telegram*, March 14, 1944.

Thomason, John W. Jr. Letter file dating from 1898 to 1944 and comprised of letters to Dr. and Mrs. John W. Thomason, Sr., and to James Boyd in thirty-nine folders: 1898-1906; 1907; 1908, 1909; 1910; 1911; 1912; 1913; 1914; 1915; 1916; 1917; 1918; 1919; 1920; 1921; 1922; 1923; 1924; 1925; 1926; 1927; 1928; 1929; 1930; 1931; 1932; 1933; 1934; 1935; 1936; 1937; 1938; 1939; 1940; 1941; 1942; 1943; 1944.

"Colonel John W. Thomason, Noted Marine Corps Author, Dies Here," *San Diego News*, March 13, 1944.

"The Thomason Room," Special Collections at Sam Houston State University. Library brochure, n. d.

"A Thomason Sketchbook: A Texan with a Soldier's Eye and an Artist's Hand." Review in *Spotlight*, Sunday supplement to *Houston Post*, April 20, 1969. Cover design of magazine supplement is portrait of Howdy Martin of *Lone Star Preacher*.

"Captain Thomason's Striking Biography of J. E. B. Stuart," *Baltimore Sun*, October 25, 1930.

"Dr. J. W. Thomason Taken by Death at Huntsville," *Houston Post*, March 5, 1942.

Thompson, Charles Willis. "Cavalrymen of the Confederacy: Jeb Stuart and Bedford Forrest Lead Their Johnny Reb Horsemen Into Battle in Two Excellent Biographies," *New York Times Book Review*, November 16, 1930. Illustrated with sketches from Jeb Stuart including dust jacket portrait of Stuart."

Tolbert, Frank X. Tolbert's Texas: "All Wars Needed A John Thomason," The *Dallas News*, December 15, 1956.

Turner, Martha Anne. "Amid Memories, Mrs. J. W. Thomason Honored on Birthday," *Houston Post*, October 24, 1963.

_____. "I Visit a Nonagenarian," *Southwest Review*, XLIX (Spring, 1964), 179-186.

_____. "Legend and Legacy of John W. Thomason," with side box "Keeper of
the Flame," *Marine Corps Gazette,* 204th Anniversary Issue, 63 (November, 1979), 52-73.

_____. (ed.) " 'With All My Love—John:' A World War I Letter from John W.
Thomason, Jr.," *Texas Military History,* VII (Summer, 1968), 120-128.

United States Congress, 75th, 1st Session (June 17, 1937). Private Law #165,
Chapter 365, p. 997. Awarding a Navy Cross to John W. Thomason for
extraordinary heroism in the battle of Soissons on July 18, 1918, in de-
stroying a machine gun nest and capturing two machine guns. Approved
June 18, 1937.

United States Marine Corps Historical Center Presents Its Inaugural Exhibi-
tion, "The Marine Corps As Seen Through Contemporaneous Art." Cat-
alog. U.S. Marine Corps Historical Center, Washington Navy Yard,
Washington, D.C.

"Vicksburg Monument To Honor 35 Texans," *Houston Post,* October 26,
1961.

Wakefield, Paul L. "Captain Thomason, Marine Hero, Once Cub Reporter in
Varied Life," *New York Herald Tribune,* July 2, 1927.

Webb, Walter Prescott and H. Bailey Carroll (eds.). *The Handbook of Texas.* 2
vols. Austin: Texas State Historical Association, 1952. Branda, Eldon Stephen (ed.). *The Handbook of Texas: A Supplement.* Vol. III, Texas State
Historical Association, 1976.

"What You Think About It," *Scribner's Magazine,* 78 (August, 1925), 4-6.

Wheelock, John Hall (ed.). *Editor to Author: The Letters of Maxwell E. Perkins.* New York: Charles Scribner's Sons, 1950.

White, Ann Valentine. "The War-Time Drawings of Captain John William
Thomason, Jr., USMC." Unpublished thesis for Master of Arts degree,
University of Michigan, Ann Arbor, April, 1978.

Willock, Colonel Roger. "Colonel John W. Thomason, Jr., Chronicler of The
Corps," *Marine Corps Gazette,* 41 (May, 1957), 22-26.

_____. *Lone Star Marine.* Princeton, New Jersey: privately published, 1961.

_____. "Passing in Review:" Review of —*And A Few Marines, Marine Corps
Gazette,* August, 1958, 60-61.

Woollcott, Alexander. "Introducing Captain Thomason of the Marines,"
Vanity Fair, XXIV (June, 1925), 70, 100-104.

"Young Texan Is Literary Sensation: Galveston Featured in Magazine Story of
the World War," *Times-Herald,* Dallas, April 15, 1926.

"Young Texan Literary Sensation of Today—Features Galveston in Magazine
Story of World War," *Galveston Tribune,* April 13, 1926.

Related References

Adams, Samuel Hopkins. *A. Woollcott: His Life and His World*. New York: Reynal & Hitchcock, 1945.

Allen, E. D. "Frederick Remington, Author and Illustrator," *New York Public Library Bulletin*, 49 (December, 1945), 895-912.

Anderson, Maxwell, and Laurence Stallings. *Three American Plays*. New York: Harcourt, Brace and Company, 1926. *What Price Glory*.

"Artistic Writers," *Scribner's Magazine*, 29 (March, 1901), 377-380.

Baldwin, John W. "An Early History of Walker County, Texas." Unpublished thesis for Master of Arts degree. Sam Houston State Teachers College, Huntsville, Texas, June, 1958.

Benesch, Orro. *Artists and Intellectual Trends from Rubens to Daumier as Shown in Book Illustration*. Cambridge: Department of Printing and Graphic Arts, Harvard College Library, 1942.

Bonham, Milledge Louise. "A Little More Light on Gettysburg," *Mississippi Valley Historical Review*, Vol. XXIV, No. 4 (March, 1938), 519-525. A reprint personally annotated by Thomason is in the Thomason Collection.

Broad, E. A. "Literature as a Stimulus to Expression," *Design*, 37 (October, 1935), 26-27.

Bunker, John. "Destroyer Uses Helicopter, Sonar," *Evening Tribune*, San Diego, California, February 9, 1960.

Child, H. "Modern Illustrated Books," *Creative Art*, 7 (July, 1930), 33-41.

Foster, Will. "A Day With a Sketchbook at the Front," *Scribner's Magazine*, 65, No. 4 (April, 1919), 449-455.

"Frederick Remington," *Life*, 13 (14 September, 1942), 72-76.

Gallatin, Albert Eugene. "Pictorial Records of the Great War," *American Magazine of Art*, X, 12 (October, 1919), 465-468.

Ganoe, Sergeant Arthur R. M., USMC. "War-Thunder Rocks Earth at Villers-Cotterets," *The Marines' Bulletin*, 1 (November, 1918), 3-8.

A Guide To The American Battle Fields in Europe. Prepared by The American Battle Monuments Commission, Washington, D.C.: Government Printing Office, 1927.

Harding, George. "The American Artist at the Front," *American Magazine of Art*, X, 12 (October, 1919), 450-456.

King, Edward, and J. Wells Champney. *Texas 1874*. Houston: Cordovan Press, 1974. Edited by Robert S. Gray with an Introduction by Joe B. Frantz.

Literary Writings in American: A Bibliography, Vol. 8, Tabb to Zectlin. Mill-wood, New York: Kyto Press, a U.S. Division of Kraus-Thompson Organization Limited, 1977.

March, William. *Company K.* New York: Harrison Smith and Robert Haas, 1933.

"Marines and Texans Share Glory at St. Mihiel," *The Marines' Bulletin,* 1 (November, 1918), 22.

McClellan, Edwin N., Major U.S. Marines and Officer in Charge Historical Division. *The United States Marine Corps in the World War.* Washington, D.C.: Government Printing Office, 1920.

McCracken, Harold *Frederick Remington, Artist of the Old West.* New York: J. B. Lippincott Co., 1947.

Metcalf, Clyde H. *A History of the United States Marine Corps.* New York: G. P. Putnam's Sons, 1939.

Pitz, Henry C. *A Treasury of American Book Illustrations.* New York: Holmes Press, Inc. American Studies Books, 1947.

Rankin, Melinda. *Texas in 1850.* Boston: Printed by Damrell & Moore, No. 16, Devonshire Street, 1850.

Rather, Mrs. R. S. "Social Life in Huntsville in the Eighteen Seventies," Bulletin of Sam Houston State Teachers College, Huntsville, Texas, Vol. XXI, No. 2 (July, 1931), 25-30.

Schmidt, Hans. *The United States Occupation of Haiti 1913-1914.* New Brunswick, New Jersey: Rutgers University Press, 1971.

Shaw, Dr. Albert. "Marines Compared to Holland Boy at Dike, by Magazine Editor Back from France," *The Marines' Bulletin,* 1 (November, 1918), 10.

Simpson, Colonel Harold B. "Mollie Bailey: The Circus Queen of the Southwest," in *Women of Texas.* Waco: Texian Press, 1972.

Spaulding, Oliver Lyman. *The United States Army In War And Peace.* New York: G. P. Putnam's Sons, 1937.

Springs, Elliott White. *Pent Up On A Penthouse.* Fort Mill, South Carolina: Elliott Springs and Company, 1931.

Teichmann, Howard. *Smart Aleck: The Wit, World And Life of Alexander Woollcott.* New York: William Morrow and Company, Inc., 1976.

Turner, Martha Anne. "The Flush Years: Turn of Century Saw Prosperous Huntsville," *Houston Post,* July 21, 1963.

_____. "Historian of Republic Is Buried at Huntsville," *Houston Post,* July 5, 1963.

_____. *Richard Bennett Hubbard: An American Life.* Austin: Shoal Creek Publishers, Inc., 1979.

_____. "Huntsville's Unknown Soldiers," *Parade Magazine,* August 19, 1951.

Interviews

With Leda Thomason, October 3, 1978; December 30, 1978; January 30, 1979.

With Emily (Thomason) Petersen, October 5, 1978; January 30, 1980.

With Margaret (Thomason) Cole, October 2, 1978; December 9, 1980; November 15, 1978; January 15, 1980; February 6, 1980; March 13, 1980.

With Sue (Thomason) Noordberg, February 18, 1979; May 21, 1979; November 20, 1979; January 29, 1980.

Articles by Thomason

From *American Mercury*:

"America for Americans," *American Mercury*, 46 (February, 1939), 225-232.

"The Art of Prophecy," *American Mercury*, 42 (November, 1939), 364-371.

"The Best Best-Seller," *American Mercury*, 40 (January, 1937), 116-122.

"This Business of War," *American Mercury*, 34 (March, 1936), 369-375.

"The Businessman in History," *American Mercury*, 44 (May, 1938), 85-89.

"The Captain and the Kings," *American Mercury*, 41 (May, 1937), 115-119.

"Catastrophe in Galveston," *American Mercury*, 45 (October, 1938), 228-233.

"The Conquest of Pain," *American Mercury*, 43 (January, 1938), 107-113.

"The Cure for Alcoholism," *American Mercury*, 43 (April, 1938), 473-479.

"Diseases of the Great," *American Mercury*, 39 (October, 1936), 244-247.

"The Eternal Jewish Problem," *American Mercury*, 45 (September, 1938), 101-106.

"Father Divine's Afflatus," *American Mercury*, 39 (December, 1936), 500-505.

"The Genius of Audubon," *American Mercury*, 43 (February, 1938), 235-241.

"A Great American, Forgotten," *American Mercury*, 41 (August, 1937), 491-496.

"History's Perfect Rascal," *American Mercury*, 40 (April, 1937), 497-503.

"How Pure the Puritans?" *American Mercury*, 46 (March, 1939), 361-366.

"How to be a Diplomat," *American Mercury*, 40 (February, 1937), 243-249.

"The Man Who Knew Everything," *American Mercury*, 46 (January, 1939), 99-104.

"The Man Who Shook the Earth," *American Mercury*, 39 (November, 1936), 373-378.

"A Maverick on Parade," *American Mercury*, 42 (September, 1937), 111-116.

"The Merchant Marine Is Sick," *American Mercury*, 45 (December, 1938), 485-493.
"The Murder of Abraham Lincoln," *American Mercury*, 41 (July, 1937), 366-372.
"Napoleon's Last Victory," *American Mercury*, 40 (March, 1937), 369-377.
"Notes on an Economic Royalist," *American Mercury*, 42 (October, 1937), 234-239.
"The Old South Myth," *American Mercury*, 44 (July, 1938), 344-354.
"On Facing the Next War," *American Mercury*, 42 (December, 1937), 490-495.
"The Passing of the White Man," *American Mercury*, 43 (March, 1938), 357-364.
"Reflections on Book Reviewing," *American Mercury*, 44 (June, 1938), 221-229.
"The Seat of Mars," *American Mercury*, 45 (November, 1938), 359-363.
"Six Novels," *American Mercury*, 38 (August, 1936), 497-501.
"Something of Rudyard Kipling," *American Mercury*, 41 (June, 1937), 244-250.
"The Story of Texas," *American Mercury*, 44 (August, 1938), 482-489.
"They Got What They Wanted," *American Mercury*, 38 (July, 1936), 361-364.
"We've Paid Our Debt to Lafayette," *American Mercury*, 46 (April, 1939), 493-498.

Miscellaneous Articles:

"Approach to Peiping," *National Geographic Magazine*, LXIX (February, 1936), 275-309.
"The Capture of John Brown," *Marine Corps Gazette*, XIV, 2 (September, 1929), 153-158.
"The Case for the Soldier," *Scribner's Magazine*, 97 (April, 1935), 208-213.
"Chang's Men Bar Chinese Retreat," *New York Times*, March 5, 1931.
"Brigadier General Robert Henry Dunlap," Printed typescript in four pages by Thomason, np, nd. Inside caption reads "The Sword and the Services of Robert Henry Dunlap, Brigadier General, United States Marines." Thomason wrote the tribute at the request of Katherine Dunlap in 1933. Mrs. Dunlap distributed the pamphlet widely, sending a copy to the King of England among others.
"Dear Mr. Stallings," *Vanity Fair*, June, 1925. Quoted by Alexander Woollcott in his article "Introducing Captain Thomason of the Marines," *Vanity Fair*, 1929. Thomason defends Captain Flagg, protagonist of *What*

Price Glory, and adds his own perceptive commentary on war as he experienced it. Five illustrations by Thomason.

"Fix Bayonets!" *Scribner's Magazine,* 77 (June, 1925), 563-581.

"Fleet Comes Slipping Into Harbor as War Game Ends," *Dallas Morning News,* June 9, 1935, Section V, 1-2.

"Four Soldiers From Four Countries," in collaboration with Erich Maria Remarque, R. C. Sheriff, and Henri Barbusse, *McCall's Magazine,* December, 1929, 13, 78-91.

"Guinea Hunting by Ear," *Outing,* 78 (August, 1921), 208-210.

"Guinea Shooting in Cuba," *Outing,* 78 (April, 1921), 26-27.

"How the Groundhog Lost Prestige Back in the Days of Old Noah and Why He Now Predicts The Weather," *Houston Post,* January 31, 1914. Illustrated with drawing of groundhog wearing cap, with a bird on a limb in the background.

"Huntsville," *Southwest Review,* XIX (Spring, 1934), 233-245.

"Into Belleau Wood," *Scribner's Magazine,* 79 (March, 1926), 306-313.

"Marine Air Reserve," *Flying,* 40 (January, 1947), 30.

"Marines at Blanc Mont," *Scribner's Magazine,* 78 (September, 1925), 226-242.

"The Marine Brigade," *United States Naval Institute Proceedings,* 54 (November, 1928), 963-969.

"Marines See the Revolution," *Scribner's Magazine,* 82 (July, 1927), 13, 82-83.

"Meet The Major," in Keeping Posted, *Saturday Evening Post,* 209 (November 14, 1936), 144.

"Monkey Meat," *Scribner's Magazine,* 78 (November, 1925), 489-495.

"Monumental Four-Volume Biography Is Complete and Detailed Portrayal of Every Phase in Life of Robert E. Lee," *Dallas Morning News,* March 10, 1936, Ten-III.

"My Debt to Rockefeller," *Readers Digest,* XXXII (January, 1939), 32; 34-36. Condensed version of "Notes on an Economic Royalist."

"On Becoming a Teacher." Original holograph copy in Thomason Sketchbook, Thomason Collection, Sam Houston State University Library. Nd, but undoubtedly written at the outset of Thomason's teaching career in 1911.

"Our Disappearing Ducks," *Saturday Evening Post,* 207 (May 11, 1935), 16-17.

"Pilgrim from the North," *Outing,* 78 (June, 1921), 113.

"Read This And Know Just What Spring Is Like," *Houston Chronicle,* Sunday, March 25, 1917.

"Rice Students Write and Act Their Own Drama and Survive; 'Brain Trust' Scores a Hit," *Houston Chronicle,* March 24, 1917. Illustrated by sketches of the players by Thomason. See also *The Thresher,* Rice Institute, Houston, Thomason, April 6, 1917, and *The Campanile,* university yearbook, Volume 2, 1917.

"The Scissor-Tail Flycatcher," *The University of Texas Magazine*, XXVII (March, 1913), 267-270.

"20,000 Sightseers Visit Ships At Turning Basin: Hard Day For 'Jackies'," *Houston Chronicle*, Sunday, March 25, 1917.

"Washington Was a Man Long Before He Became a Hero," *Houston Chronicle*, February 22, 1917.

"When the Marines Fought with Mangin's Men, Roaring through the Woods to Victory July 18th, 1918 — Shall We Forget the Men Who Turned the Tide in the Great War?" *Houston Chronicle*, September 18, 1919. Thomason's first account of his combat experience and a precursor to *Fix Bayonets!*

"With the Marines," *Philadelphia Record*, November 10, 1929. Illustrations by the author.

"With the Marines, November 11, 1918," *New York World Magazine*, November 10, 1929. Illustrations by Thomason.

"With The Special Service Squadron," *Marine Corps Gazette*, XII (June, 1927), 77-82.

Books Written and Illustrated by Thomason

(All books are published by Charles Scribner's Sons and are listed in the order of publication.)

Fix Bayonets!, 1926
Red Pants And Other Stories, 1927
Marines And Others, 1929
Jeb Stuart, 1930
Salt Winds And Gobi Dust, 1934
The Adventures of Davy Crockett, edited and with an Introduction by Thomason, 1934
Davy Crockett And His Adventures In Texas, edited and with an Introduction by Thomason, 1934
The Adventures of General Marbot, edited by Thomason, 1935
Gone To Texas, 1937
Lone Star Preacher, 1941
—and A Few Marines, 1943

Contributions to Books by Others

Carroll, Gordon (ed.). *The Post Reader of Civil War Stories.* Garden City, New York: Doubleday, Doran, & Company, 1958. Includes three chapters from *Lone Star Preacher.*

Cox, Mamie Wynne. *The Romantic Flags of Texas.* Dallas: Banks Upshaw & Company, 1936. Foreword by Thomason.

Dobie, J. Frank (ed.). *The Sou'wester,* Southwestern University yearbook. Georgetown, Texas: The Athletic Association of Southwestern University, 1910. Contains "Classroom Manners," an essay by Thomason, a parody of the *Twenty-Third Psalm,* and several pen-and-ink drawings.

Greer, Hilton Ross (ed.). *Best Short Stories from the Southwest.* Dallas: Southwest Press, 1928. *The Conquest of Mike* by Thomason.

Harris, Abbie (ed.). *Alcalde.* Yearbook of Sam Houston Normal Institute, Huntsville, Texas, 1916. Essay by Thomason titled "Rare Collection of Relics of General Sam Houston."

Hemingway, Ernest (ed.) in collaboration with Lt. Col. John W. Thomason, Charles Sweeny, and Maxwell Perkins. *Men At War: The Best War Stories of All Time.* New York: Bramhall House, 1942. Includes two selections from *General Marbot* — "Lisette at Eylau" and "The Sun of Austerlitz;" one from *Fix Bayonets!* — "The Marines At Soissons;" and the three final chapters of *Lone Star Preacher* — "The Stars in Their Courses," "A Man's Bound to Fight," and "A Name and a Flag."

Hudson, Arthur Palmer, *et al.* (eds.). *The College Caravan.* New York: The Ronald Press Company, 1942. Includes "The Old South Myth" by Thomason.

Long, Ray (ed.). *Literary Treasures of 1926.* New York: Hearst's International-Cosmopolitan Magazine Corporation, 1927. *Red Pants* by Thomason.

Mason, F. Van Wyck (ed.). *The Fighting American.* New York: Reynal & Hitchcock, 1942. "Gaines Mill" by Thomason.

McMillan, George. *The Old Breed: History of the First Marine Division in World War II.* Washington, D.C.: Infantry Journal Press, 1949. Thomason quoted on "The Leathernecks, the old breed. . . ."

Metcalf, Clyde H., Colonel USMC. *The Marine Corps Reader.* New York: G. P. Putnam's Sons, 1944. Includes *Red Pants* and *Crossing the Line with Pershing.*

Peery, William (ed.). *21 Texas Short Stories.* Austin: The University of Texas Press, 1954. Lead story is "A Preacher Goes to Texas" from *Lone Star Preacher.*

Perry, George Sessions (ed.). *Roundup Time: A Collection of Southwestern Writing.* New York: Whittlesey House, 1943. Dedicated to John McGinnis with an introduction by Perry. Includes "A Name and a Flag" from *Lone Star Preacher*

Post Stories of 1935. Boston: Little, Brown and Company, 1930. Includes "A Preacher Goes to Texas."

Sellars, David K. (ed.). *Texas Tales*. New York: Noble and Noble, 1955. Includes "A Name and a Flag."

Sonnichsen, C. L. (comp. and ed.). *The Southwest in Life & Literature*. New York: The Devin-Adair Company, 1962. Includes "A Preacher Goes to Texas" from *Lone Star Preacher*.

Spaulding, Colonel Oliver Lyman, Field Artillery, and Colonel John Womack Wright, Infantry. *The Second Division American Expeditionary Force in France: 1917-1919*. New York: The Hillman Press, Inc., 1937. Gives only indirect credit to Thomason for his dedicated work on the committee.

The United States Army In The World War: 1917-1919, 17 vols. Washington, D.C.: compiled by the Second Division historical committee at the Army War College at Fort Humphreys and published in 1948.

Van Gelder, Robert and Dorothy (eds.). *American Legend*. New York: Appleton-Century, 1946. Includes "Gone to Texas" from the novel by the same name.

Williams, Blanche Colton (ed.). *O. Henry Memorial Award Prize Stories of 1930*. Garden City, New York: Doubleday, Doran & Company, 1931. Includes *Born on an Iceberg*, by Captain John W. Thomason and lists the author's story "Advance Guard," which appeared in *Hearst's International & Cosmopolitan* in April. Text examined — a special three-quarter leatherbound edition, with an introduction by the editor, was the presentation copy for winners of the award and finalists in the competition.

Woollcott, Alexander (ed.). *As You Were*. New York: Viking Press, 1943. Includes "A Preacher Goes to War" and "The Confederate Army."

Publications Illustrated by Thomason

Alcalde, Yearbook of Sam Houston Normal Institute, Huntsville, Texas, 1911. As art editor of the volume, Thomason contributed most of the art work and illustrations. Jesse Felder edited the book.

Blackford, Lieutenant Colonel W. W., C.S.A. *War Years With Jeb Stuart*. New York: Scribner's Sons, 1945. Three illustrations by Thomason including title page.

Botkin, Ben A. (ed.). *A Treasury Of Southern Folklore*. New York: Crown Publishers, 1940. Front cover design and drawing on title page by Thomason.

Boyd, Thomas. *Through The Wheat*. New York: Scribner's Sons, 1927. Numerous illustrations by Thomason.

Burlingame, Roger. "The Doctor's Confession," *Scribner's Magazine*, February, 1926.

Davenport, Walter. "Geoffrey John of Amiens," *Liberty Magazine,* May, 1925.

Dobie, J. Frank, Mody C. Boatright, and Harry H. Ransom (eds.). *Mustangs And Cowhorses.* Austin: Texas Folklore Society, 1940. One illustration by Thomason.

____. *Guide to Life And Literature of The Southwest.* Austin: The University of Texas Press, 1943. "Praxiteles Swan, fighting chaplain, by John W. Thomason in his *Lone Star Preacher.*

____. *Guide to Life And Literature of The Southwest.* Revised and enlarged edition. Dallas: Southern Methodist University Press, 1952. Same illustrations with cutline "John W. Thomason in his *Lone Star Preacher* (1941)."

Henry, Robert Selph. *'First With The Most' Forrest.* Indianapolis, Indiana: The Bobbs-Merrill Company, 1944. Frontispiece by Thomason.

Hunt, Frazier. *Custer: The Last of The Cavaliers.* New York: Cosmopolitan Book Corporation, 1928. Eight illustrations by Thomason.

Johnson, Thomas M. and Fletcher Pratt. *The Lost Battalion.* New York: Bobbs Merrill Books, 1938. Jacket drawing by Lieutenant Colonel John W. Thomason.

Logan, Harlan. *Fiftieth Anniversary Edition, Scribner's Magazine, 1887-1937,* Scribner's Sons Publisher, New York, 1937. One illustration by Thomason.

Longlaner, Chief Buffalo Child. "The Secret of His Sioux," *Hearst's International & Cosmopolitan,* June, 1927.

Mackin, Elton. "Suddenly We Didn't Want to Die," *American Heritage,* February / March, 1980. Includes 13 Thomason illustrations, some of which were sketched under fire. Five of the drawings were originals from the Thomason Collection, provided by specialist librarian Charles Lee Dwyer of Sam Houston State University Library.

Meredith, Roy. *The American Wars.* New York: The World Publishing Company, 1955. Three illustrations by Thomason.

Mitchell, Brigadier-General William. "Leaves from My War Diary," *Liberty Magazine,* March, April, and May, 1928. Part I illustrated by Thomason.

[Mosely, J. A. R.] *Stonewall Jackson and Praxiteles Swan by John W. Thomason. Greetings from Bob Moseley, Christmas* 1949. [El Paso, Carol Hertzog.] French fold. Text and drawing by John W. Thomason. Listed as item No. 302, p. 98, under Selected Ephemera in *Printer At The Pass: The Work of Carl Hertzog* compiled by Al Lowman. The University of Texas Institute of Texas Cultures At San Antonio, 1972.

Nason, Leonard H. "The Award of Valor," *Liberty Magazine,* July, 1925.

____. "The Tank and the Doctor," *Liberty Magazine,* September, 1925.

Page, Thomas Nelson. *Two Little Confederates.* New York: Scribner's Sons, 1932. Cover design and numerous illustrations by Thomason.

Pitz, Henry C. *A Treasury of American Book Illustration.* New York: Watson-Guptill Publications, 1947. One illustration by Thomason.

"Polo in China," *Caravan*. Vol. 3, No. 1 (May, 1938), 18-20. Two Thomason full-page sketches of Mongolian ponies and riders in action with focus on the grace with which the animals perform.

Roosevelt, Theodore, Jr. *Rank And File*. New York: Scribner's Sons, 1928. Ten illustrations by Thomason.

_____. and Grantland Rice. *Taps, Selected Poems of the Great War*. Garden City, New York: Doubleday, Doran & Company, 1932. Numerous illustrations by Thomason.

Sullivan, Mark. *Our Times 1900-1925*. 6 Vols. V, *Over Here* (1914-1918). New York: Charles Scribner's Sons, 1936. Contains the sketch of "Mademoiselle from Armentiers" from Thomason's *Fix Bayonets!*.

A Thomason Sketchbook: Drawings by John W. Thomason, Jr. Edited with a Foreword by Arnold Rosenfeld. Introduction by John Graves. Austin: The University of Texas Press, 1969.

Welles, Harriet. "An Uncharted Course," *Scribner's Magazine*, August, 1925.

_____. "The Stranger Woman," *Scribner's Magazine*, December, 1926.

INDEX

A

Ackerman's Art Gallery: 123
Adventures of Davy Crockett, The: 255; see also Thomason, John W., Career in the World of Art
Adventures of General Marbot: 266-267; see also Napoleon Bonaparte
Aeschylus: 99
American Congress: 97
American Legation Guard: a Marine Corps obligation, 236; see Thomason, John W., Career in the Marine Corps . . .
American Mercury, the: see Thomason, John W. — Literary editor of,
American War College: 201-221
— *and A Few Marines:* 256, 325, 337, 338; see also Thomason, John W., Career in the Marine Corps and World of Art
Andrew, Bishop James Osgood: 7
Andrew Female College: 6, 8, 12, 14
Andrews, Roy Chapman: American explorer, 238; and Thomason, 238; sits for bust sculptured by Thomason, 325; final tribute to Thomason, 342-343
Appomattox: 28, 212
Arlington: 17, 272, 343
Army of Northern Virginia: 27, 80, 267, 270
Art Institute of Newport: 113
Art Students League: 44-50, *passim;* 83, 334
Atkinson, Susanne Thomason: 344
Audubon, John J.: 288
Austin College: 6, 7, 9, 14, 20

B

Bailey, Molly and troupe: 12
Baker, Daniel: 7
  Newton D.: author of *War in the Modern World,* 279
Balboa, Panama: Thomason stationed at, 175; as crossroads of the world, 177-178; 179, 189
Baltimore, Maryland: 69, 120
Balzac, Honoré: 23
Bancroft, Hubert Howe: 13
Banner, The Texas: 6
Barbusse, Henri: collaborator with Thomason and others on war article in *McCall's Magazine,* 218-219
Barnett, Major General George: 59
Bass, Mr. and Mrs. Sidney John: parents of Leda Thomason, 42, 53; attend daughter's wedding, 65; visit Thomasons in Cuba, 105
Batista: 97
Beauregard, General Pierre Gustave: 21
Bedias Indians: 3
Belleau Wood: 80, 81, 82, 124, 216; see also A Marine Goes to War
Benchley, Robert: 124
Benet, William Rose: 341
Berkeley, Colonel Randolph C.: 118
Bible: Doré edition of, 23, 289; chapters, 24; battles, 32, 41 King James version, 288; influence on Kipling, Pearl Buck, and Hemingway, 288; on Thomason, 333
Blake, Colonel Robert: 311
Blanc Mont Ridge: 87, 88-89
Boetticher, General Friedrich Von: attaché of German embassy, 305, 306
Boston Herald, the: 222
Boyd, James (Jim): author of bestseller *Drums,* 263; background, 263; correspondence with Thomason, 263; reviews *Adventures of General Marbot,* 267; author of *Long Hunt,* 221-222; Thomason corresponds with, from the Pacific, 335-336; death of, at Princeton, 340

Katherine: 212
Thomas: author of *Through the Wheat* and *Points of Honor*, 193; reviews Thomason's *Fix Bayonets!*, 193-194
Branch, John: 7
Breckenridge, Colonel James C.: commanding officer of the Legation Guard of Peking, 226; presents eleven-year-old Jack Thomason with sergeant's warrant, 247
Bridgeman, George: 48
Bridges, Robert: 125-126
Broaddus, Lieutenant Carl: close friend of Thomason, 123, 128; predicts Colonel Roosevelt's death, 271
Carl Jr.: 123, 128, 129, 258
Virginia: 123, 128, 244, 258
Brooklyn Navy Yard: 50
Brown, Captain Julian: 237-238
Owen: 45
Brownell, William C.: mentor of Maxwell Perkins, 185
Buck, Pearl S.: 288
Burt, Katherine Newell: 212
Struthers: 212
Bush family: Huntsville pioneers, 4
Byron, the English poet: 23, 279

C

Caesar, Julius: 279
Callio, Peru: 187
Canal Zone: 179, 180, 184, 195
Caribbean: 67, 96, 117, 176
Carroll, Gordon: 322
Castro, Fidel: 99
Cathedral of St. John the Divine: 46-48
Central America: 176
Century's: 100
Champagne, the: 87; see also Meuse-Argonne offensive
Chapin, Joseph H.: 126, 180
Charles Scribner's Sons: publishers and booksellers, 125, 126; see also Perkins, Maxwell (Max)
Charleston, S.C.: 63, 64, 66, 67,

69, 71, 176, 286
Château-Thierry: 79, 80, 81, 82; see also A Marine Goes to War
Chaumont-en-Vixen: 77
Chiang Kai-shek: note on, 225; occupies new capital at Nanking, 236; control over National Army, 236; interviewed by Frazier Hunt, editor of *Cosmopolitan*, 254
Christy, Howard Chandler: painter of portraits of President and Mrs. Calvin Coolidge, 210
Churchill, Winston: 310, 312
Cincinnati, Texas: stage stop and port on Trinity River, 5-6; 17
Civil War, the: see Thomason, John W., Boyhood in Huntsville; see also listings under war
Clemens, Samuel Langhorne (Mark Twain): 23, 99, 281, 284
Colby, Lester B.: 56
Cole, Margaret Thomason: Thomason's youngest sister, 57, 224, 258; marries Dr. Cole, 300; reference to, in father's record book, 329; 330
Dr. Thomas C.: 300, 330
Columbus, Christopher: 96, 279
Confederate flag: 12, 28, 321
Confederate States of America: 212
Confederate States Provisional Army: 21, 292; see also listings under war
Congress of the Republic of Texas: 6
Coolidge, President Calvin: 187; and Mrs. Coolidge, 210
Crozier, Harry: 320
Cuba: life in, 97, 101, 104, 186; festivals, 102-104; struggle for independence, 97, 105; disintegration of, 109; see also Thomason, John W., Career in the Marine Corps . . .

D

Dallas Morning News, The: 34, 296
Dante's *Inferno*: 23, 48
Davies, Marion: hostess to Thoma-

son and others at Hearst Ranch
on West Coast, 264
Davis, Jefferson: 12, 212
  N. L.: author of *Honey in the
  Horn,* 281
  Mrs. Virginia Stuart Waller: 217
Dickens, Charles: 23, 99, 113, 289-
  290
Dobie, J. Frank: upperclassman and
  friend of John Thomason at
  Southwestern University, 36;
  first publication, 36; hails *Lone
  Star Preacher* as supreme Civil
  War novel, 319, 320; com-
  ments on *Lone Star Preacher* in
  A Texan in England, 322; says
  goodbye to Thomason in
  Southwest Review, 342
domestics of Thomason family: 26,
  69
Dover, New Jersey: 118, 119, 123ff,
  destruction of arsenal at, 130
Dowling, Dick: 8
Dumas, Alexander: 77, 113

E

East Texas: 9, 338, 343
Eisenhower, President Dwight D.:
  345
Elkins family: Huntsville pioneers, 4
Estill, Dr. Harry Fishburne: 9-10
Euripides: 99
extraterritoriality, system of: 236

F

Father Divine: 279
Ferguson, Dr. John V.: 233
Fitzgerald, F. Scott: Thomason com-
  ments on, 101; discovered by
  Perkins, 185
Fix Bayonets!: see Thomason, John
  W., Career in the Marine Corps
  and the World of Art
Foch, Marshall Ferdinand: 83, 85
Forrest, General Nathan Bedford:
  27, 235, 329
Forts: Bliss, Brown, Huachuca, and
  Sam Houston, 55
Foster, M. E.: 114, 282

Four Soldiers from Four Countries:
  article by Thomason in collaboration with other authorities
  on war, 218-219; see also *Hope
  of the World*
Fredericksburg, Virginia: 67, 68, 70
Freeman, Douglas S.: biographer of
  General Robert E. Lee, 214,
  269; publishes *Lee's Lieutenants* . . . , 318; deferred to by
  Thomason, 318

G

Galveston, Texas: 12, 21, 44, 294-
  296, *passim*
Genghis Khan, Temujin: 278
Gettysburg, Pennsylvania: Thoma-
  son visits, 217
Gibbs family: Huntsville pioneers, 3
Gibbs, Mrs. Lizzie: proprietress of
  Keep Hotel, 5
  Mrs. Sarah: 20
  Thomas: Huntsville pioneer, 6
Gillespie, C. B.: 282
"Girl I Left Behind Me, The:" Civil
  War song, 27
Glacis, the: see Thomason, John
  W., Career in the Marine
  Corps . . .
Goethe: 23, 64
Gomez, José Miguel: 98
Gone To Texas: 284; see also Per-
  kins, Maxwell, and Thomason,
  John W., Career in the Marine
  Corps . . .
Goree, Edwin King: 27
  Elise: wife of Robert Goree, 116;
  visits battlesites of Europe, 116-
  117
  Eliza Nolley (Manda): John
  Thomason's maternal grand-
  mother, 20; as poet and educa-
  tor, 21; 113; death, 210-220
  Langston James: 27
  Pleasant Kittrel (Uncle Scrap): 27
  Robert Daniel: 27, 116
  Sue Hayes: see Thomason, Sue
  Goree (Mrs. J. W.)
  Major Thomas Jewett (Dad):

reads poem at Confederate reunion, 12, 26; relationship with grandson John, 21ff, 42, 214; Civil War record, 21; contemporary of Sam Houston, 21; in Battle of Fredericksburg, 63; as superintendent of Texas Prison System, 20-21; survives Galveston storm of 1900, 295; death, 28, 68, 219

Goya, Francisco: 334-335

Grand Lodge of the Masonic Order: 7

Grant, General Ulysses S.: 28, 269

Gray, Pleasant: founder of Huntsville, Texas, 3, 4, 6

Guadalcanal: 330, 335, 347

Guantanamo: 97, 191

H

Haiti: 96

Harper's: 100

Hemingway, Ernest: precedes Thomason to Paris, 204; analogy with Thomason, 204-205; partiality to Thomason's Marbot, 267; publishes Men at War: The Best War Stories of All Times with the editorial assistance of Thomason, 322

Hill, A. P.: 219

Hindenberg: German marshal, 89; line of, 89

Hiroshima: 344

History of Texas: Henderson Yoakum's work, 14

Hitler, Adolf: invasion of Poland, 306; France falls to, 309; and the British, 302; invades Russia, 313

Hobby, Lieutenant Governor William F.: 346

Homer: 23, 99

Hood, General John Bell: 12, 26, 27, 42, 319

Hope of the World, The: Thomason's contribution to Four Soldiers from Four Countries in McCall's Magazine, 218-219

Horse Marines, the: 226, 233-234

Houston, Texas: 3, 4, 41ff, 58, 59; Thomason's article on, 70

Houston, Colonel Andrew Jackson: correspondence with Thomason, 213; see also Literary Editor of American Mercury

Margaret Lea: wife of Sam Houston, 14, 16

Sam Jr.: wounded at Shiloh, 8

General Sam: homes of, 6; and Dr. McKinney, 7; as Union sympathizer, 11; as legendary figure, 13, 16; hosts Indian friends, 16-17; Thomason story on, in Houston Chronicle, 57; mentioned, 4, 8, 26, 320, 343

Houston Chronicle, The: 33; employs Thomason to write special features, 54; employs Thomason, 23, reporter, 56, 114; 221, 282, 296

Houston Post, The: 31, 221

Howard, Roy Wilson: 254, 255

Hudson River: 47

Hugo, Victor: 23, 113

Hume, Major Charles E.: 13
John: 7

Hunt, Frazier: editor of Cosmopolitan, 190; contracts with Thomason, 190; visits Thomason in Peking, 254; author of Custer, the Last Cavalier illustrated by Thomason, 207

Huntsville, Texas: location and history of, 3-4; early settlers of, 3-5, 20; description, 3-4; as stagecoach capital of East Texas, 5; early churches of, 6-8, passim; educational institutions — see Austin College, Andrew Female College, and Sam Houston Normal Institute; effect of the Civil War upon, 8-9; social life and customs in the 19th century, 10-12, passim; heroes of, 13-14; legends, 14-15, passim; as

birthplace of John W. Thomason, 18; as environment of Thomason's boyhood, 23-32, *passim;*mentioned, 337, 343
Huntsville Item, The: 6, 285, 300

I

Ibañez: 104
International and Great Northern Railroad: 6, 9, 15; see also Tilly, J. Bob
Iowa (ship), the: 113
Iwo Jima: 344

J

Jackson, Andrew: 14
Colonel Gilder D. Jr.: 343
Thomas Jonathan (Stonewall): at Chancellorsville, 27; 212, 218, 319
James, Will: 246
Jeb Stuart: 212, 214-215, 217, 222-223; 318, 319; see also Thomason, John W., Career in the Marine Corps and the World of Art
Johnson, Elizabeth Thomason: 224, 258, 329
Samuel: 279; on dancing dog, 305
Jones, Paul: 50, 65, 259
Joseys: Huntsville pioneers, 4

K

Kaiser (William II), the: 49, 113, 211
Kaufman, George S.: author of *The Man Who Came to Dinner*, 308
Kipling, Rudyard: 23, 99, 288; Thomason compared with, 332-333
Kirkley, Miss Bertha: 9-10
Dr. J. E.: 10
Kittrell, Color Sergeant Norman: 12
W. H. (Will), Jr.: 320
Knoedler's Art Gallery: 123

L

Lassater, Major General William: 189

Latimer, Rear Admiral Julian L.: 175, 176
Latin America: 118
Latin American Office of Naval Intelligence: 311ff
Leatherneck: 177; Thomason, a dedicated, 214; 222, 314
Leckie, Robert: quoted, 323, 333
Lee, General Robert E.: commander of the Army of Northern Virginia, 27; greatness, 43; defeat of Burnside at Fredericksburg, 68; surrender at Appomattox, 28; Thomason's interest in, 23, 267-268; Freeman's biography of, 268; Thomason's rationale of why Lee failed, 269; manumits slaves, 292; 318, 319, 321
Lejeune, General John A.: commander, Second Infantry Division, AEF, 201; admirer of Thomason's books, 201-202; 317; selects Thomason for panel to compile history of Second Division, 201; refuses to release Thomason for field duty, 208
Liberty Magazine: 127, 190, 217, 220
Lincoln, Abraham: 43, 269, 288
London *Times:* acclaims *Fix Bayonets!*, 193
Lone Star Preacher: See Pearl Harbor and Lone Star Preacher and Thomason, John W., Career in the Marine Corps and the World of Art
Longfellow, Henry Wadsworth: 23, 290
Longstreet, General James: friendship with Major Goree, 12, 21; author of *From Manassas to Appomattox*, 23, 214, 319
Lorimer, George Horace: editor-in-chief of *Saturday Evening Post*, 285; assessment of Thomason's *Gone To Texas*, 285
Lusitania, the: sinking of, 52; see also listings under war

M

Magruder, John: 8
Mansfield, Battle of: 8
Marine Corps Gazette: 200, 220
Marines and Others: 213, 218
Markham, Dr. T. W.: 14-15
Marquis, Don: 124
Mason, F. Van Wyck: reprints chapter from *Lone Star Preacher* in *The Fighting American,* 322
Masters, Edgar Lee: 113
Maverick, Captain Louis: 59
Congressman Maury: 294
McGinnis, John E.: Thomason's English instructor at Southwestern University, 34; characterization of Thomason, 34; recognizes Thomason's genius, 35; encourages the writing of essay, *Huntsville* for *Southwest Review,* 258
McKinney, Dr. Samuel: 7
McMein, Neysa: 124; New York artist and designer of magazine covers, 125, 126; appraiser of Thomason's art, 125, 180
Melbourne, Australia: 335
Mencken, Henry L.: co-founder and editor of *American Mercury,* 277; quoted, 277
Meuse-Argonne offensive: 86, 87; see also A Marine Goes to War
Mitchell, the Rev. F. T.: 12
Montgomery Patriot, The: early Huntsville newspaper, 6
Moore, Dr. John E.: employs Thomason to sketch surgical illustrations, 54
Morgan, Sir Henry: 178-179
Munda: seizure of, 335
My Debt to Rockefeller: abridged version of Thomason's *Notes on an Economic Royalist* in *Reader's Digest,* 245

N

Nagasaki: 344
Nanking: seat of Chinese government under Chiang-Kai-shek, 225, 236

Napoleon Bonaparte: books on, in Thomason library, 23; line he led, 79; as object of John Thomason's admiration, 38, 269; comparison of Woodrow Wilson with, 215; see also *Adventures of Marbot;* 288
Nathan, George Jean: 277
National Defense Act: 55
National Guard, the: 55
New Caledonia: 335
New Hebrides: 335
New Orleans: 61, 63, 179
New York: see Thomason, John W., Quest for identity; 48, 51, 52, 65, 100, 123, 124, 128, 180, 190, 191, 254
New York Herald Tribune: 59, 223, 332
New York Evening Post: 192
New York Times: 325
New York World: 125, 127, 192; cables Thomason on success of *Fix Bayonets!,* 180
Nicaraqua: 195ff
Niederbreitbach, Germany: 92-94
Nimitz, Admiral Chester W.: 333, 334, 336
Noordberg, Henri: 307
Sue Thomason: introduces John to Leda Bass, 42; characterization of, 224; John's correspondence with, 207, 328; marriage and life in Holland, 307; family concern about during World War II, 307; death of father, 328; appraisal by father in his record book, 329; mentioned, 258, 330
North, the: 8, 122, 214, 270
North American Newspaper Alliance: Thomason's affiliation with, 250, 325
Notes on an Economic Royalist: Thomason article on Rockefeller in *American Mercury,* 245

O

Oakland: ancestral Thomason home in Huntsville, Texas, 20, 278

Oakwood Cemetery: 7, 17; place of burial for Thomason and Jack, 343, 347

Office of Naval Intelligence: 311ff

Old, Mrs. Flora Stuart: descendant of Jeb Stuart, 217

"Old Breed," the: an established Marine Corps tradition, 302; decline of, with advent of World War II, 302-304

Old Main: 6

Old Panama: 178

Old Testament: 23, 218, 289

P

Panama Canal Zone: 175ff

Panama City: 178

Paris: 77, 79, 82, 91

Pearl Harbor: United States Naval, installation at, 264; Japanese attack on, 313-314; as base of Admiral Nimitz's Pacific Fleet, see chapter titled Pearl Harbor and *Lone Star Preacher*

Pearl of the Antilles: 96-109; see also Cuba, and Thomason, John W., Career in the Marine Corps . . . first tour of duty

Peery, William: 322

Peiping (northern peace): 225

Peitaho Beach: see references to the Legation Guard in Peking

Peking: 225-256

Peking Union Medical College: see Rockefeller, John Davison, and Thomason, John William (Jack) III

Perkins, Maxwell (Max): editor at Scribner's, 185; assigned to Thomason, 185; development of life-long friendship with Thomason, 185; commends Thomason's success on *Fix Bayonets!*, 192; proposes Stuart biography, 214-215; correspondence with Thomason, 214-215; recommends *General Marbot* to Hemingway, 267; impatient to publish Thomason's

manuscript on Lee, 267-268; proposes series of stories laid in Texas, 284; publishes *Gone to Texas,* 284; quotes Thomason to Hemingway on imminence of World War II, 308; urges Thomason to submit *Lee's Men,* 318; proposes book on Civil War based on battlefields, 318; lauds *Lone Star Preacher,* 320; arranges display of *Lone Star Preacher,* 321; welcomes Thomason home from Pacific Theater, 337

Perry, George Sessions: 322

Pershing, General John J.: conducts punitive expedition into Mexico, 55; commands Saint-Mihiel salient, 86; as chairman of the Chile-Peru Commission to settle the Tacna-Arica controversy, 186-187; and John Thomason, 187; relinquishes duties to Major General William Lassater, 189; inspires Thomason story, 188

Peru, Republic of: 187

Petain, General Henri Phillipe: 82

Petersen, Emily Thomason: 224, 330

Dr. Henry A.: 330

Platt Amendment: 98-99

Plutarch: 23

Poe, Edgar Allan: 99

Porter, William Sidney (O. Henry): and Thomason, 221; see also *Born on An Iceberg* and Williams, Blanche Colton, *O. Henry Memorial Award.* . . .

Potomac River: 67, 211, 216

Pritchett, Henry Carr: 10

Professor J. L.: 9, 14, 213

Q

Quantico, Virginia: 67; Thomason trains at, 69-70; 123, 299

R

Rainbow Division, the: 87

Randolph, Judge Benton: 12
Red Pants And Other Stories: 199-
    200; 206, 218; see also Thoma-
    son, John W., Career in the
    Marine Corps . . .
Reed, George C.: 7
Remarque, Erich Maria: collaborates
    with Thomason and others on
    war article for *McCall's Maga-*
    zine, 218-219
Remington, Frederick: 334
Republic of Costa Rica: 185
Republic of Texas: 6, 13
"Revised Version of 23rd Psalm:"
    35-36
Rhine: 92
Robertson, General Felix D.: 13
Robinson, George: 6
Rockefeller, John Davison: founder
    of the Peking Union Medical
    College (The Fu), 245; Thom-
    ason's indebtedness to, 245;
    biography of, 245
Rodman, Rear Admiral Hugh: 110,
    121
Rogers, Will: visits Peking in 1931,
    254
Romanoff, Peter: 279
Roosevelt, President Franklin Del-
    ano: 211, 260, 263-264, 265;
    New Deal policy, 277; prepares
    for war, 312; wins third term,
    312-313
Assistant Secretary of the Navy
    Henry L.: Thomason named
    aide to, 258; entertains Thom-
    asons, 259; assumes full re-
    sponsibility for the U.S. Navy,
    260; uses Coast Guard Cutter,
    260; and Franklin Delano Roo-
    sevelt, his cousin, 263; tours
    installations on West Coast
    and Honolulu, 264; becomes
    ill in Honolulu, 265; delivers
    address prepared by Thoma-
    son, 265; cooperates with Pres-
    ident Roosevelt on national
    preparedness, 265; forced to
    curtail activities, 269; dies at

United States Naval Hospital
    in Washington, 271; burial in
    Arlington Cemetery, 272; see
    also Thomason, John W., Ca-
    reer in the Marine Corps . . .
Theodore: *Rank and File* illus-
    trated by Thomason, 207

S

Saint-Mihiel: 86; see Pershing, Gen-
    eral John J.
Salt Winds And Gobi Dust: 233,
    255
Sam Houston Normal Institute: 6,
    8, 9, 33, 53; see also Thoma-
    son John W., Quest for identity
Sam Houston State University: 9
Sandburg, Carl: 113
San Jacinto, Battle of: 13; 26
Saturday Evening Post, the: 100,
    256, 317, 325, 330
Scott, Sir Walter: 23, 99
Scribner's Magazine: see Perkins,
    Maxwell; and Thomason, John
    W., Career in the Marine Corps
    and the World of Art
Sergeant Bridoon of the Horse Ma-
    rines: 305, 343
Sergeant Houston stories: see Thom-
    ason, John W., Career in the
    Marine Corps and the World of
    Art
Seton, Ernest Thompson: influence
    on Thomason, 29
Shakespeare, William: 23, 24, 99
Shanghai: 300
Sheppard, Senator Morris: 258
Sherman, General William Tecum-
    seh: Thomason's appraisal of,
    270
Shivers, Governor Allan: accepts oil
    portrait of Thomason, 345
Smith, J. C.: 7
    Mrs. Morrow Stuart: 217
Smither family: 4
Smither, J. Mark: 27, 115
    Robert: 6, 7
Soissons: 82, 83, 85
Solomon Islands: 330

Somme Pye: 87

South, the: 3, 8, 9, 10, 24, 122, 270, 292-293

Southern Confederacy: 282

Southwestern University: 33, 36; see Thomason, John W., Quest for identity; confers honorary degree upon Thomason, 297

Sou'wester, the: yearbook of Southwestern University, 35; see also "Revised Version of 23rd Psalm" and Thomason, John W., Quest for identity

Spanish-American War: see listings under war

Special Service Squadron: 175ff

Spoon River Anthology: 113

Stafford, Mary Thomason: 224

Stallings, Helen: 305
    Laurence: ships out with Thomason on *USS Henderson,* 71; friend of World War I, 123; wounded at Belleau Wood, 124; hears of Thomason's bravery at Soissons, 124-125; author of *Plumes* and co-author of *What Price Glory,* 124; introduces Thomason to staff at Scribner's, 124; as literary editor of *New York World,* 127; 180; appraisal of *Fix Bayonets!,* 192; as newspaperman in New York, 254; employed by MGM Pictures, 305; remarries, 305

State Prison System: 6, 9, 15, 20

Stevens, John W.: Methodist minister and former captain in Hood's Texas Brigade, 42; fight with yankee, 42-43; as prototype for protagonist in *Lone Star Preacher,* 318-319

Stevenson, Coke: 320
    Robert Louis: 31; quoted, 347

Stuart, Henry Carter: Jeb Stuart's nephew, 217
    James Ewell Brown (Jeb): 214-215; 217; 223, 270-271; 292; see also *Jeb Stuart* and references to Thomason's literary career

Swinburne, Algernon Charles: 99

T

Tacna-Arica controversy: see Pershing, General John J. and Thomason, John W., Career in the Marine Corps . . .

Taylor, Professor R. U.: 39

Tennyson, Alfred Lord: 23, 290

Terrell, Texas: hometown of the Bass family, 42; 58, 63, 105

Texas Independence: reviewed by Thomason, 293-294

Texan in England, A: 342

Texas, the: battleship, 52

Texas heritage: 13, 345

Texas Revolution: 3

Texas Supreme Court: 7

Thackeray, William Makepiece: 23, 99, 113

Thomas, Ruth: 113, 123

Thomason Collection, Sam Houston State University Library: 57, 323

Thomason, Dr. Betty: 330
    Elizabeth: see Johnson, Elizabeth Thomason
    Emily: see Petersen, Emily Thomason
    Emily Jane Fisher: John Thomason's paternal grandmother, 20
    Dr. Herbert: enrolls at the University of Texas with John, 38ff; characterization of, 38-39; at Johns Hopkins, 70; bids John goodbye, 71; 224, 330
    Dr. J. W.: father of John W. Thomason, Jr., 19; background, 20; education, 20; medical practice, 20, 21-22; as man of character and diversified interests, 22-24; as family man, 22; library, 23; exposure of children to classic literature and the Bible, 23-24; man of sentiment and philosophy,

329; record book, 329-330; stature in the medical profession, 329; death of, 328-329

John W.: Provenance — birth in Huntsville, Texas, 18, 19; parentage, 19-20; ancestry, 19-21; formative influences, 21-24; relation to servants, 25-26; relationship with siblings, 26

— Boyhood in Huntsville: impact of Southern heritage and Civil War veterans, 26-28 *passim;* proximity to nature, 28-30; as budding artist, 30; as schoolboy, 30-31; devotion to reading, 31; influence of Bible, 33; first published sketch, 31; influence of Huntsville scene on Thomason's art, 26-32

— Quest for identity: matriculation at Southwestern University, 33ff; transfers to Sam Houston Normal Institute for sophomore year, 37; teaches in rural Texas school, 37-38; enrolls at the University of Texas, 38; neglects studies for art and extracurricular activity, 39-40; accepts principalship at Penn City, 40-44, attends Art Students League in New York City, 44-52; effects of the metropolis and the European War on art, 48-50; accepts teaching job in Houston, 54-55; enrolls in San Antonio training camp, 55-56; as reporter on *Houston Chronicle* staff, 56-60, *passim;* paints war posters, 59

— Courtship and marriage: Thomason meets Leda Bass, 42; first impressions of Miss Bass, 42; progress of love affair, 53; Leda as heroine in story *Luck,* 53; *Chronicle* feature on meaning of spring, 58; mixed parental reaction to romance, 62; marries Leda in Washington, D.C., 65-66;

couple settle in Charleston, 66; Thomason trains at Quantico with home base in Fredericksburg, 67-68; first Christmas away from Texas, 69-70

— Regeneration in World War I: Thomason enlists in the United States Marine Corps, 60; assigned to First Texas Battalion, New Orleans, for basic training, 61; commissioned second lieutenant in Marine Corps branch of National Naval Volunteers, 61; promoted to first lieutenant, 66; completes training at Quantico, 70; assigned to Third Replacement Battalion in command of platoon of 65, 70; undergoes six-weeks training in open and trench warfare, 71; bids wife, mother, and brother Herbert goodbye in Baltimore, 71; says farewell to father in letter, 72-73; sails from Philadelphia Navy Yard on *USS Henderson* for overseas duty, 71; arrives in France, 77; begins training with the Fourth Marine Brigade of the First Battalion, Fifth Marines, 77; first letter home, 77-79; at Chateau-Thierry, 79-82; at Belleau Wood, 81; sketches war scenes under shellfire, 80; participates in charge at Soissons, 82-85; destroys German machine gun nest, 84-85;

Assigned to Infantry Specialist School at Andilly, 85; rejoins unit for Saint-Mihiel offensive in the Meuse-Argonne, 86-87; learns of promotion to captain, 87; Thomason leads 49th Company of Marines in assault on Blanc Mont Ridge, 88; close brush with death, 89; a costly victory, 89; Fifth and Sixth Marine Regiments cited

by General Petain, 90; armistice signed at Compeigne, 90; Thomason hospitalized, 90-91; writes from hospital of proximity to death, 91; observes celebration of war's end in Paris, 91-92; receives orders to rejoin men marching to the Rhine with the American Army of Occupation, 92; resumes command at Remagen, 92; stationed at Niederbreitbach, 92; Christmas in Germany, 93-94; impact of combat on Thomason's regeneration, 94-95; as Corps leave officer for American Army of Occupation at Coblenz, 95; transfer from Coblenz to Brest, France, 95; arrival in New York, 95
— Career in the Marine Corps and in the world of art: first tour of duty — Cuba, 96; Camaguey, base of operations, 96-98; embraces ambitious reading regimen, 99; observes strict schedule of sketching and writing, 99-100; publishers reject submissions on war, 100; sells articles on hunting and tourism, 101; indulges in sport of caiman hunting, 101-102; attends religious festival with Leda, 102-104; observes Cuban customs, 104-105; rank of captain made permanent, 107; pride in siring first Thomason heir, 105-107; end of tour, 109; Base legal officer, Fifth Naval District, Hampton Roads, Virginia, 110; duties, 110; Thomason encounters Marshall Foch, 111-112; develops fatalistic philosophy, 112; continues extensive reading program, 113; renews artistic activity, 113; exhibits under auspices of Ruth Thomas, 113; visits Yorktown with family, 114; notes

progress of son, 115-116; second year at Hampton Roads, 117;
Thomason begins third tour of duty at Naval Ammunition Depot, Dover, N.J., 120; reasons for transfer, 120-121; enjoys outdoor life, 122; writes and engages in landscape painting, 123; exhibits at Newark and New York galleries, 123; introduced by Stallings to editors of Scribner's, 124; accepts commissions to illustrate stories for *Scribner's Magazine* and *Liberty*, 126; Scribner's purchases Thomason's combat material, 127; Thomason obtains additional commissions to illustrate articles and books, 127-128; attends production of *What Price Glory*, 129-130;
First tour of sea duty aboard the *USS Rochester*, 175ff; Thomason's multiple duties, 177; first combat article — *Fix Bayonets!* — published in *Scribner's Magazine*, 180; Thomason's reply to cable from *New York World*, 180; letters of praise flood Scribner's, 180-184, *passim; Scribner's Magazine* features *Marines at Blanc Mont*, 183; Thomason illustrates *An Uncharted Course*, 184; *Scribner's Magazine* quotes Thomason on *What Price Glory*, 184; see also Woollcott, Alexander; Scribner's accepts *Monkey Meat* and announces forthcoming publication of *The Conquest of Mike*, 184-185; book consisting of combat articles planning by Scribner's, 185; Thomason visits San Jose by train, 185-186; provides escort for General Pershing to Republic of

Peru, 186-187;

Thomason and Marine Guard provide security for Pershing's quarters, 186-187; reception of *Marines at Blanc Mont*, 187; *Monkey Meat* appears in *Scribner's Magazine*, 187; tour of duty in Peru results in *The Conquest of Mike, Crossing the Line with Pershing*, and *Mail Day*, 188; *Mail Day* quoted, 188-189; reunion of Thomasons in New York, 189-190; social courtesies extended the couple, 189-190; Hearst International Magazine Corporation contracts with Thomason for twelve stories for 1926 and 1927, 190; Thomason completes book manuscript for *Fix Bayonets!*, 191; Thomason's discomfiture at being a celebrity, 191; terminates leave in New York, 191; final segment of Marine Brigade articles appears in *Scribner's*, 191;

Thomason conducts training in small arms at Guantanamo Bay, 191-192; phenomenal success of *Fix Bayonets!*, 192-193; Thomas Boyd's "green" review, 193-194; at Port Limon, Costa Rica, 195; on duty in Nicaragua, 195-198; tour of duty aboard *USS Rochester* ends, 198; representative stories based on tour: *One Razor-Strop — Sixty-five Cents* and *Marines See the Revolution*, 198; publication of *Red Pants and Other Stories*, 199-200; *With the Special Service Squadron* appears in *Marine Corps Gazette*, 200;

Thomason assigned to Army War College at Fort Humphreys, Washington, D.C.: 201; obtains leave to collect data in Germany and France, 202; letters to son quoted, 202, 203; disembarkation at Antwerp, 203; inspects official records at Berlin and Potsdam, 203; journey through Rhineland, 204; visit to Paris, 204-205;

Return to Washington, 205; reunion with Jack, 205-206; literary and artistic activity, 206-207; active social life, 209ff; Easter in Washington, 211; overland trip into Virginia and North and South Carolina, 211; visit to Richmond, 212; guests of the Boyds and Burts, 212; Thomason agrees to illustrate for *Red Book* magazine, 213; visit with Elliott White Springs, 212; return to Washington, 213;

Family vacations in Maryland, 213; Thomason takes inventory of career, 213-214; begins research of Jeb Stuart biography, 214-215; resumes Second Division history project, 215; begins third year at capital, 216; interviews Stuart descendants, 217; sells story to *Liberty Magazine*, 217; collaborates with three other war authorities for article in *McCall's Magazine*, 218-219; observation on the death of Manda, 220; *The Capture of John Brown* appears in *Marine Corps Gazette*, 220; *Special Cases* and *Born on an Iceberg* published in *Liberty*, 220; parallels between Thomason and O. Henry, 222; expiration of tour of duty, 222; *Jeb Stuart* published in six segments in *Scribner's Magazine*, 222; unanimous critical acclaim, 222-223; return to Huntsville before assignment to the American Legation in Peking, 223; family reunion in Texas, 223-224;

Thomasons arrive in Peking, 225; discovery of the Great Wall, 226; temporary living quarters, 227; household staff, 227-228; the Legation Quarter, an international community, 227-229; colorful life in Peking, 229-231; organization and responsibilities of the Marine Guard, 231-232; duties of Thomason as commander of the Thirty-eighth Machine Gun Company, 232-233; Thomason's company awarded the All Arms trophy for excellence, 233; encampment at Peitaho, 233-234; *Missionary's Daughter* based on experience at Peitaho, 233; *Sergeant Bridoon of the Horse Marines* influenced by the mounted Marine, 234; *The Sergeant and The Bandit* inspired by life in Peking, 234; *The Collector,* another story inspired by the Oriental scene, 234;

Commentary on Marines' occupation of China station, 235-236; social activity at the Legation, 237; Thomason's racing activities, 237; race horse Temujin inspires *The Sergeant and The Siren,* 237; racing companions Roy Chapman Andrews and Julian Brown, 237; Thomason and Andrews explore the Orient, 238; care exercised in the writing of *Fix Bayonets!,* 238; promenading on the Great Wall, 238; short stories influenced by the Great Wall — *Love Story of a Marine, The Sergeant and the Spy,* and *The Sergeant and the Bandit,* 238; areas of northern capital, 239-242; travel in the Orient, 241-242;

Disadvantages of the Peking climate, 242; prevalence of disease, 242; illness of Jack, 243-245; Thomason's indebtedness to John Davison Rockefeller, 245; sales of *Jeb Stuart* mount, 245; Thomason rejects Army War College's invitation to rewrite Second Division history, 245-246; orders sergeant's uniform for Jack, 247; extension of Asiatic tour, 247; Japan invades Manchuria and launches attack on Shanghai, 247; Thomason makes observation tour to Shanghai, 248; describes findings in letters to Boyd and to Dr. Thomason, 249; assessment of the Japanese soldier, 250; return to Peitaho Beach with family, 250-251; Thomason named as post adjutant, 251-252; maintains peace in Peking through strategy, 252-253; admiration for the Chinese soldier, 251, 253; guests of the Thomasons in Peking, 253-255; Thomason illustrates Thomas Nelson Page's *Two Little Confederates* and *Taps, Selected Poems of the Great War,* edited by Theodore Roosevelt and Grantland Rice, 255; begins editing and illustrating *The Adventures of Davy Crockett,* 255; completes *Salt Winds and Gobi Dust,* 255; typical selections — *Mixed Marriage, The Story of a Princess, Note on Justice, The Marine and The Emerald Sweeps,* another Sergeant Houston story; *With a Dust Storm Blowing,* and *Advance Guard,* 255-256; Thomasons embark on *USS Chaumont* at close of tour, 256; sculpture, 256;

Thomason returns to Texas to await assignment, 257; essay *Huntsville* appears in *South-*

west Review, 257-258; *The Mating of a Stamp Collector* published in *Scribner's Magazine*, 258; Thomason assigned the detail of junior aide to Assistant Secretary of the Navy Henry L. Roosevelt, 258; settles family in Spring Valley, 258; acquires wire-haired terrier Winkie, 259; Washington society, 259; weekend at Skaneateles, New York, 259-260; professional duties, 260; commission as major, 261;

Thomason awarded Silver Star for gallantry at Soissons in 1918, 261; considers writing biography of General Lee, 261-262; "Socratic Dialogues," correspondence with James Boyd, 261-263; Thomason and President Roosevelt, 263-264; inspection tour to the West Coast and Honolulu, 264; entertained by Marian Davies at the Hearst Ranch, San Simeon, California, 264;

Thomason writes and sketches on tour of Naval installations, 265; as Horse-and-Buggy man, 266; preparation for book on Napoleon's officer, Marbot, 267; release of *Adventures of General Marbot* by Scribner's, 266-267; slow progress on Lee, 267; Thomason writes for the *Saturday Evening Post*, 268; *Note on the Employment Situation, Shanghai Racket, Service with a Smile,* and *Washington Racket* appear in the *New Yorker*, 268; *Our Disappearing Ducks* runs in the *Saturday Evening Post*, 268; Sergeant Houston stories appear in the *Saturday Evening Post*, 268; Thomason writes the foreward to *Romantic Flags of Texas* by Mamie

Wynne Cox of Huntsville, 268; Thomason writes 2,500-word review of Freeman's biography of Lee, 268-269; takes month's leave to visit with family in Texas, 269; interviewed by state press, 269-270; returns to Washington, 271; Thomason and senior aide take charge of Roosevelt funeral arrangements, 271; Thomason assures smooth transfer of office to Admiral Standley, 272-273; the Thomasons vacation in Canada with the Boyds, 273; Literary editor of the *American Mercury* — Thomason accepts post as he returns to the Army War College in 1936, 277; nature of duties, 278; first submissions — reviews of Newton D. Baker's *War in the Modern World;* Norman Thomas's *War: No Profit, No Glory, No Need;* T. H. Wintringham's *The Coming World War*, 270-280; reviews Booth Tarkington's *The Lorenzo Bunch;* H. L. Davis's *Honey in the Horn;* Charles Nordoff's and James Hall's *Hurricane*, 281-282;

Begins novel as a six-part serial in the *Saturday Evening Post*, 282; attention to fan mail, 283-285; publication of *Gone to Texas* by Scribner's, 284-285; *Scow-Gun Marriage* written and illustrated for the *Post*, 285; Thomason assigned to the Naval War College at Newport, 285; elevated to the rank of lieutenant colonel, 285; family settles on Washington Street, 286; advantages of the tour, 287;

Thomason presents *The Rebel Yell* painting to the Reading Room of the Club, 287; world profile projected by Thomason through *Mercury* essays, 288; *The Best Best-Seller*, prompted by Ernest Sutherland Bates's *The Bible Designed To Be Read As Living Literature*, 288-289; *Reflections on Book Reviewing* recalls horse-and-buggy days of Thomason's boyhood, 289-290; fan mail and editorial praise, 290; *The Old South Myth*, quoted, 293; analysis of the Southern viewpoint and the essay's impact on American literary scene, 291-293; *History's Perfect Rascal*, review of Wilfred Hardy Calcot's biography of Santa Anna, 293;

The Story of Texas, review of General Andrew Jackson Houston's *Texas Independence*, 293; *Maverick on Parade*, review of Congressman Maury Maverick's autobiography *Maverick American*, 294-295; *Catastrophe in Galveston*, account of the storm of 1900 and Major Goree's involvement in it, 294-295; Sam Acheson's *35,000 Days in Texas . . .*, 296; Thomason's observation on the reporter, 296; Southwestern University confers honorary degree upon Thomason, 297; hospitalization and death of Winkie, 297-298; *The Conquest of Mike* and *The Odyssey of a Little Dog*, 298; as commander of the Second Battalion, Sixth Marines, 299ff; Thomason rejects option for motion picture rights to *Gone to Texas*, 300; plans to send Jack to Princeton, 301;

Thomason and the "Old Breed," 302-303; assessment of Thomason by command, 303-304; resigns *American*

Mercury editorship, 304; visit to Laurence Stallings and his second wife Louise in Culver City, 305; *The Wicked Do Not Always Prosper* appears in *Saturday Evening Post*, 305; Thomason paints oil portrait of a Marine with son as model, 305; letter to General Boetticher of German Embassy, 306; concern for the safety of Sue Noordberg in Holland, 307; mobilization for war in the Pacific, 308; Thomason's reunion with Alexander Woollcott, 308; release from duty in Fleet Marine Force, 309; odyssey across continent, 309-310; Thomason assigned to Latin American desk, Office of Naval Intelligence, 311; Thomason's unique role in the Corps, 311-312; operations of American Navy multiply, 312-313; deterioration of Japanese-American relations, 313; extension of embargo and freezing of Japanese assets, 313;

Attack on Pearl Harbor, 313; Thomason's responsibilities double, 314; Thomason paints recruiting poster, 314; miniature of design circulated in form of stamp, 314-315; Thomason continues artistic activity, 315; desk work increases with progress of war, 315; Thomason conducts tours of Latin American and Caribbean installations, 316; exhaustion in Buenos Aires, 316; Thomason rejoins group at Rio de Janeiro, 316; inspects British base sites, 317; Air Medal awarded Thomason by War Department, 317; Release of *Lone Star Preacher* by Scribner's, 317; significance of the publication two months after

Pearl Harbor, 319; uniformly high acclaim, 320; Perkins recognizes greatness of novel, 320; subjective commentary on classic, 320-321; reprints of *Lone Star Preacher*, 321; novel influences Hemingway to publish war anthology with Thomason's editorial assistance, 322; Thomason legend gathers moss, 322-324; resume of Thomason's World War I record, 324; summary of artistic achievement, 323-326; *The Sergeant and the Ship*, Sergeant Houston story based on author's intelligence work, 326; impact of German submarine warfare on Thomason's section of Naval intelligence, 326-327; WAVES join Thomason's staff, 327-328; Naval attache posts, 328; Thomason advanced to rank of colonel, 328; attends father's funeral in Texas, 328-329; second tour of Latin American, 330; begins to curtail activities, 330; contributes *Dog Eat Dog* and *And So He Went Along* to *Saturday Evening Post*, 330-331; Assigned to Amphibious Training Command of Pacific Fleet, 331; impact of the publication of — *and a Few Marines*, 332; Thomason assumes duty at Pearl Harbor as war plans officer and inspector of Marine bases, 334; critical reappraisal of Thomason's art, 334-335; Thomason and Frederick Remington, 334; identification with Francisco Goya, 334-335; inspects installations in the area of the Solomon Islands, 335; describes illness in letter to Boyd, 335-336; Thomason returns to Amphibious Training Command at

Camp Elliott, San Diego, 337; — *and a Few Marines* sells well, 337; Thomason resumes painting of California wildlife reminiscent of boyhood in Huntsville, 337;
Final story, *The Collaborator*, accepted by *Saturday Evening Post*, 338-339; 'First with the Most' Forest, by Robert S. Henry, last book illustrated by Thomason, 339; Thomason as host at Thanksgiving to son on leave from combat duty in the Pacific, 339; in Naval Hospital in San Diego, 340ff; notes death of James Boyd at Princeton, 340; death retires Colonel John W. Thomason, 341; impact of death on literary and military worlds, 341ff; interment of Thomason in family plot in Huntsville, 343; honors conferred upon Thomason posthumously, 344-346; see also Postscript
Thomason, John William (Jack) III: birth in Camaquey, Cuba, 105-107; letter, 106-107; first train ride, 108; develops accent at Dover, 128; rejoins father at Ancon, 195; at six endowed with habit of command, 195; observes Valentine's Day, 208-209; launches sailboat, 211; remains in Texas during parents' European tour, 202-203; illness in Peking, 243-245, 256; see also listings under Thomason, John W. and Thomason, Leda Bass; recovery and adoption of new hobby, 246; recipient of pony, 246; models sergeant's uniform at Christmas party, 247; visits Pietaho Beach, 250-251; sits for sculpture portrait by father, 256, 326;
Enrolls in cathedral school of

St. Albans in Washington, 259; takes first plane trip, 266; maturity at 16, 266; as chauffeur for Dr. Thomason, 273; graduates from St. Albans, 305; makes dean's list at University of Virginia, 309; poses for oil portrait of a Marine, 305; withdraws from University of Virginia to enroll in Marine Corps Reserve, 326; transferred to First Marine Division stationed in Australia, 331; —*and A Few Marines* dedicated to, 332; spends Thanksgiving with bride Ruth and his parents in La Jolla, California, 339; delivers funeral oration at the burial of his father, 343; awarded Silver Star for gallantry at Iwo Jima, 344; dies in plane crash near Calcutta, India, 347; buried beside father in Huntsville's Oakwood Cemetery, 347

Dr. Joshua Allen: John Thomason's paternal grandfather, 20

Leda Bass: see Courtship and marriage under Thomason, John W.; background, 42, 53, 62; description of, 53; as homemaker in Charleston, 66-68; in Fredericksburg, 71; "good soldier herself," 71; reunited with husband in New York after World War I, 95; life in Cuba, 96-109; gives birth to son, 105; care of Jack in infancy, 108-109; at Hampton Roads, 110-119; rejoins husband in Dover, 118; celebrates with husband on leave in New York, 189-190; rejoins husband in Panama Canal Zone, 195;

Dedication of *Red Pants and Other Stories* to, 199; enjoys first White House reception, 209-211; as part of the Lega-

tion Guard in Peking, see chapter 11, mentioned in *Saturday Evening Post*, 282; attends son's graduation exercises at St. Albans, 305; pilgrimage across country with John, 309-310; active in hospital and other auxiliary activities during World War II, 339

Margaret: see Cole, Margaret Thomason

Mary: see Stafford, Mary Thomason

Dr. Robert: 224, 258, 330, 341

Ruth Wynne: 339

Sue Goree (Mrs. J. W.)—mother of John W. Thomason, Jr.: marriage to Dr. J. W. Thomason, 19, background and Southern heritage, 20-21; 24; as homemaker and mother, 24-26; transfers Southern heritage to children, 21, 24; as hostess to Methodist dignitaries and Confederate brigadiers, 25; encourages John's artistic propensities, 30; relationship to domestics, 25-26; visits John before he ships overseas, 71

Sue: see Noordberg, Sue Thomason

Susanne: see Atkinson, Suzanne Thomason

Tilley, J. Bob: 15

Times Bulletin Board: 49

Tolstoy, Count Leo: 23

Toul: 87

Travis, William Barret: 26

Trinity River: 6, 8

U

United States Army: in joint operation with Marine Corps in seizure of Munda, 335

United States Army in the World War, 1917-1919, The: 222; see also Potomac Potpourri

United States Marine Corps: 59, 69, 66, 70, 81, 75; 89-90; 97, 175ff,

222, 235-236; Thomason's place in, 311-312; 332, 333; 335, 336, 341
United States Naval Hospital at San Diego: 118, 340-341
United States Navy: 52, 176, 177, 178, 271
University of Virginia: 28, 309, 326; memorial plaque to Confederate dead, 28
USS *Chaumont:* 256
USS *Henderson:* ship on which Thomason and Stallings sailed for overseas duty in World War I, 71; arrives at St. Nazaire, 77; 179
USS *Houston:* 265
USS *John W. Thomason* (DD 760): 346
USS *Kittery:* "an ancient bucket," 97
USS *New York:* 56
USS *Rochester:* flagship of the Special Service Squadron, 175; history and description of, 176; significance of, 176-177; see also Thomason, John W., Career in the Marine Corps . . . ; 184ff; 189, 255

V

Vanity Fair: 124, 184
Vicksburg, Mississippi: 345
Vicksburg National Military Park: 345-346
Villa, Pancho: 55

W

WACS, WAAFS, and WRENS: 328
Wakefield, Paul: 59ff, 249, 320; represents Governor Stevenson at Thomason's funeral, 343
Walker, Stanley: acclaims *Lone Star Preacher*, 319
Walker County, Texas: 3
war: Napoleonic campaigns, 334; see *Adventures of General Marbot* and Napoleon Bonaparte; American Revolution, 20; Texas War for Independence, 3, 13; see Houston, Sam; San Jacinto; Travis, William Barret: Yoakum's *History of Texas*, Thomason's *The Adventures of Davy Crockett*, and Andrew Jackson Houston's *Texas Independence;*
Civil War, 7, 8, 9, 13, 14, 27, 42-44, *passim;* see Forrest, Nathan Bedford, Goree, Major Thomas Jewett; Grant, General Ulysses S.; Hood, John Bell; Lee, General Robert E.; Lincoln, Abraham; Longstreet, James; *Lone Star Preacher, Jeb Stuart,* and *Gone to Texas;*
Spanish-American War, 97, 106, 334
World War I, 58, 66, 64, 91, 96; impact on American art and economy, 48-50; America declares war on Germany, 60; see Thomason, John W., Regeneration in World War I, *Fix Bayonets!* and *Red Pants and Other Stories;* Remarque, *All Quiet on the Western Front;* Stallings, *What Price Glory;* *Four Soldiers in Four Countries,* and *The United States Army in The World War, 1917-1919.* See also Kaiser, William II, Lejeune, General John; Pershing, General John J.; and Wilson, Woodrow;
Japanese invasion of China, 247-249; battles, 248-249; see also Chiang Kai-shek and Thomason, John W., Career in the Marine Corps . . .
World War II, imminence of, 306-308, *passim;* America's undeclared Naval war, 312-313; Pearl Harbor, 313; the United States declares war on Japan, 314; treatment of war by Thomason in *American Mercury,* 279-281; see also Hitler, Adolf; Roosevelt, Franklin

Delano; Churchill, Winston; Thomason's —*and A Few Marines* and Hemingway's *Men at War* . . . ; war in the Pacific, 308, 344ff; see also references to Nimitz, Fleet Admiral Chester; Thomason, Colonel John W. and Thomason, Lieutenant John William III and Postscript

Washington, D.C.: 65, 67, 68, 94, 95, 197, 212, 222, 257-273, 306, 309, 310, 317, 330, 336

Washington, George: Thomason's feature article on, 58

WAVES: 327

Webb, Walter Prescott: 320

Welles, Ambassador Sumner: 257

Weser, Father William: 5

West Indian trade: 97

"What a Fighter & What a Writer:" 194

What Price Glory: 124-125; 184

Wheeler, Royal T.: 7

Williams, Blanche C.: author of *O. Henry Memorial Award Prize Stories of 1930,* 221

Wilson, Hugh: 7
President Woodrow: 55, 95, 99

wine: 87, 94

With a Dust Storm Blowing: 255-256

Wolfe, Tom: "Tom Wolfe Memorial Bulletin," 300; Thomason comments on, 319, mentioned, 337

Woollcott, Alexander: introduces captain Thomason of the Marine Corps in *Vanity Fair,* 124; writes of Thomason in *Stars and Stripes,* 80; appraisal of *Fix Bayonets!* in *New York World,* 184; renews acquaintance with Thomason on West Coast, 309; plays himself in *The Man Who Came to Dinner,* 309; reprints chapter from *Lone Star Preacher* in his anthology *As You Were,* 321; 446

Wright, Blanche Fisher: 125
Lieutenant Commander Jerauld: 272

Y

yellow fever epidemic: 7

YMCA: 59

Yoakum, Eveline Connor: wife of Henderson Yoakum, 13

Yoakum family: 4

Yoakum, Henderson: 7, 13; biographical sketch of, 13-14; monument, 14; as Huntsville hero, 13; as author, 13; see also Houston, Sam

Z

Zayas, Alfredo: 99

Zouave Regiment of Louisiana: 42